ASIAN DEVELOPMENT
OUTLOOK 2015
UPDATE
ENABLING WOMEN, ENERGIZING ASIA

ASIAN DEVELOPMENT BANK

ADB

© 2015 Asian Development Bank
6 ADB Avenue, Mandaluyong City, 1550 Metro Manila, Philippines
Tel +63 2 632 4444; Fax +63 2 636 2444
www.adb.org; openaccess.adb.org

Some rights reserved. Published in 2015.
Printed in the Philippines.

ISBN 978-92-9257-119-1 (Print), 978-92-9257-120-7 (PDF)
ISSN 1655-4809
Publication Stock No. FLS157635-3

Cataloging-In-Publication Data

Asian Development Bank.
        Asian development outlook 2015 update. Enabling women, energizing Asia.
Mandaluyong City, Philippines: Asian Development Bank, 2015.

1. Economics.   2. Gender.   3. Asia.   I. Asian Development Bank.

Contents

Foreword

Growth in developing Asia is stuttering amid diverse challenges confronting economies globally. Recovery in the major industrial economies fell short of expectations as the United States (US) experienced temporary shocks early in the year and Japan was affected by weak consumption and slow investment. In light of softer demand for exports from developing Asia and of moderating prospects for the region's two largest economies—the People's Republic of China (PRC) and India—*Asian Development Outlook 2015 Update* marks down the forecast for regional expansion to 5.8% in 2015 and 6.0% in 2016.

While forecasts are reduced for all subregions, East and Central Asia will grow even more slowly than their 2014 rate. Lower investment growth and weak exports tamed growth in the PRC to 6.8% in 2015. This has affected exports from the other East Asian economies, even as the Republic of Korea responded to the threat of Middle East respiratory syndrome, a viral illness that soured business and consumer sentiment. Commodity producers with sizeable exports to the PRC are seeing growth hit by moderating demand from a key market in tandem with low international prices for their goods. On top of lower oil and gas prices, Central Asia is stymied by recession in the Russian Federation.

India's growth acceleration wavered as external demand turned anemic and reform implementation fell short of expectations, such that it is now projected to grow at 7.4%, or just slightly better than in 2014. Southeast Asia and the Pacific are now forecast to grow at the same pace in 2015 as 2014, but the five largest economies in Southeast Asia are collectively expected to grow a tad faster than in 2014, at 4.8%. Among them, Viet Nam can expect the fastest growth thanks to buoyant private consumption and foreign direct investment.

As oil prices remain low and food prices trend downward, regional inflation is envisaged declining to 2.3% in 2015 before picking up to 3.0% in 2016.

Global headwinds could further abrade the region's growth path. Capital has been flowing out of emerging markets, partly in anticipation of the upcoming US interest rate hike. Asia has felt the sting as net outflows reached $125 billion in the first quarter of 2015. The strengthening US dollar may catch short Asian corporations that have accumulated foreign debt. Corporations with high foreign currency exposure and scant foreign revenues will face more costly debt servicing. Policy makers need to explore options to ensure macroeconomic stability without undercutting growth, such as by using macroprudential policy to manage destabilizing capital flows and by strengthening local currency bond markets.

Over the past several decades, rapid growth has transformed the region into a "New Asia" that is more prosperous, urban, and globalized than ever before. Yet much work remains to ensure that the benefits of growth reach everyone in developing Asia. *ADO 2015 Update* draws attention to the unfinished agenda for gender equality, as Asian women are still disadvantaged in terms of education and workforce participation.

Bringing more women into paid work can be a catalyst for broader social change. Equality between men and women is a goal in its own right, but women are not the only ones who will benefit. Economies in developing Asia will enjoy greater prosperity if they resolve to use all of their human resources to the fullest.

TAKEHIKO NAKAO
President
Asian Development Bank

Acknowledgments

Asian Development Outlook 2015 Update was prepared by staff of the Asian Development Bank (ADB) in the Central and West Asia Department, East Asia Department, Pacific Department, South Asia Department, Southeast Asia Department, and Economic Research and Regional Cooperation Department, as well as in ADB resident missions. Representatives of these departments constituted the Regional Economic Outlook Task Force, which met regularly to coordinate and develop consistent forecasts for the region.

The authors who contributed the sections are bylined in each chapter. The subregional coordinators were Christopher Hnanguie and Dominik Peschel for Central Asia, Yolanda Fernandez Lommen for East Asia, Masato Nakane for South Asia, Sona Shrestha for Southeast Asia, and Christopher Edmonds and Rommel Rabanal for the Pacific.

A team of economists in the Economic Research and Regional Cooperation Department, led by Joseph E. Zveglich, Jr., director of the Macroeconomics Research Division, coordinated the production of the publication, assisted by Edith Laviña. Technical and research support was provided by Shiela Camingue-Romance, Cindy Castillejos-Petalcorin, Gemma Esther Estrada, Nedelyn Magtibay-Ramos, Pilipinas Quising, Aleli Rosario, Dennis Sorino, Lea Sumulong, Charisse Tubianosa, and Mai Lin Villaruel. Additional research support was provided by Emmanuel Alano, Ruben Carlo Asuncion, and Abigail Golena. The economic editorial advisors Robert Boumphrey, Joshua Greene, Richard Niebuhr, Anthony Patrick, and Reza Vaez-Zadeh made substantive contributions to the country chapters and regional outlook.

The theme chapter was reviewed by external peer reviewers Jane Falkingham, Lena Edlund, Xin Meng, and Athina Vlanchantoni, and by internal peer reviewers Sonomi Tanaka and Imrana Jalal. Margarita Debuque provided editorial advice. Support and guidance from members of the ADB Gender Equity Thematic Group is gratefully acknowledged.

Peter Fredenburg advised on ADB style and English usage. Alvin Tubio handled typesetting and graphics generation, in which he was assisted by Elenita Pura. Art direction for the cover design was by Anthony Victoria, with artwork from Design Muscle. Critical support for the printing and publishing of the report was provided by the Printing Services Unit of the ADB Office of Administrative Services and by the Publishing and Dissemination Unit of the ADB Department of External Relations. Heili Ann Bravo, Fermirelyn Cruz, Rhia Bautista-Piamonte, and Azaleah Tiongson provided administrative and secretarial support.

The Department of External Relations, led by Satinder Bindra, Omana Nair, and Erik Churchill, planned and coordinated the dissemination of *Asian Development Outlook 2015 Update*.

Definitions

The economies discussed in *Asian Development Outlook 2015 Update* are classified by major analytic or geographic group. For the purposes of this publication, the following apply:

- **Association of Southeast Asian Nations (ASEAN)** comprises Brunei Darussalam, Cambodia, Indonesia, the Lao People's Democratic Republic, Malaysia, Myanmar, the Philippines, Singapore, Thailand, and Viet Nam.
- **Developing Asia** comprises the 45 members of the Asian Development Bank listed below.
- **Central Asia** comprises Armenia, Azerbaijan, Georgia, Kazakhstan, the Kyrgyz Republic, Tajikistan, Turkmenistan, and Uzbekistan.
- **East Asia** comprises the People's Republic of China; Hong Kong, China; the Republic of Korea; Mongolia; and Taipei,China.
- **South Asia** comprises Afghanistan, Bangladesh, Bhutan, India, the Maldives, Nepal, Pakistan, and Sri Lanka.
- **Southeast Asia** comprises Brunei Darussalam, Cambodia, Indonesia, the Lao People's Democratic Republic, Malaysia, Myanmar, the Philippines, Singapore, Thailand, and Viet Nam.
- **The Pacific** comprises the Cook Islands, Fiji, Kiribati, the Marshall Islands, the Federated States of Micronesia, Nauru, Palau, Papua New Guinea, Samoa, Solomon Islands, Timor-Leste, Tonga, Tuvalu, and Vanuatu.

Unless otherwise specified, the symbol "$" and the word "dollar" refer to US dollars. *Asian Development Outlook 2015 Update* is generally based on data available up to **4 September 2015**.

Abbreviations

ADB	Asian Development Bank
ADO	*Asian Development Outlook*
ASEAN	Association of Southeast Asian Nations
CSF	Coalition Support Fund
EEU	Eurasian Economic Union
EU	European Union
FDI	foreign direct investment
FSM	Federated States of Micronesia
FY	fiscal year
GDP	gross domestic product
GNI	gross national income
GVC	global value chain
ICT	information and communication technology
IMF	International Monetary Fund
Lao PDR	Lao People's Democratic Republic
LNG	liquefied natural gas
M1	money that includes cash and checking accounts
M2	broad money that adds highly liquid accounts to M1
M3	broad money that adds time accounts to M2
OECD	Organisation for Economic Co-operation and Development
OPEC	Organization of the Petroleum Exporting Countries
PNG	Papua New Guinea
PPP	public–private partnership
PRC	People's Republic of China
RMI	Republic of the Marshall Islands
saar	seasonally adjusted annualized rate
SMEs	small and medium-sized enterprises
SOE	state-owned enterprise
TVET	technical and vocational education and training
US	United States of America
VAT	value-added tax

ADO 2015 Update—Highlights

Growth in developing Asia faced strong headwinds in the first half of 2015. Regional growth is forecast to slow from 6.2% in 2014 to 5.8% in 2015, with a slight rebound to 6.0% in 2016.

The region must strengthen its ability to respond to external shocks. Emerging markets are facing receding capital flows and depreciating currencies—a trend that may be exacerbated by the upcoming rise in US interest rates. Implementing macroprudential policies and developing local currency bond markets can bolster financial system resilience and mitigate risks to borrowers.

Currently moderating growth highlights the need to identify untapped resources in the region. As noted in the theme chapter, *Enabling Women, Energizing Asia,* developing Asia has made considerable progress in closing gender gaps in health and education over the past several decades. Today, narrowing gender gaps in the labor market is a good way to give the region a considerable growth boost—and, at the same time, do the right thing for women as individuals.

Shang-Jin Wei
Chief Economist
Asian Development Bank

Bracing for economic headwinds

Transition to a new normal

■ **Developing Asia faces considerable headwinds.** Growth forecasts for gross domestic product (GDP) in the region are revised down to 5.8% in 2015 and 6.0% in 2016 from the *Asian Development Outlook 2015 (ADO 2015)* forecast, published in March, of 6.3% for both years. Delayed recovery in the major industrial economies and moderating prospects for the large economies of the People's Republic of China (PRC) and India weigh on the outlook, slackening the projected pace below even the 2014 rate of 6.2%.

» **Recovery in the major industrial economies picks up after a slow start.** In the first half of 2015, harsh winter weather and labor disputes in West Coast ports slowed growth in the United States (US), while an unexpectedly weak recovery in consumption and investment slowed expansion in Japan. On the other hand, the receding threat of a Greek debt crisis provided a fillip to growth projections for the euro area. Together, the major industrial economies are projected to expand by 1.9% in 2015, 0.3 percentage points slower than the *ADO 2015* projection, and 2.3% in 2016.

» **Slowing investment and weak exports ease growth in the PRC.** Despite robust consumption demand, economic activity fell short of expectations in the first 8 months of the year as investment and exports underperformed. Growth is forecast to slow from 7.3% in 2014 to 6.8% in 2015. As external demand strengthens with the pickup in growth in the industrial countries, and as improved financial conditions support investment, downward pressure on growth will ease. The PRC is projected to grow by 6.7% in 2016.

» **Prospects for India's growth acceleration await a pickup in external demand and reform progress.** GDP decelerated in the first quarter of fiscal year 2015 (ending 31 March 2016), as external demand weakened and investors hesitated awaiting further action on structural reform. Forecasts in *ADO 2015* are revised down by 0.4 percentage points to 7.4% in FY2015. Growth is expected to pick up to 7.8% in FY2016 as key elements of the government's economic reform package reach fruition.

» **The pickup in Southeast Asia's large economies is delayed.** For the five large economies in the Association of Southeast Asian Nations (ASEAN), the growth forecast for this year is lowered to 4.8%—a slight uptick from 2014—before accelerating to 5.3% next year. Subdued demand from the major industrial economies and the PRC dampened exports in the first half. Faster-than-expected growth in Viet Nam was more than offset by weakness in three other economies. Planned infrastructure investment has fallen behind schedule in Indonesia and the Philippines, and Thailand's recovery to date has been sluggish.

■ **Soft global commodity prices keep inflation low.** Global oil prices have remained low and food prices declined under favorable supply conditions. Relatively soft domestic demand will let regional inflation slip from 3.0% in 2014 to 2.3% in 2015 before it bounces back to 3.0% in 2016. Although forecast inflation is much lower than the regional long-run rate of about 4%, the impending rise in US interest rates may constrain scope in the region for loosening monetary policy to boost domestic demand.

■ **Forecasts for the regional current account surplus are maintained.** Developing Asia's current account surplus is forecast to widen from the equivalent of 2.4% of regional GDP in 2014 to 2.5% in 2015 before falling back slightly to 2.3% in 2016. The projections are the same as in *ADO 2015*, as narrowing surpluses in commodity-exporting countries are offset by improved external balances for commodity importers.

Responding to capital flows

■ **Capital flows ebb from the region, and growth momentum slows.** For 11 economies in emerging East, Southeast, and South Asia, capital inflows reversed beginning in the second quarter of 2014. By the first quarter of 2015, net outflows had exceeded $125 billion. Capital outflows have likely further intensified since then as investors anticipated the upcoming US interest rate hike and growth slowed in the region. As a consequence, developing Asia has seen risk premiums rise, currencies weaken, and stock markets decline. Disruption from financial instability threatens to further slow the region's growth momentum.

■ **Monetary policy may be torn between stabilizing finance and stimulating demand.** Policy makers in the region may be forced to respond in kind to the increase in the US interest rate to maintain their domestic financial stability. Historically, capital outflows from emerging Asia closely coincide with episodes of rising US interest rates. The policy response is necessary to contain destabilizing capital flow reversals, but it constrains action to boost domestic demand and revive growth.

■ **Macroprudential policy can enable monetary policy independence.** By putting limits on destabilizing capital flows, the authorities may create scope for independent monetary policy that can be used to counter downturns in the business cycle. In this regard, implementing macroprudential policies to manage debt flows without impeding foreign direct investment (FDI) is the most effective way to gain policy independence.

Corporate debt and the strengthening dollar

■ **US dollar strength may put Asian companies with large foreign debt at risk.** Over the past few years, Asian corporations have increased their US dollar borrowings to take advantage of low US interest rates. The rising US dollar now confronts these companies with debt servicing costs that are higher in local currency terms. In addition, tighter liquidity ahead could make refinancing this debt more difficult and expensive.

■ **Some corporations with foreign debt have only limited foreign revenues as a natural hedge.** Data from a sample of large nonfinancial corporations show the share of foreign currency debt incurred by firms in Indonesia, Sri Lanka, and Viet Nam exceeding 65%. While corporations in Malaysia and the Republic of Korea have substantial foreign revenues, fewer firms in Indonesia, the Philippines, and Viet Nam can rely on overseas earnings. High leverage and short-term debt can exacerbate risk from high foreign currency exposure.

■ **Vibrant domestic finance can mitigate risk from currency depreciation.** Because firms resort to foreign borrowings if the domestic financial market is not large or liquid enough, a well-developed and liquid domestic financial system can reduce corporate reliance on foreign currency borrowings. Authorities may also limit corporations' unhedged foreign currency exposure and encourage more FDI inflows to help improve resilience.

The PRC and commodity exporters in developing Asia

◼ **Moderating growth in the PRC raises concerns for commodity exporters.** Commodity prices have fluctuated significantly since 2000, but recent trends have been decidedly downward. An index of global commodity prices fell by more than 45% from its peak in April 2011 to the end of August 2015. World prices for crude oil and metals, declining since 2011, fell more sharply in 2014. Just as rising prices coincided with periods of high growth and investment in the PRC, recent price drops mesh with the narrative of PRC deceleration and reduced reliance on investment-driven growth.

◼ **Commodity exporters that depend heavily on the PRC are more vulnerable.** Lower demand from the PRC will affect growth rates in developing Asia directly through reduced trade and indirectly through lower global commodity prices. The effects will depend on the share of commodities in each economy's export basket, hitting especially those with considerable direct commodity exports to the PRC. A declining appetite in the PRC for energy, metals, and other commodities, and soft global prices, are worries for a number of economies in developing Asia that depend heavily on commodity exports: Azerbaijan, Brunei Darussalam, Indonesia, Kazakhstan, and Mongolia.

Outlook by subregion

◼ **Growth is moderating in developing Asia over the forecast horizon.** The first half of 2015 has been softer than expected across the board, and projections for all subregions are adjusted downward from *ADO 2015* for both 2015 and 2016.

◼ **East Asia will grow more moderately in the near term.** Growth faltered in all economies in the subregion in the first half of 2015. Weaker-than-expected outcomes in the PRC and indications of softness in 2016 prompt downward revisions to growth projections for the subregion's largest economy. Growth in the PRC is expected to drop to 6.8% from 7.3% in 2014, but support from strengthening external demand plus accommodative monetary and fiscal policies should contain further growth moderation to 6.7% in 2016. East Asia is expected to expand at 6.0% in both 2015 and 2016, a considerable slowdown from 6.5% in 2014. Inflation will remain moderate and below the *ADO 2015* forecast. It is forecast to fall to 1.4% in 2015 and rise to 2.1% in 2016, mainly tracking the expected trend in global commodity prices. Although Mongolia now has inflation slowing to below double digits—to 7.6% in both 2015 and 2016—it remains the outlier in a subregion otherwise marked by low inflation.

◼ **South Asia is picking up more moderately than forecast.** Growth acceleration in India has been more modest than forecast in *ADO 2015* as slower implementation of planned major reforms have stymied the expected revival in investment, and as sagging exports have created headwinds. In Nepal, a catastrophic earthquake in April that caused great loss of life and extensive devastation, including to transport, has pared growth in 2015 and limits the pace of recovery in 2016, despite plans for extensive reconstruction. In the Maldives, a deep slump in tourist arrivals this year has undercut growth, but tourism and growth are expected to rebound in 2016. Growth in South Asia is now projected at 6.9% in 2015, below the 7.2% March forecast but up from 6.7% in 2014. Growth is forecast to rise further to 7.3% in 2016. Low world oil prices benefitted import-dependent South Asia, as did falling global food prices. Forecasts for inflation in South Asia are trimmed by 0.1 percentage points to 5.0% in 2015 and 5.5% in 2016.

- **Southeast Asia's projected growth recovery is delayed to next year.** Subdued economic growth in the major industrial economies and the PRC weakened export demand. Thailand has been sluggish recovering from its 2014 slump, while infrastructure investment has fallen behind schedule in Indonesia and the Philippines. Drought in several countries, and floods in Myanmar, have hurt agriculture. Viet Nam, by contrast, is growing faster than anticipated earlier this year, powered by FDI and buoyant private consumption. Subregional growth is forecast to be 4.4% in 2015—the same pace as in 2014 but below the 4.9% forecast in *ADO 2015*. Expected improvements in exports and infrastructure investment are seen lifting growth to 4.9% in 2016. Inflation in most economies is milder than projected in March. However, inflation that was higher than anticipated in Indonesia, the biggest economy in Southeast Asia, keeps the subregional inflation projection at 3.0% for 2015 and lifts it to 3.3% for 2016.

- **Central Asian commodity exporters endure weak prices and prospects.** Export revenues crimped by low oil and gas prices have constrained growth in the subregion's energy exporters: Azerbaijan, Kazakhstan, Turkmenistan, and Uzbekistan. Weak remittances have limited consumption in energy-importing Armenia, Georgia, Kyrgyz Republic, and Tajikistan, as well as in Uzbekistan. As it adjusts to lower global commodity prices and recession in the Russian Federation, Central Asia is expected to grow at 3.3% in 2015 and 4.2% in 2016. The sharp depreciation of the Kazakh tenge on 20 August raises the inflation forecast for Kazakhstan in 2015 from 6.0% to 8.9%, with lagged inflationary effects spilling into 2016. Subregional inflation is now expected to hit 8.1% in 2015 and subside to 7.5% in 2016.

- **The Pacific faces a dimmer economic outlook.** Papua New Guinea, the dominant economy in the subregion, was affected by the drop in oil and gas prices more than previously expected as the fall in revenue undercut public spending. Growth in the Pacific is now forecast at 6.7% in 2015 and 3.9% in 2016. Robust tourist arrivals are boosting the outlook for Kiribati and Palau, while a pickup in public investment is expected to spur growth in Fiji. As inflation in the Pacific was generally moderate in the first half of 2015—other than in Nauru—the forecast for the year is revised down from 5.0% to 4.2%. Inflation will pick up slightly to 4.4% in 2016.

Enabling women, energizing Asia

The unfinished agenda for gender equality

■ **Dramatic changes in recent decades have created a 'New Asia.'** Despite periods of crisis, developing Asia's real GDP per capita averaged 5.6% annual growth from 1990 to 2014. This helped lift nearly 1 billion people out of extreme poverty from 1990 to 2011. The region is becoming more urban as labor gravitates to higher wage opportunities in cities, and more globalized as its shares of world output and exports expand. While some economies have a window of opportunity to reap the benefits from a large share of working age population, some others are already showing signs of aging. One of the ways to harness this dividend and mitigate stagnation under an aging population is to bring more women into the workforce.

■ **Despite notable progress, gender equality is an unfinished agenda.** From 1970 to 2013, developing Asia saw primary school enrollment double, secondary enrollment triple, and tertiary enrollment multiply by sixfold. However, girls' average schooling remains significantly below the world average of 8.1 years, while boys' schooling approaches the world average of 8.6 years. Rates of infant and child mortality among girls have dropped, narrowing that gender gap, but a strong preference for sons is still felt. Along with the spread of affordable prenatal screening technology, it has motivated gender-specific abortions and caused disturbingly high ratios at birth of boys over girls, particularly in South and East Asia. Despite gains in education and health, women's workforce participation in the region fell from 56% in 1990 to 49% in 2013.

■ **Bringing women up to par with men can yield ample untapped benefits.** Erasing disparities against women has *intrinsic* value as it realizes their basic rights and promotes social justice. It also has *instrumental* value because it is good for development. Banishing job discrimination and closing gender gaps in employment improves how the available human capital is used, by deploying talent to occupations that can make the most of it. Eliminating gender disparity in the region would increase per capita income by 70% in roughly 60 years. Gender equality mitigates income inequality as well because women are on the whole poorer than men. Narrowing the gender gap thus yields twin benefits: better well-being for individual women and, for society, better use of human resources.

■ **Helping women earn independent incomes can catalyze social change.** Economic independence enables women to acquire credit, buy property, save for the future, and distribute household resources more equitably between sons and daughters, thus enhancing the family's human capital and economic well-being. As this phenomenon spreads, it inspires other women to follow suit. This creates a positive feedback loop, as the next generation of women builds on the gains made by the current generation. Equalizing opportunities puts women in a stronger position to improve conditions for other women of a mind to make the move, get jobs that use their abilities, and catch up with men in terms of pay and benefits.

Facilitating labor market entry

- **Social norms powerfully deter women's job-seeking but are not immutable.** Such factors as men's dominance in household decisions, social norms defining appropriate jobs, and restricted mobility continue to curtail women's freedom to work outside the home in many developing Asian economies. Further, women in Asia spend three times as many hours on household chores and family care as do men, severely limiting their time for other activities. However, women's greater participation in paid work in the formal sector can foster social change. Working mothers inspire their daughters to work outside the home, and they teach homemaking skills to their sons, which is partly why these boys are more likely to grow up to have working wives.

- **Appropriate education and skills improve women's employment prospects.** One-third of East Asia's remarkable economic growth from 1960 to 1985 came from sound investments in primary education. Yet girls in some Asian countries still commonly drop out of elementary school to support the family. Although girls' increased participation has reversed gender disparity in tertiary education from male advantage to female, many families send sons rather than daughters for vocational training, limiting girls' chances of taking up skilled occupations. Young women with little education are pushed into low-end manufacturing and services in the informal sector, where they endure poor working conditions for low pay. Access to high-quality education and training is essential to redress income inequality and enhance productivity and growth.

- **Improving opportunities for women requires institutional and legal reform.** The legal framework can help overcome traditional gender biases. Establishing the principle of equal treatment regardless of gender has payoffs in the labor market. For example, equal inheritance rights to property can entrust to entrepreneurial women potential collateral for loans. Regarding labor regulation, many Asian economies have laws that ensure equal treatment in hiring but still restrict women's working hours or the jobs they can take. Institutional reform to facilitate access to credit—such as Viet Nam's inclusion of microfinance institutions in credit registries—can boost female-owned enterprises. More reform is needed to remove institutional and legal hurdles and ease women's entry into the workforce.

Expanding occupational choices

- **Breaking down occupational silos expands women's workforce roles.** Poor, uneducated women often have no alternative to self-employment, as perhaps petty traders or waste-pickers. Even among educated women, those who aspire to land technical or senior positions often find themselves segregated into clerical and support positions. Because educational aspirations are formed early in life, breaking down occupational silos requires raising awareness in the home about the benefits of educating girls and providing opportunities for vocational training outside of traditional "women's work." In Nepal, vocational training and education enabled low-income women to challenge gender stereotypes and enter occupations conventionally treated as "men's work," such as vehicle repair. Improving work environments, facilitating childcare for working mothers, and expanding parental leave can help attract and retain women employees and facilitate their career growth toward more responsible positions.

■ **Fresh opportunities for women in the New Asia come with challenges.** Creating a supportive environment for women entrepreneurs and expanding job opportunities for women in the export manufacturing sector can pay big dividends toward greater gender equality.

» **Registered enterprises owned by women proliferate but face constraints.** General improvement of the business environment can enhance women's opportunities as entrepreneurs, but legal reform for gender equality is sometimes also needed, particularly where rights to property are unequal. In Bhutan, mobile banking has enhanced credit delivery to female micro and small entrepreneurs to help them build up substantial assets and hold title to land and other property.

» **Some export-oriented industries boost women's participation in the workforce.** Globalization has opened jobs for women in high-value service and manufacturing sectors: business process outsourcing in the Philippines, textile manufacturing in Bangladesh and Viet Nam, and electronic parts assembly in Taipei,China and Thailand. Further, evidence from the PRC suggests that more open trade facilitates women's entry into management and the professions. A comprehensive policy package that improves conditions in the workplace, removes restrictions on job options, and ensures rights to equal wages and work hours is needed to dismantle the multiple barriers that keep women from taking full advantage of these opportunities.

■ **Benefits to families and society accrue as women rise in the workplace.** In Bangladesh, the expansion of women's paid work in garment factories has enhanced their bargaining power at home, improving health and education options for the family. Companies with higher female representation in corporate management and the boardroom perform better on measures of leadership, work environment, and coordination and control, enabling higher profits. Yet, on average, less than 10% of Asian corporate board members are female—with Thailand standing out at nearly 14%—compared with a quarter or so in Germany and the US. To increase women's representation in boardrooms and senior management positions, Malaysia, for example, has established quotas. Women's political representation can shape social norms and the legal framework, but gender bias exists here too. Barely 10% of ministerial positions in developing Asia are filled by women, or just a third of the 29% in the euro area. Involving women in local leadership improved the provision of public goods in Bangladesh, Cambodia, Fiji, and the Philippines.

Equalizing worker compensation

■ **Women in paid employment continue to make less than men.** Women around the world earned 20% less than men on average in 2010, showing negligible improvement over the previous 2 decades. The wage gap in developing Asia is not unusual, as women in the region earned 77% of average male earnings in 2005–2011, about the same as in the advanced economies. Causes differ by economy: occupation differences are an issue in Viet Nam, for example, while a tendency toward part-time work is more important in Indonesia. Lower pay may discourage women from entering the workforce, and it may deter parents' investment in educating and training their daughters, thereby limiting their future options.

■ **Gender gaps in pension benefits leave aging women vulnerable to poverty.** About 20% of women in developing Asia are covered by some form of pension, compared with 35% coverage for men in the region and for women globally. Ensuring financial security for women in their old age requires a pension system designed with a gender dimension.

It should ensure that contributory pension schemes cover the self-employed and workers in the informal sector, that pension accounts credit time away on maternity leave, and that noncontributory pensions are provided publicly as needed. Reform should also equalize the statutory age of retirement.

■ **Maternity and childcare benefits strengthen workforce attachment.** Employers in the region commonly provide maternity leave with pay, usually 100% of the salary. Maternity leave helps employers retain workers and maintain their human resources, while the prospect of returning to the same job gives women an incentive to invest in skills. However, extended leave for maternity and childcare can let a woman's skills grow rusty and discourage return to the job. Policies to sustain women's full-time career development should therefore support early return to work by improving childcare, supporting the cost of playschool, offering tax relief for working mothers, and encouraging fathers to share the burden through paternity leave.

Unleashing women's potential

■ **Women's engagement in paid work can start a virtuous cycle.** Long entrenched social norms and cultural attitudes that clearly delineate "men's work" and "women's work" will not surrender overnight, but women who take on new roles in society are catalysts for change. In the labor market, developing Asia must address its unfinished gender agenda along three lines.

 » Enhance through better education and skills provision girls' competencies in light of the emerging needs of the labor market in the New Asia, thereby enabling them to move up the career ladder. In addition to high-quality education, girls need vocational training programs that target them specifically toward boosting their chances of landing a well-paid job or starting their own small business.

 » Remove legal props for gender discrimination by lifting constraints on entrepreneurship, expanding and facilitating women's access to information and communication technology, and ensuring fair compensation to men and women alike.

 » Emphasize policy that encourages women as they move beyond stereotypical jobs by widening the path for their ascent into decision-making roles. Even temporary quotas designed to boost their representation in corporate and political leadership can help change social norms and improve women's status, such that quotas may become unnecessary.

■ **Women earning income create a positive feedback loop for social change.** As more women take up new opportunities for paid labor, they powerfully catalyze change that challenges entrenched cultural and social norms. A woman with a job gains bargaining power within her household, which helps to mold the attitudes of the next generation. Gainfully employed women become examples for others to follow, affecting the decisions families make about young girls' future prospects. As they gain influence in business, civil service, and politics, women bring important issues of family and social dimensions to the national agenda. Eliciting women's best contributions to the workforce not only improves equality for women, it promises to boost economic growth and energize Asia. Everyone wins.

Growth rate of GDP (% per year)

Subregion/Economy	2014	2015 ADO 2015	2015 Update	2016 ADO 2015	2016 Update
Central Asia	5.1	3.5	3.3	4.5	4.2
Azerbaijan	2.8	3.0	3.0	2.8	2.8
Kazakhstan	4.3	1.9	1.5	3.8	3.3
East Asia	6.5	6.5	6.0	6.3	6.0
China, People's Rep. of	7.3	7.2	6.8	7.0	6.7
Hong Kong, China	2.5	2.8	2.4	2.9	2.7
Korea, Rep. of	3.3	3.5	2.7	3.7	3.4
Taipei,China	3.8	3.7	1.6	3.6	2.6
South Asia	6.7	7.2	6.9	7.6	7.3
Bangladesh	6.1	6.1	6.5	6.4	6.7
India	7.3	7.8	7.4	8.2	7.8
Pakistan	4.1	4.2	4.2	4.5	4.5
Sri Lanka	4.2	...	6.3	...	7.0
Southeast Asia	4.4	4.9	4.4	5.3	4.9
Indonesia	5.0	5.5	4.9	6.0	5.4
Malaysia	6.0	4.7	4.7	5.0	4.9
Philippines	6.1	6.4	6.0	6.3	6.3
Singapore	2.9	3.0	2.1	3.4	2.5
Thailand	0.9	3.6	2.7	4.1	3.8
Viet Nam	6.0	6.1	6.5	6.2	6.6
The Pacific	6.7	9.9	6.7	4.8	3.9
Fiji	5.3	4.0	4.0	4.0	4.5
Papua New Guinea	8.4	15.0	9.0	5.0	3.0
Developing Asia	6.2	6.3	5.8	6.3	6.0
Major industrial economies	1.4	2.2	1.9	2.4	2.3

Notes: In light of Sri Lanka's revisions to the GDP series in July 2015, the ADO 2015 GDP growth forecasts are not comparable with current estimates and are therefore omitted. Developing Asia refers to the 45 members of the Asian Development Bank listed below. Central Asia comprises Armenia, Azerbaijan, Georgia, Kazakhstan, the Kyrgyz Republic, Tajikistan, Turkmenistan, and Uzbekistan. East Asia comprises the People's Republic of China; Hong Kong, China; the Republic of Korea; Mongolia; and Taipei,China. South Asia comprises Afghanistan, Bangladesh, Bhutan, India, the Maldives, Nepal, Pakistan, and Sri Lanka. Southeast Asia comprises Brunei Darussalam, Cambodia, Indonesia, the Lao People's Democratic Republic, Malaysia, Myanmar, the Philippines, Singapore, Thailand, and Viet Nam.

(continued on the next page)

Inflation (% per year)

Subregion/Economy	2014	2015		2016	
		ADO 2015	Update	ADO 2015	Update
Central Asia	**5.7**	**6.7**	**8.1**	**6.6**	**7.5**
Azerbaijan	1.4	6.0	6.0	5.5	5.5
Kazakhstan	6.7	6.0	8.9	6.2	7.9
East Asia	**1.9**	**1.7**	**1.4**	**2.2**	**2.1**
China, People's Rep. of	2.0	1.8	1.5	2.3	2.2
Hong Kong, China	4.4	3.3	3.2	3.4	3.3
Korea, Rep. of	1.3	1.3	0.8	2.1	2.0
Taipei,China	1.2	0.5	−0.5	1.0	0.5
South Asia	**6.2**	**5.1**	**5.0**	**5.6**	**5.5**
Bangladesh	7.4	6.5	6.4	6.2	6.2
India	5.9	5.0	5.0	5.5	5.5
Pakistan	8.6	5.8	4.5	5.8	5.1
Sri Lanka	3.2	2.0	2.0	5.0	5.0
Southeast Asia	**4.1**	**3.1**	**3.0**	**3.1**	**3.3**
Indonesia	6.4	5.5	6.7	4.0	5.1
Malaysia	3.1	3.2	2.4	2.9	2.9
Philippines	4.1	2.8	2.0	3.3	3.0
Singapore	1.0	0.2	−0.2	1.5	1.0
Thailand	1.9	0.2	−0.7	2.0	1.5
Viet Nam	4.1	2.5	0.9	4.0	4.0
The Pacific	**3.2**	**5.0**	**4.2**	**4.1**	**4.4**
Fiji	0.5	2.5	2.5	2.5	3.0
Papua New Guinea	5.2	7.0	6.0	5.0	6.0
Developing Asia	**3.0**	**2.6**	**2.3**	**3.0**	**3.0**
Major industrial economies	**1.3**	**0.7**	**0.4**	**1.9**	**1.5**

(continued from the previous page)

The Pacific comprises the Cook Islands, Fiji, Kiribati, the Marshall Islands, the Federated States of Micronesia, Nauru, Palau, Papua New Guinea, Samoa, Solomon Islands, Timor-Leste, Tonga, Tuvalu, and Vanuatu. Major industrial economies comprise the United States, the euro area, and Japan.

Data for Bangladesh, India, and Pakistan are recorded by fiscal year. For India, the fiscal year spans the current year's April through the next year's March. For Bangladesh and Pakistan, the fiscal year spans the previous year's July through the current year's June.

1

BRACING FOR
ECONOMIC HEADWINDS

Bracing for economic headwinds

Developing Asia fared well during the global financial crisis of 2008–2009 by swiftly implementing countercyclical policy. While the major industrial economies contracted, the region managed to maintain growth at 6.0% in 2009 and return in 2010 to growth at 9.3%, as before the crisis. For 2015 and 2016, however, developing Asia anticipates growth like that experienced during the crisis but without the prospect of countercyclical measures to boost activity. Now may be the time for developing Asia to accept a slower rate of expansion that reflects the shift in the People's Republic of China (PRC) to growth driven less by investment and more by domestic consumption.

The shift to consumption in the PRC has become more evident since the release in March of *Asian Development Outlook 2015 (ADO 2015)*, and some economies in the region are experiencing the shift as slower exports and lower commodity prices. Because growth in the PRC is expected to remain modest while the major industrial economies recover gradually, this *Update* revises down earlier forecasts for growth in more than half the region's economies (Figure 1.0.1). Unfortunately, India is not yet in a position to pick up the slack in demand from a moderating PRC.

As developing Asia adjusts to slower growth over the long term, its policy makers must continue to pursue reform while addressing risks from volatile and erratic global financial flows, and impacts from changing monetary policies in advanced economies. With commodities in ample supply and energy efficiency improving, commodity prices should be under little pressure, providing incentive for commodity exporters to diversify in favor of new growth opportunities. However, geopolitical conflict continues to pose risks to oil prices. While risks remain manageable, policy makers must brace their economies for the headwinds to come.

1.0.1 Frequency distribution of *Update* forecast changes versus *Asian Development Outlook 2015*

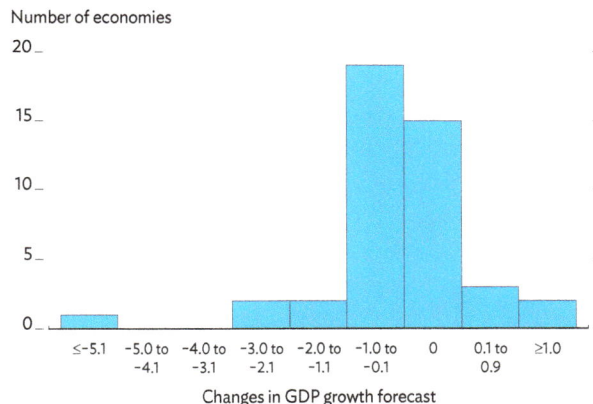

Source: *Asian Development Outlook* database.

This chapter was written by Akiko Terada-Hagiwara, Arief Ramayandi, Xuehui Han, Madhavi Pundit, Thiam Hee Ng, Shiela Camingue-Romance, Cindy Castillejos-Petalcorin, Gemma Esther Estrada, Nedelyn Magtibay-Ramos, Pilipinas Quising, and Dennis Sorino of the Economic Research and Regional Cooperation Department, ADB, Manila. Ganesh Wignaraja provided material on connecting South Asia with Southeast Asia.

Transition to a new normal

Developing Asia is now expected to grow by 5.8% in 2015 and 6.0% in 2016, substantially less than the 6.3% forecast for both years by *ADO 2015* in March (Figure 1.1.1). The revised forecast is well below the 7.6% average for the past decade up to 2014 and closer to the rate recorded in the depths of the global finance crisis of 2008–2009.

Delayed recovery in the major industrial economies and the growth slowdown in the PRC dim the region's prospects. Growth projections for all five subregions are revised down for both 2015 and 2016. Improving prospects in the major industrial economies will buoy the regional outlook somewhat in 2015 and 2016, even as growth in the PRC moderates (Box 1.1.1). However, reform to ease structural bottlenecks remains a challenge in some economies, possibly threatening demand and investment. Inflation in developing Asia is likely to remain low, reflecting lower global commodity prices and soft domestic demand. The forecast for the combined current account remains largely unchanged from March, as lower import bills largely offset the adverse effects of weaker exports of manufactured goods and commodities.

Growth across the region softened along with that of its largest economies and trading partners. All five subregions should expect growth to remain at or below the March projections. Growth forecasts were downgraded in more than half of the individual economies and maintained in about a third. Growth has slowed notably in the two commodity-driven subregions: the Pacific and Central Asia.

For the Pacific, growth prospects are substantially reduced in tandem with those of Papua New Guinea, the subregion's dominant economy, largely reflecting the impact of expenditure cuts necessitated by a worsening fiscal deficit and the temporary closure of the Ok Tedi mine. The Pacific is now forecast to grow by 6.7%, the same as in 2014 but far below the earlier *ADO 2015* forecast of 9.9%. The slowdown is expected to continue in 2016. In Central Asia, growth is now projected to slow by 1.8 percentage points in 2015 as soft commodity prices persist along with recession in the Russian Federation following a currency crisis that jolted consumer demand. Growth is expected to begin recovering next year.

Growth forecasts for the other three subregions in 2015 are lowered by about 0.5 percentage points, reflecting slowdowns in each subregion's largest economy: the PRC in East Asia, India in South Asia, and Indonesia in Southeast Asia. The Nikkei purchasing managers' index (PMI) reveals a similar pattern (Figure 1.1.2). The composite

1.1.1 GDP growth forecasts for developing Asia, 2015 and 2016

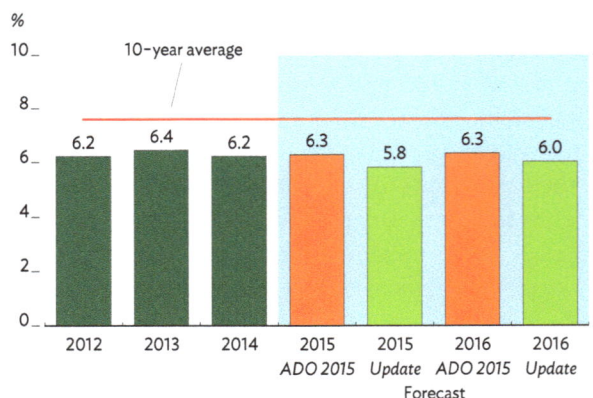

ADO = Asian Development Outlook.
Source: Asian Development Outlook database.

1.1.2 Purchasing managers' index, India, Indonesia, and the People's Republic of China

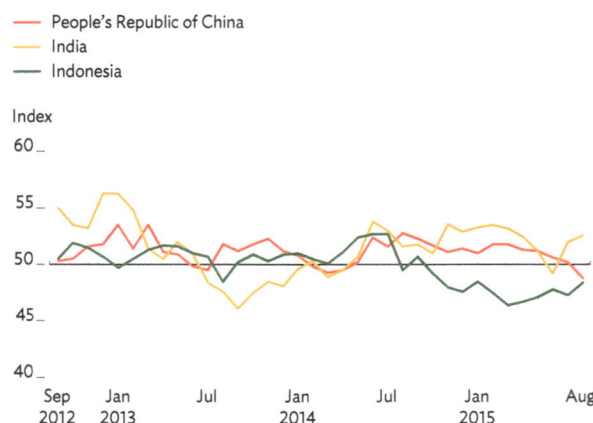

Note: Nikkei, Markit.
Source: Bloomberg (accessed 10 September 2015).

1.1.1 Fragile recovery in the industrial economies

Combined growth in the major industrial economies—the United States (US), the euro area, and Japan—is expected to accelerate to 1.9% in 2015 from 1.4% in 2014, which is less than the *ADO 2015* projection. This *Update* downgrades the growth forecast because Japan and the US were weaker than expected in the first half. A weather-related slowdown in the first quarter limited the anticipated strong US recovery, while Japan saw sluggish recovery in both investment and consumption. However, growth projections in the euro area are upgraded for the forecast period as the risk of a Greek default diminished. Inflation is expected to remain subdued in the industrial economies, as a rise in oil prices proved temporary and food prices have fallen more than expected.

GDP growth in major industrial economies (%)

Area	2013	2014	2015		2016	
	Actual		ADO 2015	Update	ADO 2015	Update
Major industrial economies	0.9	1.4	2.2	1.9	2.4	2.3
United States	1.5	2.4	3.2	2.6	3.0	2.9
Euro area	-0.2	0.9	1.1	1.5	1.4	1.6
Japan	1.6	-0.1	1.1	0.7	1.7	1.4

ADO = Asian Development Outlook.

Notes: Average growth rates are weighted by gross national income, Atlas method. More details in Annex table A1.1 on page 28.

Sources: US Department of Commerce, Bureau of Economic Analysis, http://www.bea.gov; Eurostat, http://ec.europa.eu/eurostat; Economic and Social Research Institute of Japan, http://www.esri.cao.go.jp; Consensus Forecasts; Bloomberg; CEIC; Haver; World Bank, Global Commodity Markets, http://www.worldbank.org; ADB estimates.

After a weak first quarter of 2015, the US economy surged in the second quarter, expanding at a seasonally adjusted annualized rate (saar) of 3.7%. All demand components of GDP contributed to growth. Investment continued to expand robustly, while net exports improved slightly during the first half. A healthy labor market supported growth in private consumption. Unemployment dropped from 5.7% in January this year to 5.1% in August. Other indications that the labor market has further improved include a declining average duration of unemployment, expanding nonfarm employment, and higher average weekly earnings. Housing starts and the housing price index signal continued recovery in residential construction.

Low inflation that averaged just 0.2% in June and July and is decelerating despite an improving labor market is sending mixed signals about the possible timing of the first hike in US interest rates. The US Federal Reserve is now expected to begin a gradual tightening of its monetary policy in the last quarter of this year.

With growth below expectations during the first half of 2015, growth for the full year is now projected at 2.6%, revised down from the 3.2% forecast in *ADO 2015*.

Growth is seen accelerating to 2.9% in 2016, as recent trends in investment, consumption, employment, and housing all suggest that recent growth momentum will continue next year.

Growth in the euro area slowed from a saar of 2.1% in the first quarter to 1.4% in the second. Weaker second quarter growth was evident from a decline in industrial production and soft growth in retail sales. Moreover, private and government consumption contributed less to growth in the second quarter than in the first, while investment subtracted from growth. Net exports were a bright spot, making their biggest contribution to growth in 3 years. Expansionary monetary policy, falling commodity prices, and a weak euro helped keep the region from slipping back into recession.

The seasonally adjusted unemployment rate in the euro area fell to 10.9% in July, the lowest since February 2012. This figure masks wide variation across economies, however, as unemployment is low in Germany but remains high in Spain and Greece, posing the risk that deflation may recur.

Recent indicators suggest that the euro area expanded during the third quarter. The purchasing managers' index rose to 54.3 in August, the highest since May 2011, the economic sentiment indicator increased in both July and August, and both sales and consumer confidence picked up in the early part of the third quarter. As these developments suggest a return to growth momentum, forecast growth in the euro area is revised up from *ADO 2015* forecasts to 1.5% in 2015 and 1.6% in 2016.

Japan's economy posted a surprisingly strong saar of 4.5% in the first quarter. Then activity contracted by 1.2% in the second, reflecting weaker demand both domestic and abroad. Private consumption subtracted 1.6 percentage points from growth, owing to smaller wage increases and cold weather in June. Investment presented a mixed picture, with private residential investment rising while business investment fell.

Demand for Japan's exports deteriorated in the second quarter as real exports fell across all markets. The drop was greatest in Asia, which absorbs half of all exports, followed by the US and the European Union. As the export slump outweighed the drop in imports, net exports subtracted 1.1 percentage points from growth in the second quarter.

Strong corporate profits, a weak yen, and low oil prices support a positive growth outlook for Japan, but downside risks are brewing. The recent volatility in financial markets, devaluation of the renminbi in the PRC, and subsequent depreciation of many other currencies in Asia could further depress external demand for Japan's exports. Domestic consumption and investment are expected to recover but at a slower pace as external demand is expected to remain weak. This *Update* now sees Japan expanding by 0.7% this year, accelerating to 1.4% in 2016. Both numbers are less than projected in *ADO 2015*.

Nikkei PMI for the PRC has been declining since May 2015, reaching 48.8 in August, below the 50.0 mark that separates expansion from contraction. The PMI for India improved in July and August, following a slump in June, on higher production driven largely by new orders. Indonesia's PMI has been below 50.0 for almost a year but rose slightly in August. Investment in all three economies has fallen below levels forecast in *ADO 2015*. Growth is nevertheless expected to accelerate in India and Indonesia in 2016, while it decelerates further in the PRC as the economy there shifts toward consumption-led growth. Consequently, East Asia is the one region expecting no recovery in growth in 2016, the flat 6.0% growth rate in 2016 revised down from 6.3% forecast in March.

Growth in the first half of 2015 underperformed the March forecast for the whole year in 9 of the 11 economies that offer quarterly GDP figures and outperformed the forecast in only 2 economies (Figure 1.1.3). The PRC grew by 7.0% in the first half, down from 7.3% a year earlier but in line with the government's target for the full year. The slowdown came mainly in construction and real estate, which offset acceleration in industry and services. Economies strongly linked to the PRC are feeling the effect of its slowdown. Growth in Taipei,China, an important supplier of machinery and equipment to the PRC, is now projected to slow by more than 50% in 2015 before picking up slightly next year with recovery in the major industrial economies. Growth is expected to slow as well in other economies closely linked to the PRC— the Republic of Korea; Hong Kong, China; and Singapore—but by less than in Taipei,China. Growth in these economies is expected to recover in 2016, though not to the pace anticipated earlier. In India, growth in the first quarter of FY2015 (ends 31 March 2016) slowed to 7.0% from 7.5% in the last quarter of FY2014 as exports, government consumption, and investment all weakened, and as government reform proved weaker to date than expected. Although the number of stalled investment projects had declined by the end of June 2015, much of the government's economic reform package remains to be implemented.

Only in Malaysia and Viet Nam did expansion in the first half this year exceed the forecast in *ADO 2015*. Growth in Viet Nam reached 6.3% in the first half, reflecting higher private consumption that was boosted by stable prices and wage hikes. Investment also improved, spurred by government policies to liberalize regulations and further integrate with the global economy and by the continued migration of low-end manufacturing for export from the PRC, which boosted the production of such goods. In Malaysia, first-half GDP growth slowed to 5.3% but surpassed the forecast for the year made in *ADO 2015*. Private consumption generated most of the growth, underpinned by higher wages, modest growth in employment, and government cash

1.1.3 2015 GDP forecasts in *Asian Development Outlook 2015* versus the year to date in 2015

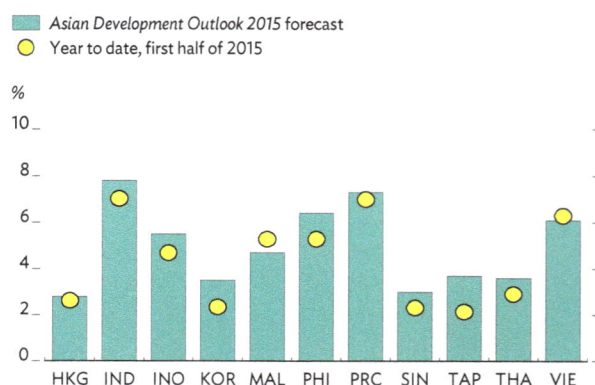

HKG = Hong Kong, China, IND = India, INO = Indonesia, KOR = Republic of Korea, MAL = Malaysia, PHI = Philippines, PRC = People's Republic of China, SIN = Singapore, TAP = Taipei,China, THA = Thailand, VIE = Viet Nam.
Note: For India, April–June 2015, which is the first quarter of FY2016.
Source: *Asian Development Outlook* database.

1.1.4 Demand-side contributions to growth, selected economies

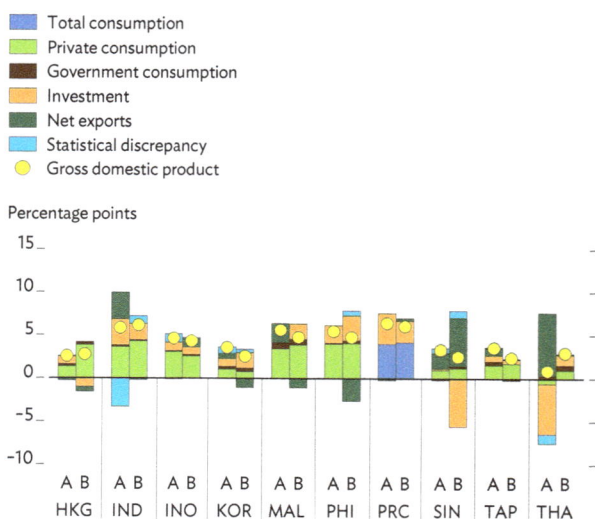

A = first half of 2014, B = first half of 2015, HKG = Hong Kong, China, IND = India, INO = Indonesia, KOR = Republic of Korea, MAL = Malaysia, PHI = Philippines, PRC = People's Republic of China, SIN = Singapore, TAP = Taipei,China, THA = Thailand.
Note: For India, April–June 2015, which is the first quarter of FY2016.
Sources: Haver Analytics; CEIC Data Company (both accessed 10 September 2015).

transfers. Growth in Hong Kong, China in the first half was a tad less than forecast in *ADO 2015* but solid as rising income, a strong labor market, and moderate inflation boosted private consumption.

While exports weakened, low energy prices helped boost consumption in 8 of 10 major regional economies (Figure 1.1.4). Consumption remained robust in the PRC, bolstered by upbeat consumer expectations and higher real disposable income, and in India, on lower inflation and inflation expectations. Retail sales in Thailand improved over a year earlier but was still held in negative territory by mounting household debt, drought, flat private investment, and feeble consumer spending. Retail sales grew in Indonesia, Malaysia, and Viet Nam, though by less than a year earlier (Figure 1.1.5). In Indonesia, consumption moderated as inflation accelerated and consumer credit tightened, while the Republic of Korea took a spending hit from rising household debt and Middle East respiratory syndrome.

Merchandise exports in developing Asia stumbled in the first half of the year, mainly because of the fall in global commodity prices and the depreciation of regional currencies against the US dollar, which depressed the value of exports in US dollar terms. Despite healthy growth in the US, euro area, and other advanced economies, merchandise exports from most developing Asia countries suffered declines year on year, as shipments fell from the PRC and India, which together account for half of the region's exports (Figure 1.1.6). Exports from Indonesia, the largest economy in Southeast Asia, and from Malaysia also deteriorated because of declining energy prices—and as the investment slowdown in the PRC and other factors limited imports of minerals and other industrial materials.

In East Asia, particularly in Taipei,China and the Republic of Korea, the slide in exports was largely the result of weak external demand for electronic products in the PRC and the major industrial economies. Meanwhile, declining oil prices and muted demand from the Russian Federation have cut exports from oil-exporting economies in Central Asia. Lower prices for cotton and rice have contributed to declines in the value of shipments from Pakistan, and lower rice prices also limited exports from Cambodia and Myanmar. Lower prices for rubber have constrained exports from Thailand and, along with poor weather, from Sri Lanka.

Imports also deteriorated because of low prices for oil and weak domestic demand. Central Asia experienced the largest declines as remittances fell in US dollar terms because of the continued recession in the Russian Federation and the depreciation of the ruble. All but a few economies in the region also saw imports decline as oil prices remained low and as weak external demand and the growth slowdown in the PRC inhibited investment and demand for intermediates for export-oriented manufactures, mostly in East and Southeast Asia.

1.1.5 Retail sales in selected developing Asian economies

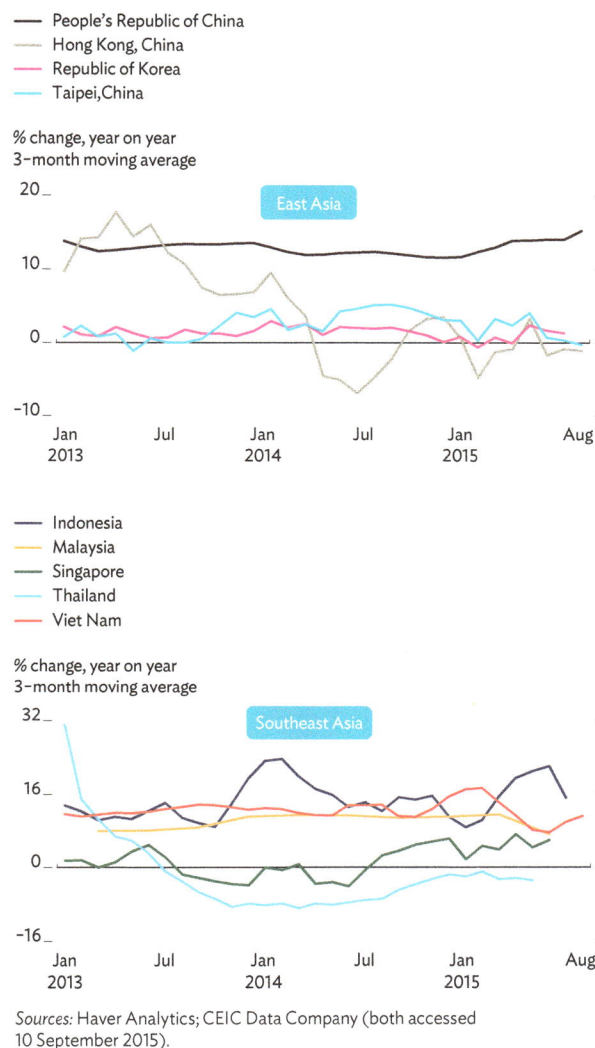

— People's Republic of China
— Hong Kong, China
— Republic of Korea
— Taipei,China

% change, year on year
3-month moving average

— Indonesia
— Malaysia
— Singapore
— Thailand
— Viet Nam

% change, year on year
3-month moving average

Sources: Haver Analytics; CEIC Data Company (both accessed 10 September 2015).

1.1.6 Change in export and import value

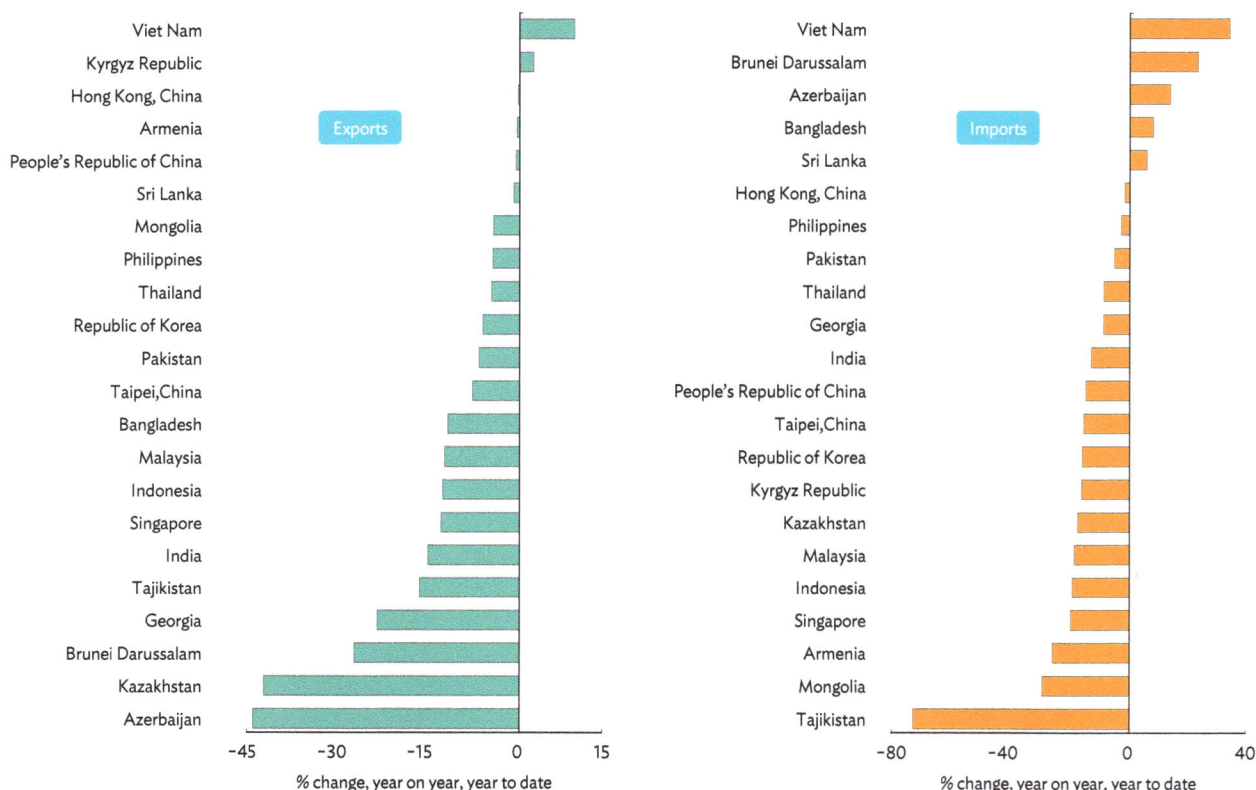

Exports

Viet Nam	
Kyrgyz Republic	
Hong Kong, China	
Armenia	
People's Republic of China	
Sri Lanka	
Mongolia	
Philippines	
Thailand	
Republic of Korea	
Pakistan	
Taipei,China	
Bangladesh	
Malaysia	
Indonesia	
Singapore	
India	
Tajikistan	
Georgia	
Brunei Darussalam	
Kazakhstan	
Azerbaijan	

% change, year on year, year to date

Imports

Viet Nam	
Brunei Darussalam	
Azerbaijan	
Bangladesh	
Sri Lanka	
Hong Kong, China	
Philippines	
Pakistan	
Thailand	
Georgia	
India	
People's Republic of China	
Taipei,China	
Republic of Korea	
Kyrgyz Republic	
Kazakhstan	
Malaysia	
Indonesia	
Singapore	
Armenia	
Mongolia	
Tajikistan	

% change, year on year, year to date

Note: Data are as of July 2015, except for the Kyrgyz Republic (May 2015); Azerbaijan, Brunei Darussalam, Georgia, Kazakhstan, the Philippines, Sri Lanka, and Tajikistan (June 2015); and the Republic of Korea and Viet Nam (August 2015).
Sources: Haver Analytics; CEIC Data Company (both accessed 10 September 2015).

1.1.7 Real and nominal changes in export and import value

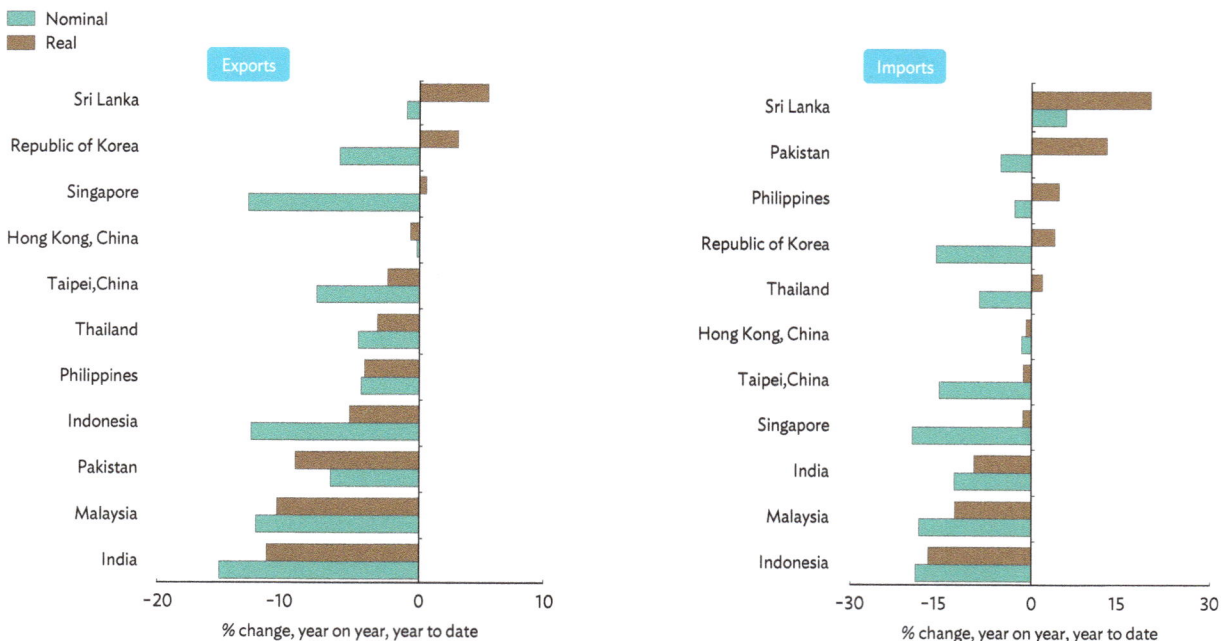

■ Nominal
■ Real

Exports

Sri Lanka	
Republic of Korea	
Singapore	
Hong Kong, China	
Taipei,China	
Thailand	
Philippines	
Indonesia	
Pakistan	
Malaysia	
India	

% change, year on year, year to date

Imports

Sri Lanka	
Pakistan	
Philippines	
Republic of Korea	
Thailand	
Hong Kong, China	
Taipei,China	
Singapore	
India	
Malaysia	
Indonesia	

% change, year on year, year to date

Note: Data are as of July 2015, except for India and Pakistan (March 2015); Sri Lanka (April 2015); Hong Kong, China (May 2015); and the Philippines and Taipei,China (June 2015).
Sources: Haver Analytics; CEIC Data Company (both accessed 10 September 2015).

In economies where volume data are available, export volumes generally declined in the first half of the year from a year earlier, though by much less than the declines in nominal terms. Volumes rose in a few economies (Figure 1.1.7). In Sri Lanka, the Republic of Korea, and Singapore, real exports have been growing, though lower export prices caused nominal exports to decline from January to August. This suggests that the primary reasons for the decline in exports are lower commodity prices and weaker currencies relative to the US dollar. Imports have shown a similar trend. Large declines in imports have resulted mainly from lower prices for imports into the Republic of Korea, Pakistan, the Philippines, and Thailand. Import volumes into these economies actually grew strongly, reflecting strong demand for consumer goods. Tempered global commodity prices helped contain import bills in these economies and kept their current account balances from worsening substantially.

In view of these trends, developing Asia's current account surplus for 2015 is expected to remain unchanged from the *ADO 2015* forecast at 2.5% of GDP this year and 2.3% next year (Figure 1.1.8). While the outlook is generally stable across subregions, commodity exporters are feeling a squeeze. In Central Asia, the projected current account balance is revised down significantly for both years, by 3.0 percentage points to a deficit of 3.2% in 2015, and from a surplus of 0.2% to a deficit of 1.6% in 2016. These developments reflect an expected widening in Kazakhstan's current account deficit and a cut in Azerbaijan's projected surplus in view of weaker prospects for petroleum exports. The Pacific still expects surpluses in both years but significantly narrower ones as energy exporters get lower receipts.

Revisions to the current account balance are minimal for the other three subregions. The East Asia current account surplus is still projected at 3.3% of GDP for 2015, as in *ADO 2015*, but for 2016 is revised up to 3.1% from 3.0% in the earlier forecast. The PRC is likely to achieve the surplus forecast in *ADO 2015*, raising the ratio for East Asia. Imports are likely to decline in 2015 on low energy prices and lower imports of raw materials for construction, in light of a large inventory of unsold housing in lower-tier cities. Imports will recover in 2016 as construction picks up again.

The projected current account deficit in South Asia is expected to worsen only slightly, by 0.1% of GDP, to 1.1% in 2015 and 1.5% in 2016. The larger countries—India, Bangladesh, and Pakistan—all have deficits within 1.5% of GDP, and revisions are slight. All three have experienced falling exports and imports to date in 2015. Falling prices have greatly helped these large oil importers. India's projected current account deficit for this year,

1.1.8 Current account balance, developing Asia

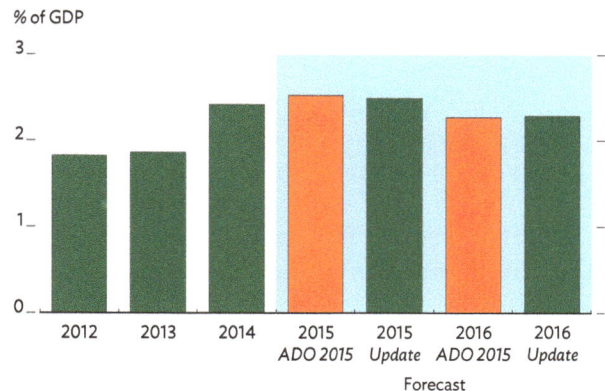

ADO = Asian Development Outlook.
Source: Asian Development Outlook database.

1.1.9 Inflation forecasts in *ADO 2015* versus year to date

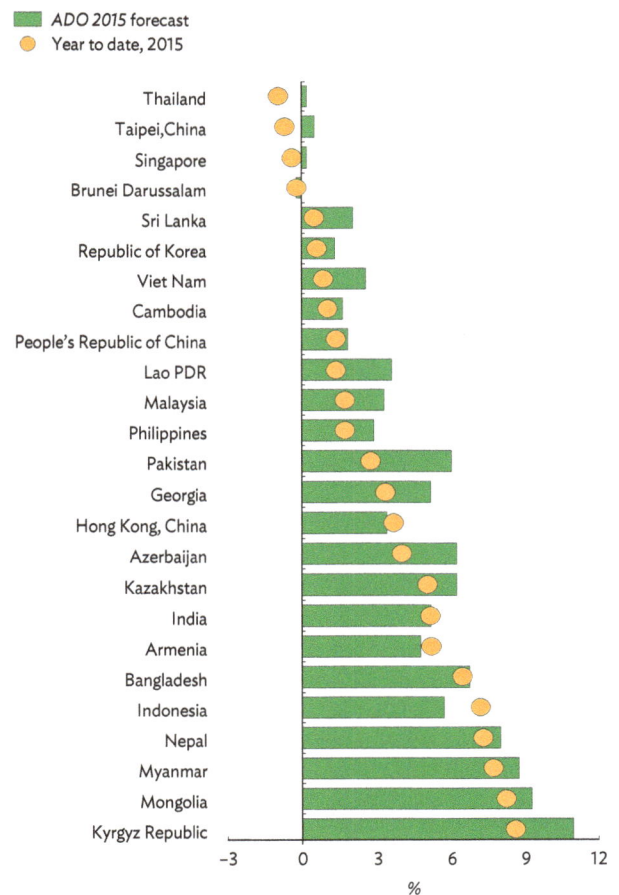

ADO = Asian Development Outlook, Lao PDR = Lao People's Democratic Republic.
Note: Data are as of August 2015 except for Myanmar (February 2015); Brunei Darussalam (April 2015); and Cambodia, the Kyrgyz Republic, Nepal, and Tajikistan (June 2015); and Armenia; Hong Kong, China; India; the Lao PDR; Malaysia; Mongolia; the People's Republic of China; Singapore; and Taipei,China (July 2015).
Sources: Asian Development Outlook database; Haver Analytics; CEIC Data Company (all accessed 10 September 2015).

unchanged from March, reflects the slump in exports over the past few months and modest growth in services, which are expected to continue for the rest of the year due to delayed recovery in the major industrial economies.

In Southeast Asia, the current account surplus is expected to drop marginally to 3.0% of GDP, as merchandise exports from much of the subregion declined in the first half of 2015 because of soft external demand and, for producers of hydrocarbons and other commodities, plunging global prices. Imports also dropped—in some cases more than exports—on account of much lower prices for imported oil, subdued investment, and reduced demand for imported inputs to supply export industries. The subregional current account surplus is seen narrowing slightly in 2016 as stronger investment in the larger economies raises imports of capital equipment.

Global oil prices have remained low, while food prices declined sharply under generally favorable supply conditions. Softening domestic demand has exaggerated these trends. Inflationary pressures have been more subdued than expected in many economies, and a few economies—notably Singapore, Thailand, and Taipei,China—have experienced deflation (Figure 1.1.9, previous page). Weaker global prices have caused prices to fall steadily in developing Asia since Brent crude last peaked at $111.87 per barrel in June 2014.

Many economies have benefitted from lower producer costs, which have helped contain the consumer price index. In the PRC, producer prices have declined for 42 consecutive months and, in August 2015, were 6.2% below those of June 2014. This reflects declines in other commodity prices and the appreciation of the renminbi in real terms, which helped dampen the impact of rising food prices and generally keep inflation at bay. However, producer price inflation was up between August 2015 and June 2014 on sharp depreciation and soft domestic demand in a few countries, notably Georgia, the Kyrgyz Republic, and Nepal (Figure 1.1.10).

Soft global commodity prices are expected to keep domestic price pressures muted, and average inflation in the region is now projected at only 2.3% in 2015, revised down from 2.6%, before rising slightly to 3.0% next year, as forecast earlier. These rates are well below the region's long-run rate of about 4%, reflecting slack domestic demand that may require a policy response if recovery in demand proves weaker than expected. Central Asia is expected to post the highest inflation rate of any subregion during the forecast period as domestic prices rise in depreciated currencies. Inflation forecasts for 2015 in the other subregions are revised down from March. For 2016, average inflation is expected to rise slightly (Figure 1.1.11).

1.1.10 Consumer and producer price inflation, selected developing Asia, June 2014 versus the present

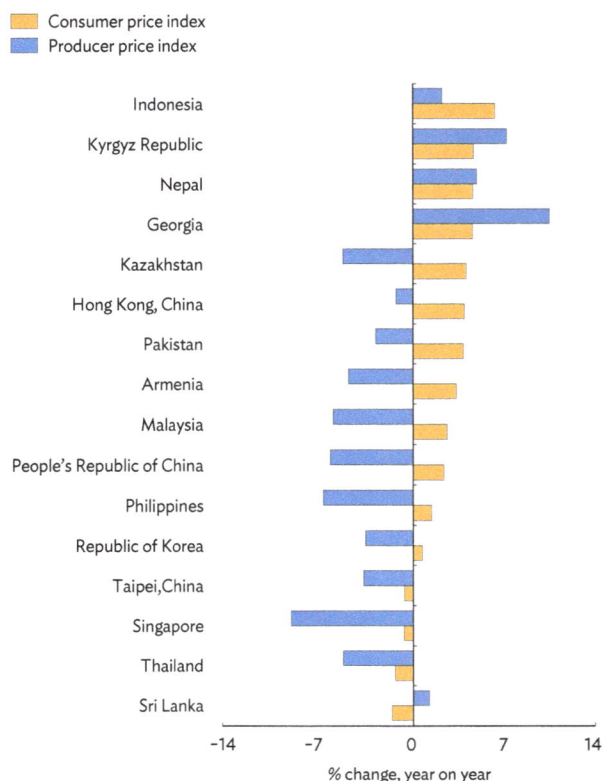

Note: Data are as of August 2015 except for Nepal and Hong Kong, China (March 2015); Armenia and Sri Lanka (April 2015); Georgia, Indonesia, the Kyrgyz Republic, the Republic of Korea, Malaysia, and Singapore (June 2015); and the Philippines and Kazakhstan (July 2015).
Sources: Haver Analytics; CEIC Data Company (accessed 10 September 2015).

1.1.11 Inflation, developing Asia

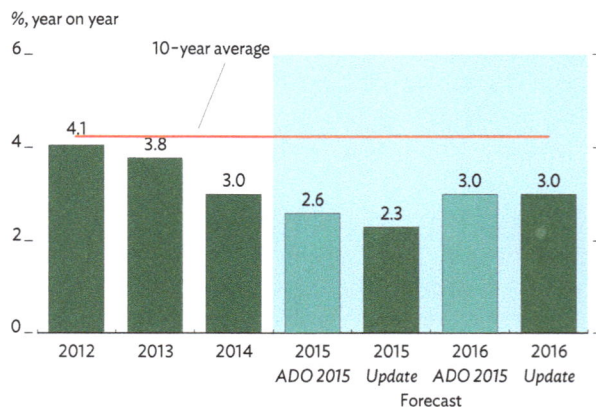

ADO = Asian Development Outlook.
Source: Asian Development Outlook database.

1.1.2 Connecting South Asia with Southeast Asia

Developing Asia—in particular the PRC, the rest of East Asia, and Southeast Asia—have become close partners through global value chains over the past decade. However, moderating growth in developing Asia and in the PRC in particular requires Southeast Asia to find a new engine of growth. As the end of this year will see the inauguration of ASEAN Economic Community, combining the 10 members of the Association of Southeast Asian Nations in an integrated market and production base, the time is ripe to strengthen trade links that look beyond the subregion. South Asia, now the fastest growing subregion in Asia but still enjoying only limited links with Southeast Asia, appears to be the place to explore. The improved political environment is an attraction, as a pro-business Indian government implements its new Act East Policy and opens up to Myanmar, the land bridge between the two subregions. Two populous subregions with a combined population of 2.3 billion people would benefit from better links.

A recent study highlighted the potential for investments in infrastructure and associated software to further economic ties between South and Southeast Asia (Wignaraja et al. 2015). The study found, using the computable general equilibrium model, that the welfare gains from infrastructure-led integration have potential to be large. Assuming the removal of all tariffs and a 50% reduction in nontariff trade barriers applicable to South Asian and Southeast Asian trade, and a 15% reduction in trade costs from improved trade facilitation and infrastructure, the benefits amount to at least $568 billion. More populous South Asia would see the larger gain of $375 billion (8.9% of combined GDP), while Southeast Asia would see a notable gain of $193 billion (6.4%). The smaller economies in South Asia would likely see the largest gains.

There are, however, impediments in the form of barriers to cross-subregional transport mainly in Myanmar, with other gaps in Bangladesh, Cambodia, the Lao People's Democratic Republic, Thailand, and Viet Nam (ADB and ADBI 2015). Missing road and railway links need to be constructed, transport links such as roads connecting to major highways need to be upgraded, and railways need to be modernized and made compatible. Major ports at Chittagong in Bangladesh, Kolkata in India, and Yangon in Myanmar suffer constrained capacity, efficiency, and connectivity to road and rail networks. Various impediments hinder energy trading, including technical barriers related to grid synchronization, gaps in natural gas pipelines, and distorted energy pricing and subsidy regimes.

ADB and ADBI (2015) further suggested that the total cost of infrastructure investment to link the two subregions would be $73 billion. This figure includes $34 billion for railway projects, $18 billion for roads, $11 billion for ports, and $10 billion for energy trade infrastructure (box figure).

Cost to connect South Asia and Southeast Asia

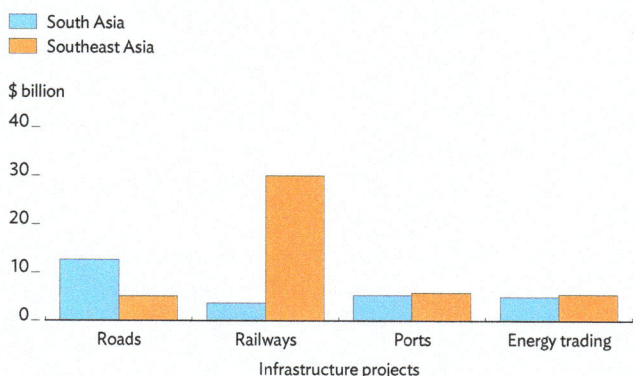

Sources: ADB; ADBI 2015.

Following analysis of infrastructure bottlenecks, the estimates cover projects to upgrade existing infrastructure connecting South and Southeast Asia and to create new infrastructure but excludes the cost of infrastructure projects wholly within either subregion.

As the study supposed that the region may be short of public finance for infrastructure-led integration on this scale, public–private partnership (PPP) would be an important part of the program. Successful PPP in infrastructure has been limited so far because private firms are leery of projects' high risks and long gestation periods, their creation of public goods and the free riding this encourages, and information asymmetries between lenders and borrowers.

Financing infrastructure-led integration would require a deepening of Asian financial markets and new instruments able to accommodate the risks. The development of bond markets and guarantees for infrastructure project bonds may encourage more uptake by institutional investors that take the long view, such as pension funds. Demonstration PPP projects backed by capacity building and advisory services could showcase how PPP works and pique the interest of the private sector, which could be stimulated as well by political risk guarantees, improved transparency and regulatory frameworks, and support for PPP coordination and governance.

Finally, the study suggested that coordinating the planning and implementation of regional infrastructure projects is another challenge because of the myriad regional institutions with different mandates that may overlap and institutions' uneven capacity to manage and finance infrastructure projects. Multilateral and regional development banks can play a useful role as honest brokers and suppliers of knowledge to facilitate regional connectivity.

Growth moderation in the PRC is set to continue in the near term as structural reforms move the economy to a more balanced, more sustainable growth path. Further, the aging population in the PRC will put downward pressure on its growth potential. Economies closely linked to the PRC need to explore new avenues for future growth. For Southeast Asia and South Asia, there is considerable untapped potential in building closer connections between the two subregions (Box 1.1.2, previous page).

As developing Asia adjusts to slower growth over the long term, its policy makers must continue to pursue reform to make their economies more resilient. Key risks to the outlook include possible shocks to crude oil prices from geopolitical strife in the Middle East and the unresolved conflict in Ukraine. Commodity producers must contend with the impact of current low prices, though, particularly those selling directly to the PRC. The anticipation of the upcoming increase in US interest rates and slowing growth in the region have led to outflows of capital and depreciating exchange rates. For a region that has benefited from generally prudent macroeconomic policies over the recent decade, what further steps can be taken to face the global headwinds?

Responding to capital flows

Volatile capital flows are yet again posing challenges to policy makers in developing Asia. While economies in the region face the challenges of maintaining growth momentum, capital flows are ebbing as uncertainty about the expected rise in the US interest rate reverses investors' earlier preference for emerging markets.

Recent trends in regional capital flows

Net flows of capital to 11 selected economies in developing Asia—the PRC; the Republic of Korea; Hong Kong, China; India; Taipei,China; Indonesia; Malaysia; the Philippines; Singapore; Thailand; and Viet Nam—have been negative since the beginning of 2014 (Figure 1.2.1). Net outflows are mainly through portfolio and other investments. Foreign direct investment is holding up well in positive territory, but mostly to the benefit of the PRC. The right panel of Figure 1.2.1, charting net capital flows in the same economies minus the PRC, shows that they have yet to return to positive territory since the capital exodus following the "taper tantrum" in the second half of 2013. Net capital outflows continue in portfolio and other investments.

The aggregate trend in capital flows masks some anomalies in the data. Despite negative net flows to most economies in the region, capital flows into India and Indonesia—the two economies badly hit during the taper tantrum in the second half of 2013—were still positive going into the first quarter of 2015 (Figure 1.2.2). Capital flows entering India

1.2.1 Capital flows to selected Asian economies

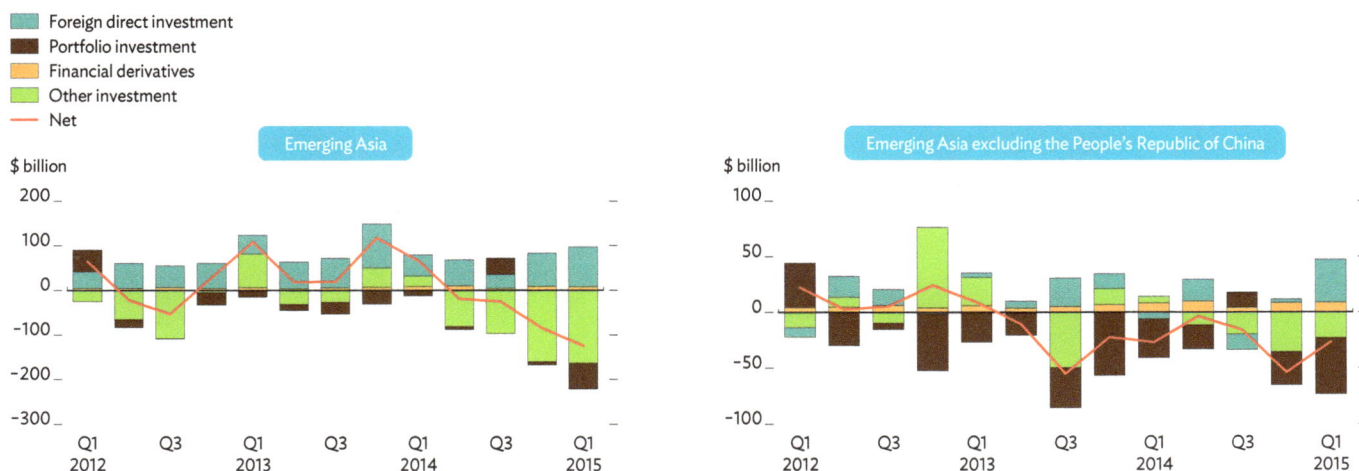

- Foreign direct investment
- Portfolio investment
- Financial derivatives
- Other investment
- — Net

Q = quarter.

Note: Emerging Asia consists of the People's Republic of China; Hong Kong, China; India; Indonesia; the Republic of Korea; Malaysia; the Philippines; Singapore; Taipei,China; Thailand; and Viet Nam. Charts are based on balance of payments data.

Source: Haver Analytics (accessed 4 September 2015).

are still trending upward, while flows to Indonesia are still largely positive, albeit slowing. Short-term flows, particularly portfolio investments, are still the dominant factor in positive net flows in the first quarter of 2015. Other investment, mostly transactions conducted through the banking system, is still positive in India but, in Indonesia, has already dipped into negative territory and started to drag on net inflows.

Are India and Indonesia genuine exceptions? While a lag in the release of data on the balance of payments makes it difficult to assess the most current circumstances, entering the second quarter of 2015, portfolio purchases by nonresidents—the net inflows that have been the major contributor to capital inflows into these economies—plunged dramatically, particularly for equity (Figure 1.2.3). So it does not seem that India and Indonesia are real exceptions to the current regional trend of receding capital flows. They may instead be just a little late in joining the declining trend in capital flows.

The anticipated monetary tightening in the US is not expected to affect financial markets in emerging economies as much as the taper talk did in 2013, but reversals in capital flows may still have considerable implications that complicate the maintenance of financial stability in the region. Risk premiums to economies around the region—represented by the credit default swap premium on 5-year sovereign bonds—have escalated since July 2015. Likewise, local currencies have been under constant depreciation pressure for about as long. Anticipated or not, recent capital outflows pose some threats to regional financial stability.

Challenges for regional monetary authorities

The continuing progress of economic recovery in the US requires the Fed to start tightening its monetary policy to forestall unwanted inflation. A US interest rate rise and associated capital flows out of emerging economies appear to put emerging market economies at risk of financial crises, especially related to foreign exchange rates and debt denominated in foreign currencies, if the capital flows are not managed appropriately (Frankel and Roubini 2001).

The expectation of a higher interest rate in the US suggests continuing pressure for more capital outflows going forward. Movement in the US interest rate in either direction coincides with capital outflow from Asia, with the exception of foreign direct investment (Table 1.2.1). Portfolio flow appears to have the strongest negative correlation with movement in the US interest rate, particularly during the episode of the US interest rate increase in 2004–2006. In light of this, there is a good chance that the upcoming interest rate increase in the US will draw capital away from the region.

1.2.2 Net capital flows, India and Indonesia

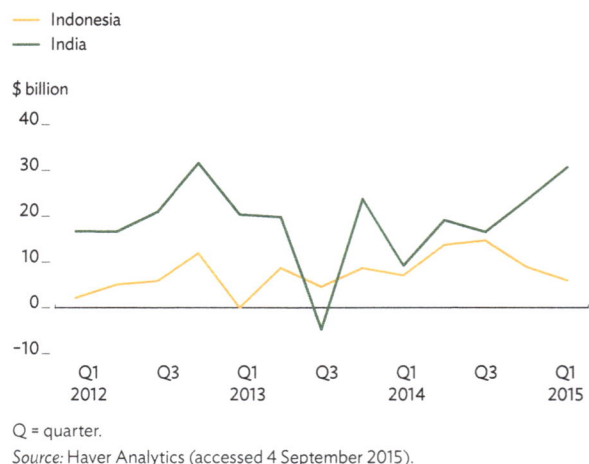

Q = quarter.
Source: Haver Analytics (accessed 4 September 2015).

1.2.3 Total nonresident portfolio equity flows, India and Indonesia

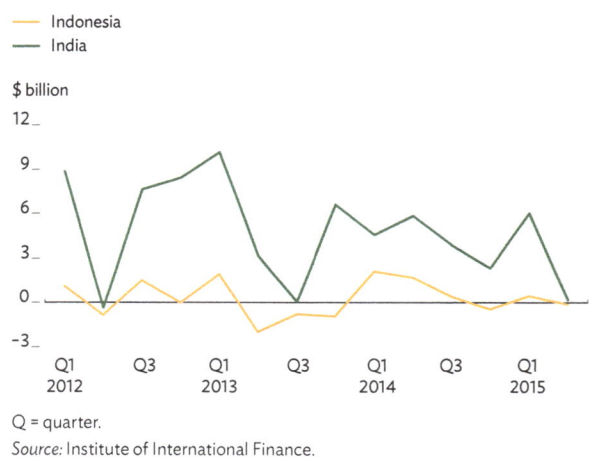

Q = quarter.
Source: Institute of International Finance.

1.2.1 Correlation between movements in the US federal funds rate and capital flows in selected Asian economies

Capital flow	Q4 2000–Q1 2009	US rate decline, Q4 2000–Q3 2003	US rate increase Q1 2004–Q3 2006	US rate decline Q2 2007–Q1 2009
Foreign direct investment	0.308	−0.223	0.328	0.564
Portfolio investment	−0.328	−0.320	−0.601	−0.027
Other investment	−0.020	0.158	−0.066	−0.119
Net	−0.073	−0.422	−0.359	−0.047

Q = quarter.
Note: The economies are the People's Republic of China; Hong Kong, China; India; Indonesia; the Republic of Korea; Malaysia; Singapore; and Taipei,China.
Source: ADB estimates.

As the threatened outflow of capital is anticipated this time, catastrophic implications for financial markets are unlikely. However, regional monetary authorities will still need to perform a balancing act to prevent an exodus of capital that may threaten domestic financial stability. In this regard, monetary authorities in the region may need to respond to the increase in the US interest rate in kind, by symmetrically tightening domestic liquidity.

Unfortunately, unlike in the US, growth is currently weakening in most of developing Asia. This difference in the momentum of economic growth points to a need for developing Asian economies to pursue monetary policies diametrically opposed to the expected policy of the US by loosening their domestic liquidity positions. Though required to catalyze economic growth, easy money policy is not what developing Asia needs now to safeguard domestic financial stability, in the current context of managing capital outflows to ease exchange rate pressures toward depreciation.

Toward independent monetary policy

Developing Asia currently has two competing macroeconomic priorities. One is to safeguard financial stability in the short term in light of uncertainties regarding the impending rise in the US interest rate and the pressures it places on regional financial stability. The other is to check the current downward momentum in economic growth. The first calls for a tighter monetary policy, while the latter demands monetary stimulation to boost domestic demand and so restore growth momentum. To resolve their dilemma, regional monetary authorities need more scope for conducting monetary policy that is more independent of conditions and policy in the US but without jeopardizing the stability of national finances.

What can emerging markets do to strengthen their resilience under foreign monetary policy disturbances? The well-known "trilemma" hypothesis in international finance literature states that a country cannot simultaneously maintain a fixed nominal exchange rate, allow free capital mobility, and pursue an independent monetary policy. In particular, if the authorities want a monetary policy that is independent of the monetary policy of the US or another large and influential foreign economy so they can pursue their domestic policy objectives, they need to either tolerate flexible exchange rates or impose some form of capital controls.

Han and Wei (2014, 2015) formally tested whether the relationship between an economy's domestic monetary policy and the policy of the dominant economic hegemon (in today's world, the US Federal Reserve) depends on a country's nominal exchange rate or on capital control regimes. After controlling for the desired policy rate changes driven by domestic needs and a financial cycle factor, the study examined the association of changes to the US policy rate and to the policy rates of peripheral economies. Economies were put into four categories, those with a fixed exchange rate and capital controls, a fixed exchange rate without capital controls, a flexible exchange rate with capital controls, and a flexible exchange rate without capital controls. The study found

1.2.4 Association of periphery policy rate changes with US policy rate changes

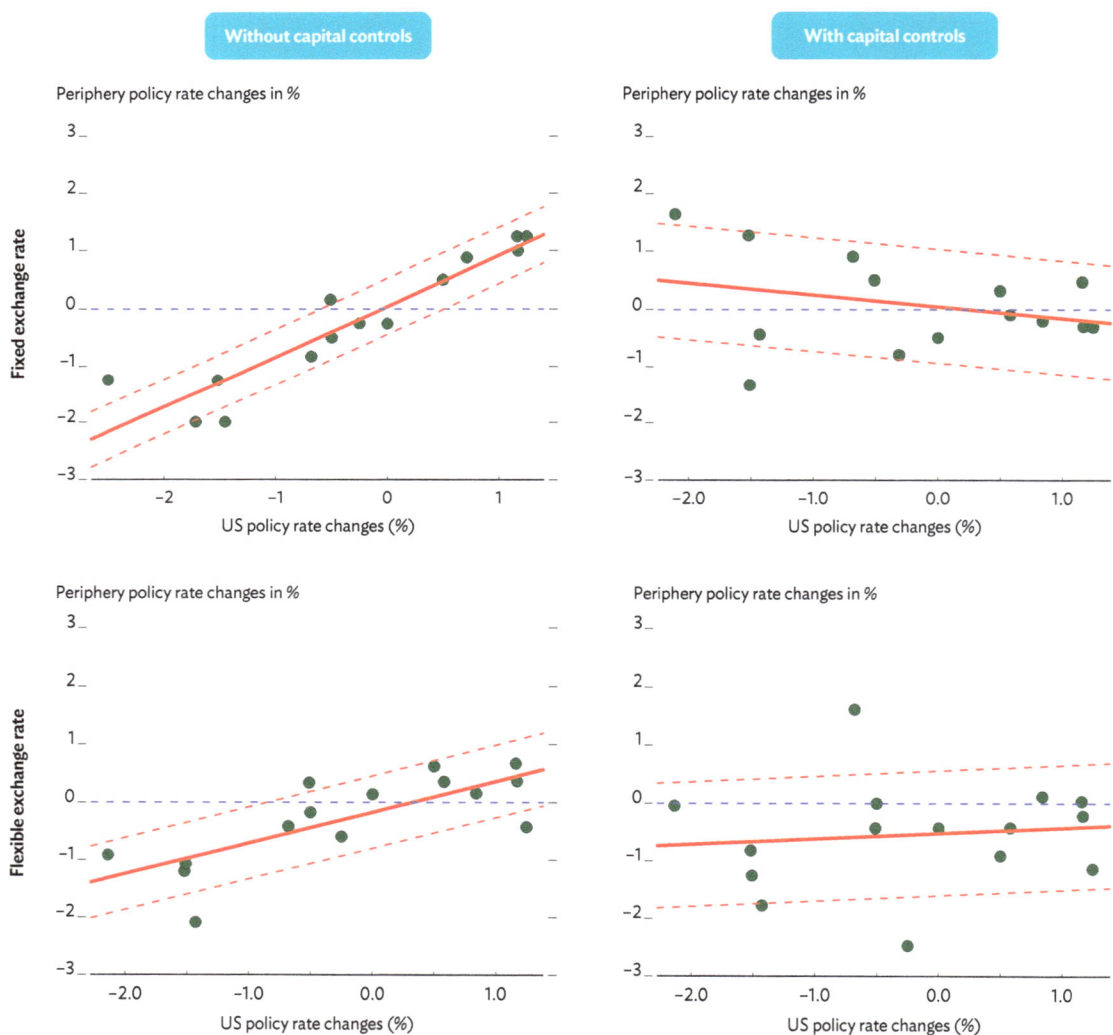

Notes: The figure is an unconditional plot of changes of periphery policy rate along the vertical axis against changes in the US policy rate along the horizontal axis. To reduce noise, observations in each regime were joined into 20 groups, each represented by the group average. Based on these constructed observations, the solid red linear regression line was fitted, along with the 90% confidence interval shown with dashed red lines. The fitted regression lines for regimes without capital controls are significantly positive, but those for regimes with capital controls are not. The 28 periphery economies were Argentina; Australia; Belarus; Bolivia; Brazil; Canada; Chile; the People's Republic of China; Colombia; Costa Rica; Ecuador; Germany; Hong Kong, China; India; Indonesia; Israel; Japan; the Republic of Korea; Mexico; New Zealand; Pakistan; Peru; the Philippines; Singapore; South Africa; Thailand; Turkey; and the United Kingdom. Germany was selected to represent the euro area. Since there were no policy rate changes in the US starting from September 2009, the baseline analysis is from May 1990 to April 2009.
Source: Han and Wei 2015.

that imposing capital controls appeared to help foster monetary independence better than abiding by a flexible exchange rate regime (Figure 1.2.4). Open economies adopting flexible exchange rate regimes are less affected by US policy rate changes than are those with fixed exchange rate regimes. However, peripheral monetary policy is found to be more independent of US monetary policy in countries with capital controls, regardless of which exchange rate regime they adopt. More specifically, the study found that, in economies with fixed exchange rates but no capital controls, a US interest rate increase by 100 basis points is followed on average by an increase in a peripheral economy's interest rate by 65 basis points. In economies with flexible exchange rates and no capital controls, the same change in the US interest rate induces an increase in peripheral interest rate of only 45 basis points. The differences between regimes with capital controls are not statistically significant.

These results imply that imposing some sort of control on cross-border capital flows can be an effective way for economies to gain a measure of monetary autonomy. However, although a flexible exchange rate regime allows for lower spillover from US monetary policy shocks, it does not fully insulate domestic monetary policy.

As emerging Asia has experienced dramatic increases in portfolio capital outflows in recent quarters, the natural question is whether prudential controls that differentiate capital flows by type are any better or less effective than undifferentiated capital controls at enhancing monetary policy independence. Han and Wei (2015) found that picking the right flows to control does make a difference. Controls on cross-border capital flows that limit debt-related instruments—particularly bonds, money market commercial and financial credits, and derivatives—are effective ways to gain autonomy in conducting monetary policy. The study suggested that controlling flows through these three debt instruments simultaneously is the most effective way to gain domestic monetary policy autonomy.

To deal with the monetary policy dilemma between stabilizing the domestic financial sector and responding to the need for domestic demand stimulation, regional authorities can achieve a degree of monetary policy independence from the US Federal Reserve by adopting careful macroprudential policy that selectively controls destabilizing capital flows. Imposing filters on several types of debt flows can make independent monetary policy more effective.

Depreciating currencies accompanying large capital outflows may support the region's exporters, but there are downsides for macroeconomic managers. In particular, foreign currency debt in the region has been on the rise as governments and corporations took advantage of the low interest rates. As the strengthening dollar raises the local currency value of foreign currency debt and debt service, it is important to analyze the extent to which this may have heightened developing Asia's vulnerability to external shocks.

Corporate debt and the strengthening dollar

Concerns have arisen about the impact of currency depreciation on regional economies. A major concern about currency depreciation is the damage it can do to corporate balance sheets. A sharp decline in currency value can force up a firm's indebtedness if it has large unhedged foreign borrowings and little foreign revenues to serve as a natural hedge. As corporations outside the financial sector are usually tightly integrated with the rest of the real economy, banks' nonperforming loans can easily proliferate when these corporations fall on hard times.

It is important to note that depreciation in developing Asia has been gradual, not at all like the sharp drop experienced during the Asian financial crisis of 1997–1998. This slower pace of change may mitigate the adverse effects of depreciation, as it allows corporations and policy makers more time to adjust. Large, sudden collapses in the value of a currency are more worrying as they can precipitate a parallel collapse in confidence in the economy.

Several studies have found that balance sheet effects from currency depreciation can exacerbate the impact of depreciation on the larger economy. Krugman (1999) warned that, when the value of a currency suffers a large fall, the harm to balance sheets may outweigh the benefits of increased export competitiveness. The analysis cautioned that firms' foreign currency borrowings can threaten the economy as a whole because they make it more vulnerable to external shocks. During the Asian financial crisis, Harvey and Roper (1999) found that corporations had borrowed foreign currency heavily in the belief that their currency would remain pegged. When the currency collapsed, corporations' foreign currency liabilities ballooned. Cavallo et al. (2005) suggested that margin constraints could induce a wave of forced selling that further drives down the value of domestic assets.

Damage to an economy from depreciation can be compounded by a liquidity or credit crunch. In an economy with a lot of debt denominated in foreign currency, local currency depreciation will likely force some companies into default. When this happens, banks become wary of extending loans, and credit tightens. This pushes corporations into production cutbacks, which further undermines their profitability and the quality of their debt. Blalock, Gertler, and Levine (2008) found that the Asian financial crisis squeezed liquidity-constrained domestic firms in Indonesia more than foreign-owned firms, which could still get credit from abroad.

Recent trends in foreign currency debt

Since the beginning of 2015, the US dollar has strengthened against almost all Asian currencies (Figure 1.3.1). The Malaysian ringgit has depreciated by 16% since the beginning of the year, and the Indonesian rupiah by 11%. As US monetary policy moves toward a tighter monetary stance while most Asian economies head the other way toward accommodation, this divergence is likely to put further downward pressure on regional currencies. Forecasters do not expect them to recover their value before the end of 2016. The strengthening dollar has raised concerns about the extent of Asian economies' foreign currency exposure.

In recent years, several Asian economies have loaded up on debt. Bonds outstanding in the PRC, India, Indonesia, the Republic of Korea, Malaysia, Pakistan, the Philippines, Sri Lanka, Thailand, and Viet Nam rose from 68% of combined GDP in 2008 to 85% in 2014. While most of the increased debt is in domestic currency, foreign currency debt has picked up strongly as well. This can be seen in the rapid growth in new issuances of foreign currency bonds in these economies, most of them denominated in US dollars, which reached a record high of $242 billion in 2014. The value of all outstanding foreign currency bonds in these economies reached $725 billion in June 2015 (Figure 1.3.2).

Corporations have been behind most of the rise in foreign currency bond issuance, as governments still favor borrowing in domestic currency, and the value of sovereign foreign currency bonds outstanding has been relatively stable. Low US interest rates and plentiful liquidity have encouraged more corporations to issue foreign currency bonds.

Corporate exposure to foreign currency debt

A careful examination of corporations' exposure to foreign currency debt assists understanding of how the dollar's rise affects their prospects in different Asian economies. Information on 346 publicly listed nonfinancial companies in 10 Asian economies was collected for analysis. The currency of bank loans and bonds outstanding for the sample companies was obtained. So was the geographical distribution of their revenue sources to estimate the extent to which overseas revenues can serve as a natural hedge for foreign currency liabilities. Generally, the sample includes the largest publicly listed firms in the countries. Table 1.3.1 shows how the firms are distributed across economies and their share of assets relative to all assets of nonfinancial corporations and to GDP. For Malaysia, the Philippines, and Thailand, the sample includes more than two-thirds of all nonfinancial corporations by asset value. In countries with well-developed financial systems, the sample firms' assets equal a sizeable portion of GDP.

The data have limitations that should be noted. The dataset is not meant to capture comprehensively all the foreign currency liabilities of

1.3.1 US dollar versus regional currencies

People's Republic of China	India
Indonesia	Republic of Korea
Malaysia	Pakistan
Philippines	Sri Lanka
Thailand	Viet Nam

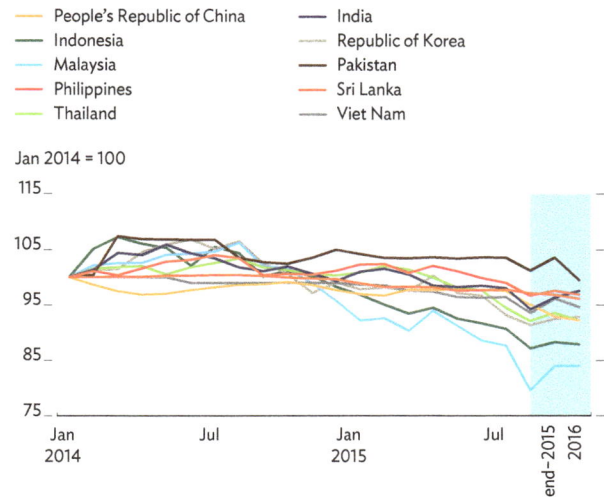

Jan 2014 = 100

Note: Measured as US dollar per local currency unit. Lower value signifies depreciation. End-2015 and 2016 are consensus end-of-period forecasts from FocusEconomics.
Sources: ADB estimates; Haver Analytics; International Monetary Fund; State Bank of Viet Nam; FocusEconomics.

1.3.2 Foreign currency bonds outstanding

■ Government
■ Corporate

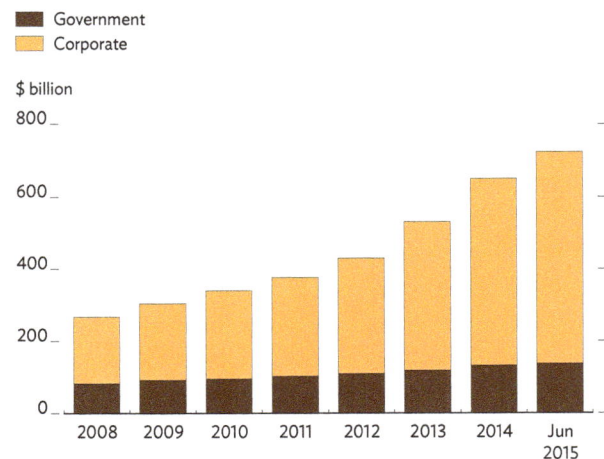

$ billion

Note: The sample includes the People's Republic of China, India, Indonesia, the Republic of Korea, Malaysia, Pakistan, the Philippines, Sri Lanka, Thailand, and Viet Nam.
Sources: AsianBondsOnline; Bloomberg (accessed 4 September 2015).

1.3.1 Share of sample firms' assets to the assets of all nonfinancial companies and to GDP

Economy	Number of firms	Share of assets[a] (%)	Share to GDP (%)
China, People's Republic of	50	29	10
India	50	57	39
Indonesia	50	45	12
Korea, Republic of	50	66	104
Malaysia	50	68	94
Pakistan	19	32	7
Philippines	19	76	54
Sri Lanka	10	38	10
Thailand	31	70	60
Viet Nam	17	22	6

[a] Sample firms' share of the assets of all nonfinancial corporations in the economy.

Source: ADB estimates based on data from Bloomberg and CEIC Data Company (both accessed 21 August 2015).

nonfinancial corporations in an economy. It excludes, for example, large firms that did not provide data on the currency breakdown of their debt. Further, information was not available on the firms' use of financial derivatives to hedge their foreign currency exposure.

Yet the data suggest differences in exposure across East, South, and Southeast Asia.

Looking at the distribution of corporate foreign currency borrowings, the vast bulk of them are denominated in US dollars. In regional economies, corporations in Indonesia, Sri Lanka, and Viet Nam have over 65% of their borrowings in US dollars (Figure 1.3.3). While corporations in the PRC carry a lot of foreign debt, it is relatively small as a share of the total debt burden, at 14%.

Across Asia, the sector that is most exposed is energy, which has 61% of its borrowings in US dollars. This likely reflects the large capital expenditure required in that sector. Another factor is that energy investments typically have long payback periods, often too long for local banks and capital markets to accommodate. Communications—another capital-intensive sector—has about 42% of its borrowings in US dollars.

While corporations have significant foreign debt exposure, some also have foreign earnings that serve as a natural hedge to mitigate risk. Among the economies in the sample, Malaysia and the Republic of Korea both have significant revenues from overseas. However, in most other economies, the share of foreign revenues is quite low (Figure 1.3.4).

Individual firms may be at risk of mismatch between their foreign currency debt and their foreign currency revenues. Calculating the ratio of foreign revenue to foreign debt for each sample firm allows an estimate of their ability to cover foreign debt payments from their own foreign revenue streams. A substantial number of firms have foreign currency debt but no foreign

1.3.3 Currency breakdown of corporate borrowings by country

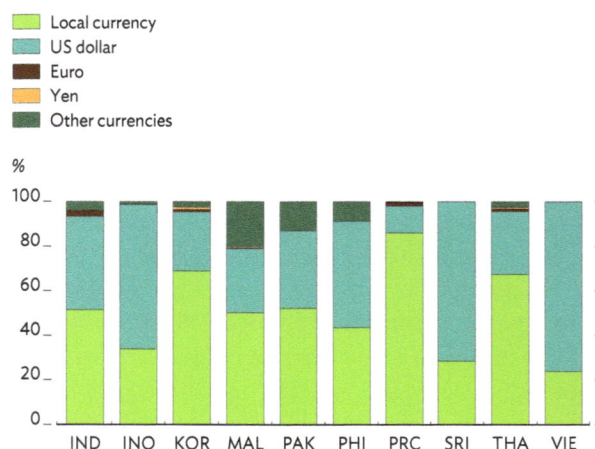

IND = India, INO = Indonesia, KOR = Republic of Korea, MAL = Malaysia, PAK = Pakistan, PHI = Philippines, PRC = People's Republic of China, SRI = Sri Lanka, THA = Thailand, VIE = Viet Nam.
Source: ADB estimates based on data from Bloomberg (accessed 21 August 2015).

currency revenue. In Viet Nam, 69% of sample firms (by asset value) that have foreign currency debt do not report any foreign currency revenue (Table 1.3.2). Similarly, a lot of corporations in Indonesia and the Philippines—firms that account for a large portion of corporate assets—do not have foreign currency revenue to match their foreign currency debt. In contrast, most corporations with foreign currency debt in the PRC, India, the Republic of Korea, and Thailand have substantial foreign earnings.

When faced with an appreciating dollar, heavily leveraged companies are the most vulnerable. The rising value of their foreign currency debts, and the higher cost of servicing them, could force them to violate their debt covenants. Pushed into distress, the companies may have no choice but to cut back on their spending and thereby forfeit hopes of digging themselves out. Leverage is commonly measured as the ratio of debt to capital. In developing Asia, corporations in the PRC, India, and Pakistan are relatively highly leveraged (Figure 1.3.5). Meanwhile, the share of corporate debt in foreign currency is relatively low in the PRC but quite high in India and Pakistan.

Another cause for concern, especially for companies with mostly short-term debt maturing soon, is that they may have trouble refinancing their debt as liquidity tightens. They are also likely to face higher costs for new borrowing. In the region, corporations in Indonesia and Pakistan have the largest share of foreign currency debt maturing by 2017 (Figure 1.3.6).

Conclusions and policy options

Analysis of the sample data shows that the nonfinancial corporate sector in some economies carries a lot of foreign currency debt, much of which is denominated in US dollars. Corporations in Indonesia, Sri Lanka,

1.3.4 Share of currency revenue by country

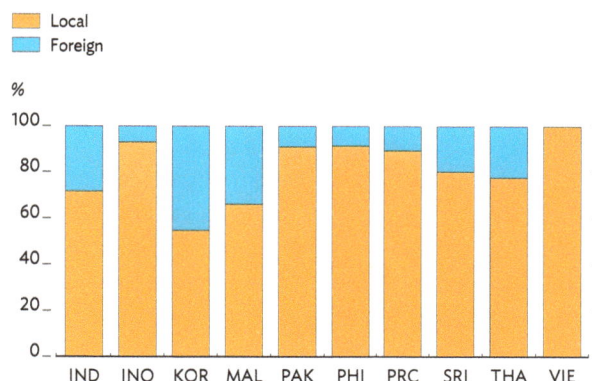

Legend: Local, Foreign

IND = India, INO = Indonesia, KOR = Republic of Korea, MAL = Malaysia, PAK = Pakistan, PHI = Philippines, PRC = People's Republic of China, SRI = Sri Lanka, THA = Thailand, VIE = Viet Nam.
Source: ADB estimates based on data from Bloomberg (accessed 25 August 2015).

1.3.2 Share of sample firms' assets by ratio of foreign currency revenue versus debt

Economy	No FCY revenue (%)	Share of FCY revenue to FCY debt		No FCY debt
		Less than 1 (%)	More than 1 (%)	
China, People's Republic of	1	11	27	60
India	33	26	31	10
Indonesia	66	10	10	13
Korea, Republic of	3	20	62	14
Malaysia	24	36	20	21
Pakistan	31	0	10	59
Philippines	72	9	6	13
Sri Lanka	48	0	19	33
Thailand	28	17	30	25
Viet Nam	69	0	0	31

FCY = foreign currency.
Source: ADB estimates based on data from Bloomberg (accessed 25 August 2015).

and Viet Nam have the highest share of foreign currency debt. Firms in the energy sector tend to have a substantial portion of their borrowings in foreign currency. Typically, the corporations that have a high share of foreign debt are also highly leveraged. This heightens their exposure to the impacts of US dollar appreciation.

Some exposure to foreign currency fluctuation can be mitigated if corporations earn revenues in foreign currency. In the Republic of Korea and Malaysia, substantial overseas earnings offset some of the exposure arising from foreign currency debt. However, companies in Indonesia, Pakistan, the Philippines, and Viet Nam are oriented more toward domestic markets and therefore earn little or no foreign revenue. This may leave them more exposed to the effect of US dollar appreciation. With US interest rates poised to rise, liquidity in the region is expected to tighten. This will pose a risk to corporations that have substantial borrowings coming due over the next few years, as in Indonesia, where 31% of corporate borrowings will mature by 2017.

Corporations' large foreign currency exposure could put the home economy at risk of balance sheet effects from local currency depreciation. This creates a dilemma for policy makers. While local currency depreciation can make exporting economies more competitive, it can also stress those with weak financial systems. Eijffinger and Karatas (2012) warned that tighter monetary policy can exacerbate financial vulnerability in developing economies. Hence, policy makers face difficult choices in the face of currency depreciation.

To minimize future exposure to currency fluctuation, authorities in the region should continue to strengthen their domestic financial systems. A better-developed domestic financial system can mitigate some of the risks of depreciation. Bordo, Meissner, and Stuckler (2010) found that economies with well-developed financial systems are more resilient under depreciation shock. With a well-developed and liquid domestic financial system, corporations can borrow more in their own currency and rely less on foreign currency borrowing. Where firms that need to borrow a lot have to rely on foreign borrowings, because the domestic financial market is not large or liquid enough, deepening the domestic financial system will give them the option of raising funds domestically in their own currency. To reduce risk in the corporate sector, the authorities can limit the unhedged foreign currency exposure of firms and promote greater use of derivatives for hedging. Encouraging more stable sources of funding such as foreign direct investment can also help improve resilience.

1.3.5 Leverage versus share of foreign currency debt

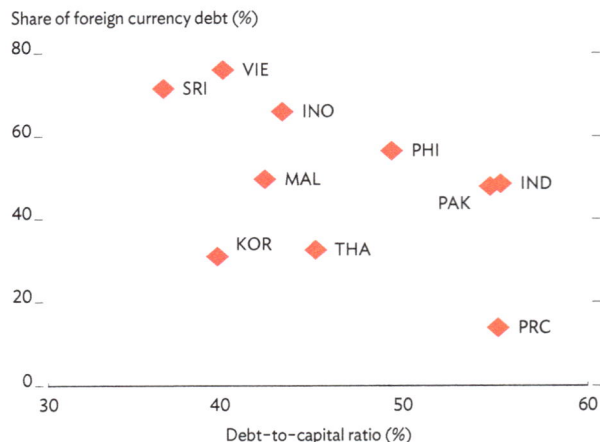

IND = India, INO = Indonesia, KOR = Republic of Korea, MAL = Malaysia, PAK = Pakistan, PHI = Philippines, PRC = People's Republic of China, SRI = Sri Lanka, THA = Thailand, VIE = Viet Nam.
Source: ADB estimates based on data from Bloomberg (accessed 25 August 2015).

1.3.6 Share of foreign currency debt maturing by 2017

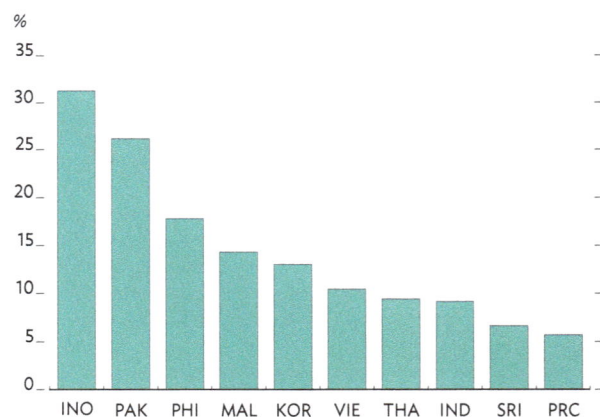

IND = India, INO = Indonesia, KOR = Republic of Korea, MAL = Malaysia, PAK = Pakistan, PHI = Philippines, PRC = People's Republic of China, SRI = Sri Lanka, THA = Thailand, VIE = Viet Nam.
Source: ADB estimates based on data from Bloomberg (accessed 25 August 2015).

The PRC and commodity exporters in developing Asia

A slowdown in the PRC has raised concern about its implications for commodity markets and therefore for commodity exporters in developing Asia. Standard & Poor's GSCI is a commodity index that tracks 18 commodity prices grouped in four categories: agriculture, industrial metals, precious metals, and energy. The measure started to decline in 2011 and sharply accelerated down in 2014, dropping by the end of August 2015 to a 6-year low. Just as rising prices in the past coincided with rapid growth in the PRC that sucked in the large supplies of commodities needed to support high investment, more recent falling prices mesh with the narrative of growth deceleration in the PRC since 2011 (Figure 1.4.1). Understanding the role of the PRC in commodity markets is essential to reading the prospects facing commodity exporters in developing Asia.

The PRC and commodity markets

The PRC is a major importer of commodities, especially energy and base metals. The PRC share of world iron ore imports averaged 67% from 2012 to 2014. Similarly, the PRC took in this period more than 30% of copper imports, as well as large shares of imports of coal and crude oil that made it either the largest or second-largest importer of some of these commodities (Table 1.4.1). In terms of apparent consumption—the sum of production and imports less exports—it is clear that the PRC was a major consumer of industrial metals, absorbing large shares of global production. While coal was the biggest source of energy in the PRC, demand for crude oil was also high. Imports and consumption of natural gas were relatively small.

Rapid growth led by investment and manufacturing for export gave the PRC a voracious appetite for commodities in the 3 decades before the global financial crisis of 2008–2009, after which growth in the PRC started to slow. Further growth deceleration may result from the leadership's current efforts to rebalance the economy toward sustainability built on greater reliance on domestic consumption.

Some forecasters envisage a hard landing for the PRC as rebalancing proceeds. Gauvin and Rebillard (2015), for example, assumes that growth will drop sharply over the next 2 years and stabilize at 3.0% over a longer horizon as investment stagnates. Projections for the PRC in this *Update* foresee a much softer landing as growth slows gradually

1.4.1 Global commodity prices and GDP growth in the PRC

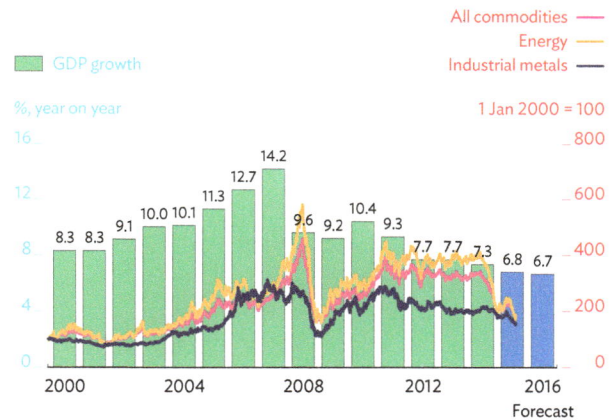

Sources: Bloomberg (accessed 29 August 2015); *Asian Development Outlook* database.

1.4.1 Imports of energy and base metals to the PRC

Commodity	Share to world imports, average 2012–2014 (%)
Iron ore	66.6
Copper	32.5
Nickel	28.1
Coal	22.0
Crude oil	14.5
Zinc	13.8
Tin	9.0
Aluminum	7.2
Natural gas	5.7

Note: Trade data are not reported annually for all countries. Averages for the period indicated based on the reported data.

Source: United Nations Comtrade database (accessed 28 August 2015).

to 6.7% in 2016. Yet, considering the importance of the PRC in the world economy, even a soft landing may undercut global recovery.

A growth slowdown would have negative spillover in other economies, as lower investment rates in the PRC bring down demand for primary commodities and potentially drive down world commodity prices. The spillover can flow to commodity-producing economies through two channels: directly through reduced trade in commodities and other exports to the PRC, and indirectly through declining world prices for commodities. Commodity exporters may find that lower commodity prices encourage other trade partners to boost their imports, diminishing the PRC share of world imports. Alternatively, exporters may respond to lower demand and prices by cutting back on production and investment, shrinking the commodity trade pie but not so much the PRC share of it. The extent to which the slowdown in the PRC affects output in commodity exporters in the short and medium run will depend on what happens to the share of the PRC in global commodity trade.

Impact on Asia's commodity exporters

Developing Asia is a major commodity producer. The region supplies significant shares of exports of metals such as tin, zinc, and copper (Table 1.4.2). Regarding energy commodities, developing Asia is a big coal exporter, providing 26% of world exports averaged for the years 2012–2014, and it contributes more than 10% of global natural gas and crude oil exports. However, as direct exports of commodities to the PRC from the rest of the region are relatively small, the impact of the PRC slowdown on producers' economies will occur indirectly through world commodity price changes. The economies that do have high direct exports to the PRC will feel the effect of reduced demand directly as well.

The share of commodities in export baskets varies across regional economies. Shares of energy-related commodities can be large. Azerbaijan and Kazakhstan export mainly crude oil, which constitutes 85% and 65% of their total exports on average for 2012–2014, and half of Brunei Darussalam's exports are natural gas. The shares of natural gas and coal in Indonesia's total exports are more than 10% each, while the share of coal in Mongolia's exports is almost 20%. With regard to industrial metals, copper constitutes 34% of Mongolia's exports in the same period. These economies are exposed to external shocks arising in world commodity markets.

For primary commodity producers, there are two channels of potential impact: the direct effect of lower PRC demand for their exports of commodities and other goods, and the indirect effect on global commodity prices. Toward estimating the impact, a model uses annual data on the export shares of 19 developing Asian economies, many of which are commodity exporters, and the global prices for commodities from 2007 to 2013 where data are available. While fluctuations in growth are determined by a number of factors,

1.4.2 Developing Asia's export share of commodities and share of its exports shipped to the PRC, average 2012–2014

Commodity	Share of world exports (%)	Share of exports shipped to the PRC (%)
Tin	70.7	5.3
Coal	26.2	6.9
Zinc	25.3	7.6
Copper	20.2	7.3
Aluminum	19.4	1.2
Nickel	15.8	0.9
Natural gas	14.2	0.4
Crude oil	10.9	9.4
Iron ore	4.0	2.9

PRC = People's Republic of China.

Note: Trade data are not reported annually for all countries. Averages for the period indicated based on the reported data.

Source: ADB estimates based on UN Comtrade database (accessed 28 August 2015).

1.4.1 Evaluating the impact of the slowdown in the People's Republic of China

A slowdown in the PRC can reduce demand for primary commodities and for other goods, and it can drive down global commodity prices, with any combination of these three effects spilling over to affect the growth rates of commodity exporters. The following method was used to evaluate the impact of the PRC growth slowdown on growth in developing Asian economies through export and price channels.

GDP growth in country i at time t is:

$$
\begin{aligned}
GDP_{it}^{gr} = \alpha + \beta_1 &\left(\frac{Nonprimary\ export\ to\ the\ PRC_{it}}{GDP_{it}} \right) \times GDP_{PRC,t}^{gr} \\
+ \beta_2 &\left(\frac{Commodity\ export\ to\ the\ PRC_{it}}{GDP_{it}} \right) \times GDP_{PRC,t}^{gr} \\
+ \beta_3 &\left(\frac{Commodity\ net\ import\ from\ the\ world_{it}}{GDP_{it}} \right) \times Price_t \\
+ \beta_4 &vol_t + \beta_5 tot_t \\
+ \eta_i &+ \varepsilon_t + \upsilon_{it}
\end{aligned} \tag{1}
$$

where, GDP_{PRC}^{gr} is GDP growth in the PRC; $Price$ is the logarithm of the real world price of a commodity, i.e., deflated by the US consumer price index; vol is the standard deviation of GDP growth in an economy over a rolling 5-year period; and tot is the change in the terms of trade.

Spillover from the PRC slowdown on growth in other economies is estimated as follows:

$$
\begin{aligned}
\frac{\partial GDP_{it}^{gr}}{\partial GDP_{PRC,t}^{gr}} = \beta_1 &\times Nonprimary\ export\ share\ to\ the\ PRC \\
+ \beta_2 &\times Commodity\ export\ share\ to\ the\ PRC \\
+ \beta_3 &\times Commodity\ net\ import\ share\ from\ the\ world \times \frac{\partial Price_t}{\partial GDP_{PRC,t}^{gr}}.
\end{aligned} \tag{2}
$$

The first element represents the spillover effect of a growth slowdown through exports to the PRC other than primary commodities. The second element represents the spillover effect through exports of primary commodities to the PRC. And the third element represents spillover through the price channel weighted by the share of net imports to GDP. The final term in equation (2) contains the response of commodity price to changes in GDP growth in the PRC, i.e., the impact of the PRC slowdown on global commodity prices. To quantify this, the estimate follows Roache (2012) in that a 1.0 percentage point increase in the growth rate of PRC output (using industrial production) is taken to result in an increase in the real price of oil and coal of around 2.0%.

The regression was estimated using panel data fixed effects methodology for 19 Asian economies in 2007–2013 for each of the commodities: coal, oil, copper, and iron (box table). Annual export data came from the United Nations' Commodity Trade Database using Standard International Trade Classification version 3 to define trade in each commodity. Yearly averages of commodity prices and the US consumer price index were taken from the International Financial Statistics database of the International Monetary Fund. The nominal GDP in US dollar terms was sourced from Haver Analytics and the *Asian Development Outlook* database. The real GDP growth series was from the *Asian Development Outlook* database. The spillover effect on GDP growth from trade and commodity price channels only, as determined by equation (2), depends on whether the coefficients corresponding to each element in the regression are significant.

Dependent variable: real GDP growth in the PRC

Variables	Coal	Oil	Copper	Iron
Volatility variable	0.0570	0.0479*	–0.0155	–0.0055
Change in the terms of trade	0.104**	–0.0834**	0.0674	0.0553
Share of nonprimary exports to total exports to the PRC	2.880***	3.446***	3.6450***	3.2750***
Share of coal to total exports to the PRC	36.100**			
Real price of coal	1.742+			
Share of crude oil to total exports to the PRC		38.3700***		
Real price of crude oil		–0.0951*		
Share of copper to total exports to the PRC			51.8700**	
Real price of copper			2.5560	
Share of iron to total exports to the PRC				45.4600+
Real price of iron				0.3250
Observations	52	86	59	57
R-squared	0.207	0.310	0.216	0.128
Number of economies	13	19	12	11

PRC = People's Republic of China.

Notes: The regression results are from a robust panel regression with fixed effects. Statistical significance at the 1%, 5%, 10%, and 15% level is denoted by ***, **, *, and +.

Source: ADB estimates.

the analysis here focuses on the direct and indirect effects through trade and commodity price channels only. The results from the regression analysis, described in Box 1.4.1 (previous page), suggest that there is spillover from all three sources: exports to the PRC of products other than primary commodities; exports to the PRC of coal, crude oil, copper, and iron ore; and price effects from oil and coal.

As Malaysia, Thailand, and Viet Nam have relatively large shares of exports other than primary commodities to the PRC, slower growth in the PRC has direct spillover through this trade channel to these economies. Indonesia, as a major coal exporter, faces a reduction in demand that drags down growth. Among the major commodity exporters in the region, all of those that export crude oil to the PRC feel the direct impact of reduced demand as a drag on their growth. However, for net importers of oil, the decline in world oil prices offsets some of the lost growth. An example is Fiji, a commodity exporter but net importer of oil whose growth rate stays essentially unchanged because of the offsetting price effect.

Net exporters with deep trade links with the PRC like Azerbaijan, Brunei Darussalam, Indonesia, Kazakhstan, and Mongolia will be doubly affected. This is consistent with the argument that a fall in export revenues from lower world prices may feed through as lower growth because commodity producers cut production and investment, and lower revenues reduce government consumption. In the simulation, a slowdown in PRC growth of 1.0 percentage point causes growth to slow by an estimated average of 0.7 percentage points in this group of economies.

The results have to be interpreted keeping in mind that the analysis is limited to spillover through trade and commodity price channels, and does not consider all determinants of growth in an economy that may mitigate or aggravate these effects. Yet the magnitude of the impact from these channels underscores the policy challenges some commodity exporters in developing Asia face from the PRC growth slowdown. Maintaining flexible monetary and fiscal policy can help buffer effects on the economy in the short run. Analysis highlights the need over a longer term for structural reform to diversify production and exports to reduce overreliance on trade in primary commodities, as well as diversify export markets.

The analysis looks at the potential effects of reduced demand from the PRC on markets for commodities. But there are also supply-side factors that can influence trade and price effects. Particularly in the case of oil, supply-side effects are extremely important determinants of world prices, as highlighted in the commodity prices section of the Annex (page 34). Further, the moderation of the PRC growth rate progressively mutes the role of the PRC in commodity markets. At the same time, other large regional economies such as India and Indonesia have potential to import more industrial metals as their investment rates rise to support stronger growth.

References

ADB and ADBI. 2015. *Connecting South Asia and Southeast Asia.* Asian Development Bank and Asian Development Bank Institute. http://www.adb.org/publications/connecting-south-asia-and-southeast-asia

Blalock, G., P. J. Gertler, and D. I. Levine. 2008. Financial Constraints on Investment in an Emerging Market Crisis. *Journal of Monetary Economics* 55(3).

Bordo, M. D., C. M. Meissner, and D. Stuckler. 2010. Foreign Currency Debt, Financial Crises, and Economic Growth: A Long-Run View. *Journal of International Money and Finance* 29(4).

Cavallo, M., K. Kisselev, F. Perri, and N. Roubini. 2005. Exchange Rate Overshooting and the Costs of Floating. *Federal Reserve Bank of San Francisco Working Paper* No. 2005-07.

Eijffinger, S. C. W. and B. Karatas. 2012. Currency Crises and Monetary Policy: A Study on Advanced and Emerging Economies. *Journal of International Money and Finance* 31(5).

Frankel, J. A. and N. Roubini. 2001. The Role of Industrial Country Policies in Emerging Market Crises. *NBER Working Paper* No. 8634. National Bureau of Economic Research.

Gauvin, L. and C. Rebillard. 2015. https://www.banque-france.fr/uploads/tx_bdfdocumentstravail/DT-562_01.pdf

Han, X. and S.-J. Wei. 2014. Policy Choices and Resilience to International Monetary Shocks. *Global Economic Review* 43(4).

——. 2015. Forthcoming. International Transmissions of Monetary Shocks. Asian Development Bank.

Harvey, C. R. and A. H. Roper. 1999. The Asian Bet. In Harwood, A., R. Litan, and M. Pomerleano, eds. *Financial Markets and Development: The Crisis in Emerging Financial Markets.* Brookings Institution Press.

Krugman, P. 1999. Balance Sheets, the Transfer Problem, and Financial Crisis. In Isard, P., A. Razin, and A. Rose, eds. *International Finance and Financial Crises: Essays in Honor of Robert P. Flood, Jr.* Kluwer Academic Publishers.

Roache, S. K. 2012. https://www.imf.org/external/pubs/ft/wp/2012/wp12115.pdf

Wignaraja, G., P. Morgan, M. Plummer, and F. Zhai. 2015. Economic Implications of Deeper South Asia–Southeast Asia Integration: A CGE Approach. *Asian Economic Papers* 14(3).

Annex: Global rebound disappoints

The combined growth forecast for the major industrial economies—the United States (US), the euro area, and Japan—in 2015 is downgraded from the *ADO 2015* projection of 2.2% to 1.9%, which still improves on growth in 2014 at 1.4%. In the US, the strong recovery projected for this year is moderated by a slowdown in the first quarter from one-off disruptions. In Japan, the pace of domestic consumption and investment recovery has been slower than expected, prompting downgrades to forecasts for both 2015 and 2016. Meanwhile, in the euro area, the overriding risk of a threatened Greek default escalating into a crisis across that region has abated for now, providing a fillip to its growth projections for the next 2 years (Table A1.1).

Low inflation has enabled the major industrial economies to continue accommodative monetary policy into the third quarter of 2015. Compared with the path of global commodity prices forecast in *ADO 2015*, the pickup in oil prices proved short-lived, and food prices have fallen more steeply. Global inflationary pressures are expected to remain subdued overall. Though the US is likely to begin raising interest rates before the end of the year, monetary authorities in Japan and the euro area will maintain their quantitative easing programs and may even expand them.

A1.1 Baseline assumptions on the international economy

	2013	2014	2015		2016	
	Actual		ADO 2015	Update	ADO 2015	Update
GDP growth (%)						
Major industrial economies[a]	0.9	1.4	2.2	1.9	2.4	2.3
United States	1.5	2.4	3.2	2.6	3.0	2.9
Euro area	−0.2	0.9	1.1	1.5	1.4	1.6
Japan	1.6	−0.1	1.1	0.7	1.7	1.4
Prices and inflation						
Brent crude spot prices (average, $ per barrel)	108.9	98.9	65.0	55.0	75.0	60.0
Food index (% change)	−7.1	−7.2	−6.0	−13.0	0.0	−1.0
Consumer price index inflation (major industrial economies' average, %)	1.2	1.3	0.7	0.4	1.9	1.5
Interest rates						
United States federal funds rate (average, %)	0.1	0.1	0.4	0.2	1.7	1.0
European Central Bank refinancing rate (average, %)	0.5	0.2	0.0	0.0	0.0	0.0
Bank of Japan overnight call rate (average, %)	0.1	0.1	0.1	0.1	0.1	0.1
$ LIBOR[b] (%)	0.2	0.2	0.5	0.2	1.8	1.1

ADO = Asian Development Outlook.

[a] Average growth rates are weighted by gross national income, Atlas method.

[b] Average London interbank offered rate quotations on 1-month loans.

Sources: US Department of Commerce, Bureau of Economic Analysis, http://www.bea.gov; Eurostat, http://ec.europa.eu/eurostat; Economic and Social Research Institute of Japan, http://www.esri.cao.go.jp; Consensus Forecasts; Bloomberg; International Monetary Fund, Primary Commodity Prices, http://www.imf.org; World Bank, Global Commodity Markets, http://www.worldbank.org; ADB estimates.

Recent developments in the major industrial economies

United States

The US economy revived strongly in the second quarter of 2015, growing at a seasonally adjusted annualized rate (saar) of 3.7% following a weak start at 0.6% growth in the first quarter due to the harsh winter and a West Coast ports dispute (Figure A1.1). Earlier in the year, the authorities had announced GDP contraction in the first quarter by 0.2%, but technical revisions to the GDP series, which were released in July, revised the estimate to modest expansion. The revised GDP series shows the US growing at a slower pace since the first quarter of 2012 than in previously published figures, requiring a recalibration of the forecast growth path.

Growth in the second quarter reflected positive contributions from all demand components of GDP. Even net exports regained a slight increase in the first half of the year as exports grew by a saar of 5.2% in the second quarter and posted a positive contribution to GDP growth.

Private consumption is still growing at a solid annualized rate of 3.1% despite the sharp loss of consumer confidence in the second quarter to an April–June average of 93.1 from 98.0 in the first quarter (2007 = 100). The fall in oil prices and favorable growth in the labor market that poised wage growth for acceleration are seen to be behind this persistently strong growth in private consumption. In August, the consumer confidence index jumped back to 98.2 from 88.0 in July (Figure A1.2), suggesting sustained momentum in consumption growth in the third quarter. The rebound also indicates a more upbeat perception of the health of the US economy and its prospects going forward.

Investment continued to improve in the first half of 2015 with growth at an average saar of 6.9%, up from 5.0% in the same period last year. Fixed investment, however, has been growing at a slower pace since the fourth quarter of 2014. The purchasing managers' index compiled by the Institute for Supply Management rose from 56.3 in January to 58.0 in August (values above 50.0 denoting increased production), the index having peaked in July at 59.4, the highest since September 2005. This increase indicates a steady pace of production, as confirmed by stability throughout the year in the industrial production index, which barely moved from 103.1 in January to 103.0 in July (2007 = 100).

The labor market further strengthened in the first 8 months of 2015. From January to August, the unemployment rate fell from 5.7% to 5.1%, the average duration of unemployment shortened from 32.3 weeks to 28.4 weeks, and nonfarm employment grew by an average rate of 2.2% year on year. Labor market improvements are

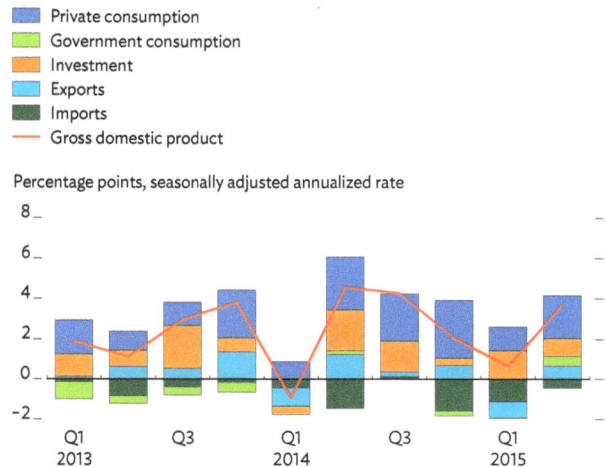

A1.1 Demand-side contributions to growth, United States

Q = quarter.
Sources: US Department of Commerce, Bureau of Economic Analysis, http://www.bea.gov; Haver Analytics (both accessed 4 September 2015).

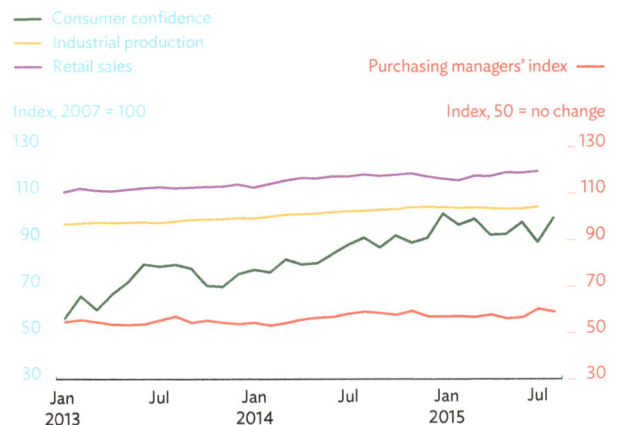

A1.2 Business activity and consumer confidence indicators, United States

Note: For the purchasing managers' index, a reading <50 signals deterioration of activity, >50 improvement.
Source: Haver Analytics (accessed 4 September 2015).

evident in the rise of average weekly earnings by 2.3% in the first 8 months of 2015, which was slightly faster than the 2.1% pace in the same period last year and should further support consumption. In addition, housing starts and the housing price index extended their upward trends that began in 2012, suggesting continued recovery in residential construction.

Inflation has continued to decelerate since December 2014, posting a rate of 0.1 in June 2015 and 0.2 in July 2015, slowed by low international commodity prices and the appreciation of the dollar (Figure A1.3). Core inflation is picking up gradually, however, and approaching 2.0%. The stronger labor market and the low inflation environment are sending mixed signals about when the US policy rate may stir. On this note, the US Federal Reserve is expected to start the tightening cycle of its monetary policy only gradually at some time in the last quarter of 2015.

The US economy is forecast to strengthen gradually through 2016, led by expanding private sector activity. Positive signs in investment, consumption, housing, and employment support this view. However, surprisingly slow growth in the first half of the year points to 2.6% growth in 2015 as a whole, lower than the 3.2% projected in *ADO 2015*. Barring extreme weather, the economy is expected to maintain its growth momentum in 2016, with GDP growing at 2.9% for the year.

Euro area

Recovery in the euro area turned sluggish as GDP growth slowed from a saar of 2.1% in the first quarter to 1.4% in the second (Figure A1.4). Yet the region, bolstered by a combination of loose monetary policy, falling commodity prices, and a low euro, managed to avoid slipping back into recession despite deepening uncertainty surrounding the Greek crisis in the second quarter. Among the major economies, Spain recorded in the quarter strong growth at 4.0%, Germany and Italy modest growth at 1.8% and 1.3% respectively, and the Netherlands meager growth at 0.3%, while France stagnated. Surprisingly, Greece grew by a strong 3.7%, a significant improvement over the poor performance of 0.2% in the first quarter of 2015.

Breaking down the region's GDP into its expenditure components revealed a slight reduction in the contribution of private and government consumption, and a drag on growth from investment compared with the first quarter. But net exports recorded the strongest contribution in 3 years.

The fall in investment is reflected in a weak industrial sector that had flat results in the first half of the year as production dropped by an average of −0.2% in the second quarter. However, the August rise in the composite purchasing managers' index to 54.3, the highest since May 2011, is a positive sign for economic expansion in the third quarter. The European Commission's economic sentiment

A1.3 Inflation, United States

—— Headline
—— Core

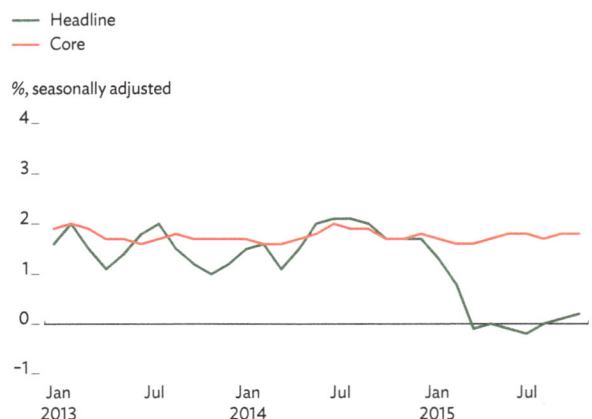

Source: Haver Analytics (accessed 4 September 2015).

A1.4 Demand-side contributions to growth, euro area

■ Private consumption
■ Government consumption
■ Total investment
■ Net exports
— Gross domestic product

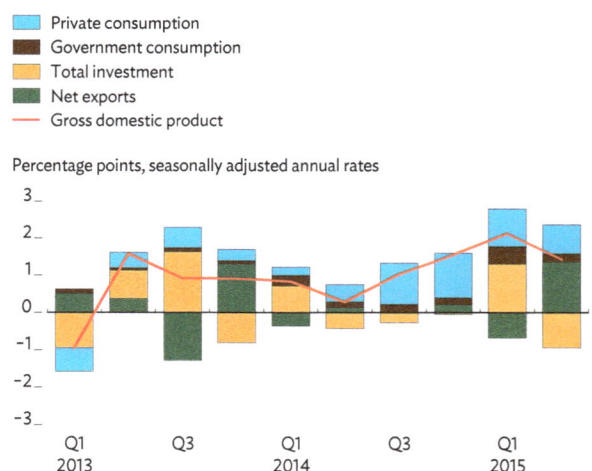

Q = quarter.
Source: CEIC Data Company (accessed 9 September 2015).

indicator also remained somewhat flat in the second quarter, possibly as uncertainty surrounding the Greek crisis spilled over to dull consumer and business confidence. It edged up again in the first 2 months of the third quarter.

As reflected in quarterly national accounts data and also by weak growth in monthly retail sales, consumer spending took a blow in the second quarter. However, sales and consumer confidence both picked up in the early months of the third quarter, which suggests that the drop in demand may be reversed, especially because labor markets appear to be strengthening (Figure A1.5).

The euro area's seasonally adjusted unemployment rate fell to 10.9% in July, the lowest since February 2012. While the decline bodes well for recovery in the region as a whole, there is wide variation in unemployment rates in individual countries. Germany had the lowest rate, at 4.7% in July, while Spain recorded a high 22.2% and, in May, Greece recorded 25.0%. High unemployment indicates that there is considerable slack in these economies, which will continue to hold down inflation.

As such, the risk of deflation is reemerging as a concern for the region. The harmonized index of consumer prices, which turned positive in May after a period of deflation, slipped from 0.3% to 0.2% in June and stayed at this rate through August. While this mainly reflects low energy prices, future declines in commodity prices and the recently rising euro will once again bear down on inflation rates.

Trade in the region benefitted from the relatively weak euro. Merchandise exports registered healthy growth at 6.2% in the first half of the year, well up from 0.8% in the same period last year. Import growth was lower at 2.5% in January–June 2015 (Figure A1.6). As a result, the external sector posted a trade surplus of €124.5 billion in the first half of the year, half again up from €86.4 billion last year. Whether or not export growth will pick up further will depend on the persistence of a low euro.

The European Central Bank is sticking to its proposed path of monetary easing by maintaining near-zero interest rates. The quantitative easing program initiated in June 2014 and expanded in January 2015 is slated to run at least until September 2016, but the central bank may extend the program further until the inflation path is consistent with achieving its 2% target. The easing of credit conditions has had some effect, as loans to households and nonfinancial corporations have been rising in recent months, albeit slowly.

The combination of better credit supply, low prices, and a low euro supported economic recovery in the region in the first half of the year that was stronger than expected. Further, the overriding risk that a Greek default could escalate into a crisis across the euro area has abated for the time being because European leaders approved a third bailout for Greece. Although problems of low inflation, high unemployment, subdued domestic demand, and high debt persist, business and consumer indicators suggest that the economy is stronger

A1.5 Selected economic indicators, euro area

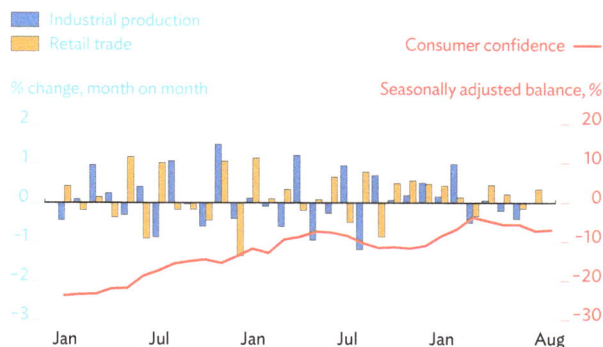

Note: Percent balance is the difference between respondents reporting an increase and those reporting a decrease.
Source: CEIC Database (accessed 9 September 2015).

A1.6 Trade indicators, euro area

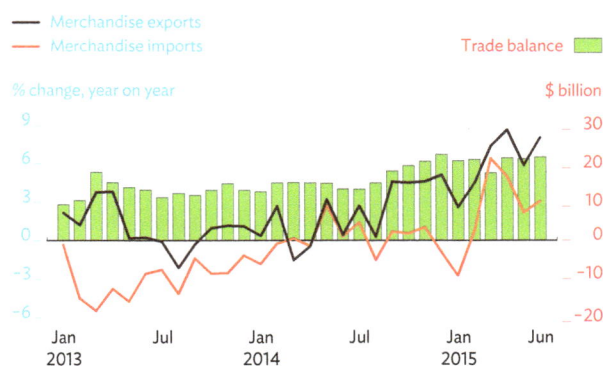

Source: CEIC Database (accessed 9 September 2015).

than a year ago and will enjoy some momentum in the coming quarters. Growth forecasts are therefore revised up from *ADO 2015* to 1.5% in 2015 and further to 1.6% in 2016.

Japan

Economic activity in Japan seesawed in the first half of 2015, as surprisingly brisk first quarter growth at a saar of 4.5% was followed in the second quarter by 1.2% contraction. In the first half as a whole, GDP grew by 2.3%, slightly slower than *ADO 2015* assumed in March. The slowdown in the second quarter was broad-based, reflecting weaker demand both domestic and external.

Slower wage growth and colder weather in June dampened private consumption, which fell by 2.7% and subtracted a sizeable 1.6 percentage points from GDP growth in the second quarter. Investment was a mixed picture. Though private residential investment continued to grow steadily by 8.0% in the second quarter of 2015, contributing 0.2 percentage points to growth, business investment lost momentum and fell by 3.6%. Soaring corporate profits, which grew by 23.8% year on year in the second quarter, did not translate into more new investment in the second quarter on top of solid 1.6% growth in the first. Although public demand contributed positively, domestic demand as a whole subtracted 0.6 percentage points from GDP growth (Figure A1.7).

Domestic weakness in the second quarter was exacerbated by deteriorating external demand. Real exports fell across all destinations. Half of Japan's exports are directed to other Asian countries, where the drop was sharpest at –4.1%, followed by –3.6% to the US and –2.7% to the European Union. External demand was particularly weak for capital goods, electronic parts and devices, and input materials, but held up relatively well for cars. While imports also fell, deteriorating exports carried more weight, such that net exports were the second biggest drag on growth after private consumption, subtracting 1.1 percentage points in the second quarter.

Recent indicators are mixed. The purchasing managers' index picked up to above 51 in July from below 50 in April, indicating further expansion. Building and housing starts once again started to rise in May this year following 15 consecutive months of decline in the wake of the boom in 2013 as purchases were brought forward to beat the new value-added tax (VAT) (Figure A1.8). Inventory destocking progressed while production slowed in response to disappointing demand. Yet, the ratio of inventory to sales remains high, rising to 144.0 in July 2015 from 133.4 in the same month last year, which suggests that production may stay anemic in the coming months. Consumer confidence is softening somewhat going into the third quarter, but private consumption of durable goods and housing investment are

A1.7 Demand-side contributions to growth, Japan

- Private consumption
- Government consumption
- Private investment
- Public investment
- Net exports
- Gross domestic product

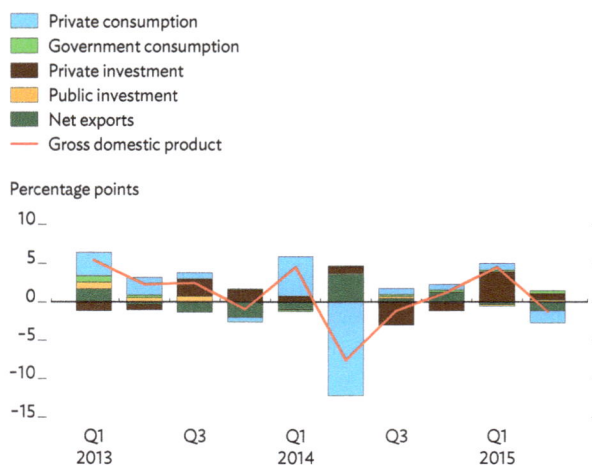

Q = quarter.
Source: Economic and Social Research Institute, Cabinet Office, http://www .cao.go.jp/en/about.html (accessed 8 September 2015).

A1.8 Housing and building starts, by floor area, Japan

- Buildings
- Housing

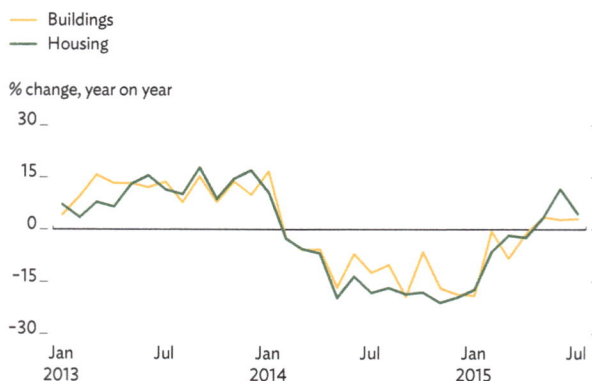

Sources: CEIC Data Company; Haver Analytics (both accessed 2 September 2015).

expected to pick up somewhat in 2016 in anticipation of a further rise in the VAT from 8% to 10% on 1 April 2017.

As the base effect from the April 2014 VAT hike faded, inflation slowed to 0.5% in the second quarter of 2015 and averaged 1.4% in the first half. Soft oil prices and limp demand continued to shave inflation. Monetary policy is expected to remain accommodative and may be loosened further if domestic demand weakens. Assuming that global oil prices rise only slightly and that GDP languishes below its potential, headline inflation (including the VAT impact) will likely be just below 1% during the forecast period (Figure A1.9).

Japan's growth prospects are supported by strong corporate profits, a weak yen, and low oil prices, but downside risks are mounting to cloud the outlook. Recent volatility in financial markets, renminbi devaluation by the PRC, and the subsequent depreciation of many currencies in Asia could affect Japan's export sector. The baseline scenario for the next 2 years is unchanged and continues to assume that domestic consumption and investment will recover—but at a slower pace as external demand, particularly from the PRC, remains weak. In sum, GDP growth in Japan is expected at 0.7% this year before picking up to 1.4% in 2016. Both projections are slower than forecast in March.

A1.9 Consumer price, GDP deflator, and real effective exchange rate, Japan

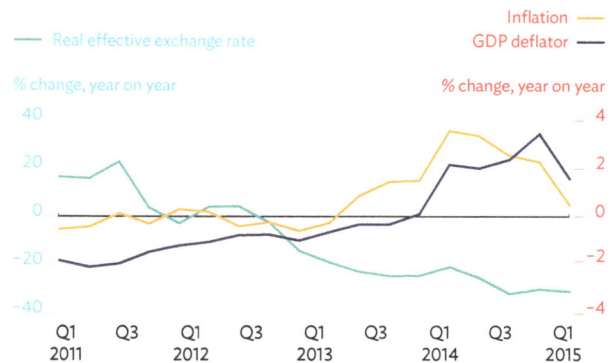

Q= quarter.

Sources: CEIC Data Company; Haver Analytics (both accessed 18 August 2015).

Australia and New Zealand

Australia is expected to grow moderately in 2015 and 2016. GDP growth dropped to a saar of 0.7% in the second quarter of 2015 from 3.6% in the first (Figure A1.10), as consumption growth balanced drag from net exports and declining inventories. The consumer sentiment index showed some improvement in the first half of the year, though it surpassed the 100 threshold separating pessimism and optimism in only 2 months: February and May. Unfortunately, consumption in the third quarter seems to be weakening, as, in July, retail sales declined by a saar of 0.1% and the consumer confidence index plummeted to 92.2. Unemployment, which averaged 6.1% in the first half of 2015, ticked up to 6.3% in July. The performance of manufacturing index of the Australian Industry Group rose above 50 in July and August, signaling an expected improvement in the sector. Inflation remains below the central bank's target of 2%–3%, having risen marginally to 1.5% in the second quarter from 1.3% in the first, and therefore leaves some scope for supportive monetary policy if need be. Panelists for the FocusEconomics Consensus Forecast expect Australian GDP to expand by 2.4% in 2015 and 2.7% in 2016.

Moderate growth is expected for New Zealand as well. The economy expanded at a sluggish saar of 0.6% in the first quarter of 2015, with the positive contribution of consumption offset by the drop in gross fixed capital formation (Figure A1.11). Some weakening in consumption is

A1.10 Demand-side contributions to growth, Australia

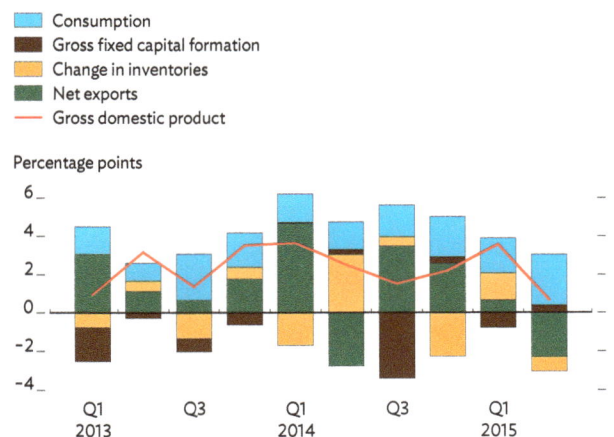

Q = quarter.

Source: CEIC Data Company (accessed 7 September 2015).

evident in slowing retail sales growth, from 1.5% in the first quarter to 0.1% in the second, and in declining consumer confidence, from 117.4 in the first quarter to 113.0 in the second. The business confidence index was positive in the early months of 2015 but then descended into negative territory, to –2.3 in June and plunging further to –29.1 in August. The performance in manufacturing index, on the other hand, stayed above the threshold value of 50 through July. Unemployment recorded a slight increase from 5.8% in the first quarter to 5.9% in the second. Inflation remains well below 1%. Although slowing growth in the PRC is expected to be a drag on dairy exports, strong domestic demand supported by a robust labor market will support the economy going forward. Consensus Forecast panelists project the New Zealand economy growing by 2.6% in both 2015 and 2016.

A1.11 Demand-side contributions to growth, New Zealand

- Consumption
- Gross fixed capital formation
- Change in inventories
- Net exports
- Gross domestic product

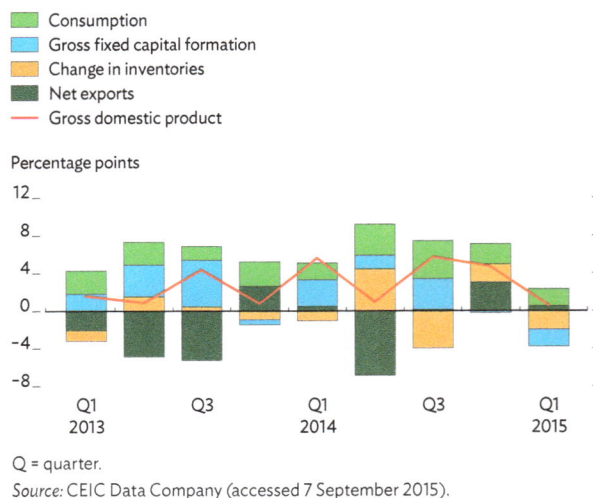

Q = quarter.
Source: CEIC Data Company (accessed 7 September 2015).

Commodity prices

International oil prices have remained low as production increases have exceeded muted growth in demand. Food prices have, at the same time, fallen sharply under generally favorable supply conditions.

Oil prices

Following a steep drop in the second half of 2014, oil prices began 2015 with a tentative recovery and then reversed course. Brent crude averaged $63 per barrel in May and June but fell sharply again in July and August, pressured by an abundance of supply, concerns about the strength of the PRC economy, and a strong US dollar (Figure A1.12). Despite a collapse in oil prices, supply in the first 7 months of 2015 from sources outside of the Organization of the Petroleum Exporting Countries (OPEC) remained 1.2 million barrels per day (mbd) higher than a year earlier, while OPEC production hit 31.5 mbd—the highest since April 2012—and averaged 58.3 mbd in the first 7 months. The International Energy Agency (IEA) estimates that the market remains oversupplied by about 3 mbd. Although imports of crude oil to the PRC in the first 7 months were still up by more than 10% by volume, slowing GDP growth there signaled weaker future demand and, more broadly, dampened expectations regarding the strength of the global recovery. On top of this, US dollar appreciation exerted further downward pressure on oil prices such that, by the end of August, the Brent crude price was half of its price a year earlier and down by almost quarter from its 2015 best showing of $66.4/barrel. The year-to-date average stands at $56/barrel.

According to the August 2015 report from the IEA, global oil demand increased in the first half 2015 by 1.7 mbd over demand in the first half of 2014 because of low oil prices, improving economic conditions, and severe winter weather in Europe. However, the IEA projects growth in global demand to decelerate in the second half of this year as prices

A1.12 Price of Brent crude

- Spot
- Annual average

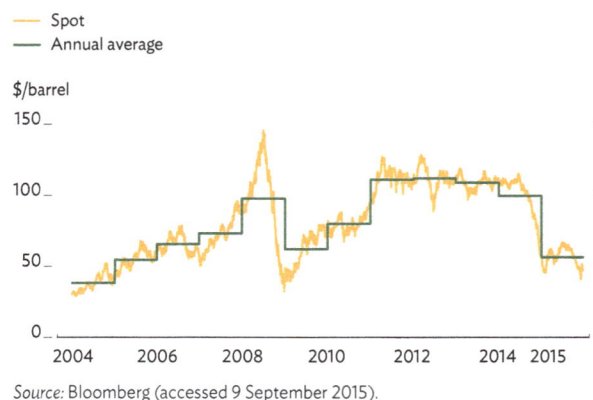

Source: Bloomberg (accessed 9 September 2015).

recover and the weather normalizes, such that the pickup in demand for the whole year will be by 1.6 mbd. As global macroeconomic conditions further improve, though, the IEA expects oil demand to rise by 1.4 mbd in 2016, mainly on increased consumption in emerging economies.

Global oil supplies were 3.3 mbd higher in the first half of 2015 than a year earlier, with growth coming from both within OPEC and outside of the cartel. Saudi Arabia and other OPEC members ramped up average production by 1.2 mbd in the first half of 2015. OPEC crude production held steady in July to average nearly a 3-year high of 31.5 mbd. Even Iraq, which is beleaguered by internal conflict, achieved production highs of 4.1 mbd. In their 5 June 2015 meeting, OPEC oil ministers agreed to maintain the production target of 30 mbd for the rest of the year. The IEA forecasts non-OPEC supply to expand by 1.1 mbd in 2015 but to decline by 0.2 mbd in 2016 in response to continued low oil prices, with US oil production falling the most.

International oil prices continue to react to economic data from major oil players. Futures prices suggest that Brent crude will trade within the narrow range of $48–$51 per barrel for the remainder of 2015 (Figure A1.13). Moving into 2016, the oil market faces several uncertainties: the speed and volume at which Iran will reenter the oil market following the easing of sanctions against it, the responsiveness of both demand and supply to low oil prices, and unexpected outages caused by unforeseen geopolitical events. Barring additional major supply disruptions, the price of Brent crude is forecast to average $55 per barrel in 2015 before recovering to $60 in 2016. As demand growth is catching up with supply growth more slowly than previously expected, the current forecast is for a milder price rebound than forecast in *ADO 2015*.

Food prices

Food prices declined by 15.6% in the first 8 months of 2015 as declines cut across all food categories (Figure A1.14). Ample global supplies of soy beans drove the edible oils subindex down by 23.4%. Grain prices have generally fallen, with wheat suffering the largest decline at 27.5%, followed by maize at 16.0% and rice at 6.1%. Near-term prospects suggest that favorable supply conditions will further soften food prices.

The US Department of Agriculture maintained its positive world agricultural outlook, increasing its forecast for global grain production for the crop year 2015/16 from 2,477 million tons in its July assessment to 2,481 million tons in its August assessment. Global wheat production is expected to reach record levels because of excellent cropping conditions in the spring wheat areas of Kazakhstan and the Russian Federation. Higher production is expected for maize as well because of wide planting and excellent yields in the PRC,

A1.13 Brent crude futures and spot price

- Average spot price
- Futures price (4 Sep 2014)
- Futures price (6 Mar 2015)
- Futures price (4 Sep 2015)

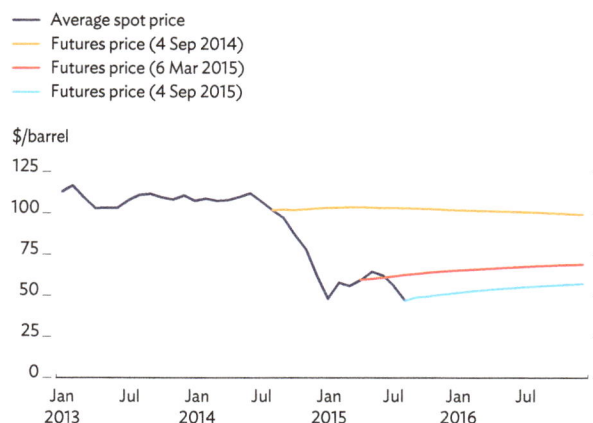

Source: Bloomberg (accessed 9 September 2015).

A1.14 Agricultural commodity price indexes

- Agriculture
- Beverages
- Food
- Edible oils
- Grains
- Other food
- Raw materials

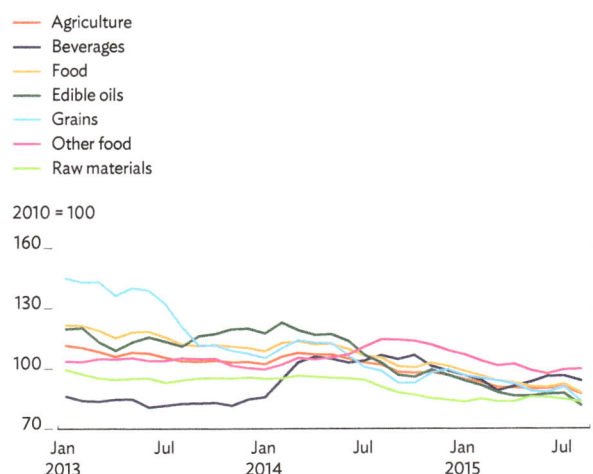

Source: World Bank, Commodity Price Data (Pink Sheet), http://www.worldbank.org (accessed 5 September 2015).

the European Union, Ukraine, and the US. Although its projection for rice production was lowered somewhat, the agency is still forecasting record output of 478.7 million tons.

The edible oil and oilseed outlook is stable as well. Soybean production is projected up by 1.1 million tons with larger harvests in Ukraine and the US. Soybean oil production is also up with high crop yields in Argentina and Brazil, and higher palm oil output is expected in Indonesia.

In 2014, meat prices shot up on a combination of drought, stock disease, and increasing demand. Conditions have since improved, but it may take some time for lower prices to pass through to consumers. World sugar prices have been on the decline since September 2014. Although sugar production is forecast to fall slightly in the crop year 2015/16, surpluses stockpiled from previous years will likely prevent price surges.

According to the latest report from the Agricultural Market Information System, El Niño conditions are well established in the equatorial Pacific and expected to strengthen through the northern hemisphere growing season, persisting into the first quarter of 2016. As a result, drier-than-average weather is being seen in Mexico, the Philippines, Spain, Thailand, and Viet Nam, while monsoon rains are delayed and subpar in the PRC and India. Despite unfavorable weather in some countries, the general supply outlook remains positive. In view of well-supplied markets for most grains, oilseeds, and edible oils, food prices are expected to fall by 13.0% in 2015—a considerably steeper decline than the 6.0% drop forecast in *ADO 2015*—and by 1.0% in 2016.

External environment in sum

The global recovery has been more tenuous than envisaged in *ADO 2015* as the growth benefits of lower commodity prices disappointed. The risk of a Greek exit from the euro, which had threatened to derail recovery in the euro area, has abated for the moment, but the euro area debt crisis remains unresolved. Declining values for many emerging economy currencies and sharp drops in equity prices across the globe—notably in the PRC—may give the US Federal Reserve pause before beginning its cycle of monetary tightening, but the Fed is still likely to act before the end of 2015 as the US economy strengthens further. Forecasts in this *Update* assume that the rise in US interest rates will not induce sharp capital flow reversals from the region like those seen in the 2013 "taper tantrum." In sum, while the risks to the growth outlook may have heightened since March, they should still be manageable for regional policy makers.

2

ENABLING WOMEN, ENERGIZING ASIA

Enabling women, energizing Asia

Over the past quarter century, developing Asia has gained a lot of economic muscle. Its macroeconomic fundamentals have improved to the extent that, while most advanced economies are still reeling under the pressures created by the global financial crisis, the region is sustaining a reasonably robust growth path. An average person in developing Asia now commands, in purchasing power parity terms, almost $10,000 in per capita GDP, a sixfold rise from $1,700 a quarter of a century ago. High incomes have encouraged the aspirations of Asians, who want a say in determining their future course of development. And the region has tremendous potential to carry forward its growth legacy.

The question most economies in developing Asia now face is how to ensure that the benefits and opportunities from growth are shared by all segments of society. Indeed, it is time to ask how effectively the region is deploying its massive resources and talent and, in particular, what Asia's improved economic status has meant for over 2 billion girls and women—half of the region's population. It is striking that, while developing Asia built its economic muscle, it did not pay equal attention to balance, as its rising growth path since 1990 has been accompanied by a stubbornly persistent gap between male and female participation rates in the labor force— the gainfully employed workforce plus active job seekers (Figure 2.0.1). Indeed, the falling rate of female participation in the region stands in stark contrast to growing or stable participation by women in every other region of the world.

Bringing more women into paid employment can raise developing Asia's prosperity. Yet centuries-old traditions in some places give husbands and fathers the authority to decide if wives and daughters can work outside the home. Employers often discriminate against women based on age and marital status—and, if they are pregnant, on that too. Viewed as homemakers and brought up to accept male supremacy as normal, women tend to be underrepresented in senior positions and leadership roles.

Can developing Asia rise to the challenge and engage its massive underutilized resource of female labor to distribute its economic benefits more evenly?

2.0.1 Gender gaps in labor force participation, developing Asia

Percentage points

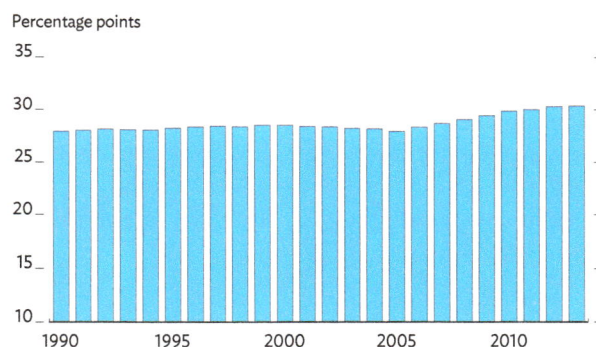

Note: The gender gap is the male labor force participation rate minus the female rate.

Sources: ADB estimates using data from International Labour Organization. Key Indicators of the Labour Market 8th Edition; World Bank. World Development Indicators online database (accessed 4 September 2015).

This chapter was written by Shikha Jha, Pilipinas Quising, Akiko Terada-Hagiwara, and Joseph E. Zveglich, Jr. of the Economic Research and Regional Cooperation Department, ADB, Manila, and Marife Lou Bacate, consultant, Economic Research and Regional Cooperation Department, ADB, Manila. It draws on the background papers listed at the end of the chapter. Background materials from Valerie Mercer-Blackman, Lea Sumulong, and Sakiko Tanaka are gratefully acknowledged.

The unfinished agenda for gender equality

Decades of rapid growth have transformed developing Asia into a "New Asia." By 2020, most economies in the region will have per capita incomes high enough for entry into the ranks of middle-income economies. The achievements of East and Southeast Asia in particular owe much to their embrace of globalization, and other subregions look to replicate their success. Developing Asia, already home to some of the largest metropolitan agglomerations in the world, will become even more urban. Changing demographics will present some countries with growth opportunities and others with the challenge of supporting aging populations.

With its economic transformation, the region has been able to make progress in narrowing gender inequalities, notably by improving women's basic literacy and life expectancy. Yet, much remains on the gender equality agenda as gaps persist in such broad dimensions as education, health, employment, and leadership. Asian women's participation in the workforce has fallen in the past 20 years more than that of Asian men, which is a worrying trend. Strengthening women's place in the labor market is a powerful way not only to narrow income inequality and boost economic efficiency, but also to hasten social change, as greater economic independence and decision-making power improves women's standing in the home and out in society, giving them voice and greater influence toward safeguarding women's welfare in their own communities and beyond.

Economic transformation to the New Asia

Asia has been transformed since the 1970s, when it was a poor, largely agrarian region locked in low growth. Despite many crises, the region's real growth in gross domestic product (GDP) per capita in purchasing power parity terms averaged 5.6% from 1990 to 2014, making it the fastest growing region in the world. This remarkable economic achievement was accompanied by significant poverty reduction. From 1990 to 2011, the portion of the population living on less than $1.25 per day declined from 55.3% to 15.3%, lifting some 950 million people out of extreme poverty. Health, education, and infrastructure improved at the same time.

The region has steadily become more closely connected with the rest of the world through trade and global production networks. The share of world exports from the economies of developing Asia doubled from about 14% in

2.1.1 Shares of global merchandise exports by world region

■ 1990
■ 2014

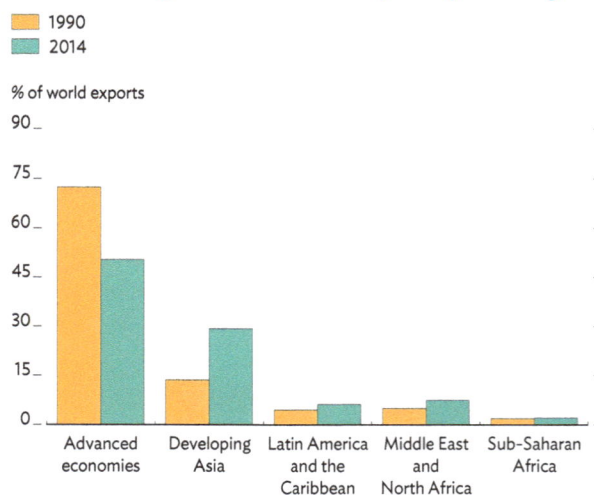

Note: Advanced economies are members of the Organisation for Economic Co-operation and Development excluding the Republic of Korea (included in developing Asia), Chile and Mexico (Latin America and the Caribbean), and Israel (Middle East and North Africa).

Source: ADB estimates using data from the World Bank, World Development Indicators online database (accessed 4 September 2015).

1990 to 29% in 2014 (Figure 2.1.1), while the region's share of world GDP grew from less than one-fifth to one-third. Export-oriented growth has expanded low-skill manufacturing jobs (Mammen and Paxson 2000). From 2010 to 2015, the estimated annual growth of the global market for low-end technologies has been an astounding 11%—faster than growth for mid-range technologies, at 10%, and for high-end technologies, at 6% (ADB 2014a). Indeed, developing Asia has emerged as the preferred location for services enabled by information and communication technology (ICT), making it home to 7 of the top 10 economies for global services that deliver ICT and undertake business process outsourcing (ADB 2014a).

The spread of ICT created new access not only to information but also to economic opportunity. A leading telecommunications database shows that the percentage of the population in developing Asia using the internet leaped from 2% in 2000 to 32% in 2014 (Table 2.1.1). In the same period, the number of mobile phone subscriptions per 100 people ballooned from 5 to 91.

The region has also become more urban and now hosts many of the largest metropolises in the world. The percentage of Asians living in cities has tripled from less than 15% in 1950 to 44% in 2015 and is forecast to increase further to over 60% by 2050. Urbanization not only creates economic opportunities but also makes them accessible through better provision of such enabling services as health care, education, public utilities, transport and communication, and finance. It creates more jobs, which attract migrant workers from rural areas, whose remittances back home can be substantial. For example, remittances to rural households represented 13% of rural income in the People's Republic of China (PRC) in 2003 (Zhu and Luo 2008). In Cambodia, hotel workers in Siem Reap and Phnom Penh remit home over $1.2 million per month (Singru 2015). City life is deeply influenced by global markets, consumerism, and information. Urban residents have fewer children, and more of their children now spend much of the day in school, which eases couples' daily responsibilities to the family in the home.

2.1.1 Mobile phone and internet access

	Mobile telephone subscriptions per 100 inhabitants		Percentage of individuals using the internet	
	2000	2014	2000	2014
Advanced economies	48.4	113.5	29.7	81.8
Developing Asia	5.2	90.8	2.2	32.0
Latin America and the Caribbean	12.1	113.9	3.9	50.2
Middle East and North Africa	5.0	109.3	1.7	38.2
Sub-Saharan Africa	1.7	70.2	0.5	19.1

Sources: ADB estimates using data from International Telecommunications Union, World Telecommunications/ICT Indicators database 2015, http://www.itu.int/en/ITU-D/Statistics/Pages/stat/default.aspx; Population Division, Department of Economic and Social Affairs, United Nations Secretariat. *World Population Prospects: The 2015 Revision.* http://esa.un.org/unpd/wpp/DVD

The New Asia is changing demographically as well, though the trends are not uniform across countries. Better access to nutrition and health services lowered death rates, leading subsequently to lower fertility rates and ultimately to longer life expectancy. The transition from high to low fertility and mortality boosted the share of the working-age population, particularly working-age youth. The resulting demographic dividend added more than 1 percentage point to average annual growth in GDP per capita in the PRC, Indonesia, the Republic of Korea, Malaysia, Thailand, and Viet Nam during the 3 decades from 1980 to 2010 (ADB 2011).

A consequence, though, is that the region as a whole is now aging rapidly. The number of people in developing Asia aged 60 years and above will surpass the number of those younger than 15 years in 2040, a decade earlier than the world as a whole reaches this milestone (Figure 2.1.2). The 60+ age group is forecast to quadruple from less than 300 million in 2015 to more than 1 billion just 50 years later. The PRC and the Republic of Korea will be notably affected. Meanwhile, a number of economies in Asia and the Pacific still have young populations. In many Pacific countries, children under 15 account for more than a third of the population, while young adults aged 15–24 account for a fifth. Other examples of young populations with potential for a demographic dividend—if the right social, economic, and human capital policies are implemented—are Afghanistan, Cambodia, the Kyrgyz Republic, the Lao People's Democratic Republic (Lao PDR), Nepal, the Philippines, Pakistan, and Tajikistan. In these countries, children and young adults account for 50%–62% of the population.

Taken together, these developments have transformed the region. The New Asia has become richer, more global, and more urban through the years, and while the region's enlarged population has started to age, the potential for growth remains high in many areas that stand to benefit from continued younger populations. How can women in particular contribute to and benefit from the transformation the region has undergone? Answering that question requires an understanding of the progress made to date in achieving gender equality, and of the challenges that remain.

2.1.2 Population projections for the young and old, world and developing Asia

- World 0–14
- World 60+
- Developing Asia 0–14
- Developing Asia 60+

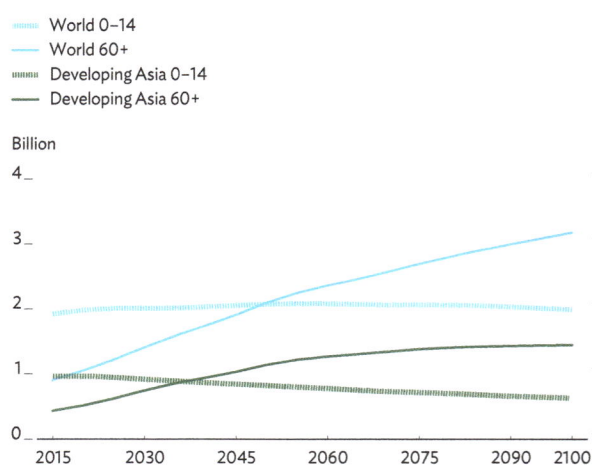

Source: Population Division, Department of Economic and Social Affairs, United Nations Secretariat. *World Population Prospects: The 2015 Revision.* http://esa.un.org/unpd/wpp/DVD

Gender equality: progress and challenges

Economic transformation to create the New Asia—combined with grassroots initiatives led by women's organizations and changes to laws and policies—helped the region achieve notable progress toward enabling women to become more productive members of the workforce. Starting with wide male–female equality gaps, the region has considerably narrowed inequality by, for instance, advancing women's basic education and literacy, extending life expectancy, and sustaining economic activity. Given the multidimensional nature of male–female inequality, its different aspects are often combined into single indicators to make the broader changes easier to understand.

Broad gender equality indicators

Gender equality entails men and women enjoying the same rights, resources, opportunities, and protections, but it does not require that they be treated exactly alike (UNICEF 2014). Special efforts to cultivate women's talents, human capital, and economic potential are not only development goals in themselves but are also necessary to achieve inclusive growth and poverty reduction (ADB 2013a).

The attempt to measure multidimensional gender inequality has spurred the development of a number of composite indexes incorporating its different aspects. Such measures have gained popularity by providing to the public an easily understood summary statistic of a complex issue.

The Gender Inequality Index of the United Nations Development Programme is among the most widely used indicators, measuring gender disparities in reproductive health, empowerment, and economic status to calculate how much potential human development is lost to gender inequality. The global average score was 0.45 in 2013, reflecting that potential loss to human development from gender inequality on average was 45%. While the index shows a decline in gender inequality in developing Asia since 2000, the reductions were uneven across countries, as is the current status (Figure 2.1.3). In 2013, Afghanistan, Papua New Guinea, Pakistan, and India in that order posted the highest continuing losses to human development, all exceeding 55%. At the other end, the lowest losses in 2013—below 20%—were recorded in order by Singapore, the Republic of Korea, the PRC (down by almost two-thirds since 2000), and Malaysia.

Another popular measure is the Gender Gap Index, which was introduced at the World Economic Forum in 2006. Starting with just 115 countries but now covering 142, this index examines gaps and outcomes to measure countries' ability to close gender inequality gaps in health, education, and economic and political participation. An index score is the percentage of the gap between women and men that has been closed. By 2014, the Lao PDR, Mongolia, the Philippines, Thailand, and Kazakhstan were among the 65 countries (46% of the total) that had closed at least 70% of the gap (Figure 2.1.4). This was a big improvement over 2006, when this milestone had been achieved by only 25 countries, or 22% and including in developing Asia only the Philippines and Sri Lanka.

Although much has been achieved toward gender equality, the loss of human development potential because of gender inequality remains considerable today. No country has fully closed the gender gap, and clearly much still needs to be done in this area—Singapore is the only economy among the top five performers by both measures. A valid concern about the use of composite indexes is that aggregation across

2.1.3 Gender Inequality Index in developing Asia, 2000 and 2013

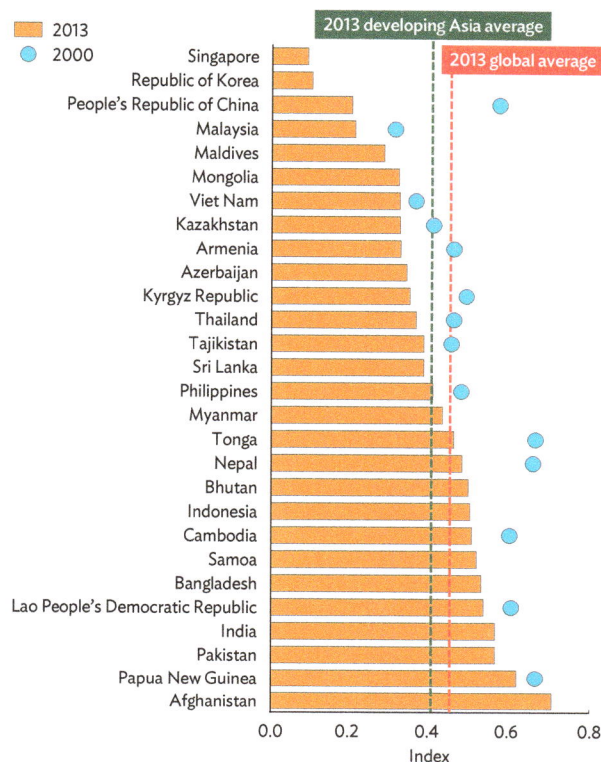

Note: The Gender Inequality Index ranges from 0 (equality) to 1 (inequality): the higher the value, the more disparity between men and women.
Source: United Nations Development Programme, http://hdr.undp.org/en/data

2.1.4 Gender Gap Index in developing Asia, 2006 and 2014

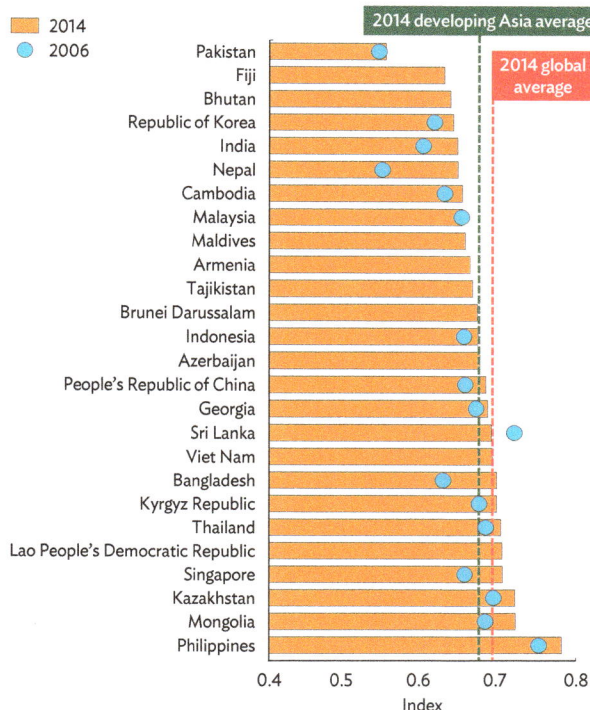

Note: The Gender Gap Index ranges from 1 (equality) to 0 (inequality).
Source: World Economic Forum, www.weforum.org

dimensions may mask important information about individual indicators and thus fail to provide policy makers with the information they need to select appropriate policies and programs (Permanyer 2013). As such, an examination is useful here of the individual dimensions of gender inequality, especially the more basic ones such as education, health, and employment.

Gender and education

Primary school enrollment in developing Asia almost doubled from 402 million students in 1970 to 714 million in 2013. The corresponding number for students in secondary school tripled from 187 million to 569 million, while the number of tertiary students multiplied by sixfold, from 33 million to 199 million. However, disparity between male and female attainment persists. From 1950 to 2010 the number of years spent in school multiplied sevenfold for girls over age 15, from 0.9 years to 6.4, against an increase by 4 times for boys, from 2.0 years to 7.8 years. Despite the improvement, girls' average schooling remains significantly below the world average of 8.1 years, while boys' schooling approaches the world average of 8.6 years (Table 2.1.2). School completion rates are found to be near parity for primary school children in the Asian countries able to report the information. However, rates are uneven at the secondary and tertiary levels, in which females outnumber males (perhaps reflecting women's rising aspirations).

2.1.2 Average years of schooling

	1950		2010	
	Male	Female	Male	Female
Advanced economies	6.6	6.2	11.7	11.5
Developing Asia	2.0	0.9	7.8	6.4
Latin America and the Caribbean	2.9	2.5	8.3	8.3
Middle East and North Africa	1.0	0.4	7.9	6.9
Sub-Saharan Africa	1.6	0.9	5.9	4.8
World	**3.3**	**2.6**	**8.6**	**8.1**

Note: Figures are weighted by population aged 15 years and above. Advanced economies are members of the Organisation for Economic Co-operation and Development excluding the Republic of Korea (included in developing Asia), Chile and Mexico (Latin America and the Caribbean), and Israel (Middle East and North Africa).

Sources: ADB estimates using data from Barro, R. and J.-W. Lee. 2013. A New Data Set of Educational Attainment in the World, 1950–2010. *Journal of Development Economics* 104; Population Division, Department of Economic and Social Affairs, United Nations Secretariat. *World Population Prospects: The 2015 Revision.* http://esa.un.org/unpd/wpp/DVD/

Improving female education has positive socioeconomic spillover, as it improves women's ability to make informed choices about family planning, nutrition, health, and education (UNESCAP, ADB, and UNDP 2009). In Viet Nam, for example, the children of mothers who received primary education have a mortality rate of 27 per 1,000 live births, or less than half the rate of 66 for the children of mothers with no education.

Gender and health

Many economies in developing Asia have seen improved health outcomes for females over the past 2 decades. Unsustainably high fertility rates have been sharply curtailed. Rates of infant and child mortality among girls have similarly dropped, narrowing the gender gap in this area. Adult female and maternal mortality rates have also declined and, like mortality rates for infants and children, are now uncommonly low for national income levels, with many Asian economies plotting below the curve that shows the average relationship of mortality statistics with GDP per capita (Figure 2.1.5).

2.1.5 Female mortality indicators and income

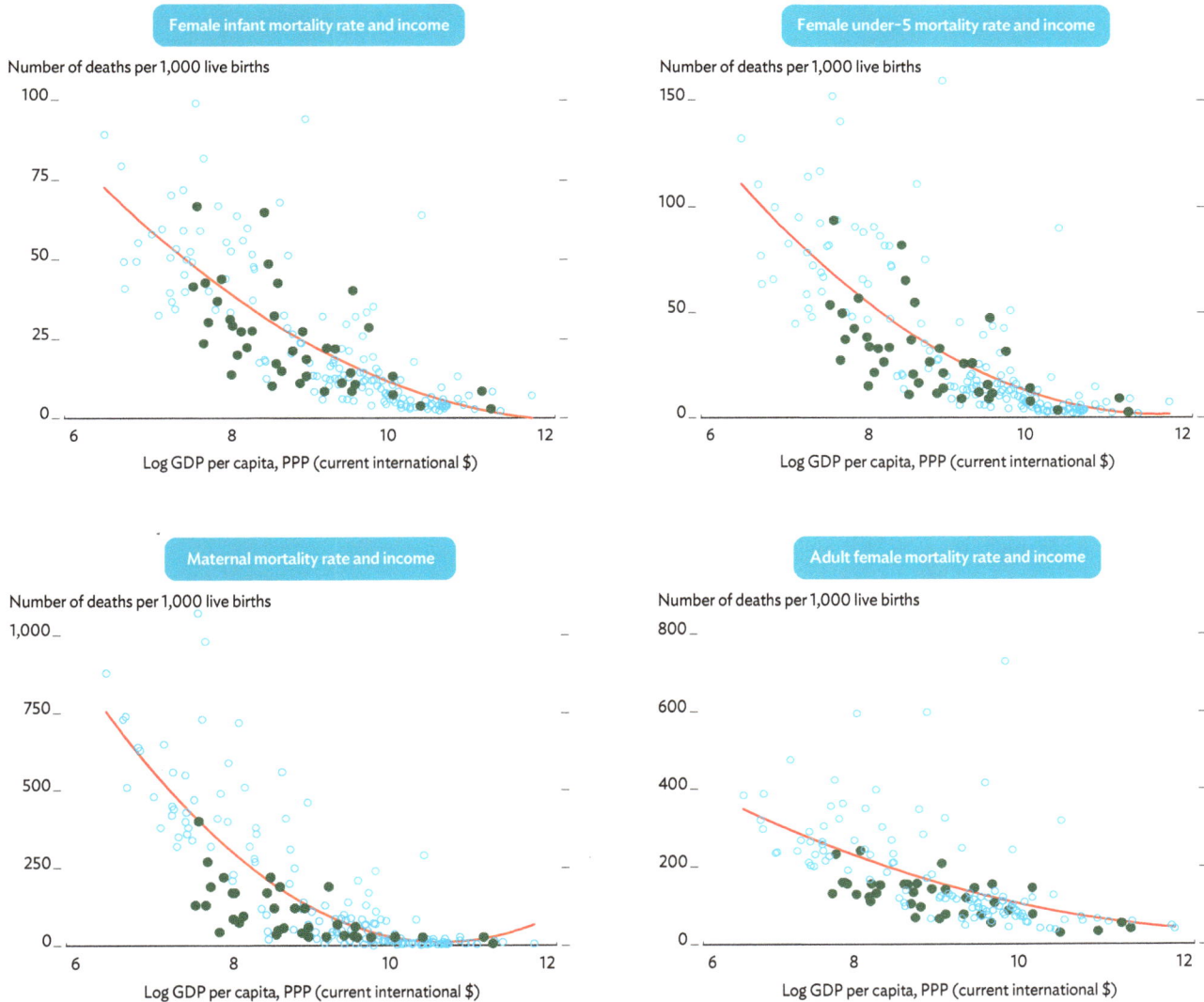

PPP = purchasing power parity.

Note: Green dots indicate developing Asian economies.

Source: World Bank. World Development Indicators online database (accessed 4 September 2015).

2.1.3 Life expectancy at birth, regional averages

| | Life expectancy at birth (years) | | | | Healthy life years | |
| | 1950–1955 | | 2010–2015 | | 2013 | |
	Female	Male	Female	Male	Female	Male
Advanced economies	68.3	63.4	82.8	77.4	72.6	68.6
Developing Asia	42.8	41.1	72.9	69.4	63.9	61.0
Latin America and the Caribbean	53.0	49.5	77.9	71.2	67.9	63.2
Middle East and North Africa	42.8	41.9	73.6	70.0	63.0	61.3
Sub-Saharan Africa	37.8	35.3	59.0	56.4	50.8	48.9
World	48.3	45.4	72.7	68.3	64.0	60.0

Note: Advanced economies are members of the Organisation for Economic Co-operation and Development excluding the Republic of Korea (included in developing Asia), Chile and Mexico (Latin America and the Caribbean), and Israel (Middle East and North Africa).

Sources: ADB estimates using data from Population Division, Department of Economic and Social Affairs, United Nations Secretariat. *World Population Prospects: The 2015 Revision.* http://esa.un.org/unpd/wpp/DVD/; World Health Organization. Global Health Observatory Data Repository. http://apps.who.int/gho/data/view.main.700?lang=en

Female life expectancy has also improved in the region, more so than most other regions (Table 2.1.3). Women were expected to live for 42.8 years on average in the early 1950s, and men were expected to live for a shorter 41.1 years. Women advanced at a faster pace, doubling by 2013 their lifespan advantage over men. Living longer brings its own difficulties, however, as it leaves women more likely than men to be widowed or otherwise single in their twilight years (ILO 2009). Moreover, women in the region can expect a slightly longer spell of unhealthy life years: 9 years compared with 8 for men. On average, based on data for 2013, the number of years of healthy life is 64 in a life span of 73 for Asian women and 61 in 69 for Asian men.

Although female mortality and life expectancy indicators have improved in developing Asia, a persistent issue at the other end of life is the disturbingly high ratio of boys to girls at birth (Box 2.1.1). While boys have always outnumbered girls at birth—left to nature, the sex ratio at birth should be 105–106 boys per 100 girls—a distorting factor is a strong preference for sons in the region, which motivates gender-specific abortions, particularly in South and East Asia. Sons are preferred to daughters, especially in agrarian economies, for their perceived higher wage-earning capacity, their ability to continue the family line in patriarchal settings, and their status as the main recipients of inheritance. Daughters, by contrast, are perceived as economic burdens, especially where dowry payment is the cultural norm (Guilmoto 2012).

Women in the workforce

Across the globe, the labor force participation rate—the proportion of the population 15 years of age and older that is employed or looking for work—has declined slightly for both men and women over the past quarter of a century (Figure 2.1.6). But looking at what underlies the global trends, developing Asia stands out as the only region with declining

2.1.6 Annual change in labor force participation rates, 1990–2013

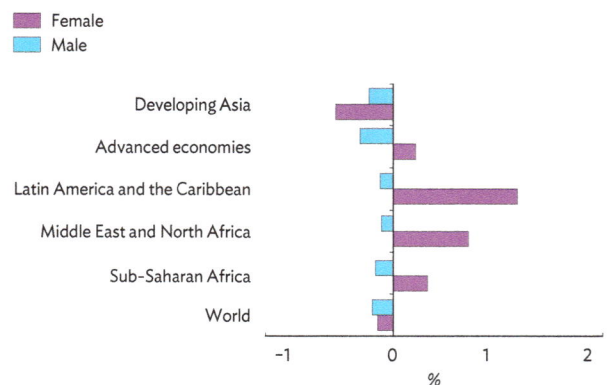

Note: Advanced economies are members of the Organisation for Economic Co-operation and Development excluding the Republic of Korea (included in developing Asia), Chile and Mexico (Latin America and the Caribbean), and Israel (Middle East and North Africa).

Sources: ADB estimates using data from the International Labour Organization. Key Indicators of the Labour Market 8th Edition; Global Employment Trends; CEIC Data Company (all accessed 4 September 2015).

2.1.1 Sex ratio at birth: distortions and unintended consequences

While sex ratios at birth fluctuate naturally, the widespread availability of affordable means to discover the sex of an early fetus has caused wide distortions in sex ratio in some parts of developing Asia. Falling fertility rates, whether through strict controls on family size as in the PRC and Viet Nam or other causes, have combined with a strong social norm favoring sons to make improved prenatal diagnosis technology a tool for prenatal sex selection (UNFPA 2012). The phenomenon has become more pronounced in the past 20 years, easing only in the Republic of Korea, Taipei,China (where a rapid increase in the sex ratio at birth occurred earlier, between 1985 and 1995), and Uzbekistan. It is no longer confined to Asia but manifests as well in developed countries among ethnic communities of South and East Asian origin (Guilmoto 2012). The global sex ratio has been rising steadily, from 106 in 1950–1955 to 108 in 2005–2010. While developing Asia as a whole has been tracking this global trend, gender imbalances in some regional economies have grown at a much faster pace—in particular in Armenia, Azerbaijan, the PRC, Georgia, India, and Viet Nam (box figure).

Such imbalances can have unintended social and economic consequences. Female infanticide leaves a shortage of brides. Intense competition for brides may drive men to work harder to secure higher income. Wei and Zhang (2011a) estimated that 20% of the growth rate of GDP per capita in the PRC in recent years can be attributed to hard work and entrepreneurship driven by a rise in the sex ratio. Chang and Zhang (2012) found evidence that, during periods of fierce competition in marriage markets in Taipei,China, young men typically worked longer hours, saved more, amassed more assets, and engaged in more entrepreneurial activities.

Wei and Zhang (2011b) found an increase in the local sex ratio in rural areas of the PRC associated with a higher savings rate by households with sons. Horioka and Terada-Hagiwara (2015) revealed parallel results in the Republic of Korea and the opposite effect in India, where the bride's family pays a dowry to the groom. In both the PRC and the Republic of Korea, the groom bears most marriage-related expenses. Tan, Wei, and Zhang (2015) argued that low ratios of girls to boys at birth makes parents harder workers and more tolerant of unsafe workplace practices.

Other possible impacts of disturbing the natural sex ratio at birth include higher prices for more upscale urban housing in the PRC intended to attract brides (Wei, Zhang, and Liu 2012), worsening property crime in the PRC (Edlund et al. 2013), loneliness and marginalization causing psychological problems among unmarriageable men

(Hesketh 2011), greater incidence of parental smoking and alcohol use as coping mechanisms (Chen 2014), higher male suicide rates (Kuroki 2014), and women more prone to sexually transmitted infection because they have multiple partners (Trent and South 2012).

Measures to reduce sex selection at birth must include outlawing female gendercide and ensuring its strict enforcement, guaranteeing equal rights and opportunities for women, and raising awareness about the perils of skewed sex ratios. The story of the Republic of Korea reversing its gender imbalance is noteworthy, including the role women's movements played in demanding reform to family law and, in 1958, the civil code (Chung and Das Gupta 2007). Regular monitoring of demographic trends is likewise essential. A reliable civil registration system allows timely interventions by governments and independent agencies to address gender imbalances.

Sex ratios at birth in developing Asian economies

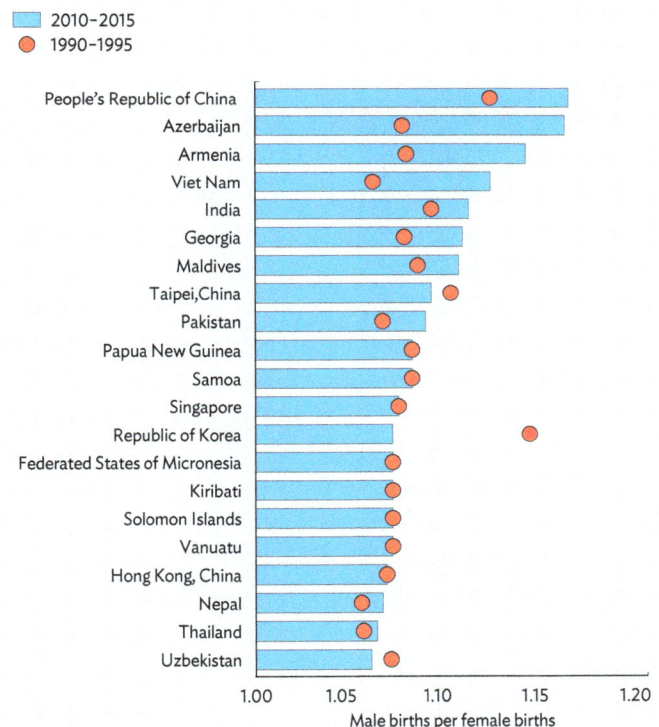

Legend:
- 2010–2015
- 1990–1995

Categories (top to bottom): People's Republic of China, Azerbaijan, Armenia, Viet Nam, India, Georgia, Maldives, Taipei,China, Pakistan, Papua New Guinea, Samoa, Singapore, Republic of Korea, Federated States of Micronesia, Kiribati, Solomon Islands, Vanuatu, Hong Kong, China, Nepal, Thailand, Uzbekistan

x-axis: 1.00, 1.05, 1.10, 1.15, 1.20 — Male births per female births

Source: Population Division, Department of Economic and Social Affairs, United Nations Secretariat. *World Population Prospects: The 2015 Revision.* http://esa.un.org/unpd/wpp/DVD

female labor force participation, dropping from 56% in 1990 to 49% in 2013. The trend in developing Asia largely reflects declines in East Asia from 71% to 63% and in South Asia from 36% to 31% (Figure 2.1.7). Within Asian subregions, the trends are driven by the larger economies, mainly the PRC in East Asia and India in South Asia. The men's participation rate exceeds that of women by over 50 percentage points in South Asia. Within individual economies, the gender gap varies greatly from as high as 63.7% in Afghanistan to as low as 2.8% in the Lao PDR. The drop started before the global financial crisis of 2008–2009. Moreover, the Asian financial crisis of 1997–1998, which was much more severe in the region, brought no change.

Recent economic and social changes have brought higher educational attainment, fewer children, safer childbirth, and longer life expectancy—and so would be expected to smooth women's access to labor markets—but have so far had only a minimal effect on the female-to-male ratio of labor force participation rates overall. Although more women are migrating to towns and cities in search of better job opportunities, they remain vulnerable to exploitation, targeted violence and abuse, and low pay as they tend to take informal jobs with poor working conditions.

2.1.7 Trends in the female labor force participation rate within developing Asia

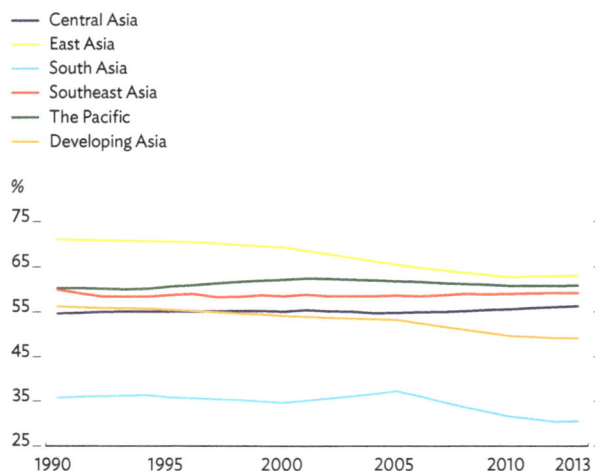

Sources: ADB estimates using data from the International Labour Organization. Key Indicators of the Labour Market 8th Edition; Global Employment Trends; CEIC Data Company (all accessed 4 September 2015).

Gains both intrinsic and instrumental

Gender equality has *intrinsic* value, as it ensures equal basic rights to women and promotes a sense of social justice. This makes it a development goal on its own. It also has *instrumental* value as a powerful means to foster economic growth and development by making institutions more representative and enhancing productivity, thereby reducing poverty (World Bank 2011). The misallocation of talent in a labor market that places highly capable women in low-skilled, low-return occupations significantly hinders growth. Efficiency gains occur naturally when women can develop and market their talents to maximum effect. Encouraging female empowerment therefore yields gains in both equity and efficiency.

Intrinsic equity gains

While closing gender gaps remains on the development agenda in developing Asia, rising income inequality from the 1990s to the late 2000s in economies that are home to over 80% of the region's population has shifted the focus toward more equitable sharing of the economic pie. Righting rich–poor disparity became the centerpiece of national development plans in the PRC, India, Indonesia, the Philippines, and Thailand, among others. Meanwhile, because women as a group are poorer than men, better gender equality can bring more equitable income distribution. It therefore deserves similar attention (Box 2.1.2).

2.1.2 Income equality and gender equality moving in tandem

Inequality is a broad concept referring not just to income differences, or vertical inequality between the rich and the poor, but more generally to gaps between diverse groups of people. Horizontal inequality between "culturally formed groups" is equally important to individual welfare and social stability (Stewart 2002). For example, if girls regularly have less access to education than boys, two groups of equal merit acquire unequal shares of resources, disadvantaging one group and its individual members. If it persists, such inequality depresses the contribution that the marginalized group can make to its own prosperity and that of the larger society.

To the extent that women remain poorer than men because they have no independent sources of income, income distribution intertwined with the gender gap affecting access to economic opportunity and its rewards. Data gathered from around the world show that countries marked by greater narrowing of gender gaps in the half

decade from 2006 to 2012 also distributed incomes more equitably (box figure).

This finding is corroborated by household income inequality in members of the Organisation for Economic Co-operation and Development (OECD), where women have made substantial progress toward narrowing gaps in participation, pay, and career advancement, and this development has put a brake on worsening inequality. Having more households with women in paid work, especially full-time work, means less income inequality. Data from OECD members show an increase in the proportion of households with women working full time in a high-skilled job from 1985 to the late 2000s. These changes reduced the Gini measure of income inequality by almost 2 percentage points over that time period (OECD 2015). However, women are still 16% less likely to have a paid job, and they earn 15% less than men. This calls for a continued focus on reducing gender disparities.

Initial gender equality and average income inequality

- ● Developing Asia
- ○ Rest of the world

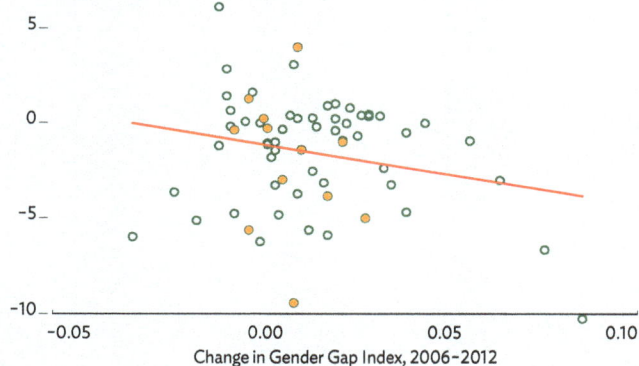

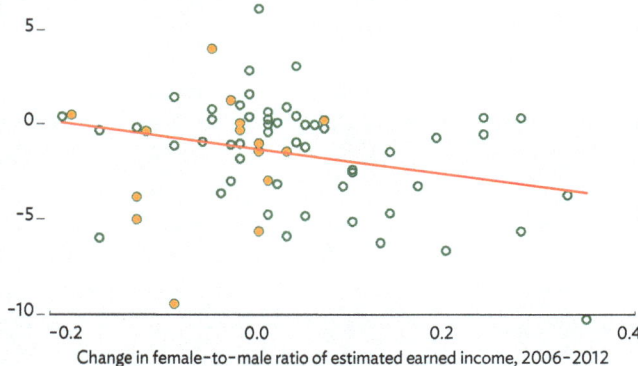

Source: ADB estimates using data from the World Bank, World Development Indicators online database and World Economic Forum. *Global Gender Gap Report 2014* (both accessed 4 September 2015).

Instrumental efficiency gains

Women's employment can be viewed as influencing economic growth through three main channels (Morrison, Raju, and Sinha 2007). It boosts the productivity of labor and complementary inputs such as schooling for women. It improves efficiency by enabling better allocation of resources by, for example, removing barriers to women's employment in certain sectors or occupations and to their unfettered use of land, capital, and other productive inputs. Finally, it harnesses women's incentive to save more than men do toward building homes, securing social insurance against shocks, and bequeathing adequate resources to the next generation.

Gender gaps in employment mean that available human capital is not used well or the talent is misallocated across different occupations. If women are not in the workforce, their potential contribution to productivity and GDP are lost, as their talent and skills are diverted to homemaking. On the other hand, if women who are qualified for senior positions are assigned to jobs requiring lesser skills while the more senior positions are given to less qualified men, the investment in human capital embodied in these women is unable to contribute to economic output. Therefore, narrowing the gender gap by avoiding discrimination and appropriately allocating workers across occupations will improve efficiency.

To illustrate, a study in the US found that efforts to end racial discrimination in hiring and allow black men and women to realize their potential explained 17%–20% of the output growth in the US from 1960 to 2008 (Hsieh et al. 2013). Likewise, an analysis of data from the mid-1990s to the 2000s showed that the increased employment of women in developed economies contributed more to global growth than did growth generated in the PRC (*The Economist* 2006). This analysis vividly captures the instrumental value of gender equality.

If added over generations, the effect on economic growth can be substantial as women redirect their time from the home to market production through workforce participation. Estimates for developing Asia point to a potential 30% gain in per capita income achieved after one generation and 70% after two generations after the elimination of gender disparity (Box 2.1.3). In aging economies in particular, higher female workforce participation can moderate shrinkage in the productive workforce and the slowing of growth that it causes.

The relation between female workforce participation and per capita income is not linear however (Figure 2.1.8). Evidence gathered worldwide suggests that, as economies develop, women's workforce participation relative to men's displays a U-shaped relationship (Goldin 1995). In primarily agricultural economies with high poverty rates, women contribute to household income by working on the family farm or outside the home. Female workforce participation usually declines as incomes rise, the focus of economic activity shifts from agriculture to industry, and opportunities now available in the labor market become less attractive to female workers because of their physical demands or social norms that prohibit women from engaging in manual labor. Participation swings back up as further development (and less social stigma) encourages women to study beyond elementary school and take advantage of more attractive employment opportunities.

The U-shaped relationship suggests that increasing national income will not necessarily propel women into the workforce. On the other hand, having more women in paid jobs and therefore in control of their income is associated with higher total factor productivity (Loko and Diouf 2009) and broader economic development (Heintz 2006). While the gain in GDP from closing gender gaps is impressive—varying

2.1.8 Female-to-male ratio of labor force participation versus income per capita, 2013

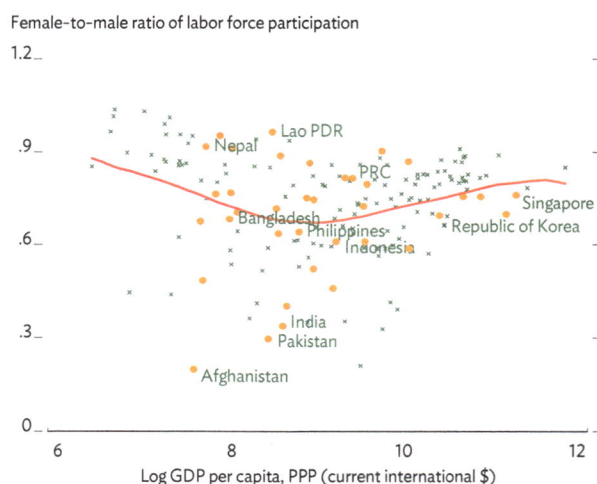

Female-to-male ratio of labor force participation

Lao PDR = Lao People's Democratic Republic, PPP = purchasing power parity, PRC = People's Republic of China.

Sources: ADB estimates using data from the International Labour Organization. Key Indicators of the Labour Market 8th Edition; CEIC Data Company; World Bank. World Development Indicators online database (all accessed 4 September 2015).

2.1.3 Women and their potential contribution to growth in Asia

In a model to examine the growth effects of higher gender equality, Kim, Lee, and Shin (forthcoming) considered an economy with three generations in which every individual lives for three periods: childhood, adulthood, and retirement. The model assumed that a male adult divides all his time between market production (i.e., working in the official labor market) and home production. A female adult divides her time between home production, market production, child rearing, and child education. The more children she has, the more time she spends on child rearing. Women in this model spend more time educating their sons than their daughters, reflecting the parental preference for sons that is common in some parts of the region.

Children's education—determined by children's time for schooling, mothers' time spent educating them, and government expenditure on education—determines their human capital when they become adults, which determines in turn their productivity in the workforce. Parents' investment in the human capital of their children can therefore help sustain economic growth.

The bargaining power of a woman determines not only the time she must spend on home production but also the time her husband spends on it (box figure). Because he spends the rest of his time on market production, the male essentially has no decision problem regarding time allocation. Additionally, discrimination in the labor market means that female workers receive lower wages than men.

The model was fitted to the data for an average economy in developing Asia. The results from this model indicated that eliminating the disparities between men and women at home and in the labor market can increase per capita income in developing Asia by over 70% in roughly 60 years.

Woman's time allocation

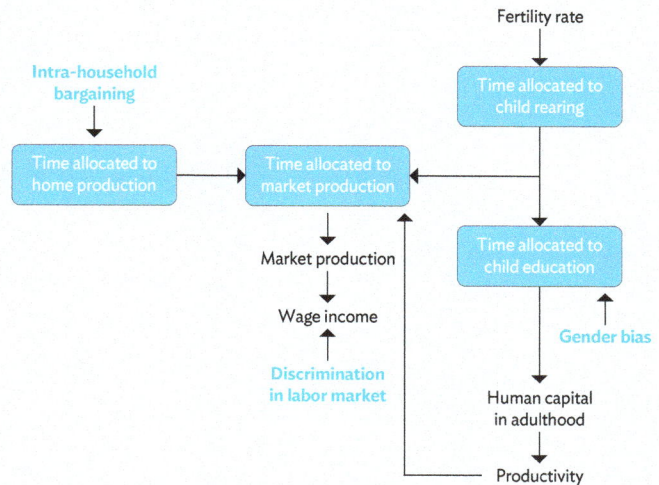

Source: Pande, Ford, and Fletcher, forthcoming.

However, policies to achieve gender equality are not without side effects. As women increase their market participation, the opportunity cost to their time rises and their fertility rate falls. On the other hand, higher childcare subsidies can increase the fertility rate but reduce women's participation in the labor market. And encouraging men to engage in childcare promotes women's participation in the workforce and higher economic growth but at the cost of lower fertility. A judicious combination of policies is therefore needed to achieve multiple goals.

from 15%–20% in Indonesia, Malaysia, and the Philippines to 25%–30% in Bangladesh, India, and Pakistan—economic growth continues to be impeded by gender gaps in workforce participation, entrepreneurial activity, and education (IMF 2015).

While the emphasis has traditionally been on equality of outcomes (e.g., women achieving parity with men in terms of income, wealth, assets, paid work, and the division of housework), equality of opportunity is no less important, ensuring that women have formal and legal equality in terms of access to education, health services, and employment. Equality of opportunity creates an enabling environment for a woman to participate in decision making and to have a voice within the household and outside of it, strengthening her place in society.

As women generally place greater emphasis on the welfare of their families and children than do men, gender equality enhances household welfare. Studies have shown that women tend to spend more on nutrition and preventive health care and invest more in children's education (Goldman Sachs Global Markets Institute 2009). Qian (2008) found that raising incomes for women improved survival rates for girls and educational attainment for all children, while raising incomes for men worsened girls' survival rates and educational attainment. Similarly, in Indonesia, raising mothers' bargaining power, as measured by transfers at marriage and assets brought to marriage, lowered the risk of child labor (Galasso 1999). As women are responsible for a disproportionate number of household spending decisions, and as they spend more on education and health, they create human capital that can drive growth in a world of constrained resources (Goldman Sachs Global Markets Institute 2014). Narrowing the gender gap therefore gives twin benefits—to the society and to individuals (UNICEF 2006). Investing in the potential offered by the female half of the world's population is thus a priority and very expensive to ignore.

Employment that fosters social change

When a woman takes up a job with income flows, the benefits of being a part of the workforce give her the resources she needs to ease the constraints she began with (Figure 2.1.9). Her economic independence enables her to access credit, buy property, distribute household resources more equitably between sons and daughters, and save more for the future, enhancing the family's human capital and economic well-being. As this phenomenon spreads through a region, it inspires other women to follow suit and changes perceptions of gender inequality, especially among younger people. The dynamics of households where women are active workforce participants thus creates a powerful feedback loop for social change as it empowers women to break through the barriers that prevented them from working outside the home.

Evidence shows that women in developing Asia are disadvantaged by unfair laws on inheritance and property rights (World Bank 2015). Across East Asia and the Pacific, households headed by women own less land than households headed by men. Few women own farms despite 40% of the region's women being employed in agriculture (World Bank 2012). If women had the same access to productive resources as men in agriculture, they could increase yields on their farms by 20%–30%. This could raise total agricultural output in developing countries by 2.5%–4.0%, which could reduce the number of hungry people in the world by 12%–17% (FAO 2011).

A woman's ability to command income from outside of the home strongly influences the autonomy she has within it (Eswaran 2014). This pattern has been observed in rural Bangladesh (Anderson and Eswaran 2009) and in Ahmedabad, India (Kantor 2003). General increases in household income can loosen constraints that pressure parents to prioritize one gender over the other, particularly in terms of education, health, and nutrition.

Women tend to save more than men. One study found that a 1 percentage point increase in women's share of employment raises aggregate saving by one-quarter of a percentage point—comparable with a 1 percentage point increase in the growth rate of GDP (Seguino and Floro 2003).

2.1.9 Constraints on working for income and the feedback loop

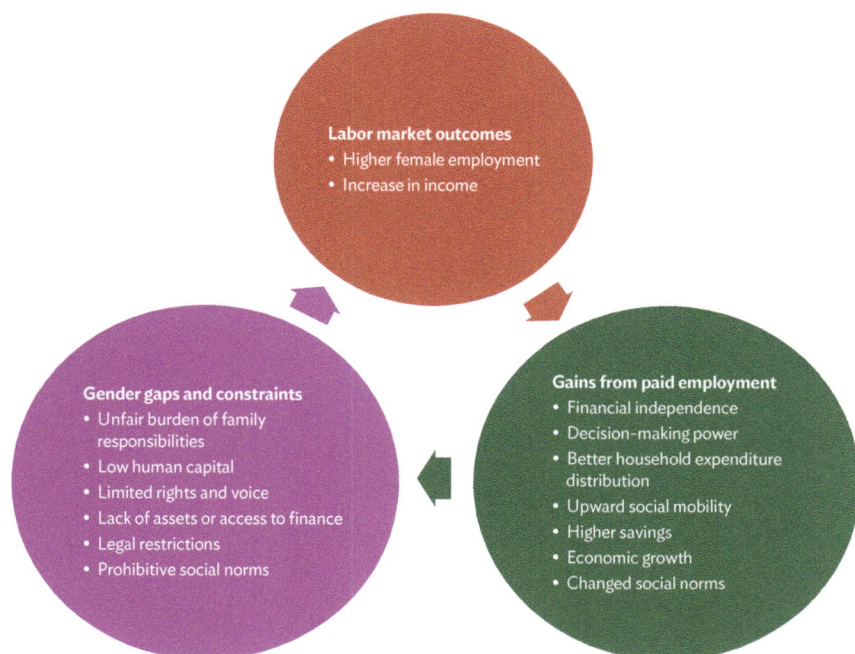

Labor market outcomes
- Higher female employment
- Increase in income

Gender gaps and constraints
- Unfair burden of family responsibilities
- Low human capital
- Limited rights and voice
- Lack of assets or access to finance
- Legal restrictions
- Prohibitive social norms

Gains from paid employment
- Financial independence
- Decision-making power
- Better household expenditure distribution
- Upward social mobility
- Higher savings
- Economic growth
- Changed social norms

Source: Authors.

Women's subpar contribution to the workforce can have serious macroeconomic consequences: a less-skilled workforce in light of women's rising educational attainment, an unused pool of talent, lower productivity in female-owned companies, and lower per capita GDP (IMF 2013). The Asia-Pacific loses an estimated $89 billion in income every year because women are underrepresented in the workforce (UNDP 2010). If their representation increased to 70%, as in the advanced economies, annual GDP would be 4.2% higher in India, 2.9% higher in Malaysia, and 1.4% higher in Indonesia. It would be a huge missed opportunity for developing Asia if its women were not fully enabled to participate in the workforce.

With equal opportunity, women in the workforce would have a say at home and in the society, enabling them to improve conditions for other women to enter the labor market or better themselves by taking the initiative, getting the jobs they are best suited for, and catching up with men regarding pay and benefits.

Facilitating labor market entry

Women's greater assumption of income-earning work can promote economic growth and foster social change. Yet, despite significant improvements to labor markets around the world in recent decades, most remain divided along gender lines, not least in developing Asia. The wide variation in female labor force participation rates among economies in the region suggests that the factors that inhibit women's joining the workforce differ from place to place. Differences in access to education, legal frameworks, and cultural and social norms may explain why women in some countries find it easier than others to enter paid employment outside the home.

Education is a must for better employment prospects. Developing Asia has made great strides in educating girls but has left a yawning gap between girls and boys in the training that imparts skills that employers need.

The legal framework can be a powerful tool to level the playing field. Yet laws in many Asian economies do not provide for equal opportunity in hiring, or they perversely apply to women stricter limits on statutory working hours than they do to men.

Perhaps the most daunting barriers to change are convention, tradition, and cultural practices that affect how work in the home is shared among husbands, wives, sons, and daughters. As a result, women often cite family responsibilities, including housework and caring for the elderly and children, as barriers to joining the workforce. Social norms and cultural practices may limit the types of jobs women may take or restrict their ability to travel to work.

Social norms and cultural practices

Entrenched social norms can be powerful deterrents to women's pursuit of work outside the home. These barriers take many forms: traditional views of "men's work" and "women's work," attitudes regarding acceptable behavior for women and girls outside the home, or even the stigma a man may bear by having a working spouse. Figure 2.2.1 maps the prevalence of female employment against expressions of bias, finding an inverse relationship and indicating that developing Asia (its economies shown as red dots) harbors somewhat more bias against women's employment than the global average, especially where women are seen to compete with men.

In Pakistan, for example, restriction imposed by men appears to be a critical constraint that keeps female workforce participation low (Figure 2.2.2). While 40% of unemployed women report having free time on their hands, a quarter of unemployed women say they would like to work if they could find a suitable job. Female workforce participation could easily double if these women were employed. The incentive is quite strong, as highly educated women who work outside the home earn twice as much as those who stay at home.

In the Republic of Korea, many women drop out of the workforce in their mid-20s to marry and raise children, and some return to it only in

2.2.1 Attitudes about gender roles and female employment

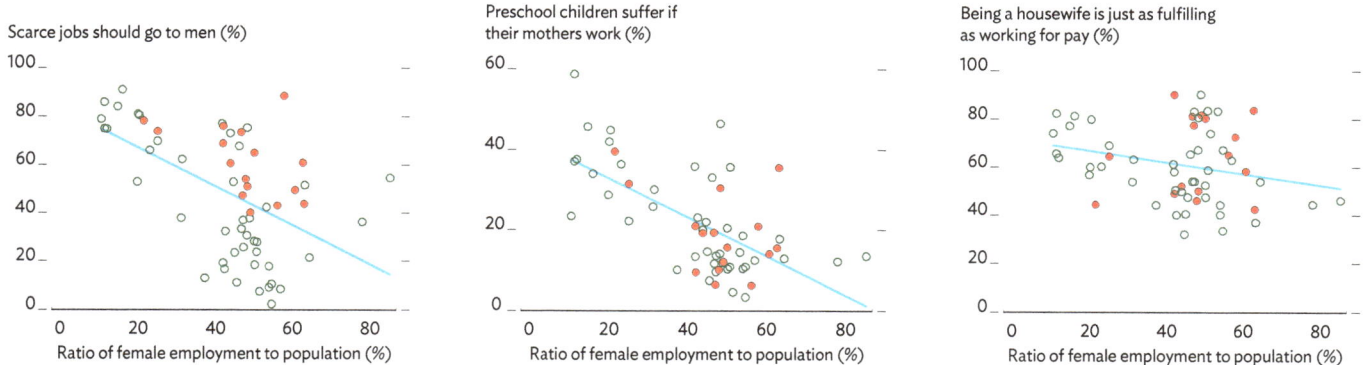

Note: Data pertain to the percentages of male and female responses to each question. Red dots indicate developing Asian economies.
Source: World Values Survey Association. World Values Survey Wave 6: 2010–2014. www.worldvaluessurvey.org

their 40s. This suggests that domestic responsibilities are a major factor keeping women out of the workforce and seriously interrupting their career development.

    Inequitable time allocation within the household—especially for unpaid caregiving and such domestic chores as cooking and cleaning—reflects individual preferences, bargains struck within the family, and social norms (World Bank 2011). Around the world, the amount of time women spend on unpaid housework and caregiving varies from 50% more than men to six times more (World Bank 2014). A different source reported that many women in South Asia devote more time to housework than men by a factor of 10, and that the average differential in developing Asia is three (OECD 2014). Although more women now enter the workforce and men share more domestic work, men have yet to take up all the slack (UN 2010).

    This limits women's participation in the workforce. Data comparing countries show an inverse relation between women's labor force participation rate and the hours they devote to housework and caregiving (Figure 2.2.3). That is, the more time women spend on household activities in comparison with men, the less they participate in the workforce. This relation is much stronger in developing Asia than in most other places in the sample. Clearly, domestic responsibilities limit options for paid work. These chores may use time inefficiently if women are more productive workers than some men in the workforce. Figure 2.2.4 shows gender inequality in unpaid caregiving related inversely to per capita income. At the household level, the gender gap in hours allocated to unpaid work declines the richer and more educated couples are (World Bank 2011).

    Social and cultural norms can be strongly entrenched, but they are not immutable. Creating the opportunities for more women to join the paid workforce can be a powerful catalyst toward changing long-held cultural and social norms. Individual data derived from surveys in 24 countries distributed across North and South America, Asia and

2.2.2 Reasons for not working in Pakistan

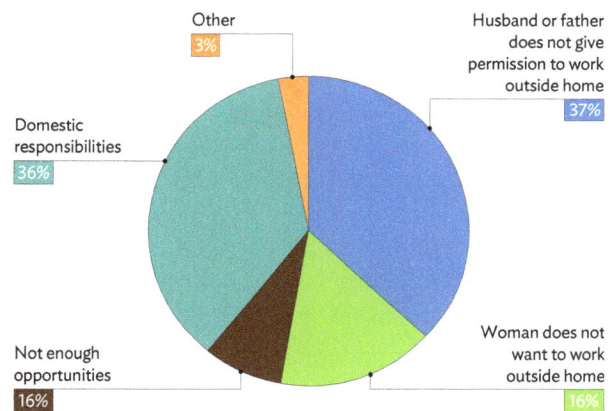

Source: Pande, Ford, and Fletcher, forthcoming.

2.2.3 Female labor force participation versus unpaid housework and caregiving

Female labor force participation rate (%)

Ratio of female employment to population (%)

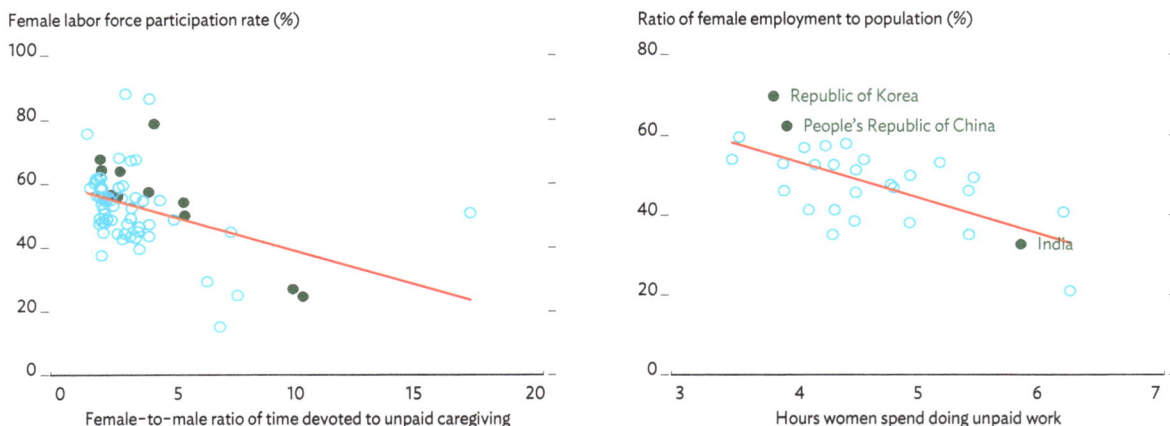

Female-to-male ratio of time devoted to unpaid caregiving

Hours women spend doing unpaid work

Note: Green dots indicate developing Asian economies.

Sources: World Bank. World Development Indicators online database; OECD. Gender, Institutions, and Development online database (both accessed 4 September 2015).

Australasia, Europe, and the Middle East show that female respondents raised by mothers employed outside the home are themselves more likely to be employed and hold supervisory responsibility. Further, they work more hours and earn higher hourly wages than do women whose mothers stayed at home full time. Meanwhile, children of employed mothers—who are exposed to parental division of housework that is less traditional and more equitable—are found to spend more time caring for family members as adults than do the children of mothers who never worked outside the home (McGinn, Castro, and Lingo 2015).

These observations suggest that parents often succeed in transmitting their gender attitudes to children, and that teaching by example is one way that progressive parents can counter social and cultural norms that inhibit more equitable participation in paid employment. Governments and other public institutions can, for their part, lead the pursuit of change through formal education and vocational training.

Appropriate education and skills

Educational trends have long presaged change in society and livelihoods. They are no less potent when used to encourage and guide social change and to improve economic outcomes through gender equality. In particular, investment in schooling for girls and vocational training for women strengthens human capital, boosts growth over the long term, and breaks down social and cultural barriers to women's entry into the workforce. This ultimately helps to close persistent gender gaps.

As much as one-third of East Asia's remarkable growth performance from 1960 to 1985 derived from sound investments in primary education for a rapidly growing working-age population—the so-called demographic dividend (World Bank 1993). This dividend promises to continue paying well into the future, as the high potential output per

2.2.4 GDP versus gender inequality in unpaid caregiving

Log GDP per capita, PPP (current international $)

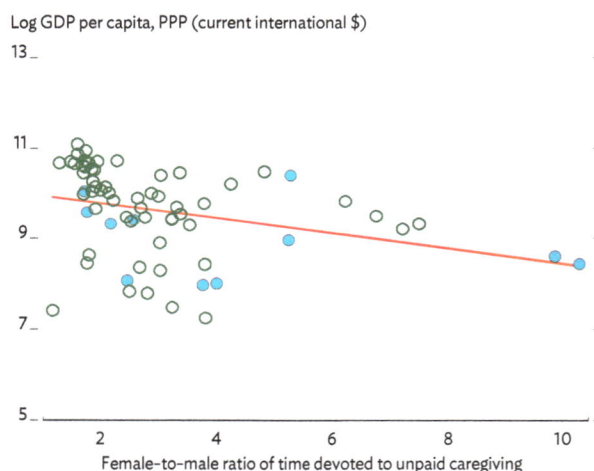

Female-to-male ratio of time devoted to unpaid caregiving

PPP = purchasing power parity.

Note: Blue dots indicate developing Asian economies.

Sources: World Bank. World Development Indicators online database; OECD. Gender, Institutions, and Development online database (both accessed 4 September 2015).

capita and savings contributed by this expanded workforce enhance long-run growth. As developing Asia reaches a new demographic transition, raising women's participation in paid employment can directly foster further growth. Where populations are still young, such as in Indonesia, the Philippines, and Sri Lanka, half of the large rising generation is female. Where populations are aging—as in the PRC; Hong Kong, China; the Republic of Korea; Singapore; Taipei,China; Thailand; and Viet Nam—employed women can moderate demographic imbalance as a shrinking workforce supports a growing number of pensioners.

Data for developing Asia from 1970 to 2010 show a positive correlation between the long-term growth rate of GDP per capita and the female-to-male ratio of average years of schooling (Figure 2.2.5). Employing women in the workforce appears to greatly raise the chances of high economic growth. Educated women in particular provide a more skilled workforce. Education also improves women's incomes and their ability to make informed choices about family planning, nutrition, health, and education for their children. Investing in female education advances not only their own welfare but also that of their families and communities by making them role models for their gender.

The past quarter century has seen substantial growth in educational opportunity worldwide that has bridged gender gaps across grade levels. Almost all regions are now near parity in terms of primary and secondary enrollment (Table 2.2.1). Indeed, enrollment in tertiary education has reversed gender disparity from male advantage to female. In a number of regions including East Asia and the Pacific, girls are now more likely than boys to benefit from secondary education as well as tertiary. Longer years in school mean that girls are more mature when they begin to seek work outside the home (Figure 2.2.6). This finding is corroborated by analysis of cross-section data from five Asian economies: the PRC, India, Indonesia, the Republic of Korea, and the Philippines. It shows that women in the 15–24 age group, who are likely to be enrolled in secondary and tertiary education, now participate less in the workforce than do people in general (ADB 2015).

Notwithstanding the exceptional narrowing of the education gender gap, inequality is still wider in poor countries than in middle-income and rich countries (Duflo 2012).

In developing Asia, primary enrollment is nearly universal at 95% or higher for both girls and boys, but there is considerable variation across countries. In 2013, gender parity indexes for primary enrollment in the region ranged from 0.7 in Afghanistan to 1.1 in Nepal. In tertiary education, 15 of the 20 countries with data in the region had gender parity indexes greater than 1.0, indicating that

2.2.5 Growth rate of GDP per capita versus female-to-male ratio of average years of schooling, 1970–2010

- ▲ Central Asia
- ● East Asia
- ◆ South Asia
- ■ Southeast Asia
- + The Pacific
- ○ Rest of the world

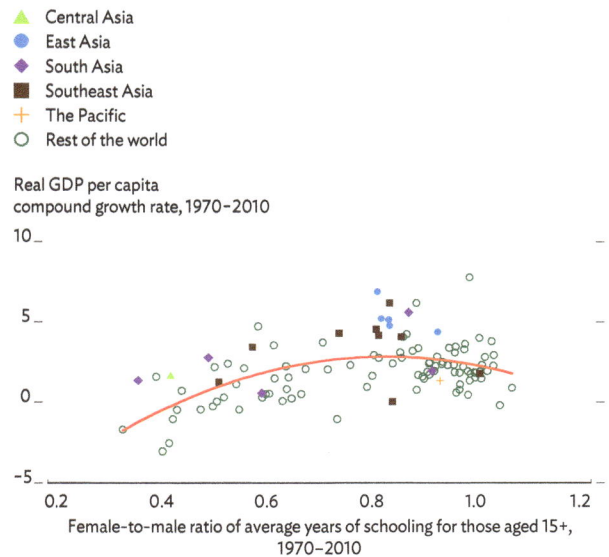

Real GDP per capita compound growth rate, 1970–2010

Female-to-male ratio of average years of schooling for those aged 15+, 1970–2010

Notes: Economies with initial female-to-male ratios >1 are excluded. Real GDP per capita growth (constant 2005 $) is compounded and adjusted for purchasing power parity.
Sources: ADB estimates using Penn World Table 8.1; Barro and Lee. 2013. A New Data Set of Educational Attainment in the World, 1950–2010. *Journal of Development Economics* 104.

2.2.6 More education for delayed labor market entry

- ▲ Central Asia
- ● East Asia
- ◆ South Asia
- ■ Southeast Asia
- + The Pacific
- ○ Rest of the world

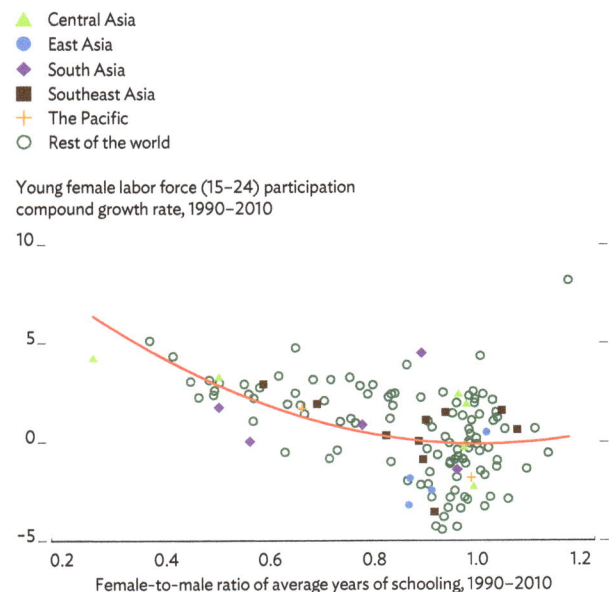

Young female labor force (15–24) participation compound growth rate, 1990–2010

Female-to-male ratio of average years of schooling, 1990–2010

Note: Economies with initial female-to-male ratios >1 are excluded.
Sources: ADB estimates using data from International Labour Organization. Key Indicators of the Labour Market 8th Edition; Barro and Lee. 2013. A New Data Set of Educational Attainment in the World, 1950–2010. *Journal of Development Economics* 104.

2.2.1 Gender parity index by level of education

Region	Primary enrollment		Secondary enrollment		Tertiary enrollment	
	1990	2013	1990	2013	1990	2013
World	0.88	0.98	0.84	0.97	0.90	1.10
Arab states	0.82	0.94	0.75	0.94	0.71	1.06
Central and Eastern Europe	0.97	1.00	0.97	0.98	1.17	1.17
Central Asia	1.00	0.99	...	0.99	...	1.11
East Asia and the Pacific	0.93	0.99	0.82	1.01	0.67	1.10
Latin America and the Caribbean	0.99	0.98	1.07	1.06	0.96	1.28
North America and Western Europe	1.00	0.99	1.01	1.00	1.11	1.29
South and West Asia	0.74	1.00	0.59	0.94	0.49	0.92
Sub-Saharan Africa	0.83	0.93	0.76	0.86	0.47	0.70

... = data not available.

Note: The gender parity index is the ratio of the female gross enrollment ratio divided by the male gross enrollment ratio for each level of education. The regions are as classified by the United Nations Educational, Scientific, and Cultural Organization (UNESCO) Institute of Statistics.

Source: UNESCO Institute of Statistics. http://data.uis.unesco.org/ (accessed 13 August 2015).

women were more likely to pursue higher education than were men. At the extreme is the Philippines, where girls are 1.3 times more likely than boys to be in primary school and 1.8 times more likely to be in secondary school (Albert et al. 2012).

Despite progress in school enrollment, gender differences in education persist. In many countries, poor families often enroll only their boys in primary school, seeing them as future breadwinners, and marry off their daughters, seeing them as future liabilities or simply destined for customary child marriage (and the consequent social ill of preteen or teenage pregnancy). Such treatment of girls merely shifts them from one poor household to another, perpetuating gender inequality through generations. In South Asia, where such practices are prevalent, almost half of women remain illiterate. A study in Madagascar found that teen pregnancy makes females 42% more likely to drop out of school and worsens by 44% their likelihood of completing lower secondary school (Herrera and Sahn 2015). The lifetime opportunity cost of teen pregnancy measured by foregone annual income over the lifetimes of women who become mothers at age 15–19, is estimated at 1% of annual GDP in the PRC, 11% in Bangladesh, and 12% in India (Chaaban and Cunningham 2011).

Many girls drop out of school to help with unpaid housework, thus missing their chance to enter the workforce, or to take low-paying dead-end drudge work to supplement family income. High direct and indirect education costs that are beyond the means of low-income households are the main cause of the early dropping out (World Bank 2002). Gender parity in education must be promoted for educational investments to bear fruit and for women to realize their potential. More importantly, what matters to labor markets is not just access to schooling but also strong learning outcomes. Narrowing disparities in access to high-quality education holds the promise not only of redressing income inequality but also of higher productivity and growth-enhancing returns. Sianesi and Van Reenen (2003) published a survey of the issue.

Even though girls receive the same number of schooling years as boys, young women lose out to young men in the race for jobs as they transition from school to the workforce. Finding a job after attending school may take years, imposing a large opportunity cost in terms of earnings foregone. In Indonesia, the Philippines, and Thailand, the average waiting time after finishing school and before finding a job is 4–5 years (ADB 2008). Gender, education, and social status affect the waiting time, as data from the Philippines show (Box 2.2.1).

Individuals may become discouraged after a long search for work and drop out of the labor market. The jobless rate, a broad measure of unutilized human resources, adds to the job-seeking unemployed the long-term unemployed who are not looking for work (Figure 2.2.7).

Young women are far more likely than young men to be unemployed over the long term, particularly in low- and middle-income countries, for a number of reasons (OECD 2012). One important factor is limited information about job availability and the returns on educational investments, without which some young people fail to acquire the knowledge and skills necessary to land high-quality wage jobs. Another is early marriage and childbearing, because of which married young women are more likely to be unemployed than unmarried women of the same age, especially in developing countries.

In general, the odds of long-term unemployment ease as educational attainment rises. Because conditions for young women in the labor market are significantly more difficult than for young men, they need more support in terms of education, training, and counseling to minimize the risk of becoming irretrievably discouraged and alienated from the labor market.

Technical and vocational education and training (TVET) programs are vital to expanding women's employment. Education augmented with job training directly benefits not only women's workforce participation but also their economic and health prospects (ADB 2013b). However, because many Asian education systems are not geared to the region's emerging personnel requirements, a mismatch persists between demand for labor with particular knowledge, skills, and experience and the supply available. Livelihood and skills training cannot improve access to local labor markets unless it is adjusted for relevance to market needs.

Young Asian women require targeted TVET programs to smooth their transition from school to the labor market and enable them to compete for better-paid jobs on an equal footing with young men, including in traditionally male areas of employment. Training and scholarships to encourage young women to take up nontraditional employment can

2.2.1 Disparity in the transition from school to work in the Philippines

The average time required to find a job in the Philippines varies by gender and educational attainment; the search time is shortest for those with some college education. The transition to work is particularly slow for women with relatively meager qualifications. While young men who complete high school have similarly paced transitions as men who finish college, young women who complete high school have slower transitions than women with college degrees. Wage employment eventually rewards 71% of college graduates, 52% of high school graduates, and 37% of high school dropouts (Bird, forthcoming).

Social status affects employment prospects too. Children from better-off families have wider social networks and access to job information, and better job-search techniques, that improve their chances of finding wage employment. Evidence indicates that the transition to work is slower for men whose family incomes are higher, though, perhaps because financial support in the interim is not an issue. It is faster for women in households whose head is self-employed, possibly reflecting the ready availability of positions in family businesses. In families with more children, men tend to be employed while women stay at home to attend to housework and child care (Bird, forthcoming).

2.2.7 Jobless and unemployment rates for youth aged 15–24 years, latest year available

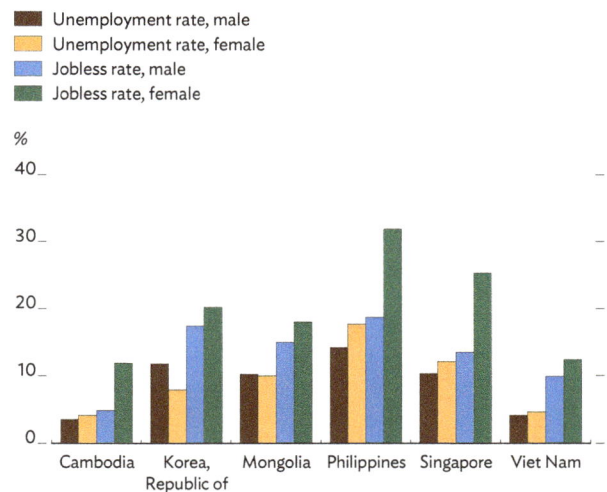

- Unemployment rate, male
- Unemployment rate, female
- Jobless rate, male
- Jobless rate, female

Notes: Data pertain to share of youth not in education, employment, or training. The "unemployed" are those looking for work, and the "jobless" include the unemployed and those not looking for work.

Source: International Labour Organization. Key Indicators of the Labour Market 8th Edition.

be included in the design of employment projects in line with project objectives (ADB and ILO 2013). Targeted and well-delivered TVET programs can significantly increase women's incomes and improve rural livelihoods (FAO, IFAD, and ILO 2010). TVET programs ideally incorporate information about entrepreneurship.

As technological advance and process automation play ever larger roles in raising productivity, workers need stronger technical skill sets. Policy interventions to facilitate the school-to-work transition should therefore ensure a solid foundation of high-quality education, establish better links between educational institutions and employers, and provide job seekers with adequate labor market information. Gender-sensitive TVET programs should be promoted that are tailored to local contexts, attract women to trades and professions beyond stereotyped "women's work," and offer placement and counseling services. Before they can be scaled up, such programs need first to be run as pilot projects and then carefully evaluated.

Institutional and legal reform

Laws can influence various aspects of gender gaps. In general, the legal and institutional framework can be a powerful instrument for establishing the general principle of gender equity. Particular laws, on the other hand, can impinge directly or indirectly on women's ability, relative to men, to enter the labor market or launch a business venture.

In the past half century, numerous changes have been made to the gender aspects of national legal frameworks worldwide. Changes include the addition of nondiscriminatory clauses in constitutions, status revisions that allow women to take jobs and conduct business transactions, and the granting of female property rights. Naturally, a constitutional right to freedom from discrimination is expected to guarantee gender equality in the labor market. Yet a key finding of World Bank (2015) is that 33% of the countries covered globally, or 56 of 173, do not have any such constitutional provision. More than half of the advanced economies do not constitutionally guarantee freedom from discrimination (Figure 2.2.8). Likewise, in developing Asia, a third of national constitutions do not guarantee freedom from discrimination on gender. This inhibits women's pursuit of opportunities in these job markets, even if they are well-qualified.

In short, laws can open up equal employment opportunities for women or obstruct their access to the labor market. Among the countries in the World Bank's *Women, Business, and the Law* database, almost 90% still have at least one legal limitation on women's economic opportunities. In some countries, husbands can legally object to their wives working and prevent them from accepting jobs.

On the other hand, the database shows that 9 economies have legal quotas for women's representation on the boards of publicly listed companies, while 16 have legal quotas for women in the national legislature. Such a quota system may ensure that women are represented but does not guarantee that they are influential. The greater ambition is to go beyond quotas and ensure that women representatives play active roles when and where decisions are made.

2.2.8 Percentage of national constitutions with no nondiscrimination clause

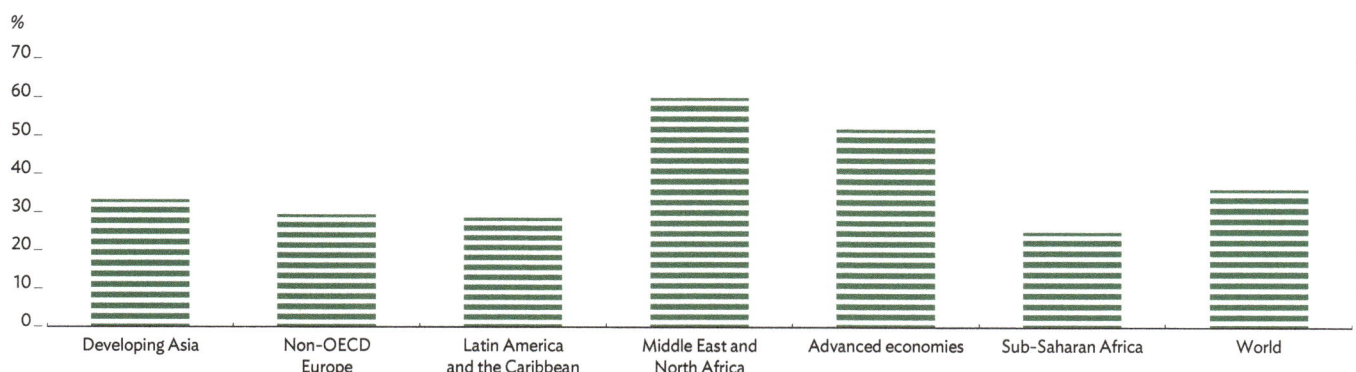

Note: Advanced economies are members of the Organisation for Economic Co-operation and Development (OECD) excluding the Republic of Korea (included in developing Asia), Chile and Mexico (Latin America and the Caribbean), and Israel (Middle East and North Africa).
Source: World Bank. *Women, Business and the Law* database. http://wbl.worldbank.org/data (accessed 11 September 2015).

More than half of economies reporting in the World Bank's database do not have laws that explicitly prohibit corporate discrimination by gender in such areas as hiring, statutory work hours, and wages. More than 70% of the sampled developing Asian economies do not have such laws (Figure 2.2.9). The bias in hiring and wages is further aggravated by occupational segregation, as 19 of the 34 developing Asian economies in the sample restrict which jobs women can take. In these economies, women cannot work in mining, construction, or metal works, even if they are neither pregnant nor nursing.

Significantly, laws remain that restrict the number of hours or times of day a woman can work (Table 2.2.2). Discrimination can be casual and arbitrary, as an employer who believes that women are inherently less able may favor male workers. This can prevent women from getting the jobs they are best qualified for, hampering personal and professional development and productivity in the economy as a whole.

Although gender parity under the law has improved globally, many laws, regulations, and policies continue to hinder women's efforts to start a business.

Women are disadvantaged, professionally as well as personally, by unfair laws on property rights. The absence of laws that foster equality and poor implementation of existing policies and laws limit their access to or ownership of land and other productive resources (UN 2013). Women are less likely than men to exercise control over land, buildings, or other assets, or to have access to the credit, technology, and information that are useful when setting up or expanding a business. In almost 20% of the 173 countries included in the World Bank's database, daughters' inheritance rights to property are unequal to those of sons.

While men and women have equal rights to property ownership in most developing Asian economies, some countries in South and Southeast Asia do not grant equal property inheritance rights to sons and daughters, or to surviving female and male spouses (Figure 2.2.10). Equal property rights give women greater latitude on whether to go out to work, how far to travel for work, and other decisions that influence the quality of work.

2.2.9 Asian economies with no laws to prohibit job discrimination based on gender

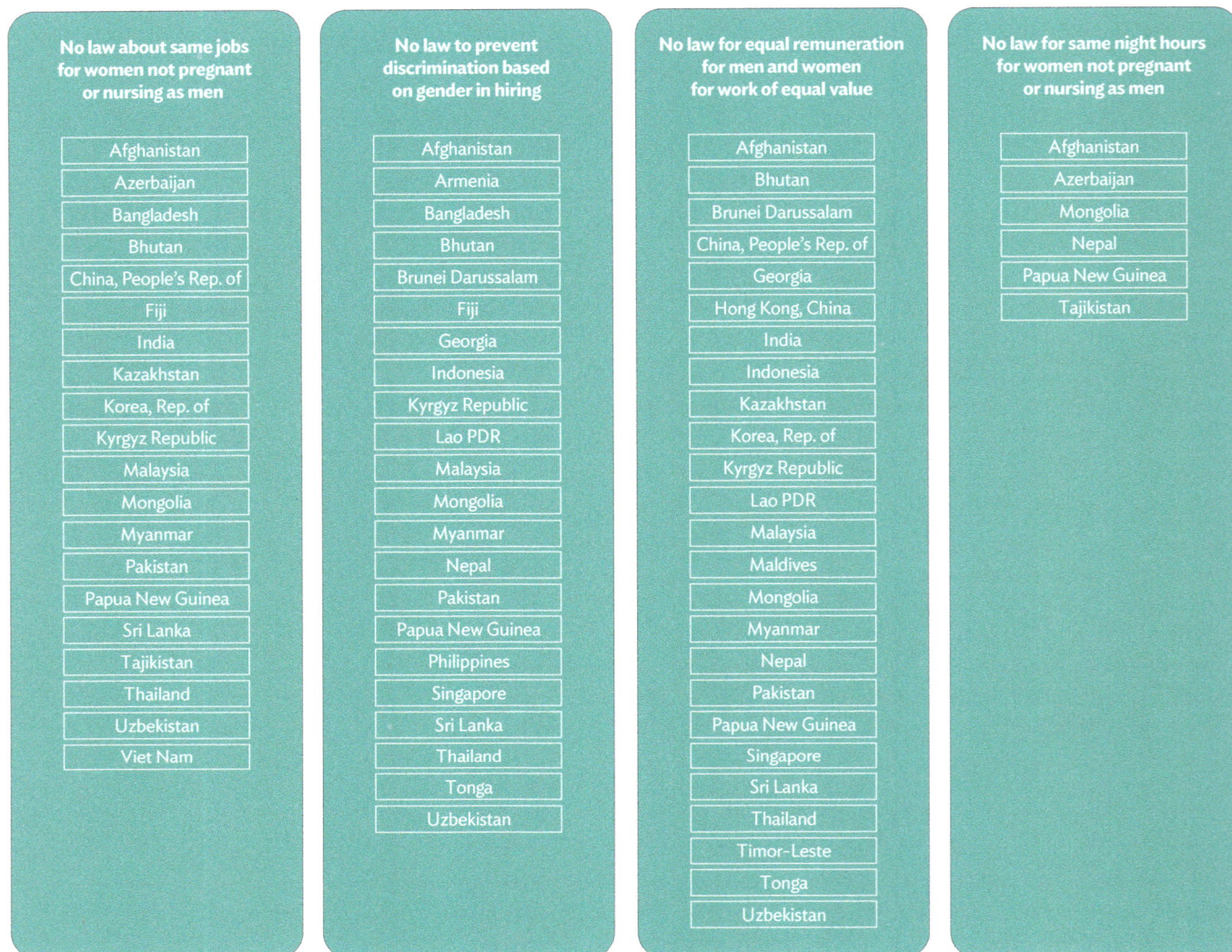

No law about same jobs for women not pregnant or nursing as men	No law to prevent discrimination based on gender in hiring	No law for equal remuneration for men and women for work of equal value	No law for same night hours for women not pregnant or nursing as men
Afghanistan	Afghanistan	Afghanistan	Afghanistan
Azerbaijan	Armenia	Bhutan	Azerbaijan
Bangladesh	Bangladesh	Brunei Darussalam	Mongolia
Bhutan	Bhutan	China, People's Rep. of	Nepal
China, People's Rep. of	Brunei Darussalam	Georgia	Papua New Guinea
Fiji	Fiji	Hong Kong, China	Tajikistan
India	Georgia	India	
Kazakhstan	Indonesia	Indonesia	
Korea, Rep. of	Kyrgyz Republic	Kazakhstan	
Kyrgyz Republic	Lao PDR	Korea, Rep. of	
Malaysia	Malaysia	Kyrgyz Republic	
Mongolia	Mongolia	Lao PDR	
Myanmar	Myanmar	Malaysia	
Pakistan	Nepal	Maldives	
Papua New Guinea	Pakistan	Mongolia	
Sri Lanka	Papua New Guinea	Myanmar	
Tajikistan	Philippines	Nepal	
Thailand	Singapore	Pakistan	
Uzbekistan	Sri Lanka	Papua New Guinea	
Viet Nam	Thailand	Singapore	
	Tonga	Sri Lanka	
	Uzbekistan	Thailand	
		Timor-Leste	
		Tonga	
		Uzbekistan	

Lao PDR = Lao People's Democratic Republic.
Source: World Bank. *Women, Business and the Law* database. http://wbl.worldbank.org/data (accessed 11 September 2015).

Ownership of property and other assets affects women's workforce participation through several channels. Owning property helps women support themselves by, for example, cropping land to grow food for household consumption or partitioning home space for a small shop. They can use property as collateral to start a small business. The money thus earned can finance the TVET of family members and free up time through the hiring of household help or the purchase of modern conveniences. Property ownership may increase women's bargaining power in the household (Floro and Meurs 2009).

A critical constraint on women, especially those trying to start small businesses, is a dearth of credit. Women entrepreneurs in the Maldives, for example, find their inability to borrow to finance business startups a major stumbling block (ADB 2014b). A number of economies in developing Asia have instituted positive reforms with regard to credit: In Viet Nam, public credit registries now include information from

2.2.2 Laws governing work hours and overtime

	Night work	Overtime limits		
	Restricted hours	Statutory work hours	Limits for men	Limits for women
Central Asia				
Armenia		40/week	4/day, 180/year	Same
Azerbaijan	10:00 p.m.–6:00 a.m.	8/day, 40/week	2/day	0/day[a]
Georgia		41/week		
Kazakhstan		40/week	2/day, 120/year	0/day[b]
Kyrgyz Republic		40/week	4/day	Same
Tajikistan	10:00 p.m.–6:00 a.m.	40/week	120/year	0/day[c]
Uzbekistan		40/week	4/day, 120/year	Same
East Asia				
China, People's Republic of		8/day, 40/week	3/day, 36/month	Same
Hong Kong, China				
Korea, Republic of		8/day, 40/week	12/week	2/day, 6/week, 150/year[d]
Mongolia		8/day, 40/week		
Taipei,China	10:00 p.m.–6:00 a.m.	8/day, 40/week	4/day, 46/month	Same
South Asia				
Bangladesh		8/day, 48/week	2/day, 12/week	Same
India	7:00 p.m.–6:00 a.m.	9/day, 48/week	3/day, 12/week, 50/quarter	0/day[e]
Nepal	6:00 p.m.–6:00 a.m.	8/day, 40/week	4/day, 20/week	Same
Pakistan	7:00 p.m.–6:00 a.m.	9/day, 48/week		0/day[e]
Sri Lanka		9/day, 48/week	3/day, 12/week	Same
Southeast Asia				
Cambodia				
Indonesia		40/week	3/day, 14/week	Same
Lao People's Democratic Republic		8/day, 48/week	3/day, 45/month	0/day[f]
Malaysia	10:00 p.m.–5:00 a.m.	8/day, 48/week	104/month	Same
Philippines		8/day		
Singapore		8/day, 44/week	4/day	Same
Thailand		48/week	36/week	0/day[g]
Viet Nam		8/day, 48/week	4/day, 200/year	Same
The Pacific				
Fiji		48/week		
Papua New Guinea	6:00 p.m.–6:00 a.m.	44/week		

[a] Women workers who are pregnant or have children under 3 years of age may not be called on to work the nightshift, overtime, or on a weekend, holiday, or other day that is not work day, or to undertake job-related travel (Labor Code, Sec 242).

[b] Overtime work is not permitted for pregnant women.

[c] Pregnant women or women who have children under 3 years old may not be called on to work overtime work or on weekends or holidays, or to go on business trips.

[d] An employer shall not have a female within 1 year of childbirth work overtime exceeding 2 hours per day, 6 hours per week, or 150 hours per year, even if agreed in a collective agreement.

[e] No exemption is made for women to the 9-hour workday.

[f] Pregnant women and women with children under 12 months of age may not be called on to work overtime or during a holiday.

[g] The following shall be added as Section 39/1 of the Labour Protection Act B.E. 2541: "Section 39/1 An Employer shall be prohibited to require a female employee who is pregnant to work between 10:00 p.m. and 6:00 a.m., to work overtime or to work on holidays. Where the female employee who is pregnant works in an executive position, academic work, clerical work, or work relating to finance or accounting, the Employer may require the employee to work overtime in the working days as long as there is no effect on the health of pregnant employee and with prior consent of the pregnant employee on each occasion."

Sources: World Bank. *Women, Business, and the Law* database. http://wbl.worldbank.org/data/exploreeconomies (accessed 11 September 2015); various government documents.

microfinance institutions. Cambodia and Tajikistan have new credit bureaus that collect information from microfinance institutions and offer loans with no lower limit on the amount. The Lao People's Democratic Republic also has a new credit registry that includes information from microfinance institutions.

More reforms are clearly needed covering other areas. In some countries, women still face institutional hurdles to using financial services because they lack collateral, must pay higher interest rates than men, and receive no business incentives that specifically target women (ADB 2014c). Collateral for loans is scarce primarily because land and other property is often registered in the name of male household members—fathers, husbands, brothers, and sons—despite family codes guaranteeing equal rights to own, use, and dispose of joint property. The collateral accepted by banks is limited to property that is generally given to the eldest son or acquired under the name of men, such as land and houses.

Legal reforms can remove some barriers that block women's entry to paid work, but that is just the beginning. Women face further hurdles when it comes to the type of work they can pursue.

2.2.10 Equal rights to property inheritance by gender

No
Yes

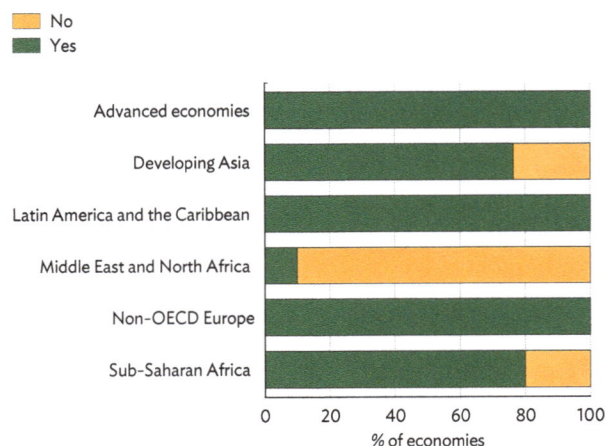

OECD = Organisation for Economic Co-operation and Development.
Notes: Advanced economies are OECD members excluding the Republic of Korea (included in developing Asia), Chile and Mexico (Latin America and the Caribbean), and Israel (Middle East and North Africa). Gender refers to sons versus daughters, surviving male spouse versus female spouse.
Source: World Bank. Women, Business, and the Law database. http://wbl.worldbank.org/data (accessed 11 September 2015).

Expanding occupational choices

Once a woman has decided to enter the workforce, her career choices may be restricted. Limited education and skills, the need to balance work with household responsibilities, and discrimination put women at a disadvantage to men. As a result, women in developing Asia tend to be concentrated in unpaid or low-paid occupations. When gainfully employed, they are likely to be in "soft" jobs and underrepresented in public office and in senior corporate positions, leaving them unable to realize their full economic potential. However, structural change, urbanization, and globalization in the region are opening up jobs for women that can help them move up the socioeconomic ladder. Moreover, the expansion of ICT across developing Asia is creating opportunities for women to earn income from home while balancing family responsibilities.

To seize these opportunities, appropriate policies are required to enable greater access to finance and pursue legal reform that would bestow on women equal rights. Enlarging and broadening women's scope in the labor market requires breaking down the silos of occupational segregation. Gender stereotypes teeter when barriers to entry into various occupations are eased by enhanced safety in the workplace and public spaces, and when training programs for women provide new skills. Women can become better represented in corporate and political leadership through affirmative action that establishes job quotas and raises awareness of gender inequality, which can help change social norms and improve women's status.

Redefining 'women's work'

A woman's choice of work is determined by a complex set of factors such as the extent and quality of her education, her decision-making power in the household, and the prevalence of social norms that perpetuate stereotypes. Employers operate within the same social norms when it comes to hiring women, but they may also impose rigid working arrangements or simply discriminate against women if, for example, they think women less productive than men. Such gender biases have many sources. Inequity in households often places heavier time burdens on women as they perform unpaid housework and caregiving. Formal state institutions perpetuate laws that favor men or fail to provide adequate public infrastructure such as roads and electricity and water systems, which contributes to women's domestic work burdens. Markets are skewed by unequal access to credit, agricultural inputs, and investments in human capital. And informal institutions can include employers' discriminatory attitudes toward women workers and social norms that restrict women's engagement in paid work. Avenues for self-employment may be blocked by a woman's lack of property rights or access to finance and technology, which can perpetuate wide disparity in the types of work that women and men do.

Figure 2.3.1 shows developing Asia ranked below some other regions on two subindexes of the gender gap index that measure inequality in workforce participation: wages and job advancement ("economic participation and opportunity") and senior decision making ("political empowerment").

Women account for a significant proportion of unpaid family workers and own-account workers throughout the developing world (Figure 2.3.2). Developing Asia had in 2013 a slightly larger share of women in this group than men—nearly 60% women and 58% men—but within the category, women were more likely to be unpaid contributing family workers. Looking across subregions shows considerable variation. The proportion of working women who are unpaid or self-employed was 6–7 percentage points higher than that of working men in East, South, and Southeast Asia and the Pacific.

Most Asian women are in informal employment, often in seasonal or casual jobs with an erratic income flow. Unable to find jobs in the formal sector and facing the prospect of extended spells of unemployment, many poor, uneducated, and marginalized women find self-employment to be the only survival strategy available to them. Though entrepreneurship is popularly associated with independence, flexible work hours, and high job satisfaction, this is not usually the case for women forced into self-employment. Women in the informal sector who are not self-employed and working at home are most commonly either street vendors or else they court even more risk as waste-pickers or construction workers (UN-Habitat 2012).

Learning through apprenticeship or technical and vocational education and training (TVET) programs is an important way to obtain better-paid employment. However, girls are less likely than boys to receive such training, which limits their chances of working in automated manufacturing. In Kazakhstan, for example, industry accounts for a larger share of men's employment than women's. Within industry, the mining and quarrying industry is an important source of high-paying jobs, but in 2011 it and the related transport and storage industries employed about three times as many men as women. Women are expressly prohibited from almost 300 types of jobs, many of them in the high-remuneration mining and transport industries. These legal barriers, combined with social norms about appropriate gender roles pertaining to work, help explain the lower female share of technical education enrollment.

Although gender differences in TVET are often driven by traditional practice, cultural norms, and legal restrictions, these notions are not immutable. Notwithstanding the difficulties of gender-segregated employment, TVET and job placement in Nepal, for instance, strengthened links between schools and industry to enable over 22% of female graduates to find employment in engineering, a well-paid industrial sector of the labor market historically closed to women (Jalal 2013).

2.3.1 Gender gap subindexes

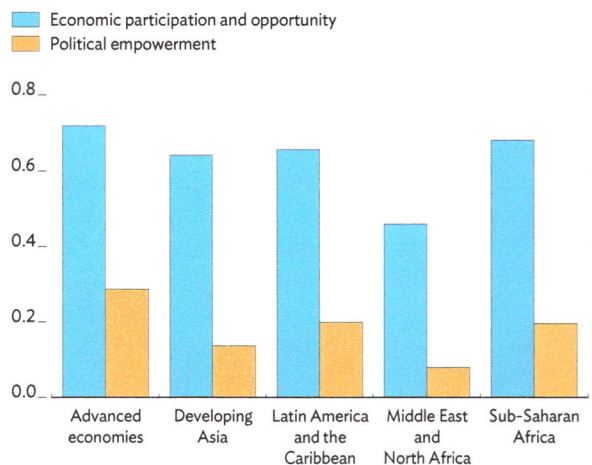

Notes: Figures refer to unweighted average scores. The highest possible score is 1 (full equality) and the lowest 0 (no equality). Advanced economies are members of the Organisation for Economic Co-operation and Development excluding the Republic of Korea (included in developing Asia), Chile and Mexico (Latin America and the Caribbean), and Israel (Middle East and North Africa).
Source: World Economic Forum. Gender Gap Report 2014.

2.3.2 Employment status by gender, 2013

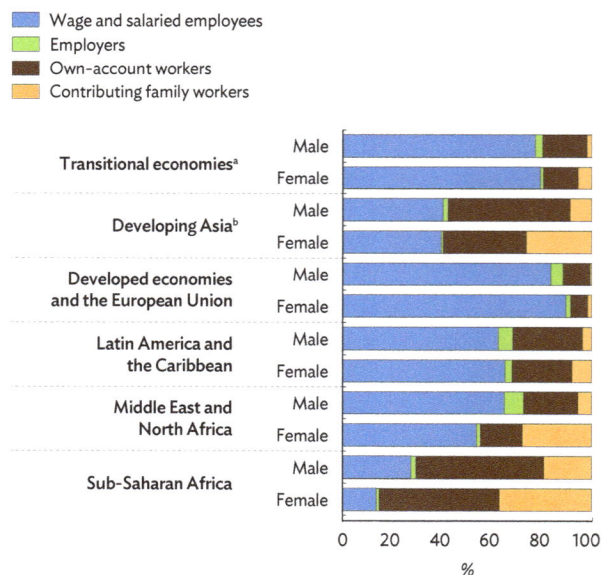

a The Commonwealth of Independent States and other economies in Central and Southeastern Europe that are not in the European Union.
b Excluding Central Asia and the Pacific.
Source: International Labour Organization. Key Indicators of the Labour Market 8th Edition.

In the Philippines, employment in manufacturing generally offers better pay and working conditions than does agriculture, where a high percentage of women are unpaid family workers. Yet, the Philippines' export-oriented development strategy, producing primarily electronics, processed food, automobile parts, textiles, and garments, has not spurred an expansion of women's employment in manufacturing relative to other industries (Figure 2.3.3).

Educated women also face obstacles in their career paths, as they are usually relegated to soft jobs in clerical and support positions, stunting their representation in senior positions (Grant Thornton 2013). When women do manage to land better jobs and attempt to continue climbing the career ladder, they bump against the infamous glass ceiling. Differences in gender roles at home reinforce this bias because women are more likely to interrupt their careers to bear and rear children and assume other family responsibilities. Women are also more reluctant than men to ask for promotions, and those who do can be perceived as "aggressive" or "unlikable" by their supervisors and peers (Bertrand 2011). Women shying away from competitive jobs for this reason further reinforces occupational segregation.

Fewer women than men reach high positions in scientific and technical disciplines, which are growth areas in the knowledge-driven New Asia. Educational aspirations are formed early in life at home, in school, and in society, and discouragement in any of these realms can keep even those with exceptional mathematical and scientific aptitude from pursuing scientific and technological fields of study. Women in general are less likely to take up careers in hard academic disciplines and, when they do, tend to leave these fields at higher rates than men at all career points. This is a cause for concern given skills shortages in the labor market, the generally more promising career and earnings prospects in science and technology, and the likelihood of positive spillover into innovation and growth (OECD 2014).

Gender stereotyping is self-perpetuating, as it undermines girls' confidence and discourages women from pursuing highly competitive positions, further reinforcing the stereotype. Low female representation in top jobs comes at a cost because women bring a distinct set of skills, work styles, and attitudes to the table that have potential to enhance productivity at all levels. Yet, even among highly qualified, educated, and skilled women, occupational choice is sometimes determined by gender stereotyping. Such stereotyping can, however, be challenged (Box 2.3.1).

Breaking down the silos of occupational segregation requires the expansion of educational and skills-training facilities, incentives for employers to provide parental leave, and legal reform. Because gender stereotypes affect attitudes at a young age beginning at home and in school, these are the places to begin to counter them by raising awareness in families through widespread public campaigns about the benefits of educating girls and their potential in the labor market. This entails sharing information about how Asian girls have been

2.3.3 Female employment by sector in the Philippines

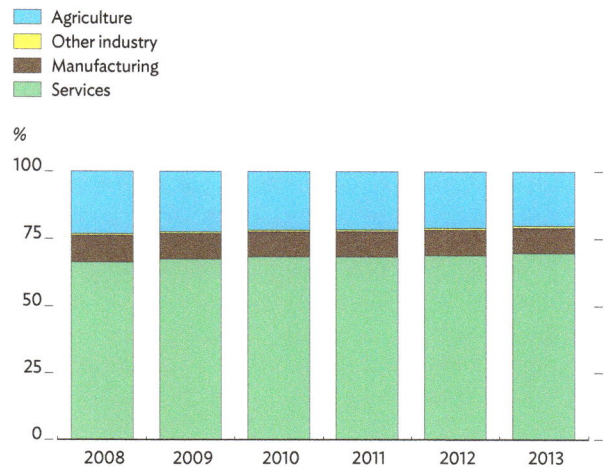

Source: Bureau of Labor and Employment Statistics. 2014. Gender Statistics on Labor and Employment. http://labstat.psa.gov.ph/PUBLICATIONS/Gender%20Statistics/Gender_Home.html

2.3.1 How gender stereotypes sap women's confidence and potential

Gender stereotyping can arise in roundabout ways. The quality of parents' work in terms of interest and job autonomy affects their ability to be responsive and nurturing toward their children, which can affect children's cognitive skills, performance in school, and social behavior (Caproni 2012). Children whose mothers have complex, responsible jobs perform better in verbal, math, and reading tests. Meanwhile, schools that employ mostly female teachers at the primary level and male teachers at the secondary level, especially in math and science, send the wrong signal to boys and girls about their respective capabilities (OECD 2012). Likewise, textbooks that cast women as nurses and men as engineers convey beliefs about girls' and boys' aptitudes, whether intentionally or not.

Gender stereotyping affects women even at the top rung of high-skilled professions, notwithstanding their possession of education, experience, and other qualifications on a par with men. Apart from having to bear an unequal share of the care burden, girls must overcome their lack of confidence, which is instilled in them from early school days. It seems to persist for a lifetime and keeps women trailing men in their earnings profiles.

Using a web-based survey of recipients of masters of business administration (MBAs) degrees from the University of Chicago in graduating classes from 1990 to 2006, Bertrand, Goldin, and Katz (2010) found that, although male and female MBAs have nearly identical earnings at the outset of their careers, their earnings soon diverge, with the earnings advantage for males reaching a high a decade after MBA completion. The divergence is largely explained by greater career discontinuity and shorter work hours for female MBAs—differences largely attributable to motherhood. The unfair distribution of childcare and other family responsibilities causes women to drop out of top careers at high rates, just as it does women at the bottom rung of the career ladder. However, the normally held view that having a working mother is damaging for children is a myth, because full-time housework is so time consuming and tiring that stay-at-home mothers spend only 22 hours per week with children, while working mothers spend an almost equal amount of time, 19 hours per week (Hofferth 1983, cited in Caproni 2012).

In the groves of academe, men tend to dominate in the high-salary "hard" fields of science—technology, engineering, and mathematics—with "soft" and relatively poorly paid fields such as history, psychology, and anthropology considered the academic areas of "women's work" (SciELO in Perspective 2015). Using data from a survey of top academic economists holding full tenure positions at leading US universities, Sarsons and Xu (2015) found that, although women have earned a third of doctorates in economics since the early 2000s, only 28% of assistant professors, 22% of associate professors, and 12% of full professors were female in 2012. This is an example of the leaky pipeline that leaves women less likely to be promoted than men. The survey data show that women in general avoid extreme views and are less confident about some of their views than men. While being equally confident as men when answering questions from their own fields, they become less certain than men when asked about topics outside their expertise (box figure).

Confidence in assessing own and other fields of expertise

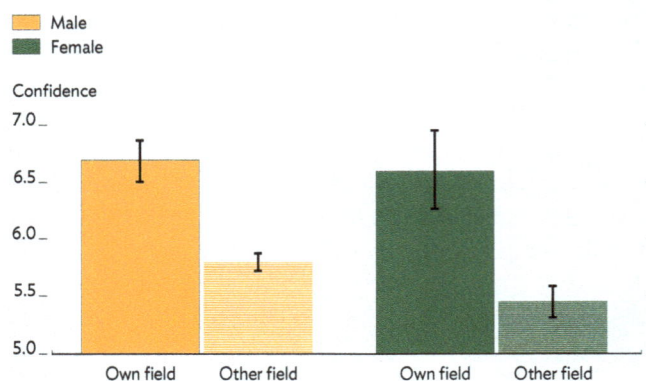

Note: The confidence level ranges from 1 (not confident) to 10 (very confident).
Source: Sarsons and Xu 2015.

consistently outperforming boys in middle and high schools, and how much families can gain by letting them compete freely with boys in all arenas.

Schools will need to further promote these views, teaching by example through the diversification of faculty and staff. Information about labor markets and appropriately designed TVET and skills provision may remove some labor market friction and skills mismatch. Improving work environments, facilitating childcare, and expanding parental leave are some of the ways to attract and retain women and to better utilize their skills as employees, senior administrators, and entrepreneurs in the formal sector.

Opportunities in the New Asia

Rapid urbanization will place half of the Asian population in urban areas by 2020. Towns and cities offer both opportunities and challenges. As urban businesses generate jobs and capital, and as trade integrates local and global markets, new economic opportunities arise. Tight labor markets leave entrepreneurship as an alternative option, especially in urban settings. Entrepreneurship promotes innovation and competitiveness and offers other means to narrow gender gaps. Motivated and enterprising Asian women are trying to move up the socioeconomic ladder by venturing into high-productivity, high-profit small enterprises that are formally registered, leaving behind traditional low-productivity, low-profit informal enterprises.

Formally registered enterprises owned by women are now spreading across the region but remain unevenly distributed. The growth of small and medium-sized enterprises (SMEs) has been fastest in Southeast Asia. Viet Nam is far ahead of the pack with an annual growth of 43%, followed by Malaysia with close to 10%, Indonesia with 8%, and Singapore, the Philippines, and Thailand below 5% (ADB 2014c). An enterprise survey by the International Finance Corporation estimates that the proportion of formal SMEs with one or more female owners is 38%–47% in East, Southeast, and Central Asia and the Pacific but only 8%–9% in South Asia, where female-owned enterprises rely on family support. The survey data show that, in economies such as Hong Kong, China; the Republic of Korea; Malaysia; and Singapore, female entrepreneurship is a matter of choice for women. However, for women in the PRC, India, Indonesia, the Philippines, and Thailand, self-employment is more likely forced upon them by circumstance.

Asian women entrepreneurs share strikingly common features with their counterparts in advanced economies: Their business is usually needed to support family income. Women tend to manage smaller firms than men, running them while taking care of their families. Women are less likely than men to take out loans for lack of self-confidence and to avoid paying high interest rates. They earn significantly less than their male counterparts because their enterprises are less productive and profitable. As firm size grows, female ownership sharply declines. In general, women entrepreneurs in the region face tighter constraints because their access to information and technology is weak, cultural restrictions require that they secure permission from a male family member, and they suffer legal discrimination (ADB 2014a).

As situations with similar characteristics do not necessarily arise from similar circumstances, policy actions cannot be blindly imported from the advanced economies. The business environment in developing Asia is much weaker than in the advanced economies, especially in South Asia and the Pacific.

Limited exposure to and capacity in business development and employee management hamper the growth of SMEs owned by Asian women, as do undeveloped networking and organizational skills (ADB 2014c).

Women's lack of credit, which traces to their lack of collateral and lenders' complex application processes, can be a particularly pernicious problem for aspiring women entrepreneurs (ADB 2014c).

In Papua New Guinea, for example, a woman is often required to obtain, aside from the many documents required for her loan application, the signature of her husband or another male relative affixed to her loan application form. Female entrepreneurs may have to settle for more expensive financing terms than men (UNESCAP, ADB, and UNDP 2013; Hughes and Jennings 2012).

Because many public credit registries and private credit bureaus do not record small loans or loans from microfinance institutions—to which many female entrepreneurs turn for credit—women have difficulty establishing the good credit histories needed to borrow larger amounts at lower interest rates (World Bank 2014). Bhutan is a contrasting example, as enhanced credit to women entrepreneurs through mobile banking helped them build up substantial assets and hold land and property registration titles. Viet Nam, on the other hand, could boost growth in national GDP per capita by over 170 basis points by closing its large credit gap for formal SMEs owned by women, estimated to equal 2% of GDP (Goldman Sachs Global Markets Institute 2014).

Growth and structural change, worsening landlessness, and rural-to-urban migration have increased the share of women's employment in services. However, women are being pushed into services that offer only low returns. For example, the wholesale and retail trade and services subsector—typically including self-employed workers and microenterprises selling food or household goods or making small repairs—is the largest employer of women in the Philippines and, after agriculture, the second largest in Cambodia and Kazakhstan (ADB 2013b). The female share of employment is about 60% in all three countries. Even in the public sector, Cambodian and Kazakh women work mainly in such traditional areas as health and education and are underrepresented in the higher-paying civil service. Filipinas have benefited from gender mainstreaming programs but are paid less in the civil service even when they have the same educational attainment as men (ADB 2013b).

Globalization and manufacturing for export have brought women-oriented jobs to the fore. Across the developing world, exporting firms employ a significantly higher share of women than do firms that do not export (World Bank 2011). In the PRC, the female share of employment is 13 percentage points higher in exporting firms than in others (Chen et al. 2013). However, the significant increase in women's paid employment that comes with trade expansion is not matched by an equal reduction in poverty, especially in households headed by women.

In developing countries, international trade may generate jobs in the formal sector that are highly available to women, but most of the tasks are low-skilled and labor-intensive, adding little value. In many cases, export-oriented industries have targeted women for employment because they can take advantage of existing gender inequality to tamp down costs and become more competitive. Women workers are attractive to export-oriented industries because they are usually less unionized, have less bargaining power, and so can be dragooned into working in substandard conditions (UNCTAD 2013).

For example, Cambodia's large export-oriented garment and footwear industry is a major employer of women, who comprise 90% of its workforce. However, employer preferences and gender stereotypes assign most women to sewing, while men are given higher-paying jobs in quality control. Close to 80% of female workers are below 30 years of age, 43% have not completed primary school, and over 40% are single (ADB 2013b). Most of them moved from rural areas to Phnom Penh to seek jobs in garment factories.

Despite independent monitoring of working conditions by the International Labour Organization, work conditions remain poor. Employees work longer than in other industries, up to 10 hours per day and sometimes 6 days a week, under short-term contracts that violate the law. Workers are vulnerable to dismissal and have little hope for promotion. Maternity leave and social insurance requirements are often unmet. The minimum wage makes it difficult for women to cover their basic needs and remit money back to their families. In addition to discrimination in recruitment because of age, marital status, and pregnancy, women experience sexual harassment from male workers and harsh discipline from foreign supervisors (ADB 2013b).

Export processing zones have contributed to the export success of many developing economies in East and Southeast Asia since the late 1960s while employing a largely female workforce, and many women have benefited from new employment opportunities (UNCTAD 2013). Greater trade openness, lower trade barriers, and better ICT have increased the returns for women working in export-oriented industries, strengthened incentives to remove gender biases and discrimination, increased women's access to markets, and in some cases raised women's wages relative to men's.

As the global economy has become increasingly connected through trade and global production networks over the past 3 decades, trade volumes have expanded and technology has advanced. Global value chains (GVCs) emerged as the production process was broken down into distinct tasks and distributed to economies according to their competitive advantage (ADB 2014d). The PRC took on the role of the hub in what has come to be known as Factory Asia, and GVC trade seems to have opened opportunities for women (Box 2.3.2). Other Asian countries served as the spokes by assembling parts and components. Currently, Bangladesh, India, and Viet Nam are among the economies pursuing growth through GVC trade.

There are two contending views about the effects of trade expansion on labor market discrimination. According to one view, the lowering of trade barriers opens domestic markets to competition, pitting sometimes complacent domestic firms against leaner foreign firms that often operate at lower cost. As firms must employ labor efficiently to be competitive, and women can usually be hired for lower wages, firms cannot afford to discriminate against women to the point of alienating them, which improves social welfare across the population (Becker 1971). The other view is that open borders may exacerbate gender inequality because export-oriented firms with female-specific tasks endlessly seek out the cheapest labor, eliminating jobs for women in one labor market when another opens up (Seguino 2000). Another way to look at it is that when firms move they boost female employment in the neediest areas where wages are the lowest.

2.3.2 Global value chain trade and female workers in the People's Republic of China

The global value chain (GVC) trade has been a force driving economic transformation, urbanization, and social change in the PRC. Rapid urbanization in coastal regions over the past 30 years has underscored the PRC's integration into the global economy, enabling double-digit rates of economic growth (Ursula 2012). Wang et al. (forthcoming) examined how the country's rapid development in GVC trade affected women's welfare outcomes.

Female migrants account for a large share of the workforce in GVC production centers, which were initially established in coastal provinces and gradually spread to less-developed inland provinces. Data show that the spatial distribution of migrant flows followed closely the regional growth of manufacturing for export. From 1990 to 2010, the top seven destinations for migrant inflows were Beijing, Fujian, Guangdong, Jiangsu, Shanghai, Tianjin, and Zhejiang, which are ranked among the top 10 provinces and municipalities in the PRC in terms of manufacturing and trade. Together, they attracted over 57% of all migrants in 2010.

Nationally, women benefited disproportionately from the economic and structural changes as some gained admittance into higher professions. In managerial occupations, women's share increased from 10% in 1982 to 25% in 2010.

The integration of the PRC into GVC trade is reflected not only in the scale of its manufacturing output. Its product composition has evolved significantly (Baldwin 2013). During the early phase from 1980 to 2000, GVC manufacturers assembled or processed for export mainly low-technology, labor-intensive goods such as apparel, textiles, and electronic products. However, in recent years, rising wages and currency appreciation crimped the economy's cost competitiveness, inducing most multinational producers of labor-intensive goods to diversify beyond the PRC to reduce costs and mitigate supply-chain risks. Investment data indicate that the PRC is losing new factory investment to lower-cost locations such as Bangladesh, India, and Viet Nam (Eloot, Huang, and Lehnich 2013).

As manufacturing in coastal regions has started to shift away from low-skilled assembly to activities that entail more technology and services, the skills demanded of local and migrant workers also changed, with potential to open more opportunities for female migrants. However, to take advantage of them, women need economic policies that promote their education and upgrade their skills, and thereby close male–female gaps in skills.

In some cases, trade openness has given rise to high-quality employment for women. Some developing countries provide evidence that locating export-oriented firms with female-specific jobs where women were not previously employed increases women's workforce participation. This is particularly true in manufacturing, where low wages may be adequate to attract women but not men. For example, Mammen and Paxson (2000) noted how export-oriented growth has spread low-skilled manufacturing jobs all over the world, and Edlund (2015) suggested that export-led growth in the PRC was partly fueled by increased female employment.

Other factors, such as gender-based restrictions on working hours and differential skills levels, may alter the effects of trade on female employment. The balance of the evidence suggests, however, that fostering trade and export-oriented industries improves job prospects for women by reducing discrimination in hiring and wages and by creating new areas for job growth (ADB 2015). In the PRC, rural migrants are paid half of what similarly skilled urban residents are paid, but the migrants stay on because they still earn more than they would in rural areas (World Bank and the Development Research Center of the State Council, PRC 2014). In Viet Nam, young female migrants in export-oriented factories have less diverse employment opportunities than male migrants (Tacoli and Mabala 2010). Although cross-border integration in the Greater Mekong Subregion has increased the earnings of female labor, these earnings were substantially lower than those of men (Hung, Nhung, and Tuan 2011). Slots for women in high-value services and manufacturing have come into being in business process outsourcing in India and the Philippines; the footwear industry in Cambodia and Viet Nam; the readymade garment industry in Bangladesh; and electronics assembly in the PRC, Thailand, and Taipei,China.

The transformation of the region into the New Asia through urbanization, structural change, and globalization has created numerous possibilities for employing women and advancing female entrepreneurship that can help women improve their economic prospects. However, a comprehensive policy package is needed to take full advantage of these opportunities by addressing multiple barriers: improving conditions in the workplace, removing restrictions on women's job options, instituting policies to ease credit constraints and support business development capacity, and promulgating legal reform to grant women equal rights regarding wages, work hours, property, and inheritance.

Women can secure a voice in the formulation of such policies through greater representation in corporate and political leadership. Augmenting the power of women to make decisions at home and in the community can be a powerful impetus for change.

Women exercising authority

A woman's decision-making authority begins at home. A woman with greater bargaining power in the household will, after all, have greater freedom outside of it to find employment, start a business, or join an organization. Engagement outside the home strengthens her autonomy not only within the family but also in society. Apart from social norms that shape gender roles, a number of other factors affect the degree to which women can make independent decisions: education, wealth, employability, freedom of movement, and access to government benefits and social networks.

In developing Asia, women customarily lack a commanding voice within the household, in line with tradition. This situation has potential to change with economic transformation. Research in Bangladesh, for example, revealed a positive link between women's bargaining power and their employment, educational attainment, and access to information and financial resources (Box 2.3.3).

Given the choice, people want to work in environments that enable their best performance, make them feel comfortable, and reward them appropriately. The lack of such environments perhaps explains why women remain underrepresented in managerial and legislative positions. Women's decision-making authority has been weak in Asian corporate settings—though males have conventionally dominated corporate leadership around the world.

2.3.3 Women's bargaining power in Bangladeshi households

Structural change in Bangladesh over the past 3 decades has significantly improved the lives of Bangladeshi women. Female employment has expanded in manufacturing, particularly in garments, and female participation in the labor force has increased significantly in rural areas (from 23% in 2001 to 36% in 2011) and in urban areas (from 27% to 34%), though it still falls far below the male participation rate of more than 80% in both urban and rural areas. Women now have better employment options, which contribute to their greater bargaining power and improved status at home. Health and education outcomes have generally improved. Birth control has shrunk household size, infrastructure has proliferated, and women's educational attainment has risen, narrowing gender disparity.

With a demographic and health survey of married women aged 15–49 in Bangladesh, conducted in 1999, 2007, and 2011, Meurs et al. (forthcoming) revealed positive linkage between women's employment and their bargaining or decision-making power, which the study defined in four areas: own health care, child health care, household purchases, and visits with friends and relatives. Moreover, the study found this linkage to have strengthened over time, and that wages need not be high for employment to convey some bargaining power at home.

Relative status appears to matter, the study suggested. While women with secondary or tertiary education report significantly more bargaining power, so do women whose educational attainment is higher than that of their spouse. Outside influences—access to information such as from reading a newspaper and such resources as membership in a microcredit or similar organization—likewise expand women's decision-making role. Social norms seem to matter as well. Women who are older and those with more sons have significantly greater decision-making power. And bargaining power may itself contribute to employment in Bangladesh, where social norms may not be broadly accepting of female employment.

As McKinsey and Company (2007) showed, firms with three or more women on their senior management teams tend to perform better. Such companies score higher on leadership, quality of the work environment, and values such as coordination and control, which are associated with higher operating margins. This result is supported by Catalyst (2004), which found a positive correlation between gender diversity and financial performance in terms of return on equity and total return to shareholders. Analytical evidence has shown that, if all women were excluded from managerial positions, output per worker would fall by over 10% (Cuberes and Teignier 2014). Qian (forthcoming) provided consistent evidence from 10 Asian economies that improvements to gender diversity in the boardroom and the appointment of new female directors are positively associated with a firm's performance in the subsequent year.

With this background, many governments have urged corporations to increase the number of women in boardrooms and senior management positions. To ensure female representation in boardrooms, the United Kingdom proposes a minimum quota of 25%, Norway mandates 40%, and Germany mandates 30%. Similar quotas have been established in Malaysia and India. The Malaysian cabinet approved a policy on 27 June 2011 mandating that women must comprise 30% of senior management positions by 2016 in firms with more than 250 employees. Indian law requires all listed firms to have at least one female on the board by March 2015. Across Asia, however, males continue to dominate firms' top management (Box 2.3.4).

Political representation is the other significant area where the region lags in terms of women's representation in senior positions—an area that deeply affects efforts to shape social norms and reform the legal framework. A 2008 survey by the Inter-Parliamentary Union revealed that women and men in senior political positions differ in their world views and interests and, consequently, bring different issues and concerns to the table. More than men, women focus on gender equality, community concerns, and family matters. When in high political office, women are better positioned to change societal beliefs about gender roles and create conditions that provide women with easier access to jobs, more opportunities to upgrade their skills, and power to break through the glass ceiling.

Beaman et al. (2012) found that women's political participation affects their long-term labor market outcomes by shaping parents' and children's beliefs about what women can achieve. The study found that the presence of a female leader in the village significantly increased parents' aspirations for their daughters, as well as daughters' aspirations for themselves. Such role modeling helped erase the gender gap in adolescent educational attainment, with girls eventually spending less time on household chores.

But a gender bias exists in the political field as well. According to the Inter-Parliamentary Union, the percentage of female cabinet ministers in the world increased by only 3.5 percentage points over the past 10 years, from 14.2% in 2005 to 17.7% in 2015. Developing Asia had the lowest percentage of women ministers, at only 9.6%, which is a third of the 29.0% achieved in the advanced economies (Figure 2.3.4). Most female cabinet ministers in the region oversee social sectors—the

2.3.4 Female members in senior corporate management and boardrooms in developing Asia

Data for 20 developing Asian economies plus Japan, the US, and Germany show that, while about 40% of the entire workforce consists of females, only 14.4% of corporate boardroom members and senior managers are women (box figure 1). The female share drops to below 10% if limited to the corporate boardrooms of private firms.

1 Female presence in the workforce and in the boardroom and senior management

Employed women as a share of total employed

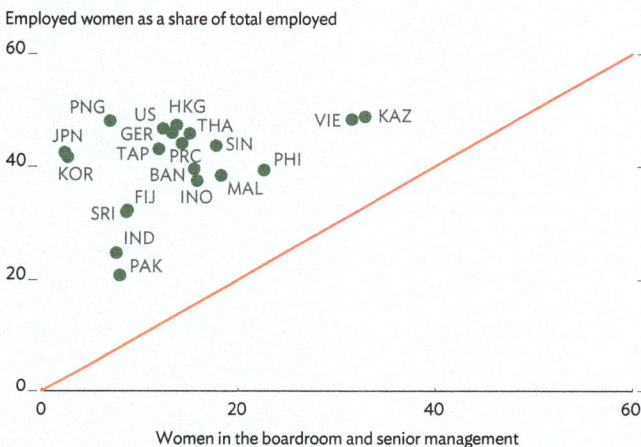

BAN = Bangladesh, FIJ = Fiji, GER = Germany, HKG = Hong Kong, China, IND = India, INO = Indonesia, KAZ = Kazakhstan, KOR = Republic of Korea, JPN = Japan, MAL = Malaysia, PAK = Pakistan, PHI = Philippines, PNG = Papua New Guinea, PRC = People's Republic of China, SIN = Singapore, SRI = Sri Lanka, TAP = Taipei,China, THA = Thailand, US = United States, VIE = Viet Nam.
Note: Employment data refers to the average for the period 2009–2013.
Source: ADB estimates using data from Orbis and International Labour Organization, Key Indicators of the Labor Market, 8th edition (accessed 31 July 2015).

However, a few economies have respectable female representation. In Kazakhstan and Viet Nam, the number of female workers in the entire workforce is on a par with males, and the female share in top management is also high, exceeding 30% in both countries. Kazakhstan and Viet Nam still rank high even if the sample is limited to representation in the boardrooms of private firms—excluding the state-owned firms that tend to have higher female representation. In general, countries in Southeast Asia perform well, with the female share of top management above the sample mean of 14.4%, led by the Philippines, Malaysia, and Singapore.

Regarding boardroom membership, the three countries in the region with the highest female share are also in Southeast Asia: in order, Thailand, Indonesia, and Viet Nam (box figure 2). Thailand's high share of representation in the boardroom, at 14%, compares reasonably well with 17% in North America and Europe. India is an exception in developing Asia, as every board has at least one female member because of a recently enacted law, but the average share in India is not significantly higher than the regional average.

2 Female share in the boardroom by economy, with maximum and minimum

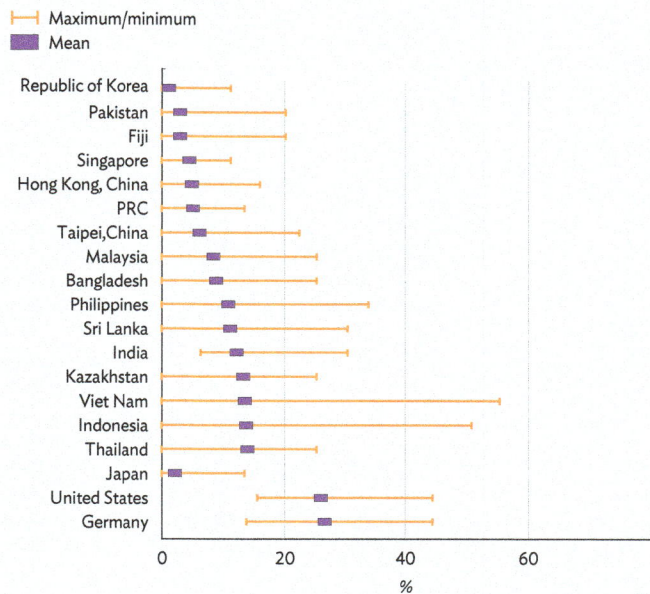

PRC = People's Republic of China.
Source: ADB estimates using data from Bloomberg and company websites of 10 largest publicly listed private firms (all accessed 31 July 2015).

Variation is more pronounced when looking at female senior management and boardroom representation by industry (box figure 3). More than half of female employees work in the service sector in Asia, and this is where female representation is highest in 13 Asian economies with comparable data. Female representation in corporate leadership remains low in the region because Asia's corporate sector is dominated by manufacturing firms, at 52% of the total. Manufacturing is still central to quite a few economies of the region, accounting for 76.5% of all firms in Taipei,China; 69.9% in the Republic of Korea; and 59.8% in the PRC. Female representation in top management tends to be extremely limited in manufacturing. This contrasts sharply with higher income groupings such as the members of the Organisation for Economic Co-operation and Development, where the service sector is more developed and can absorb more than 80% of female workers.

Boards average 10 members, and many boardrooms, especially in industry, are completely male. Females are slightly better represented in services such as health care, real estate, and finance. Female representation is consistently lower in developing Asia than in the advanced economies in the sample. Communication is the only area where developing Asia outperforms the selected advanced economies in terms of female representation.

continued on the next page →

2.3.4 continued

The general trend holds even if the sample is broadened to include the senior management of smaller firms and publicly owned firms. Two industries with relatively small firms and relatively high female representation still fail to impress, as only 15.4% of top management is female in education, and only 14.7% in public administration. These two industries are followed by real estate (box figure 4).

3 Female share in the boardroom by industry

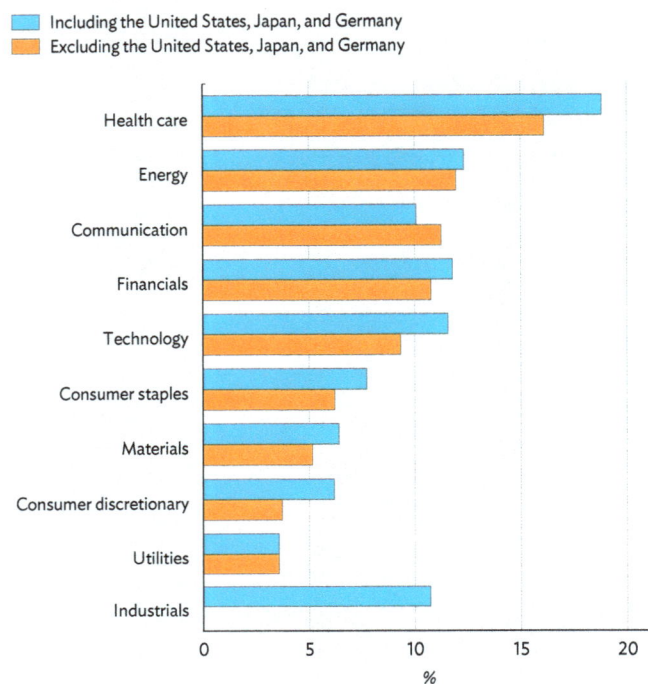

Including the United States, Japan, and Germany
Excluding the United States, Japan, and Germany

Source: ADB estimates using data from Bloomberg and company websites of 10 largest publicly listed companies (all accessed 31 July 2015).

4 Female share in top management in developing Asia by industry

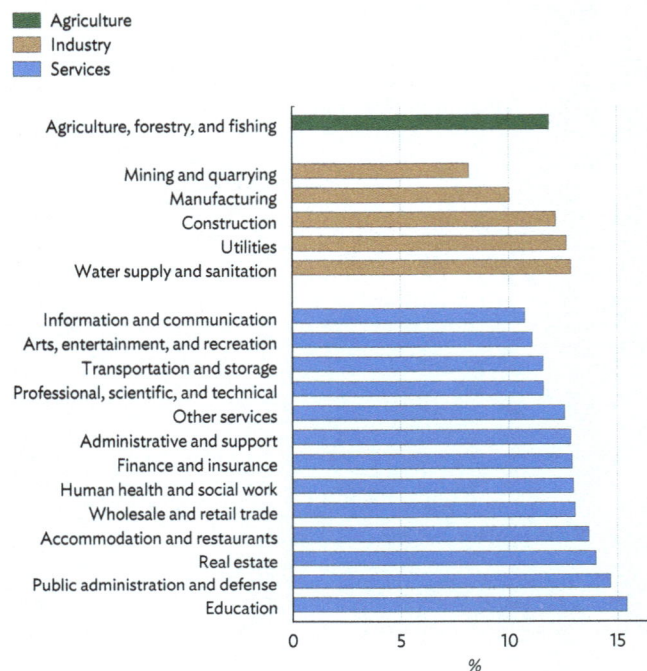

Agriculture
Industry
Services

Note: As used here, "top management" refers to board members and senior management.
Source: ADB estimates using data from Orbis (accessed 31 July 2015).

so-called "soft" portfolios—concerned with education, health, and the family, rather than the "hard" sectors such as finance, infrastructure, and defense.

Progress in local communities likewise remains slow in a wide range of Asian economies, with little improvement in women's participation or leadership in local politics recorded since 2010 (UNDP 2014). Involving women in local politics can help put on the agenda the issues women face in the community. In India, for example, a quota system that reserves one-third of the seats on village councils for women brought greater investment in infrastructure to supply clean drinking water and better provision of other public goods (Chattopadhyay and Duflo 2004). India amended its constitution in 1993 to reserve for women one-third of the seats at every level of local government. Initially, the system faltered as women felt intimidated by various social and cultural attitudes and their lack of information about and experience in running public offices. Even by 2000, there was a wide variation across states in

2.3.4 Women in ministerial positions, world regions

% of total ministers

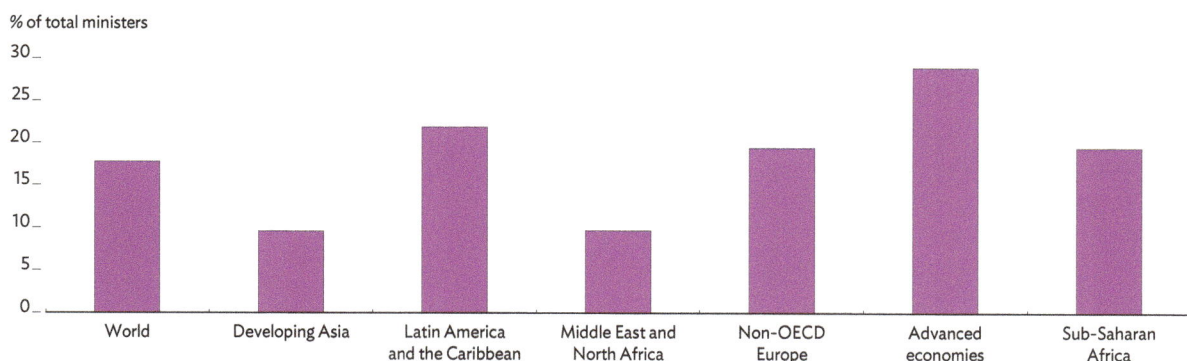

Notes: Data are as of January 2015. Advanced economies are members of the Organisation for Economic Co-operation and Development (OECD) excluding the Republic of Korea (included in developing Asia), Chile and Mexico (Latin America and the Caribbean), and Israel (Middle East and North Africa).
Source: Inter-Parliamentary Union. Women in Politics 2015. http://www.unwomen.org/~/media/headquarters/attachments/sections/news/stories/2015/femmesenpolitique_2015_web_anglais.pdf

women's representation, which was lowest in Uttar Pradesh at 25% and highest in Karnataka at 43% (Jha 2000). Doubts arose especially as the politically savvy husbands of elected officials sometimes took charge. However, over time, the quota dramatically raised the number of women serving as local leaders, from fewer than 5% in 1992 to close to 40% in 2005 (Pande and Topalova 2013). As deep-rooted traditions and norms were not easy to change, it took a decade of mandated quotas favoring women to bring about the change in raising women's political profile. Quotas have been instituted in a number of regional countries, with seats now reserved in lawmaking bodies in Afghanistan, Bangladesh, the PRC, and Pakistan.

In Nepal, a governance support program that included the development and implementation of a gender and social inclusion policy improved the allocation of public resources and community infrastructure. It also increased the allocation of state resources to benefit women and disadvantaged groups from 38% in 2010 to 46% in 2011 (Jalal 2015). Similar examples of women using local leadership roles to improve the provision of public goods have been reported in Bangladesh, Cambodia, Fiji, and the Philippines (UNDP 2014).

The reasons women participate in politics vary, ranging from interest in and advocacy of certain issues to hopes for a lucrative profession. However, a major reason many women enter politics is kinship, as they have relatives who are also involved in politics (UNDP 2014). Whatever the incentive, policies that directly raise the number of women in political bodies promise to be a big boost to women's participation in public service.

Having more women in leadership can be a powerful instrument for opening up a wider range of occupations to women. Yet choice of career is not the only barrier women face when they enter the labor market. Employed women also find their pay and benefits lag behind those of men.

Equalizing worker compensation

Beyond the question of women's paid employment and the positions open to them is the issue of compensation. Across the world, women tend to receive lower wages and fewer benefits for their work than do men. The pay gap has important consequences for closing other types of gender gaps. Lower pay may discourage working-age women from entering the workforce, disrupting the positive feedback loop by which paid work strengthens women's position in the household and society. It may also deter young women from investing in education and training, limiting their future options.

Many factors can open up an earnings gap between men and women. Men and women may have different skill levels on average or may select, or be segregated into, different industries and occupations. Different responsibilities in the household—particularly when it comes to children—may cause women to accrue less work experience than men or devote less time to paid work. But even taking these other factors into account, gender discrimination continues to play a crucial role, and thus policy change may be needed to level the playing field.

Gender wage gaps

Considerable evidence indicates that economic development mitigates the disadvantages facing women, especially in educational attainment, life expectancy, and workforce participation (World Bank 2012). Nevertheless, the experience of Asia's labor markets underscores the finding that gender equality does not come automatically with economic development. Inequality between the compensation packages of employed men and women persists in developed and developing countries alike.

Globally, there does not seem to be a clear association between economic development and unadjusted wage ratios (Figure 2.4.1). In 45 of 51 countries in a sample covering 1995–2010, Terada-Hagiwara, Zveglich, Jr., and Camingue-Romance (unpublished) found a narrowing of the wage gap, even as female and male wages increased in most of these economies. Focusing only on wage gaps in developing Asia does not change the result. Both across economies and over time in individual examples, little correlation exists between per capita income and differences in pay for men and women.

Developing Asia stands out among the regions for having the widest variation in gender wage gaps across economies (Figure 2.4.2). These gaps have narrowed in some economies as they have developed but have remained stubbornly wide in others, even as women caught up with men in educational attainment. At one end of the spectrum, female workers in Azerbaijan and Georgia in Central Asia receive less than half of the average male pay.

2.4.1 Stage of development and earnings differences between men and women, 1997–2011

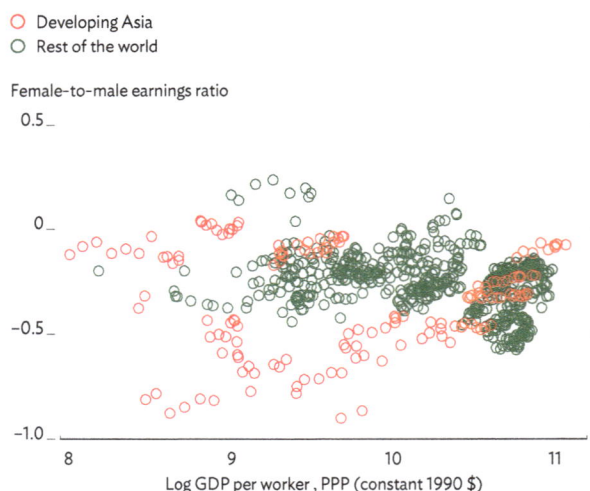

PPP = purchasing power parity.
Sources: The Conference Board. https://www.conference-board.org; International Labour Organization. Global Wage Report 2012. http://www.ilo.org

At the other end, women's pay in the Philippines and Thailand in Southeast Asia is almost on a par with men's. High-income economies in East Asia, such as Taipei,China and Hong Kong, China also perform relatively well in this regard. Variation is much narrower in Latin America and the Organisation for Economic Co-operation and Development (OECD). This suggests that country-specific factors play a bigger role in developing Asia than in the other groups of economies considered here.

While the dispersion of gender wage gaps within a region may differ, the mean values are surprisingly similar across regions. For example, in 2005–2011, female workers in OECD countries earned 76% of the wages of their male counterparts, while the corresponding figure was 77% in developing Asia.

Wage gap convergence was slightly faster in developing Asia than in OECD countries at the turn of the century, with the female-to-male wage ratio improving from 69% in 1995–1999 to 74% in the early 2000s. However, the wage ratio has since been stagnant, improving by a mere 3 percentage points to 77% by 2005–2011 (Terada-Hagiwara, Zveglich, Jr., and Camingue-Romance, unpublished).

Equal pay for work of equal value is now a recognized human right to which men and women are both entitled (Oelz, Olney, and Manuela 2013). Yet not all countries have laws ensuring in practice the equal pay principle (UN Women 2015). Among economies reporting on gender discrimination in the World Bank's database, 18 economies in developing Asia do not have laws guarding against wage difference based on gender.

Unequal pay between men and women can broadly be explained by such factors as personal and job characteristics, labor market structure, and institutional and social norms (Ñopo, Daza, and Ramos 2011). One important determinant of the earnings gap is disparity in human capital or productivity characteristics, as captured by educational attainment, work experience, type of employment, and occupation or industry type. Another is personal taste, as employers discriminate because they prefer workers of a certain type for historical or cultural reasons (Altonji and Blank 1999). Inequality may trace in part to such factors as workplace harassment, social norms that hold women responsible for housework and caregiving, and gender gaps in access to finance and in property inheritance and ownership rights.

Women may be inclined to accept lower wages in return for physical security or job flexibility in terms of hours or telecommuting. Alternatively, educated women may be offered wages that are insufficient to induce them to enter the workforce at the same rate as equally educated men. Men tend to have higher job-specific human capital than women because they generally undergo more intensive training and have more extensive work experience, even if their educational attainment is no higher than women's. Thus, women's lower labor force participation rates, greater likelihood of working part time, and more frequent career breaks can generate large cumulative gaps

2.4.2 Gender wage gap by region and group, 2005–2011

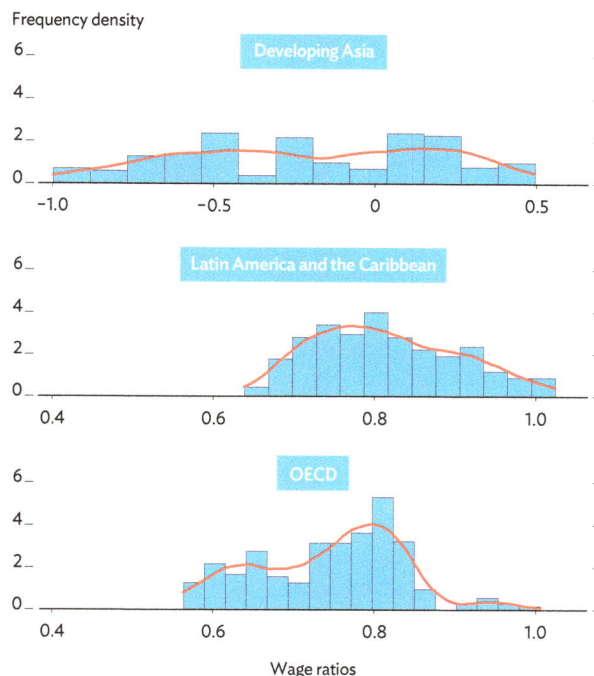

OECD = Organisation for Economic Co-operation and Development.
Note: The line represents the kernel density estimation of the average female-to-male wage ratio across economies.
Source: Terada-Hagiwara, Zveglich, Jr., and Camingue-Romance, unpublished.

in their lifetime income vis-à-vis men. Gayle and Golan (2011) found that work experience is the most important factor explaining the gender earnings gap. An important feature of the gap is its evolution over a worker's lifetime as a function of work experience. The gap is relatively small when workers are young, and it widens as they age. Between male and female workers who both work full time continuously, however, the wage gap narrows as they age.

An empirical study using pooled data from 51 economies in 2005–2011 found that variables such as a higher share of part-time workers in the workforce, a younger female working population, a higher ratio of female workers in agriculture, and a higher fertility rate induce wider gender wage gaps. Working part time and being a young worker can be associated with fewer years of work experience, which corresponds to lower pay. Similarly, having more children necessitates early and more frequent career breaks, curtailing women's work experience (Terada-Hagiwara, Zveglich, Jr., and Camingue-Romance, unpublished).

Gender gaps in education can partly explain the gender differences in earnings ratios over time. Rising incomes and globalization have provided opportunities for girls to pursue education, and for women to embark on career tracks, from which they had previously been blocked by traditional institutions. Education outcomes have narrowed significantly in most economies as they developed (Hausmann et al. 2014). Still, in most economies, women of working age are substantially more likely to have lower educational attainment than men. Moreover, men's human capital accumulated from work experience on top of education may have a role to play in creating disparities between male and female wages (Mincer and Polachek 1974).

Thus, simply closing the gap in education between men and women may not be enough to close the gap in their earnings. Indeed, even as differences in education and skill levels converge, such tendencies as clustering by gender in different occupations may perpetuate differences in average pay. However, industry and occupational segregation need not always be to women's detriment. In the Philippines, for example, half of all paid female employees work in personal services, the industry that pays the third highest in the country, compared with only 20% of men. At the other end, 20% of paid male employees work in agriculture, the lowest-paying industry, compared with 10% of women (Menon et al., forthcoming).

How much gender differences in education, experience, and industry and occupation choices account for the pay differences varies considerably across the region. Using household survey data from five developing Asian economies, Menon et al. (forthcoming) analyzed the extent to which pay gaps have closed as women caught up in terms

2.4.3 Unadjusted and adjusted female-to-male wage ratios, selected Asian economies

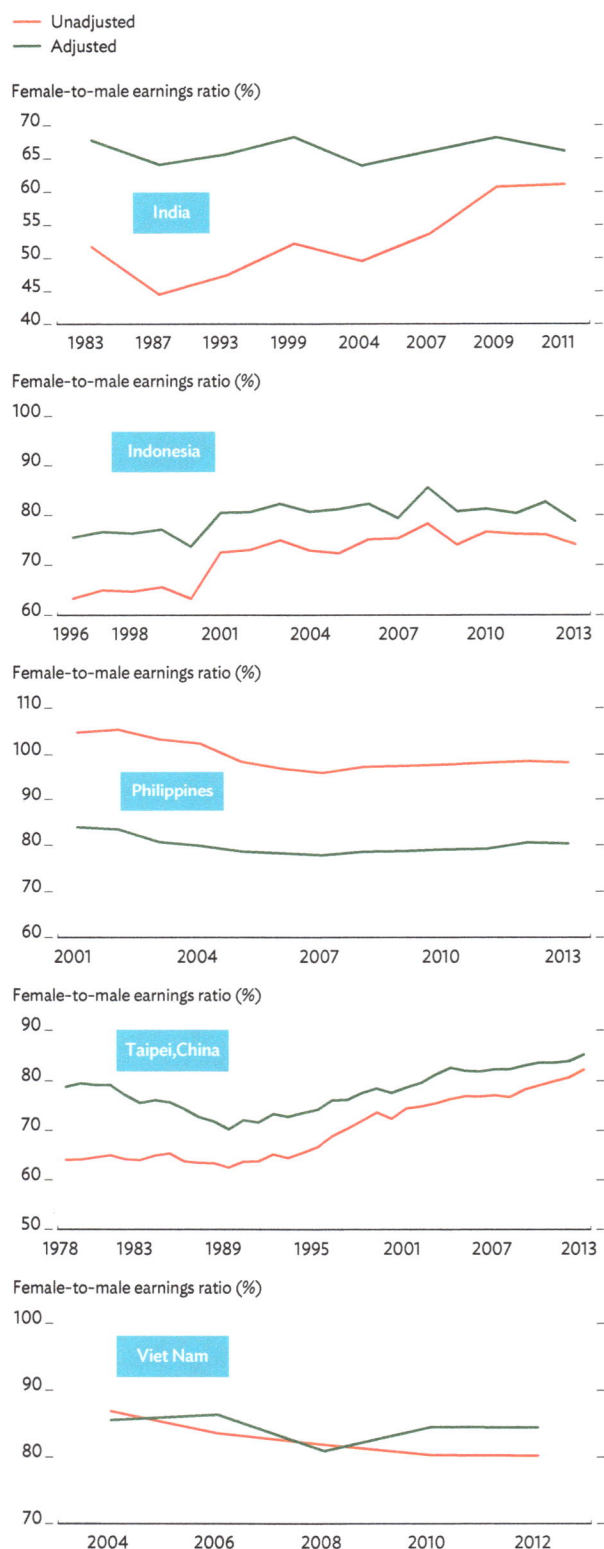

Note: Adjusted female-to-male wage ratios take into account observed productivity characteristics such as educational attainment, experience, industry and occupation choice, and individual and household characteristics such as whether work is part time or full time.

Source: Menon et al., forthcoming.

of observed productivity characteristics. As shown in Figure 2.4.3, unadjusted female-to-male wage ratios have risen substantially in India and Taipei,China and only moderately in Indonesia, while they declined slightly in the Philippines and Viet Nam. Adjusting results to account for observed productivity characteristics explained some of the pay differences in the sample countries except the Philippines. Causes differ by economy: occupation differences are an issue in Viet Nam, for example, while a tendency toward part-time work is a more important issue in Indonesia. Essentially, had women been compensated the same as men for their higher educational attainment and their clustering in better-paying industries and occupations, women would have made about 20% more than men on average. Improvement in the adjusted female-to-male wage ratios has been more modest than in the unadjusted ratios in most cases.

As the continued large residual wage gap in these cases indicates, gender differences in earnings have not disappeared even as women have closed gaps in observable characteristics. This implies that unobservable characteristics and gender disparities may be undermining any gains that women have made by accumulating education and experience. However, the technique employed in the study does not distinguish the source of the residual gap, which could be unmeasured differences in skills, differences in workforce commitment, or labor market discrimination. However, in an earlier study of Taipei,China, results of a detailed decomposition of the wage gap trend were not consistent with women losing attachment to the workforce or a widening gap in unobserved skills, which bolsters the case that wage discrimination is the culprit (Zveglich, Jr., Rodgers, and Rodgers 1997).

That competition from international trade has contributed to worsening wage discrimination is supported by evidence from Taipei,China (Berik, Rodgers, and Zveglich, Jr., 2004) and India (Menon and Rodgers 2009). In Viet Nam, earnings differentials left unexplained by observed characteristics have been attributed to changes in unobserved skills, demand or supply shocks, or discrimination, highlighting the significant influence of traditional beliefs regarding gender (Liu 2004).

Policy interventions are important, particularly toward supporting women's roles as caregivers to young children while working. Of particular merit is a transformative approach that boosts the pay and security of women's jobs, improves the compatibility of women's paid work with childcare, promotes skills development, and improves women's productivity. Policies aiming to narrow earnings gaps should account as well for the unobserved factors that explain them.

Pensions and poverty

The existence of gender pay gaps is important to consider because lower earnings, lower savings, and legal barriers to wealth inheritance deepen women's economic insecurity and financial dependence on men, which can have serious repercussions for themselves and others when they grow old. Not only do women bear more unpaid family work than men, they are also more likely to spend their income on maintaining the household and supporting its members (Vlachantoni and Falkingham 2012).

These factors affect women's ability to support themselves not only in the present but also in the future. They may eventually have to rely on handouts from family members to sustain themselves, and there may not be enough money to provide income security even at the subsistence level. In fact, women have less access than men to support systems for old age (World Bank 2009). Elderly people are vulnerable to poverty because of their declining capacity to earn, especially if they have little or no pension because they were self-employed or worked in the informal sector for poor pay (Barrientos, Gorman, and Heslop 2003).

Vulnerability in old age arises, both for individuals and for society, from complex and cumulative processes: demographic differences between men and women, sociocultural factors, and institutional factors defining old-age support systems (Vlachantoni and Falkingham 2012). Reduced capability to cope independently magnifies insecurity and heightens aging women's exposure to certain threats. Apart from this, women tend to live longer than men and so have on average more years of old age to finance with their lesser incomes. Ensuring that women have social protection is a potent way to reduce poverty in old age.

According to the International Labour Organization, only 42% of the working-age population across the globe has pension coverage under existing law of each country (Figure 2.4.4). Protection for women is lower than for men, as only one in three females of working age enjoys some form of legal coverage. Conditions in developing Asia appear worse, with only 20% of women covered by some form of pension, compared with 35% for women globally, which is about the same coverage for men in developing Asia. However, in some countries, wives can be beneficiaries under their husbands' contributory schemes even if widowed.

In countries with social protection systems, gender disparities are reflected in the often highly differentiated coverage men and women receive. To break it down, 32% of the working-age people across the globe are required by law to contribute to mandatory pensions systems through which they can receive cash in their old age. Another 7% contribute to voluntary pension systems, and another 4% are eligible to receive pensions without having contributed. The corresponding rates of coverage for women are consistently lower, with 26% covered by mandatory contributory schemes, 4% by voluntary schemes, and 5% by noncontributory schemes. In developing Asia, the average for legal coverage is about 25%, with noticeably weaker protection for women.

Effective coverage is unequal between men and women. Worldwide, almost 52% of older people above the statutory pensionable age receive pensions. Coverage ranges from 17% in sub-Saharan Africa to above 94% in Central and Eastern Europe (Figure 2.4.5). In Asia and the Pacific, effective coverage stands at 47%, but this masks significant differences across countries. Pension coverage for women

2.4.4 Legal coverage for old age pensions by region

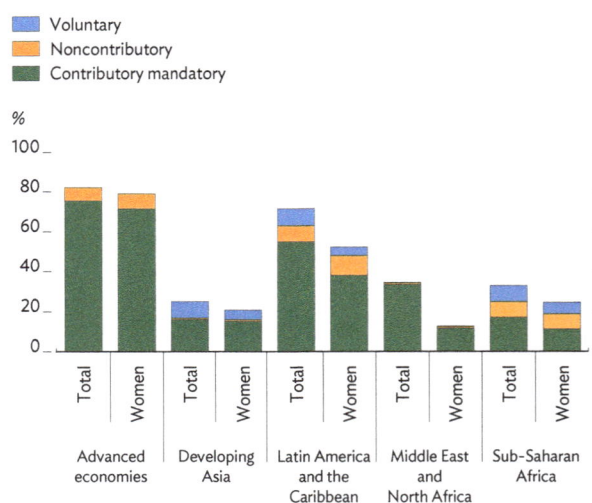

Notes: Averages are weighted using total population. Data are from latest available year. Advanced economies are members of the Organisation for Economic Co-operation and Development excluding the Republic of Korea (included in developing Asia), Chile and Mexico (Latin America and the Caribbean), and Israel (Middle East and North Africa).
Source: ADB estimates using data from International Labour Organization. World Social Protection Report 2014–15. http://www.social-protection.org/gimi/gess/RessourceDownload.action?ressource.ressourceId=37085

2.4.5 Ratio of pension beneficiaries to population above the statutory pension age by region

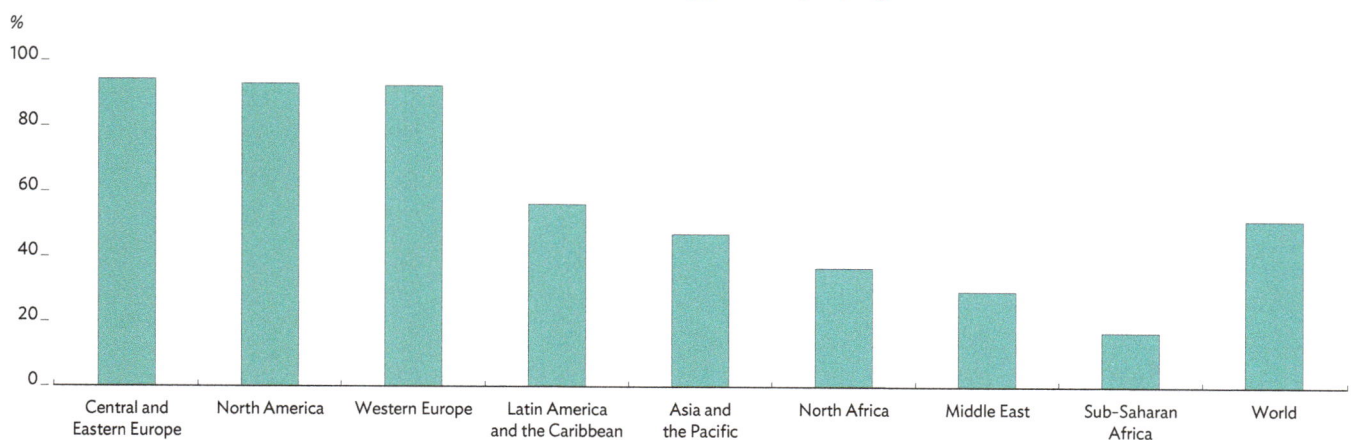

Source: International Labour Organization. World Social Protection Report 2014–15. http://www.social-protection.org/gimi/gess/RessourceDownload.action?ressource.ressourceId=37158

is not the only thing that tends to be significantly scantier than for men, but also the amount of money paid (ILO 2014). In some developing Asian economies, pension benefits received by elderly women replace a smaller share of their final wage compared with men (OECD 2013). This is a double penalty when women's lower earnings are considered.

Discrimination in regulations on retirement tends to worsen gender welfare disparity among the elderly. Formally employed Asian women, for example, still have lower statutory retirement ages than their male counterparts (Table 2.4.1). This is particularly true in Central Asia (excepting Armenia) and in some East and Southeast Asian economies such as the PRC, Viet Nam, and Taipei,China. In the PRC, the retirement age varies according to whether women live in rural or urban areas and by their type of occupation (Leckie 2012).

Ensuring old-age protection for women can promote gender equality by affording women greater financial security. Social transfers for women, for example, promote gender equity at home. Health outcomes for girls living with grandmothers who receive social transfers are better than for those living with their grandfathers who are pension recipients (Duflo 2003). For women, pensions may provide a new and reliable resource more under their control than other household income earlier in life (Ståhlberg, Kruse, and Sundén 2005).

Considering the significant gaps that have accumulated between men and women in welfare status and financial need in old age, a gender dimension included in the design of social pension schemes can improve the likelihood of such schemes succeeding in targeting those most in need. Broadening the coverage of pension systems is important, and the pension calculation formula should ensure

2.4.1 Statutory retirement age by gender, developing Asia

Economy	Men	Women
Central Asia		
Armenia	63	63
Azerbaijan	62	60[a]
Georgia	65	60
Kazakhstan	63	58
Kyrgyz Republic	63	58
Tajikistan	63	58
Turkmenistan	62	57
Uzbekistan	60	54
East Asia		
China, People's Republic of[b]	60	50–55
Korea, Republic of	56–58	56–58
Taipei,China	60	55
South Asia		
India	60	60
Nepal	58	58
Pakistan	60	60
Southeast Asia		
Indonesia	58	58
Lao People's Democratic Republic	60	60
Malaysia	60	60
Philippines	60–65	60–65
Singapore	62–65	62–65
Viet Nam	60	55

[a] More precisely 59.5 years.

[b] Retirement age is 55 for white-collar workers in urban areas and in the civil and public service, 50 for blue-collar women in urban areas, and 60 in rural areas for both men and women.

Source: ADB compilation.

earnings replacement as reliably as it sets the minimum guarantee. Closing the gender gap in pensions will not be easy, however, as it is closely linked to existing inequality in the labor market. Since the private sector provides about 90% of jobs in developing countries, involvement of the private sector would be essential in aligning pension benefits along gender lines (IFC 2013). Although considerations of gender equality are gaining ground in public debates about pensions, much still has to be done in this area. Important reforms to improve gender welfare disparity in old age include eliminating gender differences in statutory retirement ages, expanding the coverage of contributory pensions to the self-employed and agricultural workers, crediting pension accounts for time away on maternity leave, and providing publicly funded noncontributory pensions.

Maternity and childcare benefits

An aging population can place great pressure on younger women already bearing a heavy load of family responsibilities. As childbirth and infant care are full-time tasks, they can interrupt a working mother's career for a considerable length of time. In the Republic of Korea, for example, female workforce participation shows an M-shaped pattern as many women drop out in their mid-20s and some return to the workforce only in their forties (Pande, Ford, and Fletcher, forthcoming). Such breaks affect women's chances of returning to the job, retaining wage rates and their eligibility for other benefits, sustaining an income stream, and finally supporting themselves. The truncating of women's careers induces many employers to favor men for promotions and career development (World Bank 2009).

The lack of legal protection discourages women from entering the workforce or returning to their jobs after giving birth. Maternity and childcare benefits can strengthen their workforce attachment. The overwhelming preference in developing Asian economies, however, seems to be to require employers to provide break time for nursing mothers, rather than requiring them to provide maternity leave and to retain employees' positions until their return (Table 2.4.2).

Nevertheless, employer-provided maternity leave with pay is common in the region, averaging 14 weeks, which is on par with the recommendation from the International Labour Organization to provide at least 14 weeks. Although many countries do not protect the mother's wages, the balance of laws in the region favors protecting 100% of the salary. Evidence suggests that providing maternity leave keeps women in the same company and thereby strengthens its human capital. However, there is a caveat: Although maternity leave can, on the one hand, increase women's participation in the workforce, long leave may put them out of touch with their jobs, let their skills get rusty, and discourage their return to the job. Policies are needed to ensure that women return to the workforce following childbirth. Almost half of the countries in the world offer paternity leave to fathers of newborns. Paternity leave is shorter than maternity leave, as the idea is that converting only part of maternity leave into paternity leave

2.4.2 Maternity benefits in Asia, 2015

Economy	Paid maternity leave duration (calendar days)	Percentage of wages paid during maternity leave	Employers required to give employees an equivalent position upon return from maternity leave	Employers required to provide break time for nursing mothers
Central Asia				
Armenia	140	100	Yes	Yes
Azerbaijan	126	100	Yes	Yes
Georgia	183	100	No	Yes
Kazakhstan	126	100	Yes	Yes
Kyrgyz Republic	126	19	Yes	Yes
Tajikistan	140	100	Yes	Yes
Turkmenistan	112	100	...	...
Uzbekistan	126	100	Yes	Yes
East Asia				
PRC	128	100	No	Yes
Hong Kong, China	70	80	No	No
Korea, Republic of	90	100	Yes	Yes
Mongolia	120	100	Yes	Yes
Taipei,China	56	100	No	Yes
South Asia				
Afghanistan	90	100	No	Yes
Bangladesh	112	100	No	No
India	84	100	No	Yes
Maldives	60	100	Yes	Yes
Nepal	52	100	No	Yes
Pakistan	84	100	No	No
Sri Lanka	84	100	No	Yes
Southeast Asia				
Brunei Darussalam	91	100	No	No
Cambodia	90	100	No	Yes
Indonesia	90	100	No	Yes
Lao PDR	105	100	No	Yes
Malaysia	60	100	No	No
Myanmar	98	100	No	No
Philippines	60	100	No	Yes
Singapore	105	100	No	No
Thailand	90	100	No	No
Viet Nam	180	100	Yes	Yes
The Pacific				
Fiji	84	100	Yes	No
Kiribati	84	25	...	...
Papua New Guinea	0	N/A	No	Yes
Solomon Islands	84	25	...	...
Timor-Leste	84	100	Yes	Yes
Tonga	N/A	N/A	N/A	No
Vanuatu	84	66	...	...

... = data not available, N/A = not applicable, Lao PDR = Lao People's Democratic Republic, PRC = People's Republic of China.

Sources: World Bank. *Women, Business and the Law* database (accessed 16 September 2015); International Labour Organization. 2014. *World Social Protection Report 2014/15.* http://www.ilo.org/wcmsp5/groups/public/---dgreports/---dcomm/documents/publication/wcms_245201.pdf

allows the mother to get back to work sooner, in addition to permitting the father to spend more time with the baby (*The Economist* 2015).

For women with young children, the burden of household responsibilities may preclude their taking up work outside the home. Policies to sustain these women's full-time careers and career development would need to improve childcare facilities and reduce the cost of supplementary or play schools. As caring for children is one of the presumed responsibilities of women, a legal and institutional environment that allows them to manage this responsibility while working would greatly facilitate formal employment. However, a third of the Asian countries examined do not have public childcare facilities for preschool children. This is true of most countries in South Asia and the Pacific, most of which also fail to guarantee flexibility in work schedule for the mothers of minors (Figure 2.4.6).

A policy alternative to provision of public childcare is tax relief granted specifically to working mothers. Singapore is the only economy in the region to offer it, providing to each parent a parenthood tax rebate for up to three children. The lack of such legal provisions discourages women's entry in the workforce and their return to it after giving birth. Judiciously designed maternity leave may be more effective at increasing women's attachment to the workforce than even tax subsidies on the wages for reentering it.

Helping women achieve compensation parity with men is a big piece of the unfinished agenda. Decisions on investments in education and trade-offs between household responsibilities and work, for example, hinge critically on expected pay. Progress on this front is necessary to unleash women's potential.

2.4.6 Support for childcare

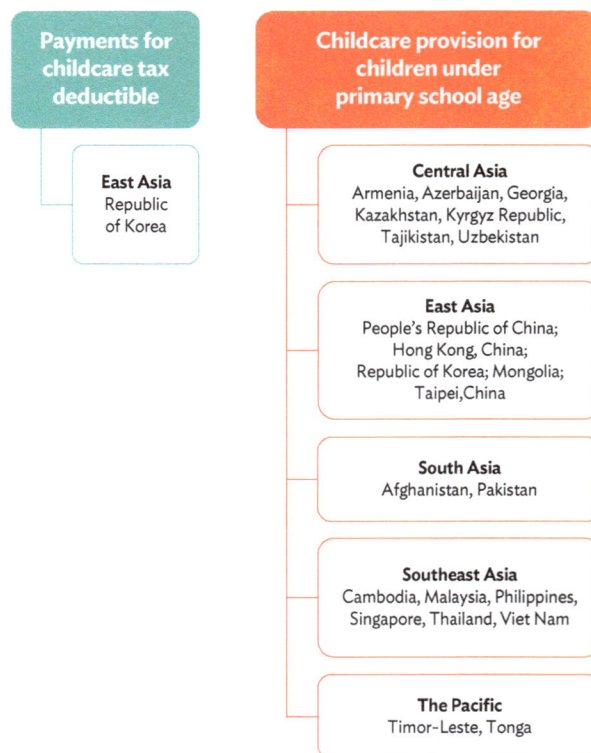

Payments for childcare tax deductible

East Asia
Republic of Korea

Childcare provision for children under primary school age

Central Asia
Armenia, Azerbaijan, Georgia, Kazakhstan, Kyrgyz Republic, Tajikistan, Uzbekistan

East Asia
People's Republic of China; Hong Kong, China; Republic of Korea; Mongolia; Taipei,China

South Asia
Afghanistan, Pakistan

Southeast Asia
Cambodia, Malaysia, Philippines, Singapore, Thailand, Viet Nam

The Pacific
Timor-Leste, Tonga

Source: World Bank. *Women, Business and the Law* database. http://wbl.worldbank.org/data (accessed 11 September 2015).

Unleashing women's potential

Opening opportunities for women to engage in paid work can start a virtuous cycle. Long entrenched social norms and cultural attitudes that clearly delineate "men's work" and "women's work" will not evolve overnight, but women taking on new roles in society can be a catalyst for change. A woman with a job gains bargaining power within her household, which helps to mold the attitudes of the next generation. Gainfully employed women become examples for others to follow, affecting the decisions families make about young girls' education and training. With women gaining influence in business, civil service, and politics, issues of general importance to women will find a higher place on the national agenda.

When it comes to the labor market, developing Asia's unfinished gender agenda must be pursued along three lines. First is enhancing women's skills to ensure they have the competencies needed to join the workforce and move up the career ladder. Second, in tandem with developing women's skills, action is required to remove legal impediments, lift constraints on entrepreneurship, expand and facilitate access to ICT, and ensure fair compensation. Finally, policies need to help women move out of stereotypical jobs, with a particular emphasis on giving women a path into decision-making roles.

Enhancing job skills

Without adequate skills, women find that they are unable to seize most economic opportunities. A large majority of Asian women work in the informal sector, often in seasonal or casual employment with low pay and poor working conditions. This is the usual case for young, inexperienced female migrants who move from villages to towns in search of better jobs, particularly in export manufacturing, but in so doing expose themselves to exploitation and abuse. Improving women's education is the foundation of the agenda to achieve greater gender equality.

While primary school girls have almost reached parity with boys in school enrollment, and girls even outnumber boys at the secondary and tertiary levels, high educational attainment alone is not enough to ensure equitable entry into the labor market. Even when girls attend school for as many years as boys, they lag behind boys in getting trained for the job market.

The importance of learning by doing needs recognition. Vocational and technical education and apprenticeship programs should be designed to open up opportunities for women to work in nontraditional areas. Ensuring that women are employed directly by government-funded projects can break down gender stereotypes and make it easier for women to be hired for jobs outside of traditional "women's work." Putting women in these jobs would help to create awareness among employers and the public through the media.

Public expenditure policies can help overcome the roadblocks women face in considering economic opportunities outside the home. Beyond traditional education, to meet the emerging and advanced needs in the labor market of the New Asia, girls would benefit from appropriately designed apprenticeships and vocational training programs including high-end technical skills and ICT training, business development training programs, and programs designed specifically to prepare young women to compete for better-paying jobs on an equal basis with young men.

To bring girls from the margins into the mainstream, it is essential to expand incentives for better learning outcomes such as through conditional cash transfers for school attendance. It would also help to design policies that ensure funding support to women for secondary and tertiary education, facilitate women's access to information about labor markets and educational facilities, and provide women with placement and counseling services.

Leveling the playing field

An appropriate legal and institutional framework is necessary to create equal employment opportunities for women. It must ensure equal opportunity for men and women regarding job placement; statutory working hours and retirement age; pay, pensions, and other benefits; and property rights. Other legal reforms should add nondiscriminatory clauses to constitutions and revise women's constitutional status to ensure their equitable treatment in jobs.

Breaking barriers to female entrepreneurship is another area that needs attention. In some economies, women still face institutional hurdles to using financial services because they lack collateral, must pay higher interest rates than men, and receive no business incentives that target women. These barriers disrupt and delay their business transactions. In addition to improving access to formal credit sources, tax incentives may be provided to give women entrepreneurs incentive to formally register their small businesses.

The expanded use of ICT in the region presents opportunities for job seekers to search for work online and for firms to provide more occupations with the option of telecommuting, which can help women balance work needs with home responsibilities. Moreover, entrepreneurs who operate on very small scales—handcrafting jewelry and preparing homemade meals, including packed lunches for office workers—can establish themselves online with low startup costs, allowing more women to set up home-based businesses (Box 2.5.1).

However, a new challenge arises: closing the digital gender gap. According to ADB (2014e), 1.3 billion people in developing Asia used the internet in 2013. This internet penetration rate of 31.9% compares with 74.7% in Europe and 60.8% in the Americas. This Asian figure includes 600 million women and girls. However, a significant finding for gender equality is that 30% fewer women than men in Central Asia use the internet and 35% fewer in South Asia. Meanwhile, 9 out of 10 women with a mobile phone report that it makes them feel more secure, connected, and productive. Yet 21% fewer women than men in low- and

2.5.1 Going online to open doors in labor markets

Worldwide, 12 million people find work through online employment sites and mobile tools such as Babajob in India (Raja et al. 2013). In the informal sector in Bangalore, the Babajob website matches job vacancies with job seekers, helping to create employment for the urban poor (Ranganathan and Sarin 2009). An ICT-enabled opportunity for women as well as men is to work from home, which removes geographic limitations for employers and employees alike. A global poll found that 17% of employees who can be connected online to their workplace frequently telecommute (Ipsos 2012). Further, the survey found that a fourth of telecommuting globally takes place in Asia and the Pacific. A strong 83% majority of those surveyed believed that telecommuting would "keep talented women in the workforce instead of leaving temporarily or completely to raise children."

Indeed, ICT innovations have enabled telecommuting and outsourcing to become standard practices today, providing millions of jobs in India and the Philippines. According to Raja et al. (2013), online services like oDesk (39% of whose subscribers are women) and Elance (41% women subscribers) posted 2.5 million jobs in 2012, and a large share of female workers and entrepreneurs online earned extra income while spending time with their families. In Bangladesh, Grameenphone's Village Phone Program facilitated women's provision of telecommunication services in their villages (Alam, Yusuf, and Coghill 2009).

ICT enables women entrepreneurs to boost their profitability by economizing on the time and travel costs of business and by expanding their marketing network, in addition to enjoying the convenience and efficiency of conducting financial transactions online.

middle-income countries own a mobile phone. In South Asia, the figure is 37% (ADB 2014e).

Closing the gender digital divide requires expanding the availability and affordability of ICT services to women and girls. Initiatives along these lines include Grameenphone's Village Phone Program in Bangladesh, which extended the commercial use of mobile phones to 350,000 women. ICT training that targets women is needed to ensure they become effective users. Bhutan, for example, has 50 community e-centers that help adolescent girls in rural areas learn computer skills and programming (ADB 2014e).

Beyond facilitating entry into the labor market, policies also need to address the gender pay gap. Women are often paid less than men for the same job. These gender wage gaps vary widely across developing Asia. While a few countries have almost achieved wage parity, the differences are still large in others. Economic growth does not automatically narrow the gender wage gap, as analysis of past trends shows. Laws guarding against wage discrimination by gender are necessary to ensure that women receive the same wage as men for work of equal value.

Women also receive lower pension benefits because of breaks in their careers and, in some countries, laws restricting their length of service. Equalizing retirement ages between men and women is needed, as is extending the coverage of existing contributory schemes to include self-employed women. Also essential to closing the gender gap are measures to ensure that the aged receive adequate protection in terms of coverage and compensation. This entails crediting pension accounts for time away on maternity leave and extending public pensions to benefit women without formal employment.

Widening career paths

Gender stereotyping can limit women's occupational choices. Even when women are well-educated and highly skilled, employers segregate men and women into their job silos according to traditional stereotypes. Jobs for women in the formal sector are usually support positions rather than managerial roles, and they are concentrated in "soft" sectors such as health care and education instead of such "hard" areas as technology and finance.

To help women avoid getting relegated to low-paying jobs, policies must be formulated to prepare them for higher-paying industries and occupations and to open up opportunities for full-time work. Promoting export-oriented industry allows women in informal employment to find work with employers that discriminate less and gives employers incentives to banish gender discrimination from their hiring policies to better compete on the global market. Ways to help women explore occupations traditionally not considered "women's work" and to get better jobs in urban areas include easing migration controls and processes, creating a work environment conducive to women's participation, providing facilities for good water supply and sanitation, and ensuring a safe environment in the workplace and along the commute to it.

Women carry a heavy burden of unpaid domestic responsibilities, and bearing children necessarily breaks their work continuity, which interrupts their career development and affects their pension benefits. Policies are needed to ensure that women return to the workforce following childbirth. Most employers in the region provide maternity leave with pay. Almost half the countries in the world also offer relatively short paternity leave to fathers of newborns. Ceding part of maternity leave in exchange for paternity leave lets the father spend more time with the baby and the mother get back to work sooner. Many Asian economies provide public care for preschool children, but this needs to be supplemented through legal reforms to provide tax incentives for provision of private childcare, tax credits targeted to women, and flexible work schedules for the mothers of small children without limiting their right to work the same number of hours and times of day as men.

Opening opportunities to women necessarily entails enabling their rise to positions of greater responsibility and decision-making authority. In developing Asia, women still play a rather traditional role in the household, customarily lacking a commanding voice. This tradition is carried over to the workplace, such that women remain woefully underrepresented in senior corporate management and government, which curtails their wider decision-making authority in society. Women in leadership positions can be instrumental in reshaping social norms and reforming the legal framework.

Money earned outside the home reinforces a woman's bargaining power in the household, strengthening her autonomy within the family and in society. Other factors that affect her decision-making power include her educational attainment, wealth, employability, freedom of movement, and access to government benefits and social networks. Expanding women's access to employment and microcredit, and building supportive infrastructure, can help women make their voices heard in the household and beyond.

Political participation and female representation in senior leadership positions is a promising approach to bridging gender gaps. It positively influences girls' career aspirations. Women's representation can be improved with reservation systems and quotas. Boosting women's presence in corporate management requires more appropriate education for women and changes in corporate culture. Affirmative action such as job quotas and awareness creation would encourage more women to step forward to assume senior leadership positions, better enabling them to advance social change and improve the status of other women.

Energizing Asia

Creating opportunities for more women to take up paid labor can powerfully catalyze change that challenges entrenched cultural and social norms. In addition to high-quality education, girls need vocational training programs that target them specifically toward boosting their chances of landing a well-paid job or starting their own small business. An appropriate legal and institutional framework is necessary to ensure equal economic opportunity for women. Even temporary quotas designed to boost their representation in corporate and political leadership can help change social norms and improve women's status, such that quotas may become unnecessary.

The household dynamics of a woman earning an independent income create a feedback loop for social change. The income earned from outside the home gives her financial independence, improves her access to credit, allows her to save more, and raises her socioeconomic status. The independent source gives her autonomy to use her income to provide equally to her sons and daughters education, health care, and nutrition, which maximizes the family's human capital. Employed mothers transmit their success to their children, in part by demonstrating to them a relatively fair parental division of housework, which directly changes children's gender attitudes and indirectly those of their peers. Over time, the more progressive attitudes of growing children change social and cultural norms.

Once these changes take root, they will allow women to break through the barriers that had been holding them back and allow them to contribute more to their own personal welfare and the betterment of society and the economy. Changes in social norms, cultural values, and beliefs then ripple through society, empowering other women to follow and thus completing another cycle of the positive feedback loop toward gender equality. Eliciting women's best contributions to the workforce not only improves equality for women, it promises to boost economic growth and energize Asia. Everyone wins.

Background papers

Kim, J., J. W. Lee, and K. Shin. Forthcoming. A Model of Gender Inequality and Economic Growth. Asian Development Bank.

Menon, N., Y. Rodgers, J. E. Zveglich, Jr., and M. Bacate. Forthcoming. Gender Earnings Gaps in Asia: Recent Trends and Explanations. Asian Development Bank.

Meurs, M., V. Slavchevska, L. Wang, R. Ismaylova, and T. Woldsenbet. Forthcoming. Structural Change and Household Bargaining Power in Bangladesh 1999–2011. Asian Development Bank.

Pande, R., D. Ford, and E. K. Fletcher. Forthcoming. Female Labor Force Participation in Asia: Constraints and Challenges (Synthesis Report). Asian Development Bank.

Qian, M. Forthcoming. Women's Leadership and Corporate Performance. Asian Development Bank.

Terada-Hagiwara, A., J. E. Zveglich, Jr., and S. Camingue-Romance. Unpublished manuscript. Gender Pay Gap: A Macro Perspective. Asian Development Bank.

Wang, L., S. Kanji, S. Jha, and M. Meurs. Forthcoming. How Women Have Fared with the People's Republic of China's Rise in Global Supply Chain Trade? Asian Development Bank.

References

Alam, Q., M. A. Yusuf, and K. Coghill. 2009. Village Phone Program, Commodification of Mobile Phone Set and Empowerment of Women. *The Journal of Community Informatics (Special Double Issue)* 5(3)/6(1).

Albert, J. R., F. M. Quimba, A. P. Ramos, and J. P. Almeda. 2012. Profile of Out-of-School Children in the Philippines. *PIDS Discussion Paper Series* No. 2012-01. Philippine Institute for Development Studies.

Altonji, J. G. and R. M. Blank. 1999. Race and Gender in the Labor Market. In Ashenfelter, O. and D. Card, eds. *Handbook of Labor Economics.* 3(c). Elsevier.

Anderson, S. and M. Eswaran. 2009. What Determines Female Autonomy: Evidence from Bangladesh. *Journal of Development Economics* 90(2).

ADB. 2008. *Asian Development Outlook 2008: Workers in Asia.* Asian Development Bank.

———. 2011. *Asian Development Outlook Update 2011: Preparing for Demographic Transition.* Asian Development Bank.

———. 2013a. *Gender Equality and Women's Empowerment Operational Plan, 2013–2020: Moving the Agenda Forward in Asia and the Pacific.* Asian Development Bank.

———. 2013b. *Gender Equality and the Labor Market—Cambodia, Kazakhstan, and the Philippines.* Asian Development Bank.

———. 2014a. *Innovative Asia: Advancing the Knowledge-Based Economy: The Next Policy Agenda.* Asian Development Bank.

———. 2014b. *Maldives: Gender Equality Diagnostic of Selected Sectors.* Asian Development Bank.

———. 2014c. *Gender Toolkit—Micro, Small, and Medium-Sized Enterprise Finance and Development.* Asian Development Bank.

——. 2014d. *Asian Development Outlook 2014: Asia in Global Value Chains.* Asian Development Bank.

——. 2014e. *Digital Revolution for Asia's Women: Bridging the Gender Divide.* Asian Development Bank.

——. 2015. *Women in the Workforce: An Unmet Potential in Asia and the Pacific.* Asian Development Bank.

ADB and ILO. 2013. *Good Global Economic and Social Practices to Promote Gender Equality in the Labor Market.* Asian Development Bank and International Labour Organization.

Baldwin, R. 2013. Global Supply Chains: Why They Emerged, Why They Matter, and Where They Are Going. In Elms, D. K. and P. Low, eds. *Global Value Chains in a Changing World.* World Trade Organization.

Barrientos, A., M. Gorman, and A. Heslop. 2003. Old Age Poverty in Developing Countries: Contributions and Dependence in Later Life. *World Development* 31(3).

Beaman, L., E. Duflo, R. Pande, and P. Topalova. 2012. Female Leadership Raises Aspirations and Educational Attainment for Girls: A Policy Experiment in India. *Science* 355(2012).

Becker, G. 1971. *The Economics of Discrimination.* University of Chicago Press.

Berik, G., Y. Rodgers, and J. E. Zveglich, Jr. 2004. International Trade and Gender Wage Discrimination: Evidence from East Asia. *Review of Development Economics* 8(2).

Bertrand, M. 2011. New Perspectives on Gender. In Ashenfelter, O. and C. David, eds. *Handbook of Labor Economics* 4(b). Elsevier.

Bertrand, M., C. Goldin, and L. F. Katz. 2010. Dynamics of the Gender Gap for Young Professionals in the Financial and Corporate Sectors. *American Economic Journal: Applied Economics* 2(3).

Bird, K. Forthcoming. *Filipino Youth Labor Market Experience: School-Work Transition.* Asian Development Bank.

Caproni, P. J. 2012. *Management Skills for Everyday Life—The Practical Coach.* Prentice Hall.

Catalyst. 2004. *The Bottom Line: Connecting Corporate Performance and Gender Diversity.*

Chaaban, J. and W. Cunningham. 2011. Measuring the Economic Gain of Investing in Girls: the Girl Effect Dividend. *Policy Research Working Paper* No. 5753. World Bank.

Chang, S. and X. Zhang. 2012. http://www.ifpri.org/sites/default/files/publications/ifpridp01203.pdf

Chattopadhyay, R. and E. Duflo. 2004. Women as Policy Makers: Evidence from a Randomized Policy Experiment in India. *Econometrica* 72(5).

Chen, X. 2014. *Gender Imbalance and Parental Substance Use in Rural China.* Mimeo. Yale University.

Chen, Z., Y. Ge, C. Wan, and H. Lai. 2013. Globalization and Gender Wage Inequality in China. *World Development* 44.

Chung, W. and M. Das Gupta. 2007. http://www.jstor.org/stable/25487621

Cuberes, D. and M. Teignier. 2014. Gender Inequality and Economic Growth: A Critical Review. *Journal of International Development* 26(2).

Duflo, E. 2003. Grandmothers and Granddaughters: Old-Age Pensions and Intra-household Allocation in South Africa. *World Bank Economic Review* 17(1).

———. 2012. Women Empowerment and Economic Development. *Journal of Economic Literature* 50(4).

Edlund, L. 2015. Forthcoming. *Female Labor Force Participation in Asia: China Country Study.* Asian Development Bank.

Edlund, L., H. Li, J. Yi, and J. Zhang. 2013. Sex Ratios and Crime: Evidence from China. *Review of Economics and Statistics* 95(5).

Eloot, K., A. Huang, and M. Lehnich. 2013. A New Era for Manufacturing in China. *Mckinsey Quarterly.* June.

Eswaran, M. 2014. *Why Gender Matters in Economics.* Princeton University Press.

FAO. 2011. *The State of Food and Agriculture 2010–11: Women in Agriculture, Closing the Gender Gap for Development.* Food and Agriculture Organization of the United Nations.

FAO, IFAD, and ILO. 2010. *Gender Dimensions of Agriculture and Rural Employment: Differentiated Pathways Out of Poverty: Status, Trends and Gaps.* Food and Agriculture Organization of the United Nations, International Fund for Agricultural Development, and International Labour Organization.

Floro, M. and M. Meurs. 2009. Global Trends in Women's Access to "Decent Work": Dialogue on Globalization. *Occasional Papers* No. 43/ May 2009. International Labour Organization.

Galasso, E. 1999. *Intra-Household Allocation and Child Labor in Indonesia.* Mimeo. Boston College.

Gayle, G. L. and L. Golan. 2011. Estimating a Dynamic Adverse-Selection Model: Labour-Force Experience and the Changing Gender Earnings Gap 1968–1997. *Review of Economic Studies* 20.

Goldin, C. 1995. *The U-Shaped Female Labor Force Function in Economic Development and Economic History. Investment in Women's Human Capital and Economic Development.* University of Chicago Press.

Goldman Sachs Global Markets Institute. 2009. *The Power of the Purse: Gender Equality and Middle-Class Spending.*

———. 2014. *Giving Credit Where It Is Due: How Closing the Credit Gap for Women-owned SMEs Can Drive Global Growth.* Global Markets Institute.

Grant Thornton. 2013. *Women in Senior Management: Setting the Stage for Growth.* Grant Thornton.

Guilmoto, C. Z. 2012. *Sex Imbalances at Birth: Current Trends, Consequences, and Policy Implications.* United Nations Population Fund Asia and the Pacific Regional Office.

Hausmann, R., L. Tyson, Y. Bekhouche, and S. Zahidi. 2014. *The Global Gender Gap Report, 2014.* World Economic Forum.

Heintz, J. 2006. *Globalization, Economic Policy and Employment: Poverty and Gender Implications.* International Labour Organization.

Herrera, C. and D. Sahn. 2015. The Impact of Early Childbearing on Schooling and Cognitive Skills among Young Women in Madagascar.

Hesketh, T. 2011. Selecting Sex: The Effect of Preferring Sons. *Early Human Development* 87(11).

Hofferth, S. 1983. Less Guilt for Working Mothers. *Good Housekeeping.* University of Michigan Institute for Social Research.

Horioka, C. Y. and A. Terada-Hagiwara. 2015. The Impact of Pre-marital Gender Ratios on Household Saving in India and Korea: the Competitive Saving Motive Revisited. Unpublished.

Hsieh, C., E. Hurst, C. Jones, and P. Klenow. 2013. The Allocation of Talent and US Economic Growth. *Working Paper* 18693. National Bureau of Economic Research.

Hughes, K. and J. E. Jennings. 2012. *Global Women's Entrepreneurship Research: Diverse Settings, Questions, and Approaches.* Edward Elgar.

Hung, N. M., N. T. Hong Nhung, and B. Quang Tuan. 2011. Earnings and Quality of Female Labor in the Border Areas of Viet Nam and Implications for Greater Mekong Subregion Cooperation. *Greater Mekong Subregion–Phnom Penh Plan for Development Management: Research Report Series.* Asian Development Bank.

IFC. 2013. *IFC Jobs Study: Assessing Private Sector Contributions to Job Creation and Poverty Reduction.* International Finance Corporation.

ILO. 2009. *Ageing Societies: The Benefits, and the Costs, of Living Longer.* International Labour Organization.

———. 2014. *World Social Protection Report 2014/15: Building Economic Recovery, Inclusive Development and Social Justice.* International Labour Organization.

IMF. 2013. *Women, Work, and the Economy: Macroeconomic Gains from Gender Equality.* International Monetary Fund.

———. 2015. Fair Play: More Equal Laws Boost Female Labor Force Participation. *IMF Staff Discussion Note* SDN/15/02. International Monetary Fund.

Ipsos. 2012. *The World of Work: Global Study of Online Employees Shows One in Five (17%) Work from Elsewhere.* Ipsos.

Jalal, I. 2013. TVET Leads to Non-traditional Jobs for Women in Nepal. *ADB Gender Network E-news.*

———. 2015. Nepal: A Chorus of Women's Voices Makes a Difference— Influencing Local Government Spending. *Gender Case Studies Series.* Asian Development Bank.

Jha, S. 2000. Fiscal Decentralization in India: Strengths, Limitations and Prospects for Panchayati Raj Institutions. Background Paper No. 2. *Overview of Rural Decentralization in India* 3. World Bank.

Kantor, P. 2003. Women's Empowerment through Home-Based Work: Evidence from India. *Development and Change* 34.

Kuroki, M. 2014. The Effect of Sex Ratios on Suicide. *Health Economics* 23(12).

Leckie, S. H. 2012. The People's Republic of China. In Park, D. *Pension Systems in East and Southeast Asia Promoting Fairness and Sustainability.* Asian Development Bank.

Liu, A. Y. 2004. Gender Wage Gap in Viet Nam: 1993 to 1998. *Journal of Comparative Economics* 32.

Loko, B. and M. A. Diouf. 2009. Revisiting the Determinants of Productivity Growth: What's New? *IMF Working Paper* 09/225. International Monetary Fund.

Mammen, K. and C. Paxson. 2000. Women's Work and Economic Development. *The Journal of Economic Perspectives* 14(4).

McGinn, K. L., M. R. Castro, and E. L. Lingo. 2015. Mums the Word! Cross-national Effects of Maternal Employment on Gender Inequalities at Work and at Home. *Harvard Business School Working Paper* No. 15-094.

McKinsey and Company. 2007. *Women Matter: Gender Diversity, a Corporate Performance Driver.*

Menon, N. and Rodgers, Y. 2009. International Trade and the Gender Wage Gap: New Evidence from India's Manufacturing Sector. *World Development* 37(5).

Mincer, J. and S. Polachek. 1974. Family Investments in Human Capital: Earnings of Women. *Journal of Political Economy* 82(2).

Morrison, A., D. Raju, and N. Sinha. 2007. Gender Equality, Poverty and Economic Growth. *Policy Research Working Paper* 4349. World Bank.

Ñopo, H., N. Daza, and J. Ramos. 2011. Gender Earnings Gaps in the World. *IZA Discussion Paper* No. 5736. Institute for the Study of Labor.

OECD. 2012. *Closing the Gender Gap: Act Now.* Organisation for Economic Co-operation and Development.

———. 2013. *Pensions at a Glance Asia/Pacific 2013.* Organisation for Economic Co-operation and Development.

———. 2014. *Social Institutions and Gender Index 2014 Synthesis Report.* Organisation for Economic Co-operation and Development.

———. 2015. *In It Together: More Women in the Workforce Lowers Inequality.* Organisation for Economic Co-operation and Development.

Oelz, M., S. Olney, and T. Manuela. 2013. *Equal Pay: An Introductory Guide.* International Labour Organization.

Pande, R. and P. Topalova. 2013. Women in Charge. *Finance & Development* 50(2). International Monetary Fund.

Permanyer, I. 2013. A Critical Assessment of the UNDP's Gender Inequality Index. *Feminist Economics* 19(2).

Qian, N. 2008. Missing Women and the Price of Tea in China: The Effect of Sex-Specific Earnings on Sex Imbalance. *The Quarterly Journal of Economics* 123(3).

Raja, S., S. Imaizumi, T. Kelly, J. Narimatsu, and C. Paradi-Guilford. 2013. *Connecting to Work: How Information and Communication Technologies Could Help Expand Employment Opportunities.* World Bank.

Ranganathan, K. and A. Sarin. 2009. *Babajob.com—Digitizing the Informal Job Sector: Case Study.* Indian Institute of Management.

Sarsons, H. and G. Xu. 2015. *Confidence Men? Gender and Confidence: Evidence among Top Economists.* London School of Economics.

SciELO in Perspective. 2015. *Gender Inequality in Science Varies Among Disciplines.* SciELO in Perspective blog. http://blog.scielo.org/en/2015/03/08/title-inequity-of-gender-in-science-varies-over-disciplines/ (viewed 29 July 2015).

Seguino, S. 2000. Gender Inequality and Economic Growth: A Cross-country Analysis. *World Development* 28(7).

Seguino, S. and M. S. Floro. 2003. Does Gender Have Any Effect on Aggregate Saving? An Empirical Analysis. *International Review of Applied Economics* 17(2).

Sianesi, B. and J. Van Reenen. 2003. Returns to Education: Macroeconomics. *Journal of Economic Surveys* 17(2).

Singru, R. N. 2015. Regional Balanced Urbanization for Inclusive Cities Development: Urban–Rural Poverty Linkages in Secondary Cities Development in Southeast Asia. *ADB Southeast Asia Working Paper Series* No. 11. Asian Development Bank.

Ståhlberg, A.-C., A. Kruse, and A. Sundén. 2005. Pension Design and Gender: Analyses of Developed and Developing Countries. *Gender Issues* 22(3).

Stewart, F. 2002. Horizontal Inequalities: A Neglected Dimension of Development. Queen Elizabeth House Working Paper Series. *Working Paper* No. 81. University of Oxford.

Tacoli, C. and R. Mabala. 2010. Exploring Mobility and Migration in the Context of Rural–Urban Linkages: Why Gender and Generation Matter. *Environment and Urbanization* 22(2).

Tan, Z., S.-J. Wei, and X. Zhang. 2015. Implications of 'Missing Girls' for Workplace Safety. Unpublished.

The Economist. 2006. *A Guide to Womenomics.*

———. 2015. *More Hands to Rock the Cradle.*

Trent, K. and S. J. South. 2012. Mate Availability and Women's Sexual Experiences in China. *Journal of Marriage and Family* 74(1).

UN. 2010. *The World's Women 2010 Trends and Statistics.* United Nations.

———. 2013. *Realizing Women's Rights to Land and Other Productive Resources.* UN Women and Office of the High Commissioner for Human Rights.

UNCTAD. 2013. *World Investment Report 2013: Global Value Chains: Investment and Trade for Development.* United Nations Conference on Trade and Development.

UNDP. 2010. Asia Pacific Human Development Report. *Power, Voice and Rights: A Turning Point for Gender Equality in Asia and the Pacific.* United Nations Development Programme and Macmillan Publishers India.

———. 2014. *Gender Equality: Women's Participation and Leadership in Governments at the Local Level.* United Nations Development Programme.

UNESCAP, ADB, and UNDP. 2009. Achieving the Millennium Development Goals in an Era of Global Uncertainty. *Asia–Pacific Regional Report* 2009/10. United Nations Economic and Social Commission for Asia and the Pacific, Asian Development Bank, and United Nations Development Programme.

———. 2013. Asia–Pacific Aspirations: Perspectives for a Post-2015 Development Agenda. *Asia–Pacific Regional MDGs Report* 2012/13. United Nations Economic and Social Commission for Asia and the Pacific, Asian Development Bank, and United Nations Development Programme.

UNICEF. 2006. *The State of the World's Children 2007: Women and Children, The Double Dividend of Gender Equality.* United Nations Children's Fund.

———. 2014. *Promoting Gender Equality: An Equity-based Approach to Programming.* United Nations Children's Fund.

UNFPA. 2012. *Sex Imbalances at Birth: Current Trends, Consequences, and Policy Implications.* United Nations Population Fund.

UN-Habitat. 2012. *Gender and Urban Planning: Issues and Trends.* United Nations Human Settlements Programme.

UN Women. 2015. *Progress of the World's Women 2015–2016: Transforming Economies, Realizing Rights*. UN Entity for Gender Equality and the Empowerment of Women.

Ursula, G. 2012. Youth and Skills: Putting Education to Work, Urbanization and the Employment Opportunities of Youth in Developing Countries. Background paper prepared for the Education for All Global Monitoring Report 2012.

Vlachantoni, A. and J. Falkingham. 2012. Gender and Old-Age Pension Protection in Asia. In Handayani, S. and B. Babajanian. *Social Protection for Older People in Asia*. Asian Development Bank.

Wei, S.-J. and X. Zhang. 2011a. Sex Ratios, Entrepreneurship, and Economic Growth in the People's Republic of China. *NBER Working Paper* 16800. National Bureau of Economic Research.

——. 2011b. The Competitive Saving Motive: Evidence from Rising Sex Ratios and Savings Rates in China. *Journal of Political Economy* 119(3).

Wei, S.-J., X. Zhang, and Y. Liu. 2012. Status Competition and Housing Prices. *NBER Working Paper* 18000. National Bureau of Economic Research.

World Bank. 1993. *The East Asian Miracle: Economic Growth and Public Policy*. Oxford University Press.

——. 2002. *Education Financing in Developing Countries: Level and Sources of Funds*.

——. 2009. *Women's Retirement Age in Vietnam: Gender Equality and Sustainability of the Social Security Fund*.

——. 2011. *World Development Report 2012: Gender Equality and Development*.

——. 2012. *Toward Gender Equality in East Asia and the Pacific: A Companion to the World Development Report*.

——. 2014. *Voice and Agency: Empowering Women and Girls for Shared Prosperity*.

——. 2015. *Women, Business and the Law 2016: Getting to Equal*.

World Bank and the Development Research Center of the State Council, PRC. 2014. *Urban China: Toward Efficient, Inclusive, and Sustainable Urbanization*. World Bank.

Zhu, N. and X. Luo. 2008. The Impact of Remittances on Rural Poverty and Inequality in China. *Policy Research Working Paper* 4637. World Bank.

Zveglich, Jr., J. E., Y. Rodgers, and W. Rodgers. 1997. http://www.jstor.org/stable/2525264

3

ECONOMIC TRENDS AND PROSPECTS IN DEVELOPING ASIA

SUBREGIONAL SUMMARIES

Central Asia
East Asia
South Asia
Southeast Asia
The Pacific

Bangladesh
People's Republic of China
India
Indonesia
Malaysia
Pakistan
Philippines
Thailand
Viet Nam

Economic trends and prospects in developing Asia

Subregional summaries

Central Asia

Subregional assessment and prospects

This *Update* lowers the growth forecast for Central Asia to 3.3% from 3.5% in 2015 and to 4.2% from 4.5% in 2016, as the subregion's economies adjust to lower global commodity prices and recession in the Russian Federation (Figure 3.1.1). Lower export revenues attributable to the drop in oil and gas prices have constrained growth in the subregion's energy exporters: Azerbaijan, Kazakhstan, Turkmenistan, and Uzbekistan. In addition, weak remittances have limited consumption in Uzbekistan and the subregion's energy importers: Armenia, Georgia, the Kyrgyz Republic, and Tajikistan.

From the supply side, services, agriculture, mining, and construction linked to public investment programs performed well in the first half of 2015, while trade and export-oriented manufacturing remained burdened by weak external demand, including lower-than-expected growth in the People's Republic of China (PRC). The lower growth forecast for 2016 reflects a more sluggish recovery in Kazakhstan and the lagged impact of the recession in the Russian Federation and weaker performance in the PRC.

The inflation forecast for Central Asia in 2015 is raised to 8.1% from the 6.7% projected in *Asian Development Outlook 2015* (*ADO 2015*), as the sharp depreciation of the Kazakh tenge on 20 August warrants a rise in the inflation forecast for Kazakhstan, to 8.9% from 6.0% (Figure 3.1.2). Price controls put in place across the subregion after currency devaluations in 2014 and early 2015 have helped keep inflation

This chapter was written by Christopher Hnanguie for Central Asia; Shiela Camingue-Romance, Donghyun Park, Gemma Estrada, Madhavi Pundit, Cindy Castillejos-Petalcorin, Akiko Terada-Hagiwara, and Reza Vaez-Zadeh for East Asia; Masato Nakane for South Asia; Anthony Patrick and Sona Shrestha for Southeast Asia; and Yurendra Basnett, Prince Cruz, Caroline Currie, Christopher Edmonds, David Freedman, Malie Lototele, Rommel Rabanal, Benjamin Radoc, Roland Rajah, Shiu Raj Singh, Cara Tinio, Laisiasa Tora, and Johannes Wolff for the Pacific. Country highlights were contributed by various ADB resident mission staff.

3.1.1 GDP growth, Central Asia

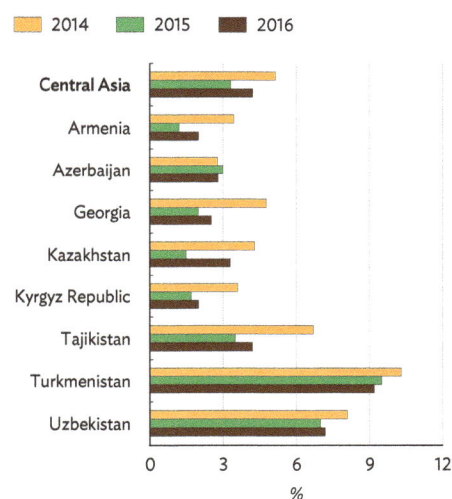

Source: *Asian Development Outlook* database.

3.1.2 Inflation, Central Asia

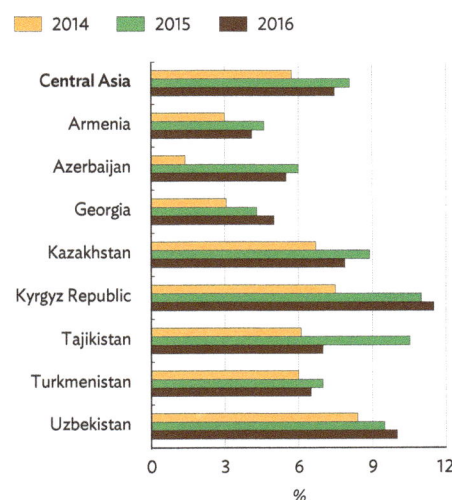

Source: *Asian Development Outlook* database.

3.1.1 Kazakhstan's economy and subregional performance

As a major commodity exporter, Kazakhstan is being hit hard by the declining oil price. And, as Central Asia's largest economy, Kazakhstan has an outsized effect on economic results for the subregion as a whole.

With the currencies of Kazakhstan's main trading partners depreciating, Kazakhstan moved to a freely floating exchange rate for the tenge earlier than planned. Consequently, the local currency depreciated by more than 21%, an even greater decline than the 16.2% devaluation in February 2014.

The new exchange rate is expected to dampen consumption and investment further. Despite lower imports, the growth forecast has been revised down to 1.5% in 2015. For 2016, GDP growth is projected to accelerate to 3.3%, reflecting government investments for Expo 2017 and improved export competitiveness. The Kashagan oilfield is expected to start production in 2017, which should support growth in Kazakhstan and help spur growth in Central Asia over the medium term.

Provided that the exchange rate stabilizes after the August floating (with some lagged impact from tenge depreciation), and that inflation targeting proves successful and some price controls are implemented, consumer prices are projected to rise by 8.9% in 2015 and 7.9% in 2016. With low oil prices reducing export earnings in 2015, the current account deficit is forecast at 5.2% of GDP, narrowing to 3.2% in 2016.

from accelerating faster, despite increases in food prices in the first half of 2015 and the recent float of the tenge (Box 3.1.1). With the lagged impact of the depreciation raising the 2016 inflation forecast for Kazakhstan to 7.9% from 6.2%, the aggregate inflation projection for Central Asia in 2016 is increased to 7.5% from 6.6% in *ADO 2015*.

The projected current account deficit for Central Asia in 2015 is now equal to 3.2% of GDP, wider than the 0.2% deficit projected in *ADO 2015* (Figure 3.1.3). This reflects an expected widening of Kazakhstan's current account deficit to 5.2% of GDP and a halving of the projected surplus for Azerbaijan from 12.0% of GDP to 6.0%, in view of weaker prospects for petroleum exports. These changes offset a narrower current account deficit projected for Armenia, revised from 9.2% of GDP to 8.7%. For 2016, the current account balance for Central Asia is now projected to be a deficit of 1.6% of GDP, compared with the 0.2% surplus forecast in *ADO 2015*, as a poorer outlook for petroleum and metal prices widens the projected deficit for Kazakhstan to 3.2% of GDP and narrows Azerbaijan's forecast surplus to 8.0%.

3.1.3 Current account balance, Central Asia

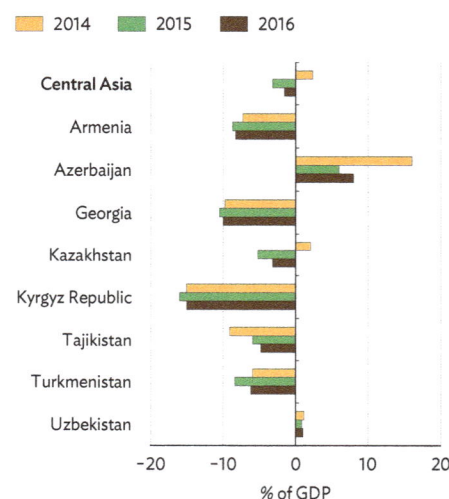

Source: Asian Development Outlook database.

Country highlights

Armenia

GDP growth accelerated to 4.0% in the first half of 2015 from 2.6% in the same period in 2014 and to 3.5% for all of 2014. All major sectors contributed to growth, but a 4.2% slump in trade slowed growth in services to 1.8% from 3.7% a year earlier. Agriculture saw double-digit growth at 15.5%, and industry including construction expanded by 3.7%. On the demand side, private consumption and investment declined, while public consumption showed only modest gains. The drag from the deficit in external trade and services moderated significantly, as exports fell much less than imports. Despite strong growth in the first half, the growth forecasts are trimmed for 2015 and 2016, as problems in Armenia's major trading partners continue to reduce trade, remittances, and investments and so depress economic growth.

3.1.1 Selected economic indicators, Armenia (%)

	2015		2016	
	ADO 2015	Update	ADO 2015	Update
GDP growth	1.6	1.2	2.3	2.0
Inflation	4.6	4.6	4.1	4.1
Current acct. bal. (share of GDP)	−9.2	−8.7	−8.3	−8.3

Source: ADB estimates.

Agriculture is still foreseen as the primary driver of growth, along with a modest contribution from industry and services. On the demand side, the pattern of growth is expected to continue for the rest of the year, with a larger deficit in external trade and services, along with weaker investment and private consumption.

The lagged pass-through of currency depreciation at the end of 2014 caused average annual inflation to accelerate to 5.0% in the first 7 months of 2015 from 3.4% in the same period in 2014 and 3.0% in all of 2014. The 12-month inflation rate of 4.2% in July remained within the central bank's target band of 2.5%–5.5%. Despite these developments, inflation forecasts remain unchanged for 2015 and 2016, as strong growth in agricultural supply, weak domestic demand, and tight monetary policy should cause inflation to recede in the months ahead.

The current account deficit narrowed to 7.3% of GDP in 2014 from 7.6% in 2013. A slight improvement in the goods and services trade deficit was partly offset by a larger deficit for primary and secondary incomes, reflecting the drop in remittances. In line with this improvement, the projections for the current account deficit are narrowed for 2015 but kept unchanged for 2016.

Azerbaijan

The economy rebounded with robust growth of 5.7% in the first half of 2015, up from 2.1% in the same period in 2014. Boosted mainly by government capital expenditure, the economy outside of the large petroleum sector was the major driver of growth. The public investment program remains a key source of economic expansion and employment, but budget revenues are under pressure from lower oil prices. Despite low prices, oil production in the first half of the year rose by 1.3%, reversing a 3.9% contraction in January–June 2014, but is expected to level off for the rest of the year to allow annual maintenance. Despite a reduction in spending from the budget plan, fiscal policy is expected to remain somewhat expansionary in 2015 to support the economy. The 2016 budget is being tightened, as low petroleum prices have led to the postponement of some investment projects. Notwithstanding these developments, this *Update* maintains *ADO 2015* growth projections for 2015 and 2016.

Official foreign currency reserves fell by more than 30% in January–August 2015 because the central bank intervened to maintain the new exchange rate after the February 2015 devaluation of the Azerbaijan manat. Oil prices, key to local currency stability, have fallen dramatically over the past year, from $103.08 per barrel of Azeri light crude in August 2014 to $46.23 a year later. Declining foreign currency reserves and oil prices are putting further pressure on the manat and could trigger another devaluation if recent trends continue over the coming months. Dollarization is the main concern in the banking sector, as US dollar deposits almost doubled after the devaluation. To limit inflation, the central bank has reduced local currency liquidity. With tepid domestic demand largely offsetting price pressures from the devaluation, year-on-year inflation rose to only 3.5% in the first half of 2015, which was nevertheless up from 1.6% for the same period in 2014. The devaluation will continue to put inflationary pressure on imports other than food.

3.1.2 Selected economic indicators, Azerbaijan (%)

	2015		2016	
	ADO 2015	Update 2015	ADO 2015	Update 2015
GDP growth	3.0	3.0	2.8	2.8
Inflation	6.0	6.0	5.5	5.5
Current acct. bal. (share of GDP)	12.0	6.0	13.4	8.0

Source: ADB estimates.

Although domestic demand and prices for imported food are expected to moderate, this *Update* retains *ADO 2015* inflation forecasts for 2015 and 2016.

The plunge in global petroleum prices caused hydrocarbon exports to plummet by 47% in the first quarter of 2015, narrowing the trade surplus and slashing the current account surplus to 0.5% of GDP in the first quarter of 2015. As oil exports are expected to remain weak and imports have been higher than projected earlier, this *Update* halves the forecast for the current account surplus for 2015 and, for 2016, reduces the forecast surplus a bit less.

Georgia

Economic growth slowed in the first quarter of 2015 to 3.2% from 4.8% for the whole of 2014. Preliminary data show a further slowdown to 2.6% in the first half of 2015. The slowdown largely reflects declines of 5.2% in manufacturing and 2.5% in trade, and it came despite strong growth of 22.9% in mining and 17.2% in construction. After expanding by 12.2% in the first quarter, bank credit fell by 1.5% in the second in line with slower growth. Despite planned fiscal consolidation, capital spending is expected to contribute to growth in the second half of 2015 and in 2016. However, net exports will remain a drag on growth, as recession in the Russian Federation and Ukraine weakens the external outlook. Growth forecasts are maintained for 2015 and 2016, but growth could be lower if recession in the Russian Federation proves worse than currently forecast, along with its impact on Georgia's other trading partners in the subregion.

Annual average inflation in August 2015 amounted to 3.2%, as large increases for tobacco and alcoholic beverages (13.1%) and for furnishings, household equipment, and maintenance (9.3%) offset smaller declines for transport (–1.6%) and clothing and footwear (–0.9%). Continuing moderate inflation, despite depreciation of the Georgia lari by nearly 33% since November 2014, reflects weakening domestic demand (as much domestic credit is denominated in US dollars) and reduced profit margins for firms, along with lower prices for imported food and energy. Inflationary expectations have recently increased, however, with the depletion of inventories accumulated at cheaper prices, rising production costs, and extensive dollarization in the economy. To counter these expectations, the National Bank of Georgia raised its policy rate in steps by 200 basis points to reach 6.0% in August. However, inflation is expected to accelerate to about 6% by year-end. With tighter monetary policy, this *Update* trims the inflation forecast for 2015 but keeps the forecast for 2016.

The current account deficit reached 14.1% of GDP in the first quarter of 2015 as the trade deficit widened and the regional economic slowdown hurt remittances. The deficit was funded largely through foreign direct investment inflows and official development assistance. Though export data for the first 6 months suggest a further cut in exports of nearly 24%, reflecting a drop in vehicle exports by nearly two-thirds, lower oil prices helped cut imports by about 9%. Sharp declines in remittances—from the Russian Federation by 41%, Greece by 19%, and Italy by 12%—caused total remittances to fall by almost

3.1.3 Selected economic indicators, Georgia (%)

	2015		2016	
	ADO 2015	Update	ADO 2015	Update
GDP growth	2.0	2.0	2.5	2.5
Inflation	5.0	4.3	5.0	5.0
Current acct. bal. (share of GDP)	–12.0	–10.5	–10.5	–10.0

Source: ADB estimates.

23% in the first half of 2015. Because a rebound in exports and a further reduction in imports are expected in the second half, the forecasts for current account deficits are revised down for 2015 and 2016.

Kazakhstan

In a surprise move, Kazakhstan instituted a freely floating exchange rate on 20 August 2015, abandoning its earlier narrow currency band linked to the US dollar and adopting a monetary policy that targets inflation. As a result, the local currency depreciated by more than 21%, an even larger decline than the 16.2% devaluation in February 2014. This move followed the depreciation of other currencies in the subregion and its environs, notably the ruble, which, along with the drop in prices for oil and other commodities, had made Kazakhstan less competitive.

Growth in the first half of 2015 is estimated to have slowed from 3.9% a year earlier to 1.7%, its slowest rate since 2009. Industry grew by only 0.6% as nearly stagnant 0.3% growth in manufacturing largely negated growth in oil production at 1.3%, metallurgy at 5.6%, and chemicals at 1.8%. Agriculture expanded by 3.0%, and construction, which benefitted from ongoing government projects, by 5.1%. While still recovering from the 2014 devaluation, low oil prices, and ruble depreciation, the economy suffered a further shock from the early move to a freely floating exchange rate and the resulting depreciation of the tenge. Over the medium term, gains from a more competitive exchange rate are likely to materialize. While the 2015 budget has been revised several times to reflect lower oil prices, the government is committed to continuing some stimulus expenditure despite sharply declining revenues. Real growth may suffer from lower private consumption in response to higher import prices, and from diminished private investment as commodity producers see profits fall. In 2016, a projected rise in exports and preparations for Expo 2017 will promote a recovery in growth despite continued weak private consumption and investment and possible downside risks from a rise in interest rates to contain inflation. The growth forecast is lowered for 2015 and 2016.

Inflation was modest at 5.3% in the first half of 2015, down slightly from 6.1% a year earlier, mainly because of weaker aggregate demand and cheaper imports from the Russian Federation after ruble depreciation. Food prices rose by 6.0%, up from 5.7% in the first half of 2014, and other goods rose by 4.4%, down from 5.8% the previous year. Price increases for services slowed to 5.1% from 6.9% a year earlier, partly reflecting regulatory restrictions on utility tariffs. In the second half of 2015, tenge depreciation will directly spur import prices, especially for nonfood imports with limited scope for substitution, and thus quicken inflation. While the government is trying to contain price increases by, for example, applying price controls and delaying to 2016 the expected salary increase for public servants, inflation is now projected to be higher by half in 2015 than the *ADO 2015* projection. For 2016, the lagged impact of the August 2015 depreciation prompts a smaller upward revision. Inflation should stay in the single digits, however, constrained by contracting private demand and lending suppressed by local banks' foreign exposure and a currency mismatch between highly dollarized deposits and loans denominated mostly in

3.1.4 Selected economic indicators, Kazakhstan (%)

	2015		2016	
	ADO 2015	*Update 2015*	*ADO 2015*	*Update 2015*
GDP growth	1.9	1.5	3.8	3.3
Inflation	6.0	8.9	6.2	7.9
Current acct. bal. (share of GDP)	–1.0	–5.2	–1.3	–3.2

Source: ADB estimates.

tenge. The newly introduced inflation targeting regime will need to strike a balance between high interest rates, which could mute economic growth, and high inflation rates, which could force further tenge depreciation and thus higher import prices.

Low oil and metal prices caused export revenues to fall by almost 47% in the first quarter of 2015 and the current account to turn negative. As commodity prices are expected to remain low in 2015 and 2016, lower export earnings outweigh lower merchandise imports, the decline in net service exports, and reduced net investment income. This *Update* forecasts a much larger current account deficit for 2015 than in *ADO 2015*. Exports are expected to recover modestly in 2016, which will ease the current account deficit despite slightly larger demand for imported goods and services in preparation for Expo 2017. The projected current account deficit is nevertheless raised from the earlier forecast. Production at the Kashagan oilfield is now expected to begin in 2017, which should boost growth and strengthen the current account balance over the medium term.

Kyrgyz Republic

GDP grew by 7.3% in the first half of 2015, or by 4.4% excluding gold. Industry expanded by 23.6%, reflecting strong mining and goods processing. Agriculture grew by 2.4%, while trade expanded by 5.8%. Growth in construction halved to 11.2% from 22.0% in 2014, reflecting more moderate expansion in capital investment—which also halved, to 6.8% from 13.5% in 2014. Despite these developments, this *Update* maintains the growth forecast for 2015, as full-year developments will depend heavily on remittances from and trade with the Russian Federation, which is experiencing a marked recession. The growth forecast for 2016 is similarly sustained on the assumption of some recovery in the Russian Federation and other subregional trading partners. The Kyrgyz Republic's accession to the Eurasian Economic Union (EEU) on 8 May 2015 and the physical opening of the EEU borders effective from 12 August 2015 add uncertainty to the country's growth prospects in the second half of 2015 and over the medium term.

Prices in the first half of 2015 averaged 7.8% higher than a year earlier, reflecting increases in energy tariffs and prices for most items, though prices at the end of June were only marginally above those of December 2014. Food prices fell by 3.5% on seasonal factors. The Kyrgyz som depreciated by about 5.4% in the first 6 months of 2015, and the exchange rate became highly volatile after 20 August 2015, following the sharp depreciation of the Kazakh tenge. By 26 August 2015, the som had depreciated by about 10.9%, from Som58.9 to the dollar on 1 January to Som65.3. Inflation may accelerate in the second half of the year, following the opening of the borders within the EEU. This *Update* raises the forecast for inflation in 2015 in view of this and of external shocks from the depreciation of the tenge and the ruble, strong growth in the first half of the year, and an expected rise in food prices. Inflation is expected to be at least as high in 2016 because of transitional price adjustments within the EEU, so the forecast for 2016 is also raised.

The January–June 2015 trade deficit narrowed by 23.1% from a year earlier as total trade declined. Imports fell by 16.8%, mainly as

3.1.5 Selected economic indicators, Kyrgyz Republic (%)

	2015		2016	
	ADO 2015	Update 2015	ADO 2015	Update
GDP growth	1.7	1.7	2.0	2.0
Inflation	10.5	11.0	10.0	11.5
Current acct. bal. (share of GDP)	−16.0	−16.0	−15.0	−15.0

Source: ADB estimates.

imports of vehicles, machinery and equipment, fertilizers, apparel, and accessories sagged, while exports fell by 2.6% with smaller shipments of fruits, vegetables, apparel, and accessories—and despite higher gold exports. Remittances were about 25.4% less than during the first 6 months of 2014, reflecting continued recession in the Russian Federation and ruble depreciation. This *Update* maintains the current account deficit forecasts for 2015 and 2016.

Tajikistan

Growth slowed to 6.4% in the first half of 2015 as industrial expansion moderated to 14.9% from 16.8% a year earlier, reflecting relatively meager 3.5% growth in aluminum, and as spillover from recession in the Russian Federation cut services growth to 0.8%. Agriculture maintained 6.9% growth. Retail trade and services are expected to decline further in the second half of 2015, offsetting moderate growth in industry and agriculture. Accordingly, this *Update* trims the 2015 growth forecast from that of *ADO 2015*. Slower expansion is expected to carry over into 2016 despite expected recovery in the Russian Federation, prompting a similar trimming of that forecast.

Average inflation moderated to 5.5% in the first half of 2015, reflecting auctions of securities by the National Bank of Tajikistan and of Treasury bills to reduce liquidity. The Tajik somoni depreciated by about 18% against the US dollar during this period and by 32% against the ruble, even with currency interventions by the National Bank of Tajikistan. While this *Update* retains the inflation forecast in 2015, the forecast is raised to 7.0% for 2016 in view of expected price increases for food and utilities reflecting in part upcoming salary hikes in the public sector. Inflation could accelerate further as a result of gradual depreciation of the Tajik somoni and currency controls that curb production and imports, thereby increasing prices for both domestic and imported goods.

A 32% fall in remittances in the first half of 2015 from the same period in 2014 contributed to a 25% decline in imports, as exports fell by about 8%. The uncertain external environment resulting from continued ruble depreciation and the weakening of the PRC renminbi and Kazakh tenge is expected to affect Tajikistan mainly through remittances, as the Russian Federation and Kazakhstan are the main destinations for Tajik migrant workers, and through external trade, as trade with the Russian Federation, the PRC, and Kazakhstan represented about 60% of all imports and 26% of exports in 2014. Despite the uncertainty, this *Update* retains the *ADO 2015* forecasts for current account deficits in 2015 and 2016, as the decline in imports resulting from lower remittances should offset a possible decline in exports caused by currency depreciation in the PRC and Kazakhstan.

Turkmenistan

Economic growth in the first half of 2015 was reported at 9.1%, lower than in the first half of 2014. Growth was driven by expansion in industry by 6.2%, construction by 12.1%, agriculture by 11.0%, and services by 11.6%. On the demand side, a 7.9% rise in investment was the main driver of growth. For the year as a whole, the decline in global

3.1.6 Selected economic indicators, Tajikistan (%)

	2015		2016	
	ADO 2015	Update	ADO 2015	Update
GDP growth	4.0	3.5	4.8	4.2
Inflation	10.0	10.0	6.5	7.0
Current acct. bal. (share of GDP)	−5.9	−5.9	−4.8	−4.8

Source: ADB estimates.

energy prices is projected to reduce export earnings and somewhat slow the pace of investment. However, strong fiscal and external buffers will help support growth in a difficult external environment. Accordingly, this *Update* slightly reduces the forecast for growth in 2015, but maintains the forecast for slower growth in 2016.

The Central Bank of Turkmenistan moved to limit inflation in the first half of 2015. Despite some food price increases and the devaluation of the Turkmen manat on 1 January 2015, price controls have also restrained inflation. The inflation forecast for 2015 is maintained in light of the pass-through effects of manat devaluation and lower state subsidies for electricity, fuel, and public transportation that will bring marginally higher prices for food, construction materials, services, and public utilities. Inflation in 2016 is expected to moderate slightly, as forecast in *ADO 2015*.

Declining energy prices are expected to reduce export receipts despite a higher volume of gas exports to satisfy gas contracts with the PRC. Under the current scenario of low prices for hydrocarbons, this *Update* maintains the forecast for the current account deficit widening in 2015 and subsequently narrowing in 2016 with some recovery in oil and gas prices.

Uzbekistan

According to government sources, the economy grew by 8.1% in the first half of 2015, the same rate as in the first 6 months of 2014. On the supply side, growth was driven by gains of 8.1% for industry and 13.1% for services. Higher production of construction materials and double-digit growth in light industry boosted total industrial output, while buoyant commercial bank lending and strong demand for information technology spurred growth in services. Agriculture grew by 6.5%, slightly below the 6.9% recorded in 2014, despite unfavorable weather. On the demand side, investment was the main source of growth in the first half, with gross fixed capital formation estimated to have risen by 9.8% over the same period of 2014, as the government continued its development programs. Based on first quarter data, the contribution of net exports to growth is estimated to have declined as external demand remains weak and economic difficulties affect major trading partners. As developments broadly correspond to forecasts made in *ADO 2015*, this *Update* maintains its projected growth rates for 2015 and 2016.

The government reported average monthly inflation in the first half of 2015 at 0.4%, or 4.9% on an annualized basis, which is well within the monetary authority's target range. The trends influencing the consumer price index remain as described in *ADO 2015*: higher government spending and continued depreciation of the local currency partly offset by lower import costs. This *Update* therefore maintains the inflation forecasts for 2015 and 2016.

The government announced an external trade surplus of only $83.4 million in the first half of 2015, or 82% below the $482.1 million trade surplus reported a year earlier. Exports remained weak due to historically low global prices for the country's natural gas, gold, copper, and cotton exports, and to slowdowns in key trading partners: Kazakhstan, the Republic of Korea, and the Russian Federation.

3.1.7 Selected economic indicators, Turkmenistan (%)

	2015		2016	
	ADO 2015	Update	ADO 2015	Update
GDP growth	9.7	9.5	9.2	9.2
Inflation	7.0	7.0	6.5	6.5
Current acct. bal. (share of GDP)	−8.4	−8.4	−6.2	−6.2

Source: ADB estimates.

3.1.8 Selected economic indicators, Uzbekistan (%)

	2015		2016	
	ADO 2015	Update	ADO 2015	Update
GDP growth	7.0	7.0	7.2	7.2
Inflation	9.5	9.5	10.0	10.0
Current acct. bal. (share of GDP)	0.9	0.9	1.1	1.1

Source: ADB estimates.

Cumulative trade with these three partners declined by 18% from the same period in 2014. At the same time, trade with the PRC grew by around 36% year on year, presumably on energy exports. Imports of goods and services declined by 6% from the same period in 2014, mainly because of lower global prices and tighter import controls. As external developments mirror those anticipated in *ADO 2015*, this *Update* maintains the earlier projections for small current account surpluses in 2015 and 2016.

East Asia

Subregional assessment and prospects

Growth faltered in all five East Asian economies in the first half of 2015 except in Hong Kong, China, where it accelerated slightly. The slowdown in the People's Republic of China (PRC) cut the exports of the other four economies, tamping down GDP growth especially in Taipei,China, an important hub in the global supply chain for electronics.

Other factors were also at work. In the Republic of Korea, an outbreak of Middle East respiratory syndrome took its toll on business and consumer sentiment, domestic demand, and industrial production. In Mongolia, investment dropped as foreign direct investment inflows almost dried up and stimulus was partly withdrawn. In Taipei,China, cutbacks on government consumption contributed to the slowdown. Hong Kong, China bucked the trend, however, as private consumption rose sharply, reflecting rising incomes and record employment.

In the PRC, declining investment and industrial production slowed growth in the first half of the year, despite fiscal policy becoming less contractionary, monetary policy remaining accommodative, and the renminbi weakening against the US dollar. Exports fell as recovery remained sluggish in major trade partners, but trade and current account surpluses were up substantially over the same period in 2014 as imports fell because of lower commodity prices and intensified import substitution.

Price pressures remained subdued throughout the subregion as global commodity prices softened. In the PRC, the impact of rising food prices was dampened by declines in other commodity prices and real renminbi appreciation, generating only a small pickup in inflation. Price increases slowed in the Republic of Korea in the first 4 months, but accelerated later as domestic demand recovered. A combination of slowing economic activity and tight monetary policy sharply reduced the inflation rate in Mongolia, which nevertheless remained the highest in the subregion.

Economic growth in East Asia will slow to 6.0% in both 2015 and 2016 (Figure 3.1.4). The growth rate will fall in all the economies in the subregion because of tepid external demand and despite fiscal stimulus in the Republic of Korea and accommodative policies in the PRC. The slowdown in 2015 will be most pronounced in Mongolia, owing to plummeting foreign direct investment, lower agricultural output, and the continuation of tight monetary policy, and in Taipei,China, where exports will be severely hit by the slowdown in

3.1.4 GDP growth, East Asia

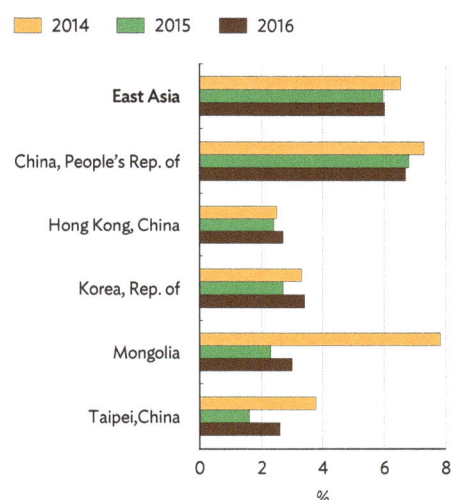

Source: *Asian Development Outlook* database.

the PRC. Assuming 2016 brings a more upbeat economic performance in the advanced economies, growth will be somewhat higher throughout the subregion, except in the PRC. There, a sluggish property sector, decelerating investment growth, and structural reform will initially tamp down growth, but accommodative monetary and fiscal policies and rising external and internal demand are expected to contain the slowdown, with GDP growth falling from a revised 7.3% in 2014 to 6.8% in 2015 and 6.7% in 2016.

Inflation in East Asia will follow a similar pattern as growth, falling to 1.4% in 2015 and rising again to 2.1% in 2016 as it tracks the expected trend in global commodity prices (Figure 3.1.5). In Mongolia, the inflation rate will drop in 2015 and be unchanged in 2016. Taipei,China will record the lowest price increases in East Asia, likely slipping into deflation in 2015 followed by a modest rise in prices in 2016. In the PRC, consumer price inflation is expected to fall to 1.5%, below the *ADO 2015* forecast, as global prices for food and other commodities remain depressed, but will likely rebound slightly in 2016 to 2.2% as those prices start to recover.

On the external front, PRC exports fell in the first half of 2015, as recovery remained sluggish in major trade partners, and imports were lower owing mainly to falling commodity prices and growing import substitution. Trade and current account surpluses were up substantially over the same period in 2014. Net capital outflows pushed the overall balance of payments into a deficit, but gross international reserves remained sizeable. The renminbi weakened against the US dollar, reflecting market trends and a change in August to how the exchange rate is fixed.

The external sectors of the other economies in the subregion suffered from weak demand in the advanced countries and from ongoing rebalancing in the PRC. Nevertheless, current accounts recorded surpluses in Hong Kong, China; the Republic of Korea; and Taipei,China in the first half of 2015. In Mongolia, the only economy in East Asia with a current account deficit, a fall in imports even steeper than for exports narrowed the deficit substantially to equal 6.1% of GDP in the first half of 2015 from 20.1% in the same period last year.

Higher growth expected in the advanced countries should improve East Asia's combined current account, but such optimism is tempered by renewed uncertainty about monetary policy tightening in the US (Figure 3.1.6). In the PRC, foreign trade will likely benefit from accelerating global growth in the forecast period, and trade and current account surpluses will remain stable as global commodity prices recover. In Mongolia, the current account deficit is expected to be narrower than earlier forecast for both 2015 and 2016, but to widen in 2016 on increased imports of equipment for underground development at the Oyu Tolgoi mine. In other economies in the subregion, current account surpluses as percentages of GDP are forecast to rise in 2015, assuming that oil prices stay low, and fall in 2016—except in Taipei,China, where the ratio will fall in 2015 and remain unchanged in 2016. On balance, East Asia's combined current account surplus is projected at 3.3% of GDP in 2015 and 3.1% in 2016, slightly higher than forecast in *ADO 2015*, as slower growth in exports and services receipts is expected to be broadly balanced by a similar trend in import demand.

3.1.5 Inflation, East Asia

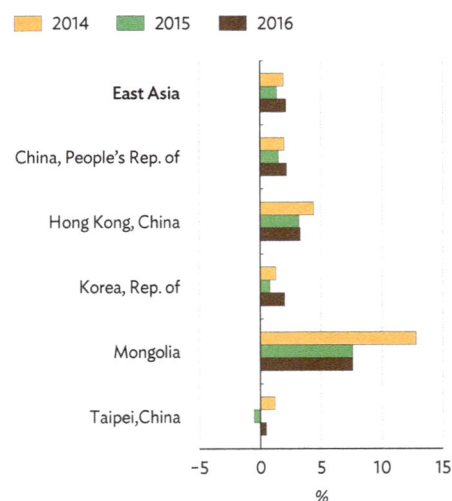

Source: Asian Development Outlook database.

3.1.6 Current account balance, East Asia

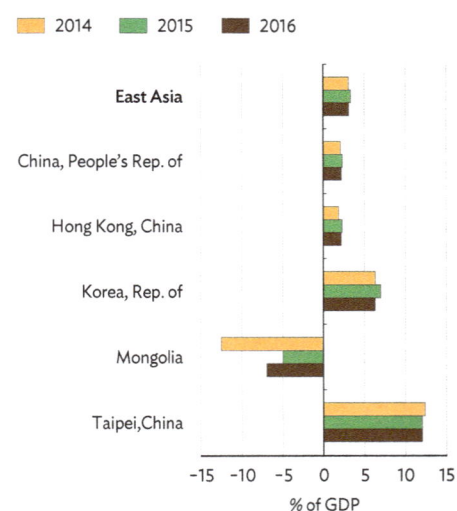

Source: Asian Development Outlook database.

Country highlights

People's Republic of China

Economic growth moderated to 7.0% in the first half of 2015 as industrial and agricultural growth slowed. Services remained the driver of growth, as equity market firms benefited from a stock market boom and correction, and as real estate transactions were lifted by lower mortgage rates and more flexible purchase conditions. On the demand side, the contributions of investment and net exports to GDP growth declined while that of consumption increased as wages rose. Inflation edged up in the first half of the year, but price pressures remained moderate as the impact of rising food prices was dampened by declines in other commodity prices and real renminbi appreciation.

Fiscal policy became more accommodative in the first half of 2015 as the consolidated budget surplus shrank; expenditure growth exceeded the budget target while revenue growth also accelerated but short of its target. Local governments' off-budget expenditures remained substantial, and plans to move them on budget progressed slowly. Monetary policy remained accommodative in the first half of the year with cuts in reserve requirements and benchmark interest rates. The broad money supply (M2) grew faster than nominal GDP, and debt continued to mount. In August, the central bank cut interest rates again in conjunction with other government policies that aimed to halt the fall in equity prices.

The renminbi weakened against the US dollar, reflecting market trends and the change in August to the procedure for fixing the exchange rate. Exports fell as recovery remained sluggish in major trade partners, and imports were lower owing mainly to falling commodity prices and growing import substitution. Trade and current account surpluses were up substantially over the same period in 2014. Net capital outflows pushed the overall balance of payments into a deficit, but gross international reserves remained sizeable.

As the economy has slowed more than expected in the first half of 2015, the growth forecast is revised down from *ADO 2015* for both 2015 and 2016. Export demand, tamped down by delayed recovery in the developed economies, should strengthen over the forecast period as global growth rises, and, together with robust consumption growth, cushion the impact of decelerating investment growth. Consumer price inflation should remain low in 2015 as global prices for food and other commodities remain depressed, but likely rebound slightly in 2016 as those prices start to recover. Inflation forecasts are revised down for 2015 but less so for 2016. Foreign trade will benefit from global growth and trade, but current account surpluses will remain stable as global commodity prices recover.

Fiscal policy is expected to stay broadly unchanged, but lower revenues may push the deficit above the indicative target of 2.7% of GDP in 2015. Further widening of the budget deficit is expected in 2016 as more of local governments' off-budget activities are brought on budget. Monetary policy has to take into account the risks associated with high credit growth, but further interest rate liberalization and lower reserve requirements cannot be ruled out.

3.1.9　Selected economic indicators, People's Republic of China (%)

	2015		2016	
	ADO 2015	Update	ADO 2015	Update
GDP growth	7.2	6.8	7.0	6.7
Inflation	1.8	1.5	2.3	2.2
Current acct. bal. (share of GDP)	2.3	2.3	2.0	2.2

Source: ADB estimates.

The projections are subject to the external upside risk of commodity prices slipping further and the downside risk of economic activity suffering a further setback in the major industrial countries. The recent stock market correction is unlikely to adversely affect consumption, investment, or financial stability. Economic activity is unlikely to be sensitive to wealth effects, as equities comprise only a small part of household wealth, corporate finance, and financial institutions' risk portfolios.

Hong Kong, China

GDP growth reached 2.6% year on year in the first half of 2015, up from 2.4% in the same period last year. Consumption was the engine of growth, contributing 4.2 percentage points and compensating for drag on growth from investment and net exports. Private consumption increased by 5.6% in the first half, brought about by rising income, a record high employment rate, and moderate prices. Gross domestic fixed capital formation grew at 7.0% in the first half of the year as large construction projects in the public sector rebounded significantly, but inventory drawdowns pulled back total investment growth.

The external sector was badly hit by weak demand from the advanced countries and ongoing rebalancing in the PRC, the economy's main trading partner. Exports of goods and services shrank by 2.7% in the second quarter from virtually no growth in the first quarter. Despite a decline in imports, the current account balance recorded a deficit of 0.2% of GDP in the first quarter, compared with a 0.9% deficit in the same quarter of 2014.

Consumer price inflation slowed to an average of 3.5% in January–July from 3.9% in the same period last year. Year on year, inflation in July was the lowest since July 2012. The lower inflation came mainly from the moderation of the increase in housing rentals, and steep drops in electricity, gas, and water tariffs and lower prices for consumer durables, clothing, and footwear.

Capital inflows, partly driven by conversions of offshore renminbi into local dollars, pushed the local currency to the strong end of its convertibility band at HK$7.75 to the US dollar. The Hong Kong Monetary Authority acted as counterparty to banks selling US dollars, purchasing $4.3 billion for the first week of September.

The GDP growth forecast for 2015 is revised down in light of the weak economic performance in the first half of the year; reduced exports, imports, and retail sales in July; and a lower purchasing managers' index in August. Assuming steady improvement in the external environment, the growth rate should rise in 2016 but not as high as the *ADO 2015* forecast. The inflation forecast for 2015 is also pared given falling world commodity prices and the absence of domestic price pressures. Reflecting the slower trade outlook, the current account will remain in surplus but narrow in the next 2 years. The main risks to the forecast include a sharp slowdown in the PRC and large capital outflows if US interest rates rise. On the upside, an unexpectedly bright business outlook for large companies could bode well for investment, while improved consumer confidence could fuel higher consumption and lift the growth rate.

3.1.10 Selected economic indicators, Hong Kong, China (%)

	2015		2016	
	ADO 2015	Update	ADO 2015	Update
GDP growth	2.8	2.4	2.9	2.7
Inflation	3.3	3.2	3.4	3.3
Current acct. bal. (share of GDP)	2.6	2.3	2.5	2.2

Source: ADB estimates.

Republic of Korea

Economic growth weakened to 2.2% year on year in the second quarter of 2015 from 2.5% in the first, as exports declined on slack demand from the PRC, and as an outbreak of Middle East respiratory syndrome (MERS) took its toll on business and consumer sentiment. Domestic demand nevertheless picked up from the first quarter to the second, with private consumption growing by 1.6% in the first half of the year and gross fixed capital formation expanding by 2.5%. GDP grew by 2.3% in the first half.

On the supply side, manufacturing continued to post anemic growth, at 0.5% in the first half, sharply down from 5.1% in the same period last year. Industrial production was hit hard by the soft external demand, dropping by 1.2% in the first half for its worst performance since 2009. The business confidence indicator for manufacturing fell dramatically from 76 in June to 67 in July, reflecting adverse sentiment among domestic- and export-oriented firms alike.

Consumer price index inflation has been below 1.0% since December 2014. After steadily easing to 0.4% in March and April 2015, it rose to 0.5% in May and 0.7% in June to August. Inflation averaged 0.6% in the first 8 months of the year, reflecting the pickup in domestic demand.

Business and consumer sentiment could improve and economic recovery should strengthen with the worst of the MERS outbreak now over, a $20 billion government stimulus package announced in July, and the Bank of Korea policy rate at a record low of 1.5% following two cuts this year, the latest by 25 basis point in June. However, despite further gradual recovery in domestic demand, weakness in external demand will continue to weigh on growth. In particular, growth moderation in the PRC, the biggest export market, will continue to dampen export growth. The GDP growth forecast is thus revised down for this year and next, but remains higher for 2016 as the economy benefits from continuing stimulus measures and more upbeat growth in the advanced economies. Inflation in both years will likewise be lower than anticipated in March, on account of unexpectedly slow recovery in domestic demand. The current account forecasts are unchanged, as slower growth in exports and services receipts than forecast in *ADO 2015* is expected to be balanced by a similar trend in import demand.

Mongolia

Growth decelerated from 7.8% in 2014 to 3.0% in the first half of 2015. Consumption increased by 2.3% over the same period last year, but gross fixed capital formation dropped by 42.7% because foreign direct investment plunged below 1% of GDP and stimulus was partly withdrawn. Exports declined by 4.5% as a 16.3% increase in copper concentrate exports (13.9% by volume) could not compensate for lower volumes and prices for both coal and iron. Net exports expanded, however, as lower foreign direct investment dragged down imports by 30.3%. On the supply side, agricultural growth softened to 9.4% and services grew by 0.3%, but industrial growth remained robust at 12.1% as production at the Oyu Tolgoi copper and gold mine picked up.

Consumer price inflation halved to 6.9% year on year in July 2015 from 14.9% a year earlier, reflecting a slowing economy and monetary

3.1.11 Selected economic indicators, Republic of Korea (%)

	2015		2016	
	ADO 2015	Update	ADO 2015	Update
GDP growth	3.5	2.7	3.7	3.4
Inflation	1.3	0.8	2.1	2.0
Current acct. bal. (share of GDP)	7.0	7.0	6.3	6.3

Source: ADB estimates.

policy tightened to contain inflation and pressure on the balance of payments. Nonperforming loans reached 5.0% of outstanding loans, and loans past due reached 6.1%, highlighting the need for continued close supervision of the financial sector.

Government revenues decreased by 5.5% in the first 7 months as value-added tax receipts and nontax revenue fell. In the first half of the year, the structural deficit was kept on par with the ceiling for 2015 equal to 5.0% of GDP, while the more important consolidated deficit—including all Development Bank of Mongolia expenditures—remained largely unchanged at more than 8% of GDP. To provide a safety margin that aligns with prudent fiscal policy, the authorities need to move quickly to adopt a credible supplementary budget.

The current account deficit narrowed sharply to 6.1% of GDP in the first half of 2015 from 20.1% in the same period last year as the goods and services balance improved. In the first 7 months, gross international reserves recovered by $0.4 billion to $1.7 billion and the togrog depreciation against the US dollar was limited to a modest 5.1%, albeit at the cost of higher external debt.

The growth forecast is lowered for 2015 and 2016, reflecting a deteriorating external environment, drought-affected harvests, necessarily tight monetary and fiscal policies, and, on the positive side, the start of underground works at Oyu Tolgoi in mid-2016. Average inflation will be lower this year than forecast in *ADO 2015*, and supply-side factors will hold inflation steady in 2016. The current account deficit will narrow more than forecast earlier but widen again in 2016 on imports for Oyu Tolgoi development. Although the poverty rate improved to 21.6% in 2014 from 27.4% in 2012, many people remain vulnerable, as does the economy as a whole, to risks stemming from downward pressure on commodity prices, fluctuating production expected from Oyu Tolgoi and other mines, severe weather that affects crops and livestock, and uncertainty regarding the authorities' success in maintaining tight macroeconomic policies.

Taipei,China

GDP grew by only 2.1% in the first half of 2015 owing to substantial export contraction that reflected the slowdown in the PRC, as well as only a modest rise in domestic demand. Despite a slowdown in tourist arrivals, especially from the PRC, private consumption advanced by 3.2%, stimulated by lower prices and rising wages and employment. Meanwhile, government consumption contracted by 1.0% in line with the objective of narrowing the fiscal deficit. In its July 2015 meeting, the central bank left the discount rate unchanged at 1.875%, where it has been for almost 4 years, but relaxed mortgage loan-to-value restrictions to aid the property market.

The GDP growth forecast for 2015 is revised down because the contraction in export orders, by 3.7% in the second quarter to the lowest level since the same quarter in 2013, is likely to weigh heavily on exports and investment this year, and because signs of declining consumer confidence could tamp down domestic demand. The growth forecast for 2016 is also revised down as continued softness in world demand, especially from the PRC, cannot be discounted, and as the economic

3.1.12 Selected economic indicators, Mongolia (%)

	2015		2016	
	ADO 2015	Update	ADO 2015	Update
GDP growth	3.0	2.3	5.0	3.0
Inflation	8.9	7.6	7.7	7.6
Current acct. bal. (share of GDP)	–8.0	–5.0	–15.0	–7.0

Source: ADB estimates.

3.1.13 Selected economic indicators, Taipei,China (%)

	2015		2016	
	ADO 2015	Update	ADO 2015	Update
GDP growth	3.7	1.6	3.6	2.6
Inflation	0.5	–0.5	1.0	0.5
Current acct. bal. (share of GDP)	12.5	12.0	13.0	12.0

Source: ADB estimates.

impact of measures to support industrial and export growth announced by the government in August 2015 have yet to take effect.

Average headline consumer inflation during the first 8 months of the year crossed to negative as prices for vegetables, fuel, lubricants, gas, and electricity softened to bring deflation by 0.6% from a year earlier. This outcome and global oil prices that are stabilizing and expected to remain low in 2016 prompt lower forecasts for consumer price inflation in both 2015 and 2016.

The current account surplus grew to 14.7% of GDP in the first half of 2015. Merchandise exports declined by 7.0% year on year, but lower oil prices reduced the import bill. A smaller ratio of surplus to GDP is expected in the second half of the year, assuming that oil prices stay low and external demand, particularly from the PRC, weakens further. The forecast for the current account surplus is revised down for both 2015 and 2016.

The main risks to the outlook include a slowdown in the PRC that is steeper than expected and stiffening competition in electronics. Domestic demand could weaken further because of falling equity and property prices. On the upside, the government may respond to the sharp slowdown by introducing additional measures ahead of the 2016 presidential and parliamentary elections.

South Asia

Subregional assessment and prospects

This *Update* lowers the growth forecast for South Asia to 6.9% in 2015 from 7.2% published in *ADO 2015*, and to 7.3% in 2016 from 7.6% (Figure 3.1.7). The downward adjustment mainly reflects more modest growth acceleration in India, for which growth forecasts are trimmed by 0.4 percentage points to 7.4% in 2015 and 7.8% in 2016. The slower expansion in India is due to unexpectedly sluggish growth in the major industrial economies, flagging global trade, and parliamentary deadlock stalling action on structural reform. Exports have disappointed expectations in several South Asian economies in 2015. This drag on growth is offset in Bangladesh and Pakistan by strong domestic demand, but weak outcomes trim growth forecasts in the Maldives, because of tourism. In Nepal, the catastrophic earthquake in April that caused great loss of life and extensive devastation to property and other infrastructure was a major setback for the economy. A rebuilding effort supported by pledges from development partners will help the economy regain momentum in 2016, though rebuilding damaged infrastructure and other facilities will likely take 5 years. Forecasts for 2016 see all South Asian economies, except the Maldives, modestly improving on 2015 growth rates, even as growth in the industrial economies is expected to remain tepid and in global trade flows subdued.

Inflationary pressures have substantially eased during 2015 because of the marked fall in global prices for crude oil and food. The *ADO 2015* inflation forecast for South Asia took these developments into account but is now revised down by 10 basis points to 5.0% in 2015 and 5.5%

3.1.7 GDP growth, South Asia

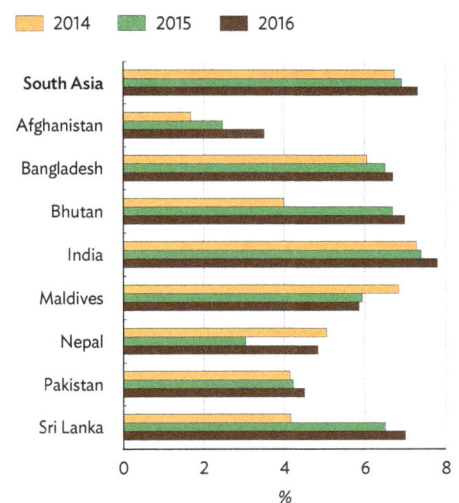

Source: *Asian Development Outlook* database.

in 2016 (Figure 3.1.8). The 2015 expected outcome is well below the
6.2% recorded in 2014. In fact, all countries in the subregion are seeing
inflation well below that of a year ago, but it remains higher than in
most other subregions in developing Asia. With a modest increase in
global oil prices expected in 2016 and essentially stable food prices,
inflation in South Asia is forecast to increase by only 0.5 percentage
points. All countries will again experience relatively moderate inflation,
but in Nepal a weak monsoon and transportation bottlenecks will push
inflation notably higher. As countries in South Asia are substantial oil
importers, the sharp reduction in oil prices has not only brought lower
inflation but also allowed the countries that maintain fuel subsidies to
reduce this fiscal burden by adjusting prices judiciously and by raising
fuel taxes.

The combined current account deficit for South Asia is forecast
at 1.1% of aggregate GDP in 2015 and 1.5% in 2016. Most countries
will have moderate current account deficits equal to less than 1.5%
of GDP in 2016 (Figure 3.1.9). However, Bhutan has a large deficit
because of imports for constructing large hydropower projects that
will export electricity to India. The Maldives deficit is smaller but
still substantial and reflects imports to construct resorts and other
infrastructure. In Nepal, the usual current account surplus from large
worker remittances is expected to turn into a small deficit in 2016
because of large imports for earthquake reconstruction. Bangladesh,
India, Pakistan, and Sri Lanka have experienced weak external demand
in 2015 and slow growth or declines in exports. However, the sharp
fall in oil prices has steeply reduced import costs to offset in large part
the fall in export sales and so constrained deterioration in the current
account deficit—except in Sri Lanka. There, a large increase in consumer
goods imports has pushed the current account deficit higher than in
the other three countries. In 2016, the expected continuation of weak
external demand will again be masked by a modest increase in oil
imports and favorable prices for food and other commodities.

Country highlights

Afghanistan

Economic activity remained slow in the first half of 2015. Investor and
consumer confidence was low as the political and security situation
worsened and the National Unity Government struggled to deliver on
anticipated reforms. Agriculture production is projected to be slightly
higher than in 2014, based on initial estimates, with good harvests
of wheat, fruit, and vegetables. Construction, trade, and services
remained depressed. Foreign direct investment declined by 30% in the
first half of the year, according to the Afghanistan Investment Support
Agency. Moreover, a business tendency survey released in August
by the Afghanistan Chamber of Commerce and Industry indicated
that business conditions deteriorated substantially from January to
June 2015.

The monthly headline consumer price index fell by 2.8% in June 2015
from a year earlier, reversing an increase of 5.6% in the year before.

3.1.8 Inflation, South Asia

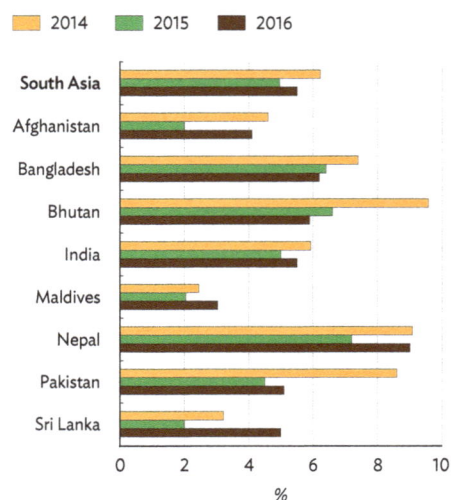

Source: Asian Development Outlook database.

3.1.9 Current account balance, South Asia

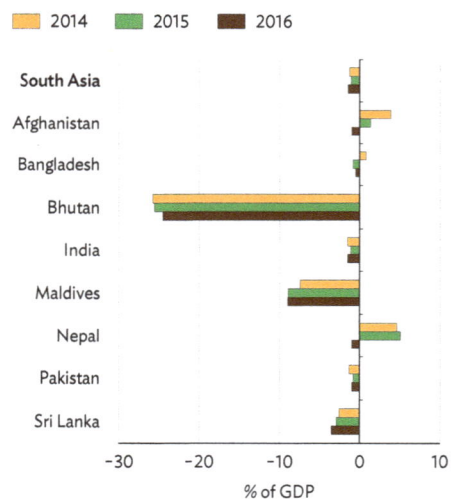

Source: Asian Development Outlook database.

The food price index dropped by 3.3% in June 2015, an even steeper reversal from the 9.7% increase in June 2014, mainly because the prices of vegetables, cooking oil, bread, and cereals were all sharply down. The nonfood index declined by 2.2%—compared with an earlier 1.2% increase. This mainly reflected the continuing decline in housing and transportation service prices.

The afghani depreciated by 5.7% against the dollar from January to June 2015, continuing a declining trend since 2011. Declining capital inflow, rising capital outflow, and flagging demand for afghanis during the period amounted to downward pressure on the currency from weakening political and security situations.

This *Update* maintains the growth forecasts for 2015 and 2016, assuming that business gains momentum in the second half of 2015. Government policy reform, better execution of the development budget, and stronger performance in manufacturing are expected to drive growth. Despite problems at the start of the year, subsequent months saw positive political developments such as the full appointment of the cabinet and two rounds of peace talks hosted by neighboring countries.

This *Update* maintains the *ADO 2015* forecasts for the current account balance including grants. Considering domestic price developments to June 2015 and the expected continuation of favorable global commodity prices, the forecast for average inflation is revised much lower for 2015 and little changed for 2016.

Bangladesh

The provisional estimate for GDP growth in FY2015 (ended 30 June 2015) is higher than the 6.1% recorded in FY2014 and projected in *ADO 2015*. Despite political agitation early in 2015 that adversely affected transport services, exports, and private investment, growth held up well because of brisk domestic demand, boosted by higher worker remittances, private sector wages, and public investment. The GDP growth forecast for FY2016 is revised somewhat higher still with the expectation that exports will grow with continued economic recovery in the US and the euro area, strong expansion in remittances will boost consumption demand, private and public investment will pick up as the business climate improves under a stabilizing political situation, and spending will increase under the annual development program.

Inflation moderated in FY2015 much as forecast in *ADO 2015* from 7.4% a year earlier, reflecting large public stocks of food grains, normal weather, a supportive monetary policy, and lower global food and commodity prices that a steady exchange rate allowed to passed through. This *Update* retains the *ADO 2015* projection for average inflation in FY2016, which matches the central bank's monetary policy statement. Although higher public sector wages and upward adjustments to administered prices for natural gas and electricity from 1 September 2015 will exert inflationary pressure, the easing of supply constraints, a cautious monetary policy, and a better crop outlook should keep inflation in check.

Export growth was 3.3% in FY2015, down significantly from 12.1% in FY2014. Garments—accounting for about 80% of total exports— grew slowly by 4.1%, reflecting supply chains disrupted by political

3.1.14 Selected economic indicators, Afghanistan (%)

	2015		2016	
	ADO 2015	Update	ADO 2015	Update
GDP growth	2.5	2.5	3.5	3.5
Inflation	5.0	2.0	5.0	4.1
Current acct. bal. (share of GDP)	1.4	1.4	-1.0	-1.0

Source: ADB estimates.

3.1.15 Selected economic indicators, Bangladesh (%)

	2015		2016	
	ADO 2015	Update	ADO 2015	Update
GDP growth	6.1	6.5	6.4	6.7
Inflation	6.5	6.4	6.2	6.2
Current acct. bal. (share of GDP)	-0.5	-0.8	0.5	-0.5

Source: ADB estimates.

demonstrations in early 2015, soft demand from the European Union and the US, and a marked decline in prices for cotton, a major input cost that can affect pricing. Imports rose by 11.2%, accelerating from 8.9% growth in FY2014. Larger imports of food grains, machinery, fertilizer, and industrial raw materials helped to propel the expansion. As exports grew significantly more slowly than imports, the trade deficit widened markedly. Despite a strong recovery in remittances, the current account recorded a small deficit slightly higher than the *ADO 2015* forecast. Export growth in FY2016 is projected to improve to 6.0% as economic growth in the euro area and the US strengthens. Imports are projected to increase by 13.0%, mainly for capital goods, industrial raw materials, and food grains. Despite the expansion in remittances, the larger trade deficit will likely mean a current account deficit narrower than in FY2015 but failing to achieve the small surplus projected in *ADO 2015*.

Bhutan

The GDP growth forecast for FY2015 (ended 30 June 2015) is revised slightly downward as industry growth was lower than expected. Sales of electricity were lower than in the previous year, despite higher hydropower production. Construction of the five major hydropower stations continued, but delays caused by geological and construction difficulties have pushed back scheduled completion by some months. Growth in services accelerated, but it did not fully offset the shortfall in industry. Export sales of major industries improved somewhat, while bank lending picked up with the removal of the credit restrictions in September 2014. Tourism performed strongly, as expected, with growth in arrivals at over 30%, much higher than in the previous 2 years. Government budget spending for FY2015 was revised slightly upward, reflecting increases in public sector wages and benefits and greater spending on crop intensification projects that should help boost agricultural production and consumption. The economy is set to expand in FY2016 as projected.

Inflation trended downward during most of FY2015, as food prices fell with increased domestic supply and declining prices for food imports from India—a trend broadly in line with global food markets. Food inflation eased to single-digits after it peaked at nearly 14% in FY2014, and nonfood inflation remained mostly stable. Reductions in fuel prices and declining housing rents helped to offset price pressures from increases in domestic power tariffs and vehicle taxes. Inflation in FY2015 was slightly lower than forecast. Notwithstanding upside pressures from increased government spending and wages, inflation is expected to ease further in FY2016 as harvests improve, world and domestic food prices remain low, and regulated fuel prices are unlikely to increase.

The current account deficit is projected to be a quarter of GDP in FY2015 and FY2016, lower than projected in *ADO 2015* but still high. Hydropower-related imports will slow toward the end of the government's Eleventh Five Year Plan, FY2014–FY2018, when most of the major stations near completion. Trade other than in hydropower will benefit from low oil prices, but the deficit will continue to reflect

3.1.16 Selected economic indicators, Bhutan (%)

	2015		2016	
	ADO 2015	Update	ADO 2015	Update
GDP growth	6.8	6.7	7.0	7.0
Inflation	7.0	6.6	6.8	5.9
Current acct. bal. (share of GDP)	−30.6	−25.6	−30.6	−24.6

Source: ADB estimates.

large private imports and lackluster exports other than hydropower. Sufficient capital and financial flows from funds tied to projects will help keep the overall balance in surplus and international reserves adequate. Risks of renewed liquidity pressures would arise if recently adopted demand-management policies are not maintained.

India

GDP growth slowed to 7.0% in the first quarter of FY2015 (ending 31 March 2016) from 7.5% in the last quarter of FY2014. The deceleration was broad-based, with private consumption, manufacturing, and services all experiencing slower growth. However, expansion in fixed investment picked up to 4.9% from 4.1% in the previous quarter, indicating a continuing gradual recovery in capital expenditure. Agriculture grew by 1.9%, but monsoon rainfall that has been 12% below normal crimped the summer crop planted area. Low global oil prices, a positive base effect, and tight monetary policy kept consumer price inflation benign at an average of 4.8% in the first 4 months of FY2015. Core inflation has trended downward for nearly 2 years and now hovers just above 4%.

The current account deficit in the first quarter of FY2015 improved to 1.2% of GDP from 1.6% a year earlier, helped by moderate monthly trade deficits and lower net outflows from the primary income account. The trade deficit benefited from a 12.1% fall in imports that reflected mainly the sharp fall in oil prices. Exports, which are substantially smaller than imports, contracted by 16.7% as sales of refined petroleum products, a major export, dropped by 53.1%. Other exports fell by 7.2% on lackluster demand in key markets.

The weak monsoon, flagging external demand, and stalled parliamentary action on structural reforms, including a revamped domestic tax system and eased restrictions on land acquisition and labor, are expected to slow the economy. With growth in the industrial economies falling short of earlier assumptions, growth forecasts are revised down for both FY2015 and FY2016. Consumer inflation is likely to remain within the central bank and government target of 4% ±2 percentage points. The inflation forecast remains in line with the forecast in *ADO 2015*, while an uptick in prices for commodities, including crude oil, is expected to boost inflation in FY2016.

With the projected 37% decline in the average crude oil price, the import bill is expected to shrink by about 10% in FY2015. The slump in exports in the first quarter is likely to continue with listless global demand and a drop in exports of refined oil products. On balance, the current account deficit in FY2015 is expected to be significantly narrower than in recent years. Some recovery in oil prices and improved demand for industry and investment will likely push import growth to 8.0% in FY2016. Exports are also likely to recover, growing by 3.5% as higher petroleum prices boost the value of exports of refined petroleum products and as external demand improves. Accordingly, the current account deficit is expected to widen marginally in FY2016.

3.1.17 Selected economic indicators, India (%)

	2015		2016	
	ADO 2015	Update	ADO 2015	Update
GDP growth	7.8	7.4	8.2	7.8
Inflation	5.0	5.0	5.5	5.5
Current acct. bal. (share of GDP)	-1.1	-1.1	-1.5	-1.5

Source: ADB estimates.

Maldives

Tourism growth in the Maldives in the first half of this year was much slower than expected, increasing by only 1.3% against 11.5% in the previous year, despite upbeat tourist arrivals globally and in Asia. Occupancy fell by 4.2%, compared with growth at 6% in 2014. Even assuming recovery in the second half and the October peak season, annual tourism growth would still be lower than assumed in *ADO 2015*. An intensified government-supported marketing campaign aims to foster a recovery that could sustain higher arrivals next year. Improved economic prospects in Europe may also help offset the effects of a marked slowdown in arrivals from the People's Republic of China, which in recent years have buoyed tourism. Construction grew more strongly than expected during the first half, with related imports growing by nearly 42% and bank credit to the industry rising by about 40%. Robust construction is likely to continue in light of the large infrastructure projects now under way and the increase in public capital spending budgeted for this year and 2016. On balance, the forecast for growth is trimmed for 2015. A revival in tourism and sustained construction and infrastructure spending at a pace higher than expected will likely extend this year's growth rate to 2016, which is an upgrade from the earlier projection.

Monthly inflation in Malé, the capital, remained low at less than 2.0%, aided by the continued decline in global food and fuel prices and low domestic fish prices during the first half of 2015. This *Update* now expects inflation in 2015 to be slightly lower than the March forecast before it picks up in 2016 as world prices advance moderately.

The current account deficit is now expected to widen in 2015 and 2016 more than previously anticipated. The deficit is expected to be higher because of unexpectedly large imports for construction, lower retained earnings from tourism, stronger domestic demand, and some increase in the prices of oil and consumer goods.

High public debt is a significant issue given the high volatility of earnings from tourism, even though the fiscal deficit has recently narrowed from the double digits. Debt sustainability is a risk because of plans to massively scale up public capital investment over the next 3 years, at least 30% financed through loans, and the demonstrated difficulty of cutting back current spending.

Nepal

The catastrophic 7.8 magnitude earthquake on 25 April and its aftershocks are estimated to have slashed GDP growth in FY2015 (ended 15 July 2015) by over 1.5 percentage points from the 4.6% *ADO 2015* projection a month before. Although the earthquake struck Nepal in the 10th month of FY2015, the impact on growth seems to be sizable, especially on the large services sector, which is now estimated to have grown by only 3.9%, compared with 6.0% forecast in the scenario with no earthquake. Inflation in FY2015 was below forecast as food and other prices moderated under good supply and lower fuel prices in the first 3 quarters of the year.

The deceleration of remittance inflows from Nepal's many overseas workers in the first 3 quarters of FY2015 initially weakened the external

3.1.18 Selected economic indicators, Maldives (%)

	2015		2016	
	ADO 2015	Update 2015	ADO 2015	Update 2015
GDP growth	6.3	5.9	5.1	5.9
Inflation	3.0	1.6	2.5	2.5
Current acct. bal. (share of GDP)	–6.3	–8.9	–6.1	–9.0

Source: ADB estimates.

3.1.19 Selected economic indicators, Nepal (%)

	2015		2016	
	ADO 2015	Update 2015	ADO 2015	Update 2015
GDP growth	4.6	3.0	5.1	4.8
Inflation	7.7	7.2	7.3	9.0
Current acct. bal. (share of GDP)	2.7	5.1	3.5	–1.0

Source: ADB estimates.

position, but the surge in transfers in the last quarter in response to needs created by the earthquake, and the slowdown in imports immediately after the earthquake, fueled a robust current account surplus.

In FY2016, a subpar monsoon will constrain agriculture growth, while the expected delay in getting reconstruction started, coupled with economic dislocation and damage to infrastructure, will curtail industry and services growth. Accordingly, GDP growth will likely be held moderately below the *ADO 2015* projection. In FY2016, inflation is expected much higher as price pressures mount owing to the expected drop in the agricultural harvest, higher demand as the pace of reconstruction picks up, and persistent supply bottlenecks. Larger imports combined with a more normal increase in remittances will likely push the current account into a small deficit.

Underspending of the budget has been a persistent problem, especially in capital spending, for which just 70% of planned expenditure is generally realized. The government's capacity for expenditure has to be drastically enhanced to ensure that reconstruction is fast and efficient. The total cost of recovery from the earthquake is estimated at about $7.1 billion (a third of GDP), about $5.2 billion to repair damage to buildings and infrastructure and the balance to cover economic losses from forgone income. Development partners have pledged about $4 billion in grants and concessional loans, to be disbursed over 5 years. Allocations for reconstruction are about $910 million in FY2016. The government is simplifying procedures for capital spending and has established the National Reconstruction Authority to speed implementation. Even with a modest increase in borrowing to finance reconstruction projects, fiscal sustainability is likely to be maintained.

Pakistan

Provisional GDP growth in FY2015 (ended 30 June 2015) matched the *ADO 2015* forecast. It was led by services as growth in manufacturing slowed. Industrial growth was hobbled by a slowdown in large-scale manufacturing to 3.3% owing to continued power shortages and weaker external demand. The resilience of small-scale manufacturing and construction sustained industrial growth at 3.6%. Agriculture growth remained modest at 2.9%. Private fixed investment slipped to equal 9.7% of GDP from 10.0% a year earlier because of continuing energy constraints and the generally weak business environment that has depressed investment for several years. GDP growth is expected to edge up to 4.5% in FY2016, assuming continued low prices for oil and other commodities, the expected pickup in growth in the advanced economies, and some alleviation of power shortages. Prospects for large-scale manufacturing remain subject to progress on power supply. Plans to build an economic corridor linking Kashgar in the PRC to the Pakistani port of Gwadar were announced in April, and this megaproject could significantly boost private investment and growth in the coming years.

Headline inflation sharply declined in FY2015 and improved on the *ADO 2015* projection. Inflation for both food and other items dropped significantly, reflecting adequate food supplies and the transmission into domestic prices of lower global prices for oil and other commodities.

3.1.20 Selected economic indicators, Pakistan (%)

	2015		2016	
	ADO 2015	Update	ADO 2015	Update
GDP growth	4.2	4.2	4.5	4.5
Inflation	5.8	4.5	5.8	5.1
Current acct. bal. (share of GDP)	−1.0	−0.8	−1.3	−1.0

Source: ADB estimates.

Inflation is now expected to be slightly higher in FY2016 than in FY2015 as oil prices recover. This *Update* sees lower inflation than forecast earlier, but inflationary pressures may come from food prices pushed higher by possible supply shortages following floods in July 2015. Monetary policy is expected to remain supportive.

The current account deficit narrowed in FY2015 from 1.3% in FY2014. The reasons were lower oil imports (which had been 35% of the total), larger inflows under the Coalition Support Fund, and robust workers' remittances. The benefit of the 18% decline in expenditures on oil imports was offset to some extent by increased imports of machinery and metal products, as well as of food and transport equipment. In FY2016, the current account deficit is expected to widen marginally as slightly higher oil prices and stronger growth in the advanced countries translates into an expansion in trade. Nevertheless, exports are expected to increase only slightly after 2 years of stagnation, as manufacturing continues to suffer under energy shortages and low cotton prices see only a modest increase.

Sri Lanka

The economy grew by 4.4% in the first quarter of 2015 and 6.7% in the second quarter (base year 2010). As expected in *ADO 2015*, the election in January of a new president and the change in government, as well as the prospect of parliamentary elections later in the year, slowed activity as investors adopted a wait and see approach. Notably, construction, which had driven growth for the previous 5 years, declined markedly in the first half of the year from the period a year earlier. Offsetting this in part, robust spending in consumption-related sectors such as wholesale and retail trade sustained relatively strong growth. The parliamentary elections on 17 August substantially expanded the majority of the new government's coalition. With political uncertainties diminished, private sector investment is expected to revive, as assumed earlier. Revisions to national accounting required that GDP growth projections be revised (Box 3.1.2).

Inflation slowed markedly, and Sri Lanka experienced deflation in July and August, with the consumer price index recording each month a 0.2% contraction year on year. Food inflation that was 12.0% in December 2014 fell to 2.5% in August, and the nonfood component has been deflationary since the last quarter of 2014, largely due to lower administered fuel prices. Reflecting declines in food and fuel prices, inflation in August averaged only 1.0% over the preceding 12-month period while core inflation stood at 3.9%. With price developments unfolding largely as expected, the *ADO 2015* inflation forecasts are maintained, with inflation rebounding in 2016.

Exports fell by 0.6% over the first half of 2015 from the same period last year, rather than improving as expected in *ADO 2015*, while imports grew by 5.7%, higher than expected. Export performance was affected by declining exports of textiles and garments to the European Union, a ban on seafood exports to that market from January 2015, and poor performance in tea production. Rapid import growth was driven mainly by goods for consumers and investment (in particular transport equipment now with a lowered tariff), despite a marked decline in fuel

3.1.21 Selected economic indicators, Sri Lanka (%)

	2015		2016	
	ADO 2015	Update	ADO 2015	Update
GDP growth	...	6.3	...	7.0
Inflation	2.0	2.0	5.0	5.0
Current acct. bal. (share of GDP)	...	-2.9	...	-3.6

Note: In light of Sri Lanka's revisions to the GDP series in July 2015, the *ADO 2015* forecasts for GDP growth and current account balance as a share of GDP are not comparable with current estimates and have been omitted.

Source: ADB estimates.

3.1.2 Rebasing national accounts

In 2015, Sri Lanka rebased its national accounts from 2002 to 2010. Together with the rebasing, several other improvements were introduced to the compiling of national accounts. These included adopting the United Nations System of National Accounts 2008 revision, the International Standard of Industry Classification version 4, and the Central Product Classification version 2, recommended by the United Nations. The production boundary has been expanded to include economic activities that were not fully captured under the previous system, such as private education, private health services, and legal services. Household economic activities are brought into the national accounts using the labor input method, which captures value created through services

such as architecture and beauty shops, among other household activities.

Rebasing and the other changes enlarged the measured size of the economy in 2010 by 14.4% over the previous GDP series. The difference was 5.2% for 2014. The structure of the economy also changed with a shift toward services, which increased their share from 54.1% of GDP to 56.5% in the first quarter of 2015, while the share of agriculture declined from 13.3% to 7.8% and of industry from 32.6% to 28.7%. A new revision policy has been introduced, allowing a 3-year period to update data that may not have been available when the new national accounts were released.

imports from lower global oil prices. Remittances expanded marginally by 2.2%, while earnings from tourism grew by 14.0%. Reflecting weakening in the current and financial accounts, the overall balance recorded a deficit of $792 million, and gross official reserves fell at the end of June to $7.5 billion, which is cover for 4.5 months of imports. The current account deficit, as revised to accommodate the rebasing of the national accounts, is expected to expand in 2016.

Southeast Asia

Subregional assessment and prospects

The projected recovery in growth is delayed. Aggregate GDP growth this year is now seen unchanged from 2014 at 4.4%, for a half percentage point reduction in the forecast from *ADO 2015*. Stronger growth is expected for the subregion in 2016, led by Indonesia and Thailand, the biggest economies in this group (Figure 3.1.10).

Forecasts for growth in 2015 are lowered from March for 6 of the 10 member economies of the Association of Southeast Asian Nations (ASEAN): Cambodia, Indonesia, the Lao People's Democratic Republic (Lao PDR), the Philippines, Singapore, and Thailand. By contrast, growth in Viet Nam, benefiting from a recovery in private consumption and buoyant foreign direct investment, is stronger than previously anticipated. Malaysia and Myanmar appear on track to meet *ADO 2015* growth forecasts, and Brunei Darussalam still looks likely to contract on weakness in oil and gas.

Unexpectedly weak demand this year from major export markets in the large industrial economies and in much of Asia, including the PRC, accounts for some of the downward revision to growth forecasts. Soft global demand and falling prices for oil and other commodities have hurt exports in several subregional economies, including Brunei Darussalam and Malaysia.

3.1.10 GDP growth, Southeast Asia

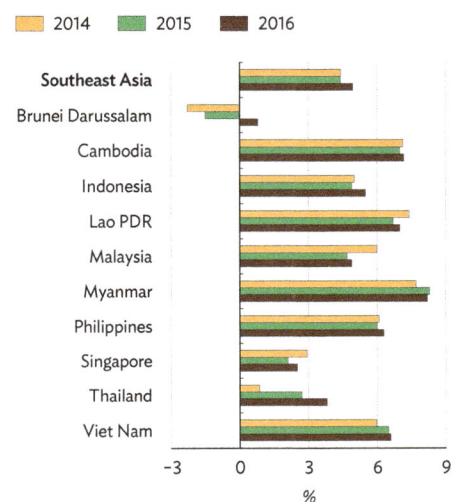

Lao PDR = Lao People's Democratic Republic.
Source: Asian Development Outlook database.

In Indonesia and the Philippines, planned increases in infrastructure investment have fallen behind schedule. The Government of Indonesia boosted its infrastructure budget for 2015, but only 10% was disbursed in the first half. Public construction in the Philippines fell early in the year before it rebounded. Public fixed investment in Malaysia has declined for a second straight year as public projects reached completion and fiscal spending tightened. Thailand has ramped up public fixed investment this year from low levels in 2014 when there were political disruptions, but disbursement still lags the target.

Private consumption across the subregion has held up relatively well, helped by growth in employment and low inflation. In the Philippines, higher remittances are key to consumption. Government cash transfers have supported private consumption in Indonesia and Malaysia. Household spending in Thailand, though, has been hit by slow growth in wages, high household debt, and lower farm incomes caused by drought and weak prices for agricultural commodities. Indeed, drought in several countries, and floods in Myanmar, have hurt agriculture and rural incomes.

Governments are rolling out fiscal stimulus packages in some economies, including Thailand and Indonesia, to spur growth. On the monetary side, interest rates were cut in Indonesia in February 2015, in Thailand in both March and April, and in the Lao PDR in August. Singapore eased monetary policy in January when it reduced the pace of appreciation for the Singapore dollar in terms of its nominal effective exchange rate and Viet Nam has relaxed some macroprudential measures.

Growth in Southeast Asia is forecast to rebound by half a percentage point to 4.9% in 2016, the inaugural year of the ASEAN Economic Community, mainly on expectations of better exports and public investment. The 2016 growth forecast is trimmed from *ADO 2015* because the global outlook has dimmed somewhat since March.

In Indonesia, growth will benefit next year from the government's push to accelerate its disbursement of funds for capital spending and from policy reform. Thailand plans to start several large infrastructure projects in 2016. Infrastructure investment in the Philippines has picked up and election-related spending will provide additional lift through May 2016. Fiscal policy in Viet Nam is seen to be supportive of growth, though it could tighten over concerns about rising public debt.

Inflation in most economies is milder than projected in March, prompting downward revisions to 2015 forecasts for seven economies in the subregion. Lower oil prices and relatively stable food prices have tamed inflation in most economies. In four economies inflation is forecast at 2.0% or less, and in another three—Brunei Darussalam, Singapore, and Thailand—consumer price indexes will likely decline over 2015. The subregional forecast for inflation at 3.0% in 2015 is down only marginally from *ADO 2015* because upward pressure on prices in Indonesia remains stubbornly strong. Inflation is high in Myanmar, too. Still, subregional inflation this year looks set to decelerate by more than 1 percentage point from 2014 (Figure 3.1.11).

For next year, an upward revision to Indonesia's inflation forecast more than offsets downward revisions for four others. As a result,

3.1.11 Inflation, Southeast Asia

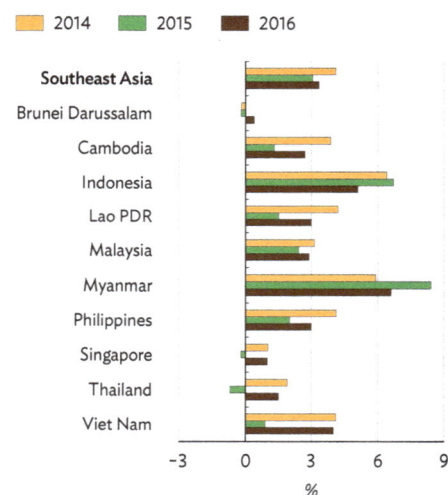

Lao PDR = Lao People's Democratic Republic.
Source: Asian Development Outlook database.

subregional inflation is expected to edge up to 3.3%, slightly above the earlier forecast. The depreciation of Southeast Asian currencies against the US dollar this year will put some upward pressure on prices of imports. Inflation could be higher than anticipated if current El Niño effects become severe.

Currency depreciation against the strengthening US dollar accelerated in August when the PRC devalued the renminbi. Sharp depreciation was recorded for the Indonesian rupiah, by 13.7% against the US dollar from the start of this year to early September, and for the Malaysian ringgit, which depreciated by 16.5% in that period. The State Bank of Viet Nam, aiming to support the country's international competitiveness, devalued the dong against the US dollar three times in the first 8 months of 2015.

This *Update* trims the projection for Southeast Asia's current account surplus this year to 3.0% of subregional GDP (Figure 3.1.12). Merchandise export receipts declined for much of the subregion in the first half owing to soft external demand and, for commodity and hydrocarbon producers, plunging global prices. But imports also dropped, in some cases more sharply than exports, due to lower prices for imported oil, currency depreciation, subdued investment, and reduced demand from export industries for imported inputs.

Forecasts of current account surpluses in 2015 are revised up for Singapore and Thailand, while current account deficits are now seen to narrow more than previously anticipated in Cambodia, Indonesia, and the Lao PDR. In Brunei Darussalam, Malaysia, the Philippines, and Viet Nam, however, current account surpluses will likely be smaller than expected in March. For 2016, the aggregate current account surplus is seen narrowing to 2.7% of GDP, largely because expected stronger investment in Thailand will push up imports of capital equipment and shrink its current account surplus.

Brunei Darussalam

Low prices and subdued production of oil and natural gas have weighed on the economy, which relies directly on hydrocarbons for almost two-thirds of GDP. Hydrocarbon production has declined over several years owing to the depletion of oil and gas fields, protracted closures to refurbish aging equipment, and government policy to manage hydrocarbon production so that it lasts until other industries can generate a larger share of GDP. Rebased data for 2014 show that oil and gas mining contracted by 2.6%, and the associated manufacture of liquefied natural gas (LNG) and methanol fell by 7.5%. The economy outside of hydrocarbons also contracted, by 0.4%, and investment fell. These developments caused GDP to contract by 2.3% in 2014.

Data for the first 6 months of 2015 show further slight year-on-year declines in export volumes of crude oil, by 0.6%, and LNG, by 0.9%. This suggests that production remained subdued, though there were signs of a pickup in exports in May and June. Prices received for oil and LNG plunged by about 45% between June 2014 and June 2015. Consequently, the value of total merchandise exports dropped by 37% in US dollar terms in the first half. Sharply lower export earnings against a 6% rise in imports slashed the trade surplus by half to $2.0 billion.

3.1.12 Current account balance, Southeast Asia

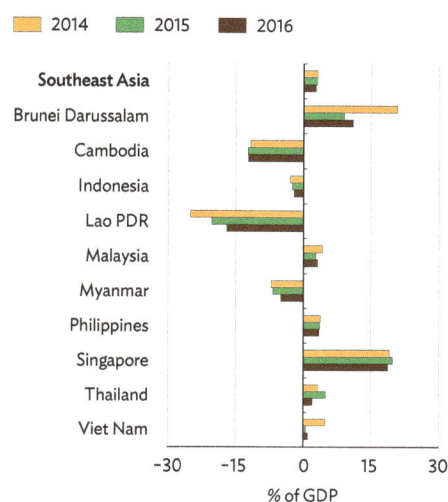

Lao PDR = Lao People's Democratic Republic.
Source: Asian Development Outlook database.

3.1.22 Selected economic indicators, Brunei Darussalam (%)

	2015		2016	
	ADO 2015	Update	ADO 2015	Update
GDP growth	-1.5	-1.5	0.8	0.8
Inflation	-0.2	-0.2	0.4	0.4
Current acct. bal. (share of GDP)	25.0	9.0	26.5	11.0

Source: ADB estimates.

Sagging oil and gas prices also dented government revenue. While the budget is expected to fall into deficit this year, the government can draw on its financial investments and reserves to sustain expenditure. Credit growth quickened from a low 1.0% year on year in 2014 to 6.3% in the first 6 months of 2015. Forecasts are retained for a small contraction in GDP this year before a modest rebound in 2016, assuming some recovery in oil and gas production.

Consumer prices have continued to ease. The consumer price index fell by 0.3% year on year in January–July following a 0.2% decline in 2014. Price declines this year have been recorded for transportation, clothing and footwear, and household equipment. Government subsidies and price controls suppress inflation in this economy. Consumer prices are projected to decline this year, as forecast earlier, and to edge up in 2016 as domestic demand improves and global commodity prices firm.

Revised data for 2014 show the current account surplus narrowed to 20.8% of GDP, largely on weaker exports of hydrocarbons. Current account surpluses for this year and next are projected to fall short of those forecast in March owing to unexpectedly low global prices for oil and LNG this year and downward revisions to oil price assumptions for 2016. The Brunei dollar, which is pegged at par to the Singapore dollar, depreciated by 5.5% against the US dollar from the end of 2014 to mid-September 2015.

Cambodia

Growth in exports and tourism slowed in the first half of 2015. Shipments of garments and footwear rose by 11.0% year on year, decelerating from 14.5% in the first half of 2014. Growth in total merchandise exports moderated to 14.0% from 18.3%. As for tourist arrivals, the rate of increase slowed to 4.6% in the first half from 5.2% a year earlier.

Agriculture is suffering from an extended period of low rainfall. However, data indicate that domestic demand is holding up, based on 33.3% year-on-year expansion of credit to the private sector in May and indications of high growth in imports.

While the expansion of garment manufacturing, construction, and services—in particular tourism, finance, and real estate services—continues to drive growth in GDP, the pace in the garment and tourism industries seems to have moderated. The garment industry faces increased competition arising from the appreciation of the US dollar, in that the Cambodian economy is heavily dollarized, and from other low-wage competitors including Myanmar. This *Update* lowers forecasts for GDP growth in 2015 and 2016.

Inflation was a mild 1.0% year on year in May 2015 and averaged just 1.1% in the first 5 months as prices declined for transportation and fuel. The inflation forecast for 2015 is trimmed, but the higher forecast for 2016 is maintained. Current account forecasts are adjusted in line with a revised narrower deficit for 2014. Gross official reserves of $4.4 billion at the end of 2014 provided cover for about 4 months of imports of goods and services.

3.1.23 Selected economic indicators, Cambodia (%)

	2015		2016	
	ADO 2015	Update 2015	ADO 2015	Update 2015
GDP growth	7.3	7.0	7.5	7.2
Inflation	1.6	1.3	2.7	2.7
Current acct. bal. (share of GDP)	-12.9	-12.3	-12.7	-12.2

Source: ADB estimates.

Indonesia

Deceleration in both fixed investment and household consumption and weak exports have dampened economic growth this year. The government boosted its budget allocation for infrastructure investment, but only 10% was disbursed in the first half. Household consumption moderated in response to higher inflation and tighter consumer credit. As a result, GDP growth slowed to 4.7% year on year in January–June.

The government has taken steps to accelerate budget execution that, in tandem with an annual pattern of much higher disbursements in the fourth quarter, should lift the contribution to growth from public investment in the second half of this year and into 2016. Household consumption will benefit in 2016 from somewhat lower inflation and from pay raises for the civil service. External demand is also seen improving in 2016. Economic growth is forecast to dip in 2015 and recover in 2016, both projections trimmed by 0.6 percentage points from March.

Inflation has abated only gradually to average 6.9% year on year in the first 8 months, prompting upward revisions to forecasts. After cutting fuel subsidies in November 2014, the government has raised prices for fuel, cooking gas, and electricity. Inflation is seen easing to 4%–5% by the end of 2015. An unexpectedly severe El Niño could damage crops and add to inflationary pressures.

Current account deficits look likely to be smaller than previously anticipated, mainly on a plunge in imports. Merchandise exports fell by 12.4% in US dollars in the first half, and they have continued to decline on soft external demand and falling prices for export commodities. Merchandise imports fell even more steeply in the first half, by 17.7%, due to rupiah depreciation, decelerating investment, and lower oil imports. The trade surplus climbed, and the current account deficit narrowed to equal 2.0% of GDP. Next year, improved demand from the major industrial economies is seen further shrinking the current account deficit, assisted by rupiah depreciation.

Lao People's Democratic Republic

Construction on electricity and real estate projects and tourism expansion are sustaining economic growth this year. Among power projects, the 1.9 gigawatt Hongsa lignite-fired power plant started commercial operations in June, and the 1.3 gigawatt Xayaburi project is one of several hydropower plants under construction. Tourist arrivals rose by 11% to 2 million in the first 5 months of 2015, helped by an increase in air services to the Lao PDR. Mine output of copper, gold, and silver rose in the first half, though prices for the metals have declined.

On the downside, drought during the planting season is expected to hurt rice production and could stem the water flow needed to generate hydropower. Moreover, government spending remains constrained by the fiscal deficit, which widened sharply 2 years ago, and from a squeeze on government revenue from lower prices for both mineral exports and oil imports. Growth in credit slowed to 13.5% year on year in May. To stimulate lending, the central bank directed commercial banks in August to lower interest rates.

3.1.24 Selected economic indicators, Indonesia (%)

	2015		2016	
	ADO 2015	Update 2015	ADO 2015	Update 2015
GDP growth	5.5	4.9	6.0	5.4
Inflation	5.5	6.7	4.0	5.1
Current acct. bal. (share of GDP)	−2.8	−2.5	−2.4	−2.1

Source: ADB estimates.

3.1.25 Selected economic indicators, Lao People's Democratic Republic (%)

	2015		2016	
	ADO 2015	Update 2015	ADO 2015	Update 2015
GDP growth	7.0	6.7	7.2	7.0
Inflation	3.5	1.5	4.0	3.0
Current acct. bal. (share of GDP)	−21.2	−20.3	−17.3	−17.0

Source: ADB estimates.

On balance, forecasts for GDP growth are edged down from *ADO 2015*. Inflation will also be lower than forecast in March, a result of falling global oil and commodity prices and moderating domestic economic growth. Inflation averaged 1.3% year on year in the first 8 months.

Exports and imports both fell at a double-digit pace in January–April. Current account deficits are now expected to be slightly narrower than previously anticipated. The Lao kip depreciated by 0.9% against the US dollar from the end of 2014 to the end of August, but it appreciated by 7.1% against the Thai baht in that period. Gross international reserves rose to an estimated $900 million in the first quarter.

Malaysia

As a major producer and exporter of crude oil, natural gas, and palm oil, this economy was bound to be buffeted by the plunge in demand and prices for hydrocarbons and other commodities. Net external demand dragged down GDP growth in the first half. Growth in private fixed investment decelerated, and public fixed investment actually declined. Private consumption held up well, though it moderated after April, when the government implemented a tax on goods and services as part of fiscal reform. GDP growth slowed to 5.3% in January–June.

The economy is seen slowing further through the second half to match in the full year the forecast made in March. Private consumption faces headwinds from sagging consumer confidence, the new tax on goods and services, slowing growth in credit to households, and signs of softening in the labor market. Business sentiment has been hurt by lackluster prospects for exports, a sharp depreciation of the Malaysian ringgit, a slide in stock prices, and spare manufacturing capacity.

In 2016, investment is projected to strengthen on prospects for improved economic growth in the major industrial economies and some improvement in demand for oil and commodities. The government is looking to stimulate growth through fiscal policy but is constrained by its pledge to narrow the budget deficit. Concerns about high household debt and capital outflows could weigh against easing interest rates. Economic growth is still seen edging up in 2016 but more gradually than anticipated in March.

Inflation was unexpectedly low at an average of 1.7% year on year in the first 7 months, even as the new tax on goods and services and the ringgit's depreciation put some upward pressure on prices from the second quarter. The inflation forecast for 2015 is revised down, but the forecast for 2016 is retained. Turning to trade, merchandise exports slid by 13.7% in US dollar terms in the first half, and imports fell by 12.0%. The current account surplus was cut by more than half from the same period in 2014. Forecasts for current account surpluses are lowered from March.

Myanmar

Severe flooding and landslides in July and August 2015 displaced 1.6 million people, caused almost 120 deaths, and damaged agriculture and infrastructure. The government declared natural disaster zones in Chin and Rakhine states and the regions of Magway and Sagaing.

3.1.26 Selected economic indicators, Malaysia (%)

	2015		2016	
	ADO 2015	Update	ADO 2015	Update
GDP growth	4.7	4.7	5.0	4.9
Inflation	3.2	2.4	2.9	2.9
Current acct. bal. (share of GDP)	3.3	2.7	4.5	3.2

Source: ADB estimates.

While the full economic impact has yet to be assessed, the floods are expected to reduce production and exports of rice and some other crops. The government has called on international partners to assist with reconstruction and rehabilitation.

The economy as a whole nevertheless continues to expand at a robust pace on investment stimulated by structural reform and generally strong domestic demand. Fiscal policy and expanded credit are contributing to growth, though both fiscal and monetary policies will likely need to be tightened in the forecast period to dampen inflationary pressures and to stabilize exchange rate expectations.

Inflation accelerated to 8% year on year in May 2015, and disruption to supplies of food and other goods from flooding could add to inflationary pressures. The Myanmar kyat depreciated against the US dollar by 24%, from MK965 in April 2014 to MK1,275 in early September 2015, largely as the result of a widening current account deficit and a stronger US dollar. Gross official reserves remain low at less than 3 months of imports.

Forecasts for GDP growth, inflation, and the current account for FY2015 (ending 31 March 2016) and FY2016 are retained from *ADO 2015*, pending data updates and the outcome of national elections scheduled for November 2015. Risks to price and external stability come from the rapid growth in credit, expansionary budget, and widening trade deficit. A prolonged decline in global prices for natural gas, a major export from Myanmar, would erode its fiscal and external positions.

Philippines

Household consumption accelerated in the first half, driven by higher employment, low inflation, and rising remittances. Private investment also rose, but government spending was sluggish early in the year before rebounding. Net external demand weighed on GDP growth, which slowed to 5.3%.

The rebound in government spending is expected to spur growth through the rest of this year and in 2016. In July, growth in public expenditure excluding interest accelerated to 31% year on year. Election-related spending will also support domestic demand through May 2016, when elections will be held. Private consumption and investment are expected to maintain solid growth in 2016. The forecast for growth in 2015 is trimmed from *ADO 2015*. Growth is projected to quicken in 2016.

Inflation forecasts are revised down in light of unexpectedly low inflation so far this year, averaging 1.7% in the first 8 months, and the assumption that global oil prices will increase only slightly in 2016 and that global food prices will be stable. Upward pressure on inflation could come from drought induced by El Niño if it damages crops and reduces hydropower supplies.

Merchandise exports fell by 12.9% in US dollar terms in the first half, and imports fell by 8.3%. The trade deficit widened, but growth in remittances and services exports, mainly from business process outsourcing and tourism, kept the current account in surplus. This *Update* trims the forecast for the current account surplus in 2015 due to the weakness in merchandise exports. It maintains the current account forecast for 2016.

3.1.27 Selected economic indicators, Myanmar (%)

	2015		2016	
	ADO 2015	Update 2015	ADO 2015	Update 2015
GDP growth	8.3	8.3	8.2	8.2
Inflation	8.4	8.4	6.6	6.6
Current acct. bal. (share of GDP)	−6.8	−6.8	−5.0	−5.0

Source: ADB estimates.

3.1.28 Selected economic indicators, Philippines (%)

	2015		2016	
	ADO 2015	Update 2015	ADO 2015	Update 2015
GDP growth	6.4	6.0	6.3	6.3
Inflation	2.8	2.0	3.3	3.0
Current acct. bal. (share of GDP)	4.0	3.7	3.6	3.6

Source: ADB estimates.

Singapore

GDP growth slowed to a lackluster 1.8% year on year in the second quarter of 2015 from 2.8% in the first, putting growth for January–June at 2.3%. Manufacturing contracted for a third consecutive quarter, weighed down by production declines in the biomedical and transport engineering industries. The modest rise in GDP in the second quarter was driven by services, mainly finance and wholesale and retail trading, and by construction as the government increased investment on public projects.

From the demand side, higher private consumption through the first half lifted total consumption expenditure, but domestic demand overall was hurt by declining inventories. Fixed investment improved in the second quarter. Exports of goods and services rose in real terms by 0.6% in the second quarter, but imports in real terms fell by 0.8%. The labor market remained tight with the unemployment rate at 2.0%. Employment grew by 2.4% in the first half, a more moderate pace than in 2014.

Data for the second half show a decline in manufacturing in July from the same month in 2014 but a slight improvement in the economy-wide purchasing managers' index in the 3 months to August. In light of the modest first-half GDP outcome and downward revisions for growth in major export markets, this *Update* trims *ADO 2015* forecasts for Singapore GDP growth.

Consumer prices fell by 0.4% year on year in the first 7 months as prices declined for housing, utilities, and transportation. Core inflation, excluding the costs of housing and private road transportation, remained positive at an average of 0.6%. The consumer price index is now forecast to fall marginally this year and to rise by just 1.0% in 2016. The monetary authority, responding in January to uncertain global growth prospects and declining domestic consumer prices, reduced the pace of appreciation of the Singapore dollar in terms of its nominal effective exchange rate. Against the US dollar, the Singapore dollar depreciated by 3.9% through the first 7 months, but it appreciated by 0.6% in nominal effective terms. Imports in US dollar terms fell at a faster pace than exports in the first half, contributing to a 40.2% jump in the current account surplus. As a ratio to GDP, the current account surplus is now projected at 19.8% this year and is seen narrowing in 2016.

Thailand

Recovery from a slump in 2014, when political unrest disrupted the economy, is unexpectedly tepid. Government expenditure rebounded in the first half of 2015, but private consumption recorded feeble growth, and private fixed investment was flat. Private consumption is constrained by falls in farm incomes, slowing growth in wages, and high household debt. Consumer confidence declined through July. Private investment is subdued because of lackluster prospects for exports, soft consumption spending, and spare industrial capacity. GDP grew by a modest 2.9% in the first half.

The government is taking steps to assist rural areas hit by drought and low prices for farm products, and in September it unveiled a stimulus package for small- and medium-sized businesses. Such fiscal measures, together with planned large infrastructure projects and improved prospects for exports to major industrial

3.1.29 Selected economic indicators, Singapore (%)

	2015		2016	
	ADO 2015	Update	ADO 2015	Update
GDP growth	3.0	2.1	3.4	2.5
Inflation	0.2	–0.2	1.5	1.0
Current acct. bal. (share of GDP)	18.9	19.8	19.3	18.7

Source: ADB estimates.

3.1.30 Selected economic indicators, Thailand (%)

	2015		2016	
	ADO 2015	Update	ADO 2015	Update
GDP growth	3.6	2.7	4.1	3.8
Inflation	0.2	–0.7	2.0	1.5
Current acct. bal. (share of GDP)	4.0	5.0	1.5	2.0

Source: ADB estimates.

economies next year, are seen lifting GDP growth in 2016 by just over 1 percentage point from 2015. Nevertheless, growth in both years will undershoot earlier projections, and forecasts are revised down.

The consumer price index fell by 0.9% in the first 8 months and is now expected to decline slightly for the full year. Core inflation has remained positive. For 2016, prices are seen turning up with inflation projected at 1.5%, this forecast trimmed from March.

A higher trade surplus in the first 6 months stemmed from a sharper fall in merchandise imports (down by 8.7% in US dollar terms) than the fall in exports by 4.9%. The trade surplus combined with stronger income from tourism to more than double the current account surplus for the same period in 2014. Current account surpluses this year and next will be above those forecast in *ADO 2015*.

Viet Nam

Faster GDP growth, at 6.3% in the first half over the same period in 2014, was driven by strong expansion in manufacturing, construction, and mining. Sustained inflows of foreign direct investment into manufacturing have propelled exports in recent years. Private consumption is growing robustly, supported by low inflation, higher off-farm employment, and improved consumer confidence.

As these trends are projected to continue, growth forecasts are raised from *ADO 2015*. Growth in credit has picked up and looks likely to exceed the government's target. Fiscal policy supports economic growth, though concerns over rising public debt could prompt a tightening next year. The outlook for trade and investment is bolstered by an easing of restrictions on foreign investment in shares and property and by the conclusion in August of a Viet Nam–European Union free-trade agreement.

Inflation subsided to 0.8% year on year in the first 8 months, continuing a steep decline since 2011, and the forecast for 2015 is revised down from March. By the end of 2015, inflation is seen rising to 2.0%. The forecast for 4.0% year-average inflation in 2016 is retained.

In contrast with most other subregional economies, Viet Nam recorded solid growth in merchandise exports in the first half. Still, imports rose at a much faster pace than exports, reflecting strong domestic demand for capital and consumer goods. A lower trade surplus cut the current account surplus. Forecasts for current account surpluses are lowered from March, in particular for 2015. The central bank devalued the Viet Nam dong against the US dollar three times in the first 8 months, by 1% each time, to support the competitiveness of exports.

3.1.31 Selected economic indicators, Viet Nam (%)

	2015		2016	
	ADO 2015	Update 2015	ADO 2015	Update 2015
GDP growth	6.1	6.5	6.2	6.6
Inflation	2.5	0.9	4.0	4.0
Current acct. bal. (share of GDP)	3.1	0.5	1.5	1.0

Source: ADB estimates.

The Pacific

Subregional assessment and prospects

Economic growth in the Pacific is now projected to average 6.7% in 2015. This is 3.2 percentage points lower than forecast in *ADO 2015*, largely reflecting disappointing growth in Papua New Guinea (PNG). The outlook, excluding the larger resource-exporting economies of PNG and Timor-Leste, remains more modest, with average growth of 3.0% this year (Figure 3.1.13).

Uncertainty regarding international oil prices clouds the near-term growth outlook, with contrasting impacts across Pacific economies. Most of these economies depend on imported energy, and continuing low prices would sustain increased purchasing power and boost consumption. On the other hand, growth prospects for energy-exporting PNG and Timor-Leste are dimming as these economies feel fiscal and economic pressure from lower revenues. Falling revenues and a rising fiscal deficit have prompted the PNG government to cut expenditure. In Timor-Leste, weak oil prices are exacerbating an earlier drop in royalties caused by declining production from its offshore oilfields.

Severe weather has dampened growth in the Federated States of Micronesia (FSM). Typhoon Maysak hit the FSM at the end of March and destroyed an estimated 90% of agricultural output, as well as hundreds of homes in Chuuk and Yap states. Despite reconstruction, the FSM economy is now expected to stagnate this year. Vanuatu's economy has also been affected by severe weather, and delays in reconstruction are seen to deepen the contraction this year by more than previously forecast.

For most of the other Pacific economies, 2015 is on track to be a good year, with half of the 14 economies anticipating stronger growth than in 2014. The one-time spike in growth projected for the PNG economy as it exports liquefied natural gas (LNG) for a full year for the first time is expected to push growth in the Pacific's largest economy to 9.0%, which is strong but considerably less than the *ADO 2015* forecast in March. Because the LNG industry is poorly integrated into the PNG economy, growth is expected to provide few benefits to most residents. In Solomon Islands, reconstruction and economic recovery following severe flood damage suffered in 2014 are expected to support 3.0% growth this year.

In the South Pacific, growth in FY2015 (ended 30 June 2015) was in line with *ADO 2015* forecasts. However, in Samoa agricultural output was modestly lower than expected, trimming the country's growth estimate for FY2015 to 2.3% from 2.5% forecast in *ADO 2015*.

In the North Pacific, rising tourist arrivals have improved Palau's near-term economic prospects while raising concerns about environmental sustainability and the carrying capacity of the country's tourist attractions and facilities. Record high tourist arrivals in Palau, led by an increase in visitors from the PRC, prompt this *Update* to raise the growth forecast for this year to 10.0% from the *ADO 2015* forecast of 8.0%.

In 2016, growth in the Pacific subregion as a whole is expected to slow to 3.9% as this year's one-time spike from the first full year of LNG exports ends and these exports become part of its base GDP. This forecast is 0.9 percentage points lower than the *ADO 2015* projection, mainly reflecting the downward revision in the PNG growth forecast.

By contrast, the outlook for Fiji next year is more promising than projected earlier, as activity picks up on infrastructure projects enabled by the country's recent reengagement with development partners, and as private investment rises.

3.1.13 GDP growth, the Pacific

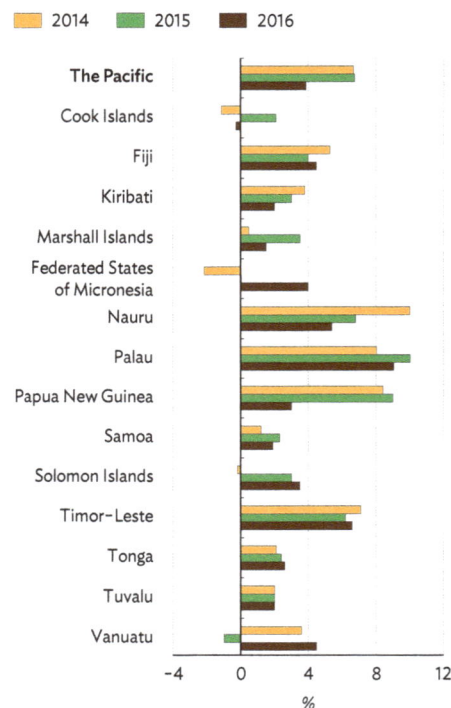

Source: *Asian Development Outlook* database.

3.1.14 Inflation, the Pacific

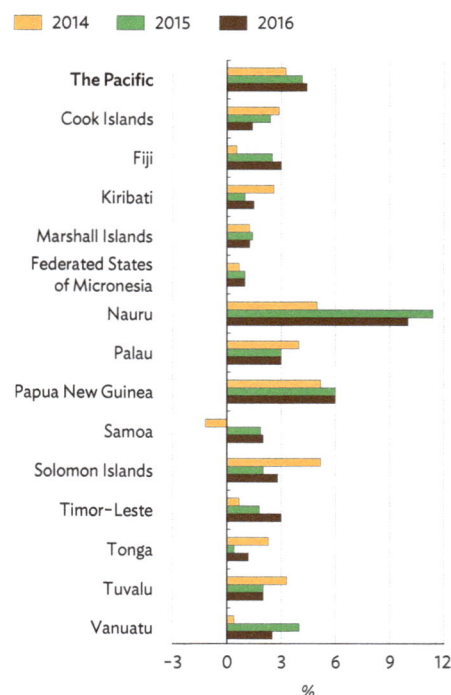

Source: *Asian Development Outlook* database.

In Timor-Leste, projected growth for 2016 is unchanged from *ADO 2015*, with large new investments—including a new international port—compensating for planned cuts in public expenditure.

In the small island economies, unexpectedly strong growth stimulus from projects assisted by development partners supports a small increase in Kiribati's 2016 growth forecast, from 1.5% to 2.0%. Projected growth in 2016 is unchanged at 2.0% for Tuvalu. In Nauru, continued fiscal expansion and recovery in phosphate exports will support growth of 5.4% in 2016, revised up from the earlier forecast of 5.0%.

Inflation in the Pacific is now projected at 4.2% in 2015 and 4.4% in 2016 (Figure 3.1.14). The 2015 projection is lower than the *ADO 2015* forecast, mainly in response to downward revisions to international commodity price forecasts. It also takes into account low inflation outcomes in Pacific economies early this year. Inflation projections for 2015 are lower for the FSM, Palau, PNG, Samoa, Solomon Islands, and Timor-Leste, but higher for the Cook Islands, Nauru, and Tuvalu.

Current account deficits are common in most Pacific economies. The subregion as a whole runs a surplus due to large royalties from offshore petroleum operations in Timor-Leste. However, these surpluses have declined in recent years as output from the main oilfield has fallen. Receipts from PNG exports of LNG have begun to offset declining surpluses from Timor-Leste, and the Pacific's combined current account surplus is projected to widen to the equivalent of 9.1% of subregional GDP in 2015 before falling back to 7.9% in 2016 (Figure 3.1.15).

Fiji

The economy is expected to grow in 2015 in line with *ADO 2015* projections as broad-based growth continues to be supported by fiscal stimulus, rising investment, and increased consumption—all aided by low oil prices. In May, Standard & Poor's raised its long-term sovereign credit rating for Fiji from B to B+, reflecting the more stable economic outlook arising from a more normalized political climate and reengagement with development partners.

As expected, tourist arrivals have grown at a steady pace—increasing by 8.7% year on year in the first half of 2015. Arrivals from the largest market, Australia, grew by 4.1%. The next two largest markets, New Zealand and the US, grew at double-digit rates. Arrivals from Asia grew even faster, increasing by over 30% and now accounting for about 9% of total arrivals. In response to the increased arrivals, Fiji Airways recently announced that it would lease two new aircrafts in 2015, which should further boost tourist arrivals. It plans to lease another one in 2017.

The Reserve Bank of Fiji reports that during the first half of 2015 new lending for investment (largely construction) soared by 82.1%, while new lending for consumption increased by 14.4%. The 2015 budget raised allocations for transport, energy, water supply, and sanitation infrastructure, and this has helped push strong growth in aggregate demand. However, because of higher spending, the government is projecting a budget deficit equivalent to 2.5% of GDP in 2015. The projection factors in the planned sale of state-owned enterprises, and the deficit will be higher if the sales are delayed or generate disappointing returns.

3.1.15 Current account balance, the Pacific

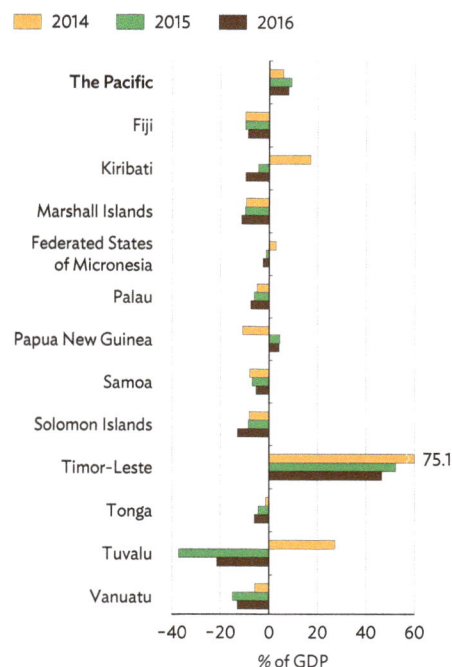

Source: *Asian Development Outlook* database.

3.1.32 Selected economic indicators, Fiji (%)

	2015		2016	
	ADO 2015	Update	ADO 2015	Update
GDP growth	4.0	4.0	4.0	4.5
Inflation	2.5	2.5	2.5	3.0
Current acct. bal. (share of GDP)	−9.8	−9.8	−8.7	−8.7

Source: ADB estimates.

The fall in oil prices kept average inflation at a moderate 1.3% year on year in the first 7 months of 2015. Low inflation is expected to allow Fiji to keep its policy interest rate accommodative at 0.5% for the foreseeable future.

Growth is now expected to accelerate in 2016 as recent trends continue and infrastructure projects are implemented with assistance from development partners. This improved outlook faces a downside risk from a possible economic slowdown in Australia linked to moderating growth in the PRC. Possible upside risks include an unexpectedly large stimulus to consumption and tourism from low oil prices.

Projected inflation in 2015 remains unchanged from *ADO 2015*, but strengthening growth prompts an increase in the forecast for inflation in 2016. Forecasts for current account deficits remain unchanged for both years.

Papua New Guinea

External and internal factors have coalesced to produce headwinds for the economy and prompt a sharp reduction in the 2015 growth forecast. Low prices for commodity exports and unfavorable weather have dimmed the outlook for agricultural output and exports. Expenditure cuts necessitated by a growing fiscal deficit, and the temporary closure of the Ok Tedi mine, further weigh on growth prospects. These headwinds are seen to slow growth in 2016 as well.

Slower growth is the main reason the 2015 inflation forecast is revised down. However, the inflation forecast for 2016 is raised as energy and other commodity prices are seen to rise modestly next year. These forecasts hinge on the government curbing expenditure and adopting more prudent monetary policies.

Driven by LNG exports, the surplus in the current account is forecast to reach about $800 million in 2015 and 2016. These forecasts are revised down significantly from March for the reasons noted above. Foreign exchange reserves will likely be maintained at $2 billion, equivalent to about 4 months of imports of goods and services.

In its midyear outlook, the government highlighted the fiscal pressures it faces this year. Without immediate cuts to expenditures, the budget deficit is projected to widen to the equivalent of 9.4% of GDP, or more than double the 2015 deficit target of 4.4%. The deficit is largely the result of disappointing revenues, particularly from mining and petroleum taxes, and consequently the government is facing short-term cash flow constraints. It has little recourse to domestic financing as PNG-based purchasers of Treasury bills have already invested heavily in short-term government debt. New sources of finance—for example, asset sales or sovereign bond issuance—are being considered but will take time to materialize and could be expensive.

The government is likely to reduce operating expenditure and defer capital expenditures by the equivalent of 2.5% of GDP. Public expenditure reform currently under way offers the most effective option for addressing the near-term cash flow constraints. However, reform should be accompanied by a clear and credible set of measures to guide fiscal policy back to balance over the medium term.

3.1.33 Selected economic indicators, Papua New Guinea (%)

	2015		2016	
	ADO 2015	Update	ADO 2015	Update
GDP growth	15.0	9.0	5.0	3.0
Inflation	7.0	6.0	5.0	6.0
Current acct. bal. (share of GDP)	13.5	4.4	15.0	4.2

Source: ADB estimates.

Proposed new investments, particularly in the mineral sector in 2017 and 2018, could boost growth in the medium term. The priority should still be to improve productivity in agriculture and service sectors because of their importance to employment and poverty reduction. This will require sustained investment in infrastructure that supports productive sectors, increased capacity in the public sector and more efficient budget execution, improved labor market institutions and labor skills, and expanded business opportunities. Greater dynamism in the non-mineral sectors would strengthen the PNG economy's resilience to commodity price fluctuations and help address concerns about rising inequality fueled by strong growth in resource extraction.

Solomon Islands

The growth forecast for 2015 is unchanged as the economy records strong export performance and progress in reconstruction following severe floods in April 2014. Despite the cessation of gold production, total exports rose by 5.3% in the first half of 2015 over the same period in 2014, largely reflecting higher exports of bauxite and agricultural commodities. The forecast for 2016 remains unchanged as growth is expected to benefit from planned fiscal expansion.

After parliamentary elections in November 2014, passage of the 2015 budget was delayed to April to give the new coalition government time to incorporate its spending priorities. The resulting 2015 budget provides for total expenditure that is 11.8% higher than the revised 2014 budget, mostly because of higher expenditure on flood recovery. Total revenues and grants are also projected to rise, but by only 3.3%. Fishing license revenue is seen to increase, but not enough to offset revenue declines from suspended operations at the gold mine. The government expects to incur a deficit (equivalent to 4.9% of GDP) for a second consecutive year and plans to draw down cash reserves to finance it.

Consumer prices have been declining in 2015 following large flood-related price rises last year. Softening international food and fuel prices have contributed. Between January and July 2015, consumer prices were 2.4% lower than in the same period in 2014, driven by reductions in prices for food, drinks and tobacco, and housing and utilities. However, core inflation remains positive, suggesting that headline inflation will rise in the latter part of the year. The inflation forecast for 2015 is revised sharply down from *ADO 2015*, but inflation is expected to pick up in 2016 as base effects from the flood dissipate.

The current account deficit in 2014 is now estimated to equal 8.1% of GDP—less than estimated in *ADO 2015*—as imports of equipment for flood reconstruction and rehabilitation were delayed. With the arrival of the delayed imports, the deficit is projected to widen slightly in 2015 and rather more so in 2016. Development assistance flows and foreign direct investment are expected to help maintain foreign reserves above 8 months of import cover through 2015 and 2016.

Timor-Leste

Projections for growth in the economy excluding the offshore petroleum sector remain unchanged from earlier estimates. Government expenditure—the main driver of the nonpetroleum

3.1.34 Selected economic indicators, Solomon Islands (%)

	2015		2016	
	ADO 2015	Update	ADO 2015	Update
GDP growth	3.0	3.0	3.5	3.5
Inflation	5.0	2.0	5.5	2.8
Current acct. bal. (share of GDP)	-15.5	-8.5	-15.0	-13.0

Source: ADB estimates.

economy—increased by 36.7% in the first 7 months of 2015 over the same period a year earlier. A rectification budget was passed in April that increased funding for the Special Administrative Region of Oecusse, with offsetting reductions in planned transport and electricity investments. The total budget for Oecusse was transferred early in the year, causing a large spike in government expenditure on transfers. However, Oecusse's high level of autonomy creates uncertainty as to future disbursements and, therefore, how much stimulus to expect from them. Expenditure on public sector wages, goods and services, and minor capital works all increased, but spending on capital investment declined significantly. The government has proposed reducing expenditure by 20%, from $1.6 billion in 2015 to $1.3 billion in 2016. If fully implemented, this would likely dampen growth in 2016.

Inflation has remained low, averaging only 0.8% year on year from January to June 2015, but picked up in recent months as food prices rose moderately. The continued appreciation of the US dollar (which Timor-Leste uses as its currency) against the currencies of trading partners has contributed to low inflation. From January to June, the dollar appreciated by 7%–13% against the currencies of Indonesia, Malaysia, and Singapore. Low inflation through the first half of 2015 prompts lower inflation forecasts for 2015 and 2016.

The value of merchandise imports in January–May fell by 55% year on year, largely because international prices for fuel and other commodities were down. However, imports of vehicles and machinery increased by 14.8%, suggesting strong underlying demand. Registrations of motorcycles, light commercial vehicles, and heavy trucks all increased in the first quarter, though car registrations fell slightly. Low oil prices are now expected to narrow the current account surplus in both 2015 and 2016 more than forecast in *ADO 2015*.

Vanuatu

The economy is now expected to contract slightly more than previously forecast. The damage wrought by Cyclone Pam in March is weighing heavily on tourism and agriculture, and reconstruction efforts have suffered delays. By June, visitor arrivals by air were down by 24% from a year earlier and arrivals by cruise ship were down by 56%. Agriculture export receipts increased in the second quarter over a year earlier because of a large but temporary increase in coconut oil exports. Exports of other major commodities fell significantly relative to a year earlier. Growth is expected to rebound in 2016 somewhat above the forecast in *ADO 2015*, as several large infrastructure projects financed by development partners get under way, reconstruction continues, and tourism and agriculture recover.

In the aftermath of the cyclone, the government responded through fiscal and monetary measures. A supplementary budget increased expenditures by 1.3%, and value-added tax and import duties were waived for building materials and relief items. The Reserve Bank of Vanuatu reduced the policy rate, lowered bank reserve requirements, and activated targeted credit facilities. These actions helped stabilize liquidity, but the weak monetary transmission mechanism limited benefits to the real economy. National Provident Fund members were

3.1.35 Selected economic indicators, Timor-Leste (%)

	2015		2016	
	ADO 2015	Update	ADO 2015	Update
GDP growth	6.2	6.2	6.6	6.6
Inflation	2.8	1.8	4.0	3.0
Current acct. bal. (share of GDP)	55.0	52.2	51.6	46.5

Source: ADB estimates.

3.1.36 Selected economic indicators, Vanuatu (%)

	2015		2016	
	ADO 2015	Update	ADO 2015	Update
GDP growth	-0.5	-1.0	4.0	4.5
Inflation	4.0	4.0	2.0	2.5
Current acct. bal. (share of GDP)	-10.0	-15.0	-7.0	-13.0

Source: ADB estimates.

permitted to withdraw up to 20% of their retirement account to finance private recovery efforts. Insurance payouts should also help to finance the economic recovery.

Reconstruction has proceeded more slowly than anticipated owing to delays in the planning and approval process, with the government finalizing its plan for recovery only in August. The bulk of reconstruction is being financed by development partners. External grants received in the first half of 2015 were up by more than tenfold over the same period last year.

The inflation forecast for 2015 is unchanged. Consumer prices rose by 5.7% year on year in the second quarter. However, underlying inflationary pressures remain contained, and softening global food and fuel prices should keep inflation on track with the *ADO 2015* forecast. The inflation forecast for 2016 is raised in line with expectations of stronger growth next year.

Projections of the current account deficit are revised for 2015 and 2016 to accommodate the doubling of the trade deficit observed in the second quarter and continued high imports for reconstruction and infrastructure projects financed by development partners.

North Pacific economies

Projected growth for FY2015 (ending 30 September 2015) is revised for two of the three developing member economies in the North Pacific. Higher growth is now expected for Palau because tourist arrivals have outpaced expectations, while the growth outlook for the Federated States of Micronesia (FSM) is now lower in the wake of Typhoon Maysak. The forecast for the Republic of the Marshall Islands (RMI) is unchanged.

Government spending is the main driver of economic growth in the RMI. The implementation of new infrastructure projects and those delayed from FY2014 will support strong growth in construction and related services in FY2015. Current government spending was up by 12.8% in the first half of FY2015 from a year earlier on higher outlays for goods and services, intergovernment grants, and transfers to households. Capital spending was up by 86.4% year on year in the same period. As infrastructure projects are completed and wind down, growth is seen to drop in FY2016 as forecast in *ADO 2015*.

In Palau, the GDP growth forecast for FY2015 is raised because of strong tourist arrivals and revised GDP figures for FY2014. Updated national accounts show Palau's economy expanded by 8.0% in FY2014, well above the previous estimate of 6.9%. The revision reflects links between tourism growth and related industries such as communication, wholesale and retail trade, and financial intermediation.

Visitor arrivals in Palau in the first three quarters of FY2015, numbering around 126,000, exceeded arrivals in the whole of the previous fiscal year. The upsurge is driven by higher arrivals from the PRC (including Hong Kong, China and Macau, China), which now accounts for more than half of arrivals, up from just 12.7% in FY2014. Most of these visitors arrive on charter flights from Hong Kong, China and Macau, China, which have increased in number since 2014. In the same period, arrivals declined from other major markets: Japan, the Republic of Korea, and Taipei,China.

There are rising concerns about the environmental sustainability of recent increases in visitor numbers, especially in terms of the carrying capacity of main attractions such as the Rock Islands (a World Heritage Site since 2013) and Jellyfish Lake. The strain on infrastructure is evident, notably on water supply and sewerage systems. Responding to these concerns, the government restricted the number of charter flights to 32 per month (from 48 per month) beginning on 15 April 2015. This reduced arrivals from the PRC from 26,205 in the January–March quarter to 20,616 in the April–June quarter, but this number is still considered high. With continued strong growth in tourist arrivals and some new investment in tourism and related sectors, Palau's GDP growth forecasts are revised substantially upward for FY2015 and FY2016.

The FSM is now projected to see no GDP growth in FY2015 following a series of devastating typhoons that affected all four states. In March 2015, Typhoon Maysak destroyed an estimated 90% of food crops and hundreds of homes in the state of Chuuk and on outlying islands in the state of Yap. In May, Typhoon Noul struck the main islands of Yap, and Typhoon Dolphin caused severe flooding and damage in the states of Pohnpei and Kosrae. Lost agricultural output and construction delays affecting infrastructure projects are expected to be offset by renewed reconstruction in the second half of FY2015.

The outlook for FY2016 is brighter, as recovery in agriculture and the scaling up of infrastructure projects are projected to support higher growth. However, growth is expected to be less than projected in *ADO 2015* as capacity constraints may hinder reconstruction.

Inflation forecasts are revised down for the FSM and Palau but unchanged for the RMI. Inflation in the RMI is still expected to rise slightly in FY2015. Consumer prices, mainly for apparel and food, rose by 1.3% in the first quarter of FY2015. Prices for household utilities, transport, health care, communication services, and education were largely unchanged, while prices for alcoholic beverages and recreation declined.

In Palau, a second of two planned hikes in the tobacco tax rate was implemented in January 2015 and helped nudge inflation to an average annual rate of 4.1% in the first half of FY2015. Prices rose despite the appreciation of the US dollar and consequent reduction in international commodity prices and import costs. Inflation in the third quarter of FY2015 dropped, however, to 0.4% as household costs and transport fell sharply. With fuel prices expected to remain low, inflation forecasts for FY2015 and FY2016 are trimmed from those in *ADO 2015*. Food inflation has remained high—at an average of 4.4% in the first 3 quarters of FY2015—reflecting rising demand from tourists.

In the FSM, minimal inflation is forecast in FY2015 and FY2016 as low prices for imported food and oil persist. The typhoons are seen to weaken domestic demand below forecasts in *ADO 2015*.

In the RMI, the cost of imports from the US declined as food and fuel prices fell. Projected current account deficits are unchanged.

The value of FSM imports from the US between October 2014 and July 2015 increased by 6.7% over the same period a year earlier. Although the value of food imports was 6.3% lower, the value of other imports—mostly machinery and transport equipment—increased

3.1.37 Selected economic indicators, North Pacific economies (%)

	2015		2016	
Marshall Islands	ADO 2015	Update 2015	ADO 2015	Update 2015
GDP growth	3.5	3.5	1.5	1.5
Inflation	1.4	1.4	1.3	1.3
Current acct. bal. (share of GDP)	−9.9	−9.9	−11.4	−11.4
Federated States of Micronesia				
GDP growth	2.3	0.0	5.1	4.0
Inflation	2.4	1.0	2.6	1.0
Current acct. bal. (share of GDP)	11.2	−1.3	6.4	−2.5
Palau				
GDP growth	8.0	10.0	6.0	9.0
Inflation	3.4	3.0	3.4	3.0
Current acct. bal. (share of GDP)	−6.4	−6.1	−8.1	−7.6

Source: ADB estimates.

by 22.3%. The forecast for the FSM current account in FY2015 is now a small deficit instead of the surplus projected in *ADO 2015* because merchandise exports and remittances have fallen while imports of services grew.

In Palau, the value of mineral imports—mainly petroleum products—dropped by 33.8% in FY2015 to July from the same period a year earlier, reflecting lower international oil prices. The value of food imports also declined slightly. The consequent 13.3% decline in the import bill and strong tourism growth prompt a downward revision to the forecast for the current account deficit in FY2015. As these trends are seen to continue, the forecast for FY2016 is also revised down.

South Pacific economies

Expansionary fiscal spending supported economic activity in FY2015 (ended 30 June 2015) in two of the three economies. In the Cook Islands, the Te Mato Vai Water Project boosted GDP growth. As anticipated in *ADO 2015*, visitor arrivals from July 2014 to March 2015 dropped by 2.2% from a year earlier. Arrivals from Australia—the largest source market—declined by 9.0%, likely because of rising costs as the Australian dollar depreciated against the New Zealand dollar, which the Cook Islands uses as its currency. Arrivals from New Zealand grew slightly, reversing the contraction observed over the same period in FY2014. The Cook Islands economy is expected to contract in FY2016 as the water project nears completion. These forecasts are unchanged from *ADO 2015*.

In Tonga, estimated growth in FY2015 matches the forecast in *ADO 2015*. The outlook for FY2016 is unchanged as the government is expected to continue its expansionary fiscal policy. Large capital outlays include expenditures for the 2019 South Pacific Games and new projects financed by development partners. The approved budget of $242.4 million for FY2016 is 17.5% higher than for the previous year, with 53.0% of expenditure expected to be funded by development partners.

Higher departure taxes and a contemplated foreign exchange levy (with revenues from both earmarked for South Pacific Games preparations) and higher excise taxes on unhealthy food and drinks, are projected to contribute to higher government revenues. However, the higher departure taxes and the foreign exchange levy risk harming tourism and remittances. Alternative sources of revenue could include import duty reform and reductions in tax exemptions. The government is prioritizing expenditure reform in line with recommendations from an ongoing public service remuneration review and the introduction of a regular formula-based wage review.

Despite growth supported by higher tourism earnings and remittance-related spending, Samoa's GDP is estimated to have grown in FY2015 by slightly less than the earlier forecast. Visitor arrivals were up by 6.1% in FY2015 to April over the same period a year earlier partly because of its hosting of a United Nations conference in September 2014. Remittances increased by 5.6% year on year during the period on higher inflows from Australia and New Zealand, which together account for nearly three-quarters of remittances. However, higher remittances were offset by declines in agricultural production and nonfood manufacturing.

3.1.38 Selected economic indicators, South Pacific economies (%)

	2015		2016	
	ADO 2015	Update	ADO 2015	Update
Cook Islands				
GDP growth	2.1	2.1	−0.3	−0.3
Inflation	1.3	2.4	1.4	1.4
Current acct. bal. (share of GDP)	...	...	...	...
Samoa				
GDP growth	2.5	2.3	2.2	1.9
Inflation	2.5	1.9	2.0	2.0
Current acct. bal. (share of GDP)	−10.9	−6.9	−9.4	−5.4
Tonga				
GDP growth	2.4	2.4	2.6	2.6
Inflation	0.4	0.4	1.0	1.2
Current acct. bal. (share of GDP)	−4.5	−4.5	−6.0	−6.0

... = data not available.
Source: ADB estimates.

Growth in Samoa is expected to moderate in FY2016 slightly more than earlier forecast in light of the recent weakness in agriculture and nonfood manufacturing. Government spending is also likely to be lower, by about 2%, following a decline of more than 20% in external grant inflows. However, strong inflows from remittances and tourism are seen to continue, augmented by receipts from the Commonwealth Youth Games.

Inflation in the South Pacific is influenced by global commodity price trends and changes in government tax policy. To curb smoking and raise revenues, the government of the Cook Islands implemented the third of three tobacco tax hikes in July 2014. The combined effect of the hikes doubled the excise tax on tobacco. Higher prices for tobacco products, as well as higher import prices resulting from the depreciation of the New Zealand dollar, contributed to inflation rising in FY2015 slightly more than projected in *ADO 2015*. The forecast for FY2016 remains unchanged given global price trends and the absence of any new tax proposals or major change in government expenditures.

Following 2 consecutive years of deflation in Samoa, consumer prices rose in FY2015, but by less than forecast in *ADO 2015*, because of higher costs for health care, restaurant food, clothing, and footwear. The *ADO 2015* projection for inflation in FY2016 still stands.

Consumer price inflation in Tonga slowed in FY2015, largely reflecting lower oil prices and transport costs but remained unchanged from the earlier forecast. Inflation in FY2016 is expected to be slightly higher than predicted as the South Pacific Games boost demand.

Current account positions in the South Pacific fluctuate depending mainly on oil prices and import needs for infrastructure projects. In Samoa, the current account deficit for FY2015 is now estimated to be lower than forecast in *ADO 2015* because of low food and fuel import costs. Following the FY2015 current account outcome, and anticipating higher net income transfers, the forecast for FY2016 is revised down as well. Higher capital outflows have drained foreign reserves such that, at the end of March 2015, gross foreign reserves covered only 4.1 months of merchandise imports, down from 5.3 months a year earlier. In Tonga, the forecasts for current account deficits remain unchanged for FY2015 and FY2016.

Small island economies

Growth in Kiribati, Nauru, and Tuvalu is driven largely by government spending on infrastructure projects.

In Kiribati, stimulus from ongoing infrastructure projects appears to have been greater than previously forecast, and low energy prices encouraged more consumption. Lending to households expanded by 26.0% in 2014 as the Kiribati Provident Fund and the Development Bank of Kiribati introduced personal lending schemes. Higher public expenditures, notably on wages and salaries, and the inclusion of a budget for contingency and infrastructure maintenance, also support output growth. Together, these developments prompt a doubling of the growth forecast for 2015.

Although infrastructure projects are scheduled to wind down next year, their positive influence on economic activity is expected to persist, as are low energy prices, so the 2016 growth forecast for Kiribati is also revised upward. The contribution of fishing license fees to GDP is seen to remain high in 2015 but lower than in 2014.

Growth in Nauru is estimated to have been slower than forecast in FY2015 (ended 30 June 2015), but is projected to exceed the forecast in FY2016. The lower estimate for FY2015 reflects underspending of the budget and problems at Nauru's port that disrupted fuel and other imports as well as phosphate exports. Despite these problems, the economy continues to be buoyed by the presence of the Australian Regional Processing Centre for asylum seekers, large increases in public spending, and higher consumer spending as households benefit from government debt repayments and the liquidation of the Nauru Phosphate Royalties Trust.

The government has adopted a number of measures intended to strengthen fiscal sustainability. It raised electricity tariffs, privatized fuel procurement and distribution, and introduced an employment and services tax for nonresidents. It plans to impose a new business profits tax in January 2016. The recent signing of a 5-year plan with the Government of Australia should bring greater stability to revenues from the processing center. The government is also aiming to establish a trust fund to save for future generations windfall revenues from the processing center, phosphate exports, and fishing licenses. The FY2016 budget allocated A$10.4 million for this purpose, bringing appropriations for the proposed fund to A$20.4 million.

Growth will slow in FY2016 as budgeted expenditures stabilize around current levels, matching the expected plateau in government revenues. Activity at the processing center is thought to have peaked in FY2015. Continued progress in budget implementation, coupled with an expected recovery in phosphate exports, should deliver continued GDP growth into FY2016, albeit at a slower pace.

For Tuvalu, *ADO 2015* projections for growth are unchanged. Expansionary fiscal measures, such as a 14.9% increase in public sector wages and construction spending, are seen to spur domestic economic activity. Higher wages and allocations for one-time development expenditures on new schools, government buildings, and outer island projects account for the 52% increase in planned government expenditures for 2015. The reconstruction of infrastructure damaged by Cyclone Pam, the commencement of other large infrastructure projects, and continued fiscal expansion promise to offset the damage and economic losses caused by the cyclone in early 2015, which are estimated at the equivalent of 10% of GDP. Fishery exports and fishing license fees continue to provide large inflows of foreign exchange, but prospects for earnings from these sources are uncertain over the medium term. Remittances look likely to remain significantly below inflows recorded in 2014, but are seen to pick up in 2016 as conditions in advanced economies improve.

For Kiribati, the annual inflation forecast is unchanged for 2015, reflecting global food and energy price trends and low inflation reported so far this year. Inflation is still seen to rise modestly in 2016, as forecast in *ADO 2015*. For Nauru, the inflation projection is revised sharply higher in both FY2015 and FY2016, reflecting the recent depreciation

3.1.39 Selected economic indicators, Small island economies (%)

	2015		2016	
Kiribati	ADO 2015	Update	ADO 2015	Update
GDP growth	1.5	3.0	1.5	2.0
Inflation	1.0	1.0	1.5	1.5
Current acct. bal. (share of GDP)	−53.0	−4.5	−48.4	−9.7
Nauru				
GDP growth	8.0	6.8	5.0	5.4
Inflation	8.0	11.4	3.0	10.0
Current acct. bal. (share of GDP)	...	...	...	...
Tuvalu				
GDP growth	2.0	2.0	2.0	2.0
Inflation	1.0	2.0	1.0	2.0
Current acct. bal. (share of GDP)	−37.2	−37.2	−21.4	−21.4

... = data not available.
Source: ADB estimates.

of the Australian dollar and disruptions to the loading and unloading of shipments.

Higher fiscal spending in Tuvalu prompts a modest upward revision to its inflation outlook. While a larger fiscal budget encourages the domestic economy, concerns linger about the sustainability of the government's recent fiscal policies. A slight increase in value-added and excise tax collections is expected, but there has been no consistent improvement in revenues from personal or corporate income taxes.

Current account deficit forecasts for Kiribati are cut substantially, reflecting new data that show much smaller historical imbalances than previously estimated. After 3 consecutive years of current account surpluses, Tuvalu is expected to record deficits in 2015 and 2016 as its import bills climb significantly. The value of imports rose sharply in the first quarter of 2015 as ongoing infrastructure projects required imports of machinery, transport goods, and other equipment and materials.

Risks to growth in small island economies include volatility in fishing license revenues stemming from uncertainty over the future terms and enforcement of the Nauru Agreement, as well as changes to the migratory patterns of tuna linked to El Niño. Small island economies are also vulnerable to disasters. Following the destruction caused by Cyclone Pam, the Kiribati Adaptation Program has begun to integrate climate risk management with national economic planning. The program's current phase aims to improve communities' capacity to store freshwater, ensure water quality, and protect coastal areas from storm surges and flooding. The Nauru Disaster Risk Management Unit is preparing a tsunami support plan to improve tsunami preparedness, as well as response and recovery processes.

Bangladesh

Growth in FY2015 outpaced the *ADO 2015* projection as industry enjoyed robust domestic demand. Inflation was subdued, as expected, but the current account deficit was modestly larger. For FY2016, growth is forecast to edge up to 6.7%, the inflation projection is retained, and the current account is now seen to remain a small deficit. Major progress on resource mobilization and structural reform is required to upgrade infrastructure and so support higher economic growth.

Updated assessment

GDP growth in FY2015 (ended 30 June 2015) is provisionally estimated at 6.5%, which is higher than the 6.1% recorded in FY2014 and projected in *ADO 2015* for FY2015 (Figure 3.2.1). Despite political protests early in 2015 that adversely affected transport services, exports, and private investment, growth held up well because of brisk domestic demand, boosted by higher worker remittances, private sector wages, and public investment.

The main demand-side contribution to growth was private consumption. Net exports markedly subtracted from growth, as exports grew much more slowly than imports. However, an unusually large statistical discrepancy in the provisional estimate of GDP makes any disaggregation of expenditure components uncertain. Investment rose to 29.0% of GDP in FY2015 from 28.6% a year earlier, largely on increased public investment. Private investment advanced only slightly, constrained by investor caution and prevailing deficits in infrastructure and skills in a generally weak investment climate.

On the supply side, agriculture grew by 3.0% in FY2015, slowing from the previous year's robust 4.4% expansion because harvests of staple and horticulture crops moderated (Figure 3.2.2). Industrial growth accelerated strongly to 9.6% from 8.2%, driven by manufacturing for the domestic market and construction. Services growth edged up to 5.8%.

Inflation moderated to average 6.4% in FY2015—close to the *ADO 2015* projection—from 7.4% a year earlier, reflecting large public stocks of food grains, normal weather, a supportive monetary policy, and lower global food and commodity prices that a steady exchange rate allowed to passed through. After a slowing trend during the first 7 months of FY2015, year-on-year inflation was broadly stable in subsequent months, ending at 6.3% in June 2015, which was down from 7.0% a year earlier. Food inflation declined to 6.3% from 8.0%, while other inflation rose to 6.2% from 5.5% (Figure 3.2.3).

Broad money grew by 12.4% year on year in June 2015, down from 16.1% in June 2014 and below the FY2015 monetary program target

3.2.1 Demand-side contributions to growth

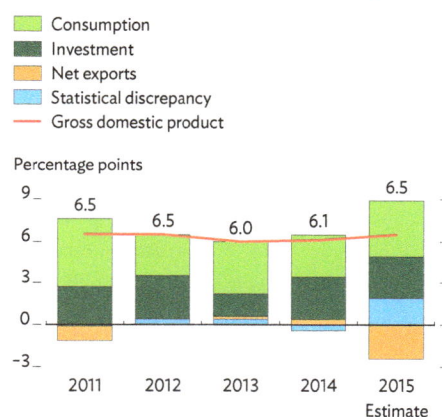

Consumption
Investment
Net exports
Statistical discrepancy
— Gross domestic product

Percentage points

Note: Years are fiscal years ending on 30 June of that year.
Source: Bangladesh Bureau of Statistics. 2015. *National Accounts Statistics.* June.

3.2.2 GDP growth by sector

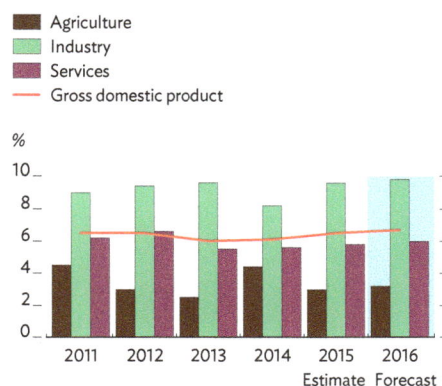

Agriculture
Industry
Services
— Gross domestic product

%

Note: Years are fiscal years ending on 30 June of that year.
Sources: Bangladesh Bureau of Statistics. 2015. *National Accounts Statistics.* June; ADB estimates.

This chapter was written by Mohammed Parvez Imdad, Shamsur Rahman, Md. Golam Mortaza, and Barun K. Dey of the Bangladesh Resident Mission, ADB, Dhaka.

of 16.5% (Figure 3.2.4). Though credit to the private sector expanded marginally to 13.2% in June 2015 from 12.3% a year earlier, it remained below the program target of 15.5%, reflecting investor uncertainty. Net credit to the government declined by 6.2% in FY2015, reversing the 6.7% expansion in the previous year as the government turned significantly more to selling savings certificates to the public. This aligned with its policy of limiting bank financing of the budget under the medium-term economic reform program. The contribution of net foreign assets to monetary growth was less than a year earlier as foreign exchange reserves grew more slowly.

Although price pressures eased over the year, the central bank kept the repo rate, its main policy rate, at 7.25%. The call money rate declined to 5.8% in June 2015 from 6.2% in June 2014 as liquidity pressures eased in the banking system. Treasury bill rates also fell. Banks' average lending rate came down sharply to 11.7% in June 2015 from 13.1% a year earlier. A lesser drop in the deposit rate narrowed the interest rate spread to 4.9 percentage points in June 2015 from 5.4 in June 2014.

Preliminary estimates of the FY2015 budget outcome indicate that, while revenue and expenditure both fell short, the budget deficit was limited to 5% of GDP as planned, financed mainly by nonbank domestic resources. Revenue equaled 10.8% of GDP, up slightly from 10.4% a year earlier, while spending strengthened to 15.8% from 14.0%. Growth in tax revenue was hampered by political disruption and slower growth in large-scale manufacturing. Development expenditure expanded rapidly by 36%, helping to maintain continued growth in investment spending during the year.

Of 48 nonfinancial state-owned enterprises, 34 had earned a combined profit of $1.7 billion as of 22 April 2015, and the remainder incurred losses of $1.3 billion, their consolidated net profit of $388.2 million modestly better than the full year net profit of $365.2 million in FY2014 (Figure 3.2.5). The Bangladesh Petroleum Corporation turned around a loss of $298.6 million in FY2014 to a profit of $444.9 million, thanks to lower global fuel prices and the decision to maintain domestic prices until earlier losses on sales were resolved. Moreover, profits increased at the Bangladesh Oil, Gas, and Mineral Resources Corporation from $57.9 million to $105.0 million. These gains were largely offset, however, by losses at the Bangladesh Power Development Board, which worsened to $1.1 billion from $875.8 million, and lower profits at the Bangladesh Telecommunications Regulatory Commission, which contracted to $888.9 million from $1.3 billion as earnings for mobile phone operators and international call termination rates both declined.

The government was able to slash its fuel subsidy by three-quarters in FY2015, to $80 million from $320 million (Figure 3.2.6). Nevertheless, preliminary estimates indicate that total subsidy spending rose by $730 million to $3.5 billion in FY2015 (equal to 1.8% of GDP) from $2.8 billion in FY2014 (1.6%) because of markedly higher subsidies for power, exports, and other priorities, paid mainly to the Rural Electrification Board, Bangladesh Inland Water Transport Authority, and Trading Corporation of Bangladesh. Despite several upward adjustments to tariffs, the power subsidy rose by $380 million to

3.2.3 Monthly inflation

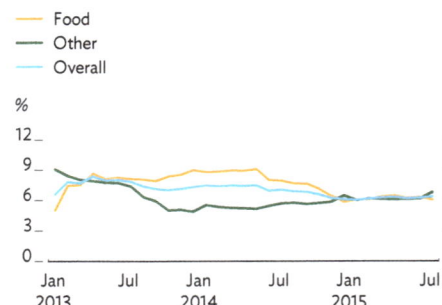

Source: Bangladesh Bank. 2015. Monthly Economic Trends. August. http://www.bangladesh-bank.org

3.2.4 Contributions to broad money growth

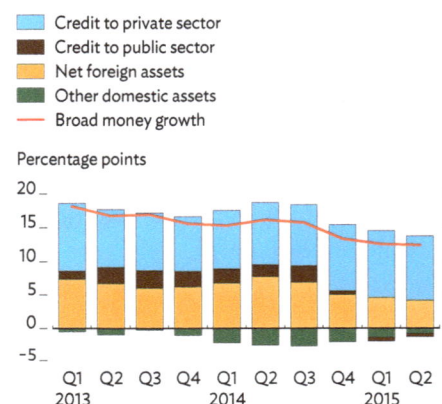

Q = quarter.
Sources: Bangladesh Bank. 2015. Monthly Economic Trends. August. http://www.bangladesh-bank.org; ADB estimates.

3.2.5 Profits and losses at state-owned enterprises

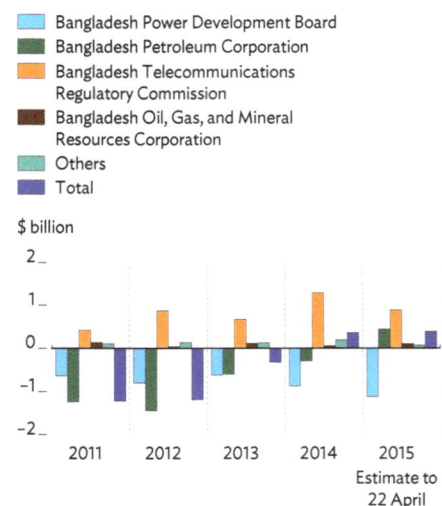

Note: Years are fiscal years ending on 30 June of that year.
Sources: Ministry of Finance. Bangladesh Economic Review 2015; ADB estimates.

$1.16 billion (0.6% of GDP) from the previous year's $780 million (0.5%) after fire forced the shutdown of one of the largest independent power plants and the consequent greater use of costly rental power plants. Fuel and power subsidies together rose by $140 million to $1.2 billion (0.6% of GDP). Agriculture continued to be the major recipient of subsidies, for fertilizer, diesel, and electric power support to farmers, but its subsidies rose only marginally to $1.16 billion.

Export growth was 3.3% in FY2015, down significantly from 12.1% in FY2014 (Figure 3.2.7). Garments—accounting for about 80% of total exports—grew slowly by 4.1%, reflecting supply chain disruption in early 2015, soft demand from the European Union and the US, and a marked decline in prices for cotton, a major input cost that can affect pricing. Continuing their weak performance of recent years, other exports grew minimally by 0.2%. Imports rose by 11.2%, accelerating from 8.9% growth in FY2014. Larger imports of food grains, machinery, fertilizer, and industrial raw materials helped to propel the expansion.

After stagnating a year earlier, remittances rose to $15.3 billion, a 7.7% increase over FY2014 as overseas employment expanded, especially in the Middle East, where new arrangements facilitated worker placement. The number of new jobs abroad for Bangladeshi workers, who number about 8 million, rose by 13.0% in FY2015 (Figure 3.2.8).

As exports grew significantly more slowly than imports, the trade deficit widened by $3.1 billion to $9.9 billion in FY2015. Despite the recovery in remittances, larger deficits in trade and the net services and primary income accounts reversed the FY2014 current account surplus of $1.4 billion to a deficit of $1.6 billion, both equal to 0.8% of GDP (Figure 3.2.9).

The combined capital and financial accounts recorded a surplus of $5.6 billion in FY2015, up from $3.4 billion a year earlier, mainly from a larger net inflow of trade credit. However, the current account deficit trimmed the overall balance to a surplus of $4.4 billion, from $5.5 billion a year earlier. Gross foreign exchange reserves rose to $25.0 billion, or cover for 6.2 months of imports, at the end of June 2015 (Figure 3.2.10).

The nominal taka–dollar exchange rate held steady in FY2015, reflecting the large net foreign exchange inflow and the sizeable reserve position (Figure 3.2.11). As the dollar strengthened markedly against other currencies, including the euro, the taka appreciated along with it. Appreciation by 14% in real effective terms over the past year will likely undercut competitiveness.

Prospects

Forecasts for FY2016 are based on several assumptions: The central bank will maintain a cautious and accommodative monetary policy to further reduce inflation without hampering output growth. Targeted domestic revenue and external resources will be mobilized, especially for financing infrastructure investment. Political calm will be maintained to restore investors' confidence. Faster growth expected in the US and the European Union, Bangladesh's main export destinations, will be realized. Normal weather is a prerequisite.

3.2.6 Government subsidies

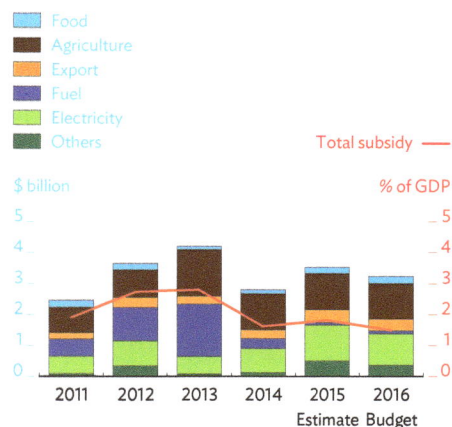

Food
Agriculture
Export
Fuel
Electricity
Others

Total subsidy ——

Note: Years are fiscal years ending on 30 June of that year.
Sources: Ministry of Finance. *Medium Term Macroeconomic Policy Statement 2015–16 to 2017–18*; ADB estimates.

3.2.7 Contributions to export growth

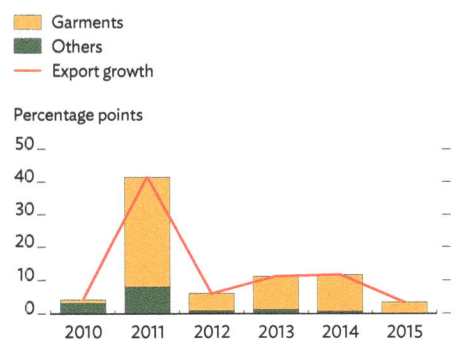

Garments
Others
Export growth

Notes: Years are fiscal years ending on 30 June of that year. High export growth in 2011 largely reflects an increase in cotton prices by more than 40%.
Sources: Export Promotion Bureau; ADB estimates.

3.2.8 Overseas employment growth

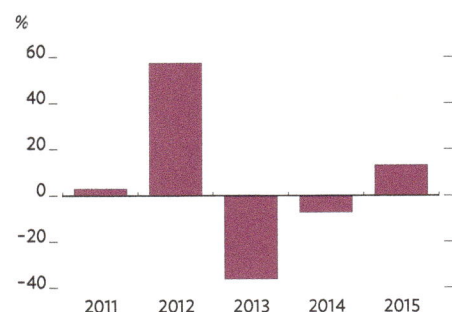

Note: Years are fiscal years ending on 30 June of that year.
Source: Bangladesh Bank. 2015. *Monthly Economic Trends.* August. http://www.bangladesh-bank.org

The GDP growth forecast for FY2016 is revised somewhat higher to 6.7% in the expectation that exports will grow with continued economic recovery in the US and the euro area, strong expansion in remittances will boost consumption demand, investment will pick up under a stable business climate, and spending will increase under the annual development program.

Growth in agriculture is forecast to accelerate to 3.2% if normal weather prevails and prices remain favorable. Industry growth is also expected to strengthen modestly to 9.8% with better performance in readymade garment exports, manufacturing for the domestic market, and construction. The government's supportive credit policies will help to boost activity in small and medium-sized industries. Growth in services is projected to edge up to 6.0% as agriculture and industry expand.

Bangladesh seeks to significantly raise investment to shift the economy to a higher growth trajectory. Government development plans indicate the need to raise investment from 29.0% of GDP in FY2015 to 34.4% by FY2020. Higher investment is required to address deficits in skills and infrastructure, especially by enhancing electric power and energy supply and efficiency, and by improving urban infrastructure and services, transport connectivity, and ports.

Simultaneously, the government needs to continue its program of structural reform toward fiscal strengthening through revenue mobilization and improved public finance management, a more welcoming investment climate, a stronger financial sector, public–private partnership, improved land management, accelerated trade liberalization, improved public services delivery, rationalized policies on subsidies and prices, and good governance.

The FY2016 budget targets a 29.5% increase in tax revenue that would lift the tax-to-GDP ratio by 1.3 percentage points to 10.6%, bringing total revenue to 12.1% of GDP (Figure 3.2.12). As the implementation of the new value-added tax law has slipped by a year to 1 July 2016, and as tax relief has been broadly granted, it will be very difficult to achieve the targeted growth in tax collection that substantially exceeds nominal GDP growth. Total budget expenditure, including current spending and the annual development program, is slated to grow by 23.1% to equal 17.2% of GDP, but achieving this large increase will also be problematic. While progress is expected toward fully implementing the budget, shortfalls will be likely on both sides of the ledger, as in previous years. Budget execution will hold the deficit to no more than 5% of GDP, as planned, but introducing the new value-added tax at the start of FY2017 would be a crucial step toward implementing the reform agenda and creating the fiscal space needed to step up infrastructure spending and support growth.

The central bank indicated in its latest monetary policy statement, issued in July for the first half of FY2016, that it would continue a cautious but pro-growth monetary policy that supports the government's growth objective and inflation target. While inflation has fallen almost to 6%, it remains at the high end of the central bank's comfort zone. Given the upward trend in nonfood inflation, the central bank kept the repo rate unchanged at 7.25%. The policy statement

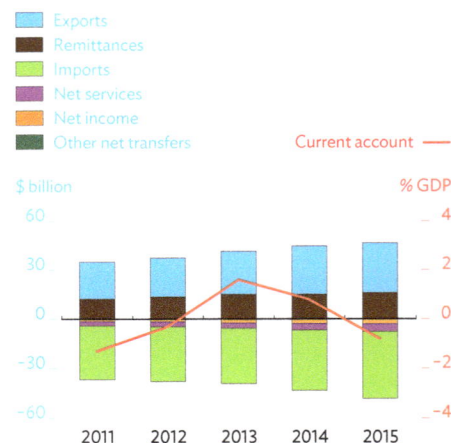

3.2.9 Current account components

Note: Years are fiscal years ending on 30 June of that year.
Source: Bangladesh Bank. Annual Report 2013–2014.
http://www.bangladesh-bank.org

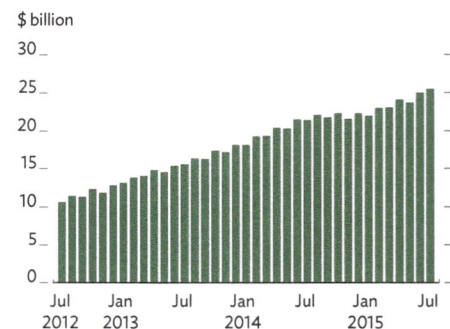

3.2.10 Foreign exchange reserves

Source: Bangladesh Bank. 2015. Major Economic Indicators, Monthly Update. August. http://www.bangladesh-bank.org

3.2.11 Exchange rates

Sources: Bangladesh Bank. 2015. Economic Trends. August. http://www.bangladesh-bank.org; Monetary Policy Department.

set the growth target for broad money at 15.6%, which is meant to take into account productive credit needs in both the public and the private sectors.

Moreover, the strategy of selective credit easing to support growth will be continued. In addition to windows for inclusive finance for small and medium-sized enterprises and for export development, a new medium- to long-term financing window—toward which the World Bank contributed $300 million of $500 million in capitalization—is now open to manufacturing enterprises and green initiatives in export-oriented textiles, apparel, and leather manufacturing.

The central bank is strengthening its supervision of bank governance. Second quarter 2015 figures for nonperforming loans show some decline since the final quarter of 2014 from the very high gross ratios at specialized banks, but those at state-owned commercial banks, which hold 25% of banking assets, remained essentially unchanged at 22.0% (Figure 3.2.13). Ratios at private and foreign banks worsened by about 1 percentage point, apparently reflecting stress on profit margins in the garment industry. For all banks the ratio was unchanged at 9.7%.

This *Update* retains the *ADO 2015* projection of 6.2% for average inflation in FY2016, matching the central bank's monetary policy statement. Although higher public sector wages and upward adjustments to administered prices for natural gas and electricity from 1 September 2015 will exert inflationary pressure, the easing of supply constraints, a cautious monetary policy, and a better crop outlook should keep inflation in check.

Export growth in FY2016 is projected to improve to 6.0% as economic growth in the euro area and the US strengthens. Imports are projected to increase by 13.0%, mainly in capital goods, industrial raw materials, and food grains. Remittance inflows are likely to grow by 9.0% as the government steps up efforts to place workers overseas. Despite higher growth in remittances, the larger trade deficit will likely mean a current account deficit equal to 0.5% of GDP in FY2016, narrower than in FY2015 but failing to achieve the small surplus projected in *ADO 2015*. Although stable over the past 2 years, the persistence of the current account deficit will likely cause the taka to depreciate against the dollar during the year. Capital and financial account inflows are seen as sufficient to boost gross foreign exchange reserves.

Several risks could derail the projections. Political stability is essential to gain the confidence of investors and consumers alike, maintain macroeconomic stability, and achieve higher economic growth. Revenue targets should be attained with matching expenditure adjustments to avoid inflationary pressure and ensure macroeconomic stability.

3.2.1 Selected economic indicators (%)

	2015 ADO 2015	2015 Update	2016 ADO 2015	2016 Update
GDP growth	6.1	6.5	6.4	6.7
Inflation	6.5	6.4	6.2	6.2
Current acct. bal. (share of GDP)	-0.5	-0.8	0.5	-0.5

Source: ADB estimates.

3.2.12 Fiscal indicators

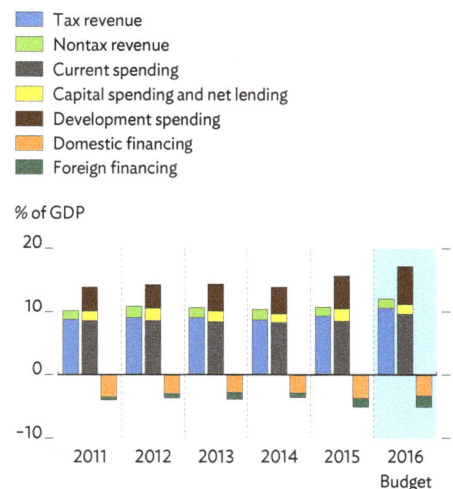

Note: Years are fiscal years ending on 30 June of that year.
Source: Asian Development Outlook database.

3.2.13 Gross nonperforming loan ratios

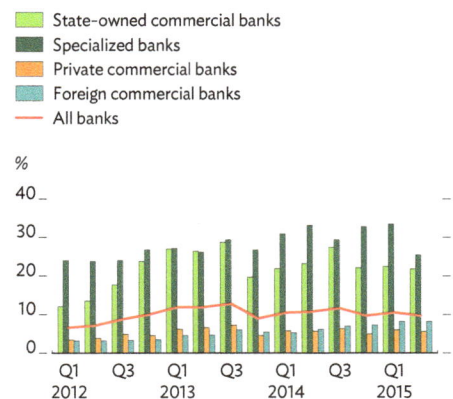

Q = quarter.
Source: Bangladesh Bank. *Bangladesh Bank Quarterly January–March 2015.* http://www.bangladesh-bank.org

People's Republic of China

Slowing more than expected in the first 8 months of 2015, economic growth is forecast to average 6.8% for the year. Export demand, tamped down by delayed recovery in the developed economies, should strengthen over the forecast period and, together with robust consumption growth, cushion the impact of decelerating investment growth.

Updated assessment

Economic growth in the People's Republic of China (PRC) moderated from a revised 7.3% in 2014 to 7.0% year on year in the first half of 2015 in line with the government's target for the full year (Figure 3.3.1). Labor markets remained healthy, as evidenced by the creation during the period of 7.2 million urban jobs, notably in services, and continued strong wage growth. The wages of migrant workers, who would be the first to suffer in an employment downturn, kept growing at near double-digit rates. Monthly purchasing manager indexes and indicators for industrial value added, retail sales, energy and cement production, and consumer confidence for July and August 2015 suggest that PRC growth performance has not fundamentally changed during the third quarter.

Services remained the key growth driver on the supply side, and domestic rebalancing from industry to services made further progress (Figure 3.3.2). Service sector growth accelerated from 7.8% year on year in 2014 to 8.3% in the first half of 2015. Growth was most pronounced in financial and real estate services. Equity market firms benefited from increased fee business during the stock market boom and subsequent correction, while real estate transactions were lifted as home sales responded to stabilization measures that included the removal of tight purchase restrictions, improved access to mortgages, and lower mortgage rates (which have declined by 1.2 percentage points since 2014), as well as to optimism that real estate prices have bottomed out at least in the larger cities.

Industry (including construction, manufacturing, and mining) expanded by 6.1% year on year in the first half of 2015, down from 7.3% in 2014 as a whole. The slowdown resulted from continued moderation of growth in construction from 9.1% year on year in 2014 to 7.0% in the first half of 2015, reflecting decelerating investment. This dampened demand for heavy equipment, mining products, and electricity, which helped reduce energy consumption per unit of GDP by 5.9% year on year in the first half. Within manufacturing, consumer-oriented enterprises did much better than heavy industries.

3.3.1 Economic growth

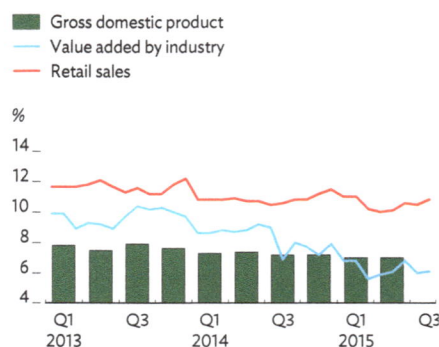

- Gross domestic product
- Value added by industry
- Retail sales

Q = quarter.
Source: National Bureau of Statistics.

3.3.2 Share of sectors in nominal GDP

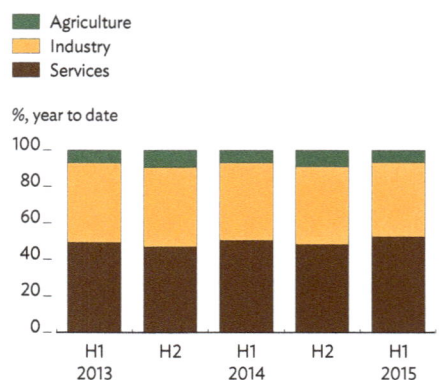

- Agriculture
- Industry
- Services

H = half.
Source: National Bureau of Statistics.

This chapter was written by Jurgen Conrad and Jian Zhuang of the PRC Resident Mission, ADB, Beijing.

Agriculture grew by only 3.5%, despite strong investment, as labor productivity improved less than expected.

On the demand side, consumption remained robust and contributed 4.2 percentage points to GDP growth in the first half of 2015 (Figure 3.3.3). The contribution of investment was 2.5 percentage points, and of net exports 0.3 points. Consumption was bolstered by upbeat consumer expectations and real disposable income growth of 7.6%. Rural households continued to enjoy faster income growth than urban households (Figure 3.3.4), helping to trim income disparities and support consumption and retail sales. Although housing sales revived, real estate investment growth remained anemic under a large overhang of unsold floor space, and growth in new housing starts languished deep in negative territory. Persistent and sizeable government support for infrastructure, shantytown redevelopment, and social housing construction could not fully compensate for decelerating private housing investment. Robust investment growth in better-performing and less capital-intensive areas of manufacturing and services could not outweigh the deceleration of investment in the more capital-intensive heavy industries, which face persistent excess capacity and a highly uncertain business outlook. Important structural changes are taking place in the PRC economy, and growth is becoming less investment driven in a measured way that aligns with government objectives. These changes and other demand-side constraints, such as limits on private investors' access to important areas of infrastructure and social service provision, are the main factors slowing investment growth—more so than financing constraints.

Price pressures remained moderate as the impact of rising food prices was dampened by declines in other commodity prices and by real renminbi appreciation, which reduced the local currency cost of imported goods. Consumer price inflation has edged up since the beginning of the year, quashing lingering deflation concerns (Figure 3.3.5). Driven by rising pork and vegetable prices, headline consumer inflation stepped up from 1.2% year on year in the first quarter of 2015 to 1.4% in the second quarter and to 2.0% in August. Core inflation rose from 1.4% in the first quarter to 1.6% in the second, and to 1.7% in August. Meanwhile, producer price deflation deepened from 4.6% in the first quarter to 4.7% in the second and to 5.9% in August. This trend reflected further weakness in global commodity prices rather than in domestic demand, given the high weighting of commodities in the PRC producer price index.

Growth in the consolidated budgetary revenue of the central and local governments accelerated from 3.9% year on year in the first quarter of 2015 to 7.4% in the first 8 months. It remained below the budget target for the full year, however, as a significant decline in the value of imports held import and resource tax revenues short of the budget, and as small and medium-sized companies received additional tax relief. Growth in consolidated budgetary expenditure also accelerated, from 7.8% to 14.8% over the same periods, which exceeded the target for the full year. A sign that fiscal policy had likely become more expansionary was shrinkage in the consolidated budget surplus, to 0.8% of GDP in the first half of 2015 from 2.0% a year earlier (Figure 3.3.6).

3.3.3 Demand-side contributions to growth

- Consumption
- Investment
- Net exports
- Gross domestic product

Percentage points, year to date

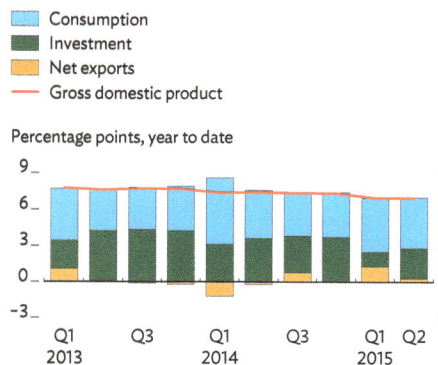

Q = quarter.
Source: National Bureau of Statistics.

3.3.4 Growth of per capita urban and rural incomes

- Urban
- Rural

%, year to date

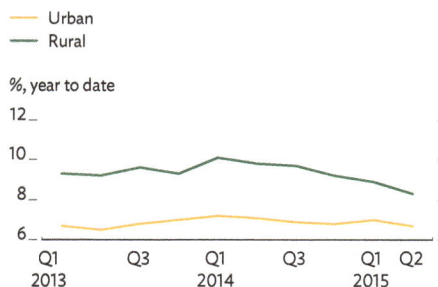

Q = quarter.
Source: National Bureau of Statistics.

3.3.5 Monthly inflation

- Overall consumer price inflation
- Core consumer price inflation
- Producer price inflation

%

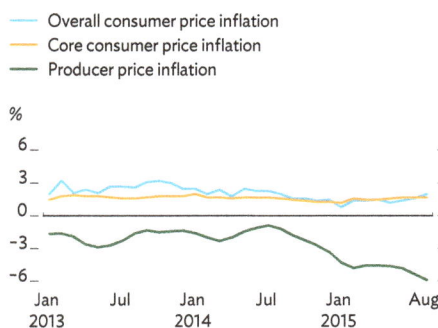

Sources: National Bureau of Statistics; People's Bank of China.

With central government revenue growth weaker than that of local governments, and the opposite holding true for expenditure growth, the fiscal burden has apparently moved a bit from local governments to the center. This shift aligns with the objective to consolidate local government finances. However, local governments' off-budget spending has apparently remained substantial, as in the past, though data are scarce. This lack of information continues to frustrate a comprehensive assessment of fiscal policy. Since January 2015, the revised budget law prohibits off-budget spending by local governments, which has been financed mainly through nonbank financing vehicles, leading to an increase in local government liabilities from CNY17.9 trillion at the end of June 2013 to CNY24.0 trillion (37.7% of GDP) at the end of 2014. However, the quota for local governments' issuance of bonds to finance deficits remains at only CNY600 million in 2015, which is too low to finance all off-budget spending if these expenditures are put on budget this year. The quota for local governments' issuance of bonds to refinance debt, on the other hand, has been increased to CNY3.2 trillion for 2015, which should be enough to cover almost all of this year's needs. Replacing maturing loans from banks and nonbank financial institutions with bonds helps to lower financing costs and makes local government finances more transparent.

The broad money supply (M2) grew by 11.3% in the first half of 2015, or 4.8 percentage points faster than nominal GDP growth, the same difference as in the first half of 2014 (Figure 3.3.7). This suggests that economic activity is not constrained by limits on credit, and that debt and its associated risks continue to mount, though less rapidly than before 2014. The People's Bank of China, the central bank, cut regulatory reserve requirements and benchmark loan and deposit rates on several occasions and injected liquidity into the banking system through open market operations and refinancing facilities for selected financial institutions, intending to stabilize money supply in light of capital outflows. Money market rates fell to historic lows as a result (Figure 3.3.8). Year on year, M2 growth moderated from 12.3% in the fourth quarter of 2014 to 11.6% in the first quarter of 2015 and 10.9% in the second, as credit demand further weakened, but jumped to 13.3% in July and August. Growth in total social financing (i.e., credit to nonfinancial enterprises and households from banks and nonbank financial institutions and capital markets) slowed more markedly, from 16.0% in the fourth quarter of 2014 to 14.9% in the first quarter of 2015 and to 13.3% in the second quarter, before recovering slightly to 13.4% in July and August. Regulatory tightening in 2013 and 2014 has forced nonbank financing, which is an important component of social financing though insufficiently captured in M2, to moderate much more than bank financing.

The renminbi, which had weakened somewhat against the US dollar in early 2015, subsequently strengthened amid market-driven fluctuations around the benchmark rate. It has weakened again since 11 August 2015, when the government moved to make the official exchange rate more market oriented and transparent by basing its determination on daily market quotes. This was another incremental step toward full exchange rate flexibility, a declared policy objective. Unchanged for the time being are the exchange rate band for the

3.3.6 Fiscal indicators and nominal GDP

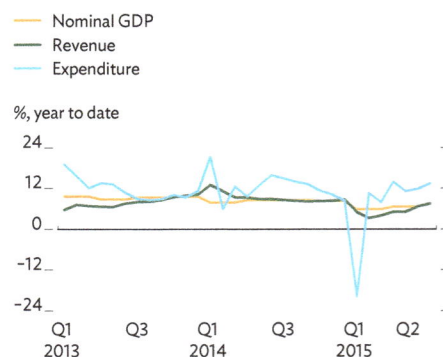

— Nominal GDP
— Revenue
— Expenditure

Q = quarter.
Sources: Ministry of Finance; National Bureau of Statistics.

3.3.7 Money supply and nominal GDP

Nominal GDP
— Money supply (M2)

Q = quarter.
Sources: National Bureau of Statistics; People's Bank of China; ADB estimates.

3.3.8 Interest rates and interbank offered rate

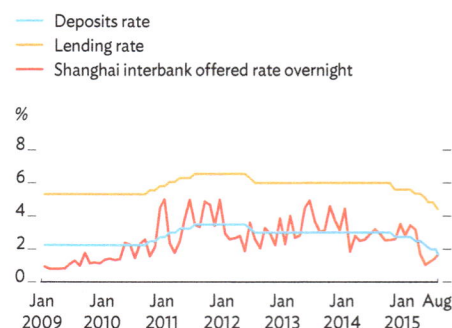

— Deposits rate
— Lending rate
— Shanghai interbank offered rate overnight

Source: People's Bank of China.

renminbi, which was widened back in March 2014 from ±1% to ±2%, and the composition of the currency basket, which remains geared toward the US dollar. However, as the dollar has risen against other currencies since last year, the renminbi has appreciated strongly in tandem in terms of its nominal effective rate (against a trade-weighted basket of currencies) and its real effective rate (taking inflation into account). During the second quarter of 2015, the renminbi was nearly 14% stronger in average real effective terms than a year earlier (Figure 3.3.9).

Exports fell by 1.4% year on year in dollar terms in the first 8 months of 2015 as recovery remained sluggish in the European Union, Japan, and the US, which directly absorb 40% of PRC exports, and as broader global demand softened. However, real export growth was stronger than the dollar figures suggest, given the weakness of other invoicing currencies like the euro and the Japanese yen. No clear evidence suggests that the PRC is losing global market share. A stronger renminbi might have narrowed the competitive edge of the PRC relative to other emerging economies, but exports have grown in line with external demand, and PRC merchandise trade surpluses are at historic highs. The PRC paid less for imports in the first 8 months of 2015 as their value fell by 14.5% year on year, owing mainly to lower commodity prices but also to important structural changes: Imports of raw materials have been declining as domestic demand for construction materials and energy weakens. Meanwhile, robust demand for consumer goods, including cars, and for intermediate products and machinery is increasingly met by domestic suppliers.

The trends in exports and imports left a trade surplus of $256.5 billion in the first half of 2015, up by more than 70% over the same period in 2014. Despite a sharp increase in the services deficit that reflects substantial overseas expenditure by outbound tourists, the PRC current account surplus rose by almost 90% year on year to $152.2 billion, or 3.1% of GDP (Figure 3.3.10). Net inflows of foreign direct investment remained strong, but net outflows of portfolio and other investment pushed the overall balance of payments into a deficit of $67.1 billion in the first half of 2015, which is close to equilibrium (Figure 3.3.11). Gross international reserves declined accordingly, but remained sizeable at $3.56 trillion at the end of August 2015.

After a pronounced stock market rally, which boosted the A-share indexes of Shanghai and Shenzhen by more than 90% from November 2014 to May 2015, both markets experienced corrections (Figure 3.3.12). Concerned about capital market and financial sector stability, the government took a number of measures. It further cut benchmark interest rates and regulatory reserve requirements, relaxed rules on margin financing, restricted short selling, suspended some initial public offerings, strengthened the capital of China Securities Finance Corporation (which provides refinancing to market participants) and pledged central bank liquidity support for it, bought exchange trade funds through the government investment company Central Huijin, convinced other securities and insurance companies to invest in shares, and initiated a share buyback program for state-owned enterprises. These measures have helped to arrest the fall in share prices for the time being, but their longer-term impact remains uncertain.

3.3.9 Exchange rates

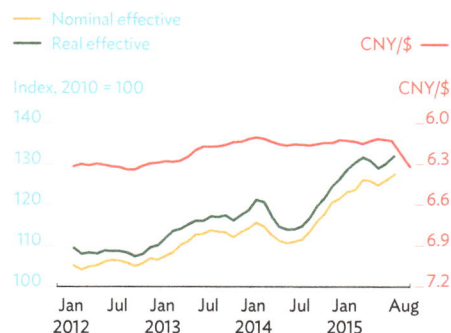

Sources: Bank for International Settlements; State Administration of Foreign Exchange.

3.3.10 Current account balance

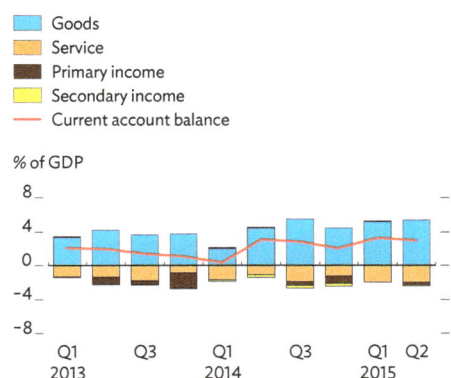

Q = quarter.
Sources: State Administration of Foreign Exchange; ADB estimates.

3.3.11 Capital and financial account

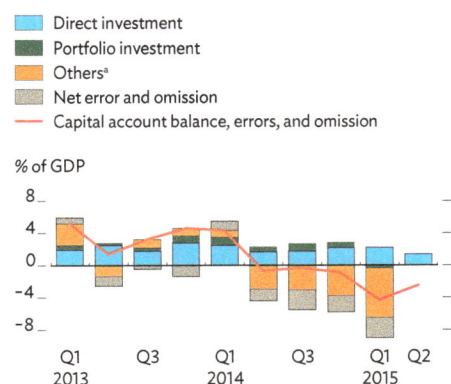

Q = quarter.
[a] Capital account, financial derivatives, and other investment.
Sources: State Administration of Foreign Exchange; ADB estimates.

Prospects

The economy decelerated more than expected in the first half of 2015, as structural changes gained traction and initially tamped down growth, and as tropical storms, the Tianjin disaster, and preparations for the Victory Day parade held back activity in a number of key manufacturing hubs during the third quarter. GDP growth forecasts are therefore revised down from those in *ADO 2015*, to 6.8% for 2015 and 6.7% for 2016 (Figure 3.3.13). Investment growth will continue to moderate, but less so in 2016 as progress toward structural reform (including deregulation of services) and better financing conditions start to invigorate private investment (Box 3.3.1). The fastest-growing investment segment will continue to be infrastructure, which the government uses as a countercyclical policy tool. Government support will increasingly be provided through policy banks such as the China Development Bank and the Agricultural Development Bank of China, which have been reformed, recapitalized, and authorized to issue infrastructure bonds. Improvements to the selection and management of infrastructure projects, partly through public–private partnership, should help to achieve the targeted growth rate with less investment. The already rapid growth of infrastructure investment is unlikely to accelerate, though, as viable projects are hard to find after years of strong investment growth (Figure 3.3.14). Real estate investment will remain the weakest segment in light of a large housing inventory overhang, particularly in lower-tier cities. However, the decline in real estate investment may bottom out in 2016 as the overhang tapers (Figure 3.3.15).

Though further progress toward financial sector reform and the opening up of the PRC economy will improve the investment climate, overall investment will continue to moderate because relatively healthy manufacturing and service industries require less capital than do construction and heavy industry, which are slowing more sharply. Consumption is expected to remain more robust than investment, its growth rate stabilizing at the level reached in the first half of 2015, provided that social expenditure goes up in line with policy objectives and that wage growth remains strong. Recovery in the developed economies, expected to unfold in the second half of 2015 and in 2016, should support PRC exports and GDP growth over this period.

At its meeting in late July 2015, the Politburo reiterated its preference for fiscal policy easing. Fiscal policy will thus likely stay broadly unchanged. Disappointing consolidated budget revenues may push the deficit above the indicative target of 2.7% of GDP in 2015 if the government sticks to its expenditure targets and lets automatic stabilizers work on the revenue side, as announced at the National People's Congress in March 2014. Further widening of the budget deficit is expected in 2016 as more off-budget activities of local governments are brought on budget. Efforts to curb local government spending will likely be rolled out over a longer period than assumed in *ADO 2015*, as soft growth in overall investment leads the government to prioritize short-term economic stability, and as consolidated public debt remains low by international standards. However, despite fine-tuning measures like allowing banks to continue to lend to local government financing vehicles for the time being, fiscal reform continues to target more

3.3.12 Stock markets

Sources: Shanghai Stock Exchange; Shenzhen Stock Exchange.

3.3.13 GDP growth

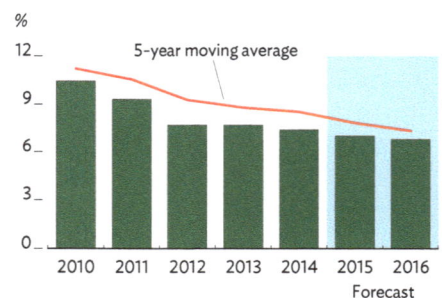

Source: Asian Development Outlook database.

3.3.14 Nominal growth of key components of fixed asset investment

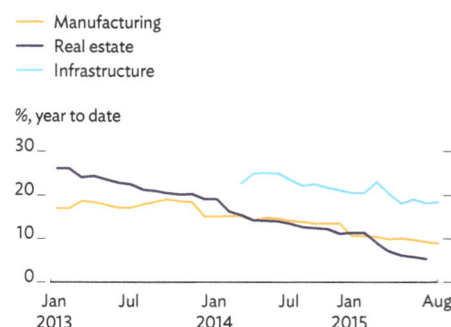

Source: National Bureau of Statistics.

efficient, accountable, and sustainable local government finance. Meanwhile, legislative and institutional preparations for a national property tax, including the establishment of a national property registry, are expected to advance over the forecast period.

The recent uptick in money supply growth will support GDP expansion in the coming months. However, monetary policy has to take into account the risks associated with high credit growth, which still substantially outpaces nominal GDP growth. In light of this, the need for further interest rate cuts is less compelling over the forecast period, particularly as (i) benchmark lending and deposit rates are already close to their historic lows after four rate cuts this year, (ii) higher US rates are expected soon, (iii) inflation will likely rise along with commodity prices, and (iv) the PRC leadership has made it clear that it sees structural reform, not monetary or fiscal stimulus, as the guarantor of sustainable growth. Nevertheless, further moves are expected toward full interest rate liberalization, for instance by deemphasizing the importance of benchmark rates. Regulatory reserve requirements—which, despite three cuts this year, remain high at 18.0% for larger banks—are likely to be further relaxed, thereby injecting liquidity in the banking system, provided that net foreign capital inflows remain moderate or negative.

With an increasingly flexible exchange rate policy, capital flows will become even more a function of progress toward opening the capital account and reforming the domestic financial sector. Over the forecast period, the government is expected to further enhance bond market access and liquidity, improve equity market governance, streamline share issuance procedures, and license more private banks to improve resource mobilization and allocation. In addition, it will launch a pilot for private cross-border capital transfers and reform existing cross-border institutional investor schemes.

Headline consumer price inflation should remain low in 2015 as global prices for food and other commodities remain depressed. This provides an opportunity for the government to further accelerate its reform of administered prices. In 2016, inflation will likely rebound as global commodity prices start to recover, which will also alleviate producer price deflation. Nevertheless, as consumer price inflation in the first half of 2015 was slightly lower than expected in *ADO 2015*, headline inflation forecasts are revised down, to 1.5% for 2015 and 2.2% for 2016 (Figure 3.3.16).

Foreign trade will benefit from accelerating global growth, even with slightly less favorable terms of trade and without much real renminbi depreciation. Trade and current account surpluses will nevertheless remain stable as global commodity prices recover.

Regarding risks to the forecast, the principal external upside risk stems from commodity prices slipping further if Iran's hydrocarbon exports increase following its long-sought nuclear deal. This may, however, be balanced by the downside risk of other events in the Middle East or North Africa pushing oil prices up. Another downside risk is recovery suffering a further delay in the major industrial economies. The Greek crisis is one factor that could undermine recovery in the euro area, for instance, and affect some of its trade partners. However, the risk of a Grexit from the euro in the short term has

3.3.1 Selected economic indicators (%)

	2015		2016	
	ADO 2015	Update	ADO 2015	Update
GDP growth	7.2	6.8	7.0	6.7
Inflation	1.8	1.5	2.3	2.2
Current acct. bal. (share of GDP)	2.3	2.3	2.0	2.2

Source: ADB estimates.

3.3.15 Real estate markets

m² = square meter.
Sources: National Bureau of Statistics; National Development and Reform Commission; ADB estimates.

3.3.16 Inflation

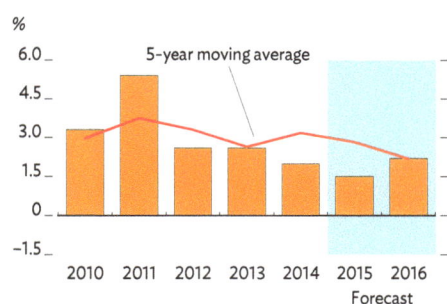

Source: Asian Development Outlook database.

3.3.1 Structural reform implemented

The comprehensive structural reform initiative launched at the Third Plenary Session of the 18th Central Committee of the Communist Party of the PRC in November 2013 has expanded effectively into many areas over the past 2 years, achieving the following milestones.

For the financial sector, the government has
- developed the regulatory framework for the Shanghai free-trade zone toward establishing a testing ground for service sector liberalization,
- strengthened regulations for trust funds and other nonbank financial institutions,
- adopted capital market development directives and streamlined the approval of public offerings,
- made benchmark deposit rates more flexible,
- introduced a deposit insurance scheme,
- licensed a number of private banks,
- doubled the renminbi trading band and made procedures for fixing the exchange rate more market driven, and
- opened a window for capital transfers between the exchanges in Shanghai and Hong Kong, China and removed the quota controlling foreign central banks' investment in onshore renminbi bond markets.

To improve public financial management, it has
- launched an enhanced pilot of local government bonds,
- amended the budget law to strengthen accountability and support local government finance reform,
- asked local governments to take stock of and report their off-budget liabilities to the central government and authorized them to replace high-interest loans from nonbank financial institutions with lower-interest bonds to improve transparency and ease the financial burden,
- improved access to such basic public services as health care and education,

- enacted enabling regulatory and institutional frameworks for public–private partnership that make it easier for private investors to provide social and infrastructure services, and
- made substantial progress toward reforming the taxation of natural resources and introducing environmental taxes.

Other reforms have
- introduced a new environmental protection law and an improved institutional framework for enforcing environmental norms that includes long-needed reform to the system for evaluating the performance of government officials,
- enhanced environmental protection agencies' independence from local authorities while institutionalizing cross-provincial cooperation and allowing third party environmental monitoring,
- launched and progressively broadened a major deregulation initiative that includes investment approvals and business licensing,
- unified urban and rural pension systems, and
- started implementing a new urbanization plan that emphasizes improving the quality of urban life and cities' ecological environment, triggering initiatives in low-income and public rental housing and shantytown renovation, revisiting the household registration system, and pursuing rural land reform on a pilot basis in several provinces.

The government's gradual approach to reform is likely to continue over the forecast period and gain traction in more areas, including the reform of state-owned enterprises, for which further details were announced in early September. The reform horizon of the Third Plenum is 5–7 years. So far, the Government of the PRC seems to be on track to meet its structural reform objectives.

been lowered by the agreement allowing another support program. The impact of a Grexit on the remaining countries in the euro area would be small in any case, and any global spillover even smaller.

The principal domestic risk is the current stock market correction possibly affecting consumption, investment, and financial stability. However, in the PRC, wealth effects have had negligible impact on consumption in the past, and equities account for only a small share of household wealth, with large household savings providing a buffer. The risk that a share price decline will engender a financial crisis is small, as only a few institutions have sizeable exposure to the stock market, and brokerages can access emergency liquidity facilities. Further, the stock market plays a relatively small role in corporate finance, which is still dominated by self-financing and bank loans. In 2014, financing through net equity issuance equaled only 4.3% of financing through bank loans.

India

Unexpectedly sluggish growth in the major industrial economies, a weak monsoon, flagging global trade, and parliamentary deadlock stalling action on some key structural reforms are expected to curb growth to 7.4% in FY2015 and 7.8% in FY2016—both below *ADO 2015* forecasts. Inflation and current account projections are unchanged. Investors are expected to favor India as the next big growth opportunity once the pace of economic overhaul picks up again.

Updated assessment

GDP growth slowed to 7.0% in the first quarter of FY2015 (ending 31 March 2016) from 7.5% in the last quarter of FY2014. The deceleration was broad-based, with private consumption, manufacturing, and services all experiencing slower growth.

On the demand side, year-on-year growth in private consumption moderated from 7.9% in the last quarter of FY2014 to a still-robust 7.4% in the first quarter of FY2015 (Figure 3.4.1). Increased urban demand in response to lower inflation and interest rates sustained the expansion and offset rural demand weakened by muted increases for minimum agriculture support prices and rural wages. Fixed investment growth picked up to 4.9% in the first quarter of FY2015 from 4.1% in the previous quarter, indicating a continuing gradual recovery in capital expenditure. The advance was driven mainly by higher government investment as the private sector continues to show little interest in launching new business ventures. With exports contracting at a faster clip than imports, net exports pulled down GDP growth by 0.2 percentage points.

Agriculture grew by 1.9% in the first quarter of FY2015 (Figure 3.4.2). While this performance reversed contraction in the previous 2 quarters, the expansion was held in check by a deficient monsoon that crimped the sown area a year earlier and produced a disappointing winter crop. Indeed, production contracted for key winter crops: rice, wheat, coarse cereals, and pulses. The growth recovery came from strong livestock, forestry, and fishery performance. Growth in industry picked up to 6.5% in the first quarter of FY2015 as faster clearances accelerated mining activity and the weak monsoon allowed construction to carry on longer than usual. Manufacturing grew by a respectable 7.2%, but less than the 8.4% expansion a year earlier, reflecting lower exports of manufactured goods, especially petroleum products from India's large private refining industry. Expansion in electricity generation also slowed markedly as distribution companies lowered their offtake.

This chapter was written by Johanna Boestel, Abhijit Sen Gupta, and Nidhi Kapoor of the India Resident Mission, ADB, New Delhi.

3.4.1 Demand-side contributions to growth

- Private consumption
- Government consumption
- Investment
- Net export
- Others
- Gross domestic product

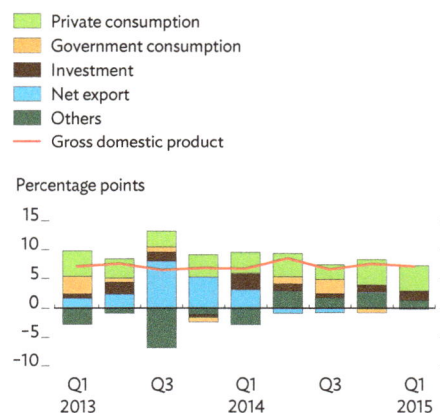

Q = quarter.
Note: Years are fiscal years; Q1 is April–June.
Source: Ministry of Statistics and Programme Implementation. http://www.mospi.nic.in (accessed 1 September 2015).

3.4.2 Supply-side contributions to growth

- Agriculture
- Services
- Industry
- Gross domestic product

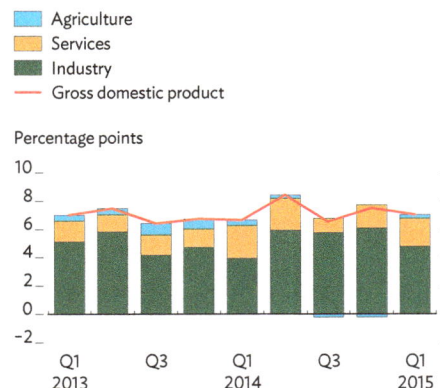

Q = quarter.
Note: Years are fiscal years; Q1 is April–June.
Source: Ministry of Statistics and Programme Implementation. http://www.mospi.nic.in (accessed 1 September 2015).

The first quarter of FY2015 saw services grow at 8.9%, a tad slower than the 9.2% recorded a year earlier. Growth in trade, hotels, transport, and communication edged up to 12.8%, mainly on growth in private hotels and restaurants, air passengers and cargo, and sales of commercial vehicles. Meanwhile, financial, insurance, real estate, and professional services growth slipped to 8.9% as property sales volume declined.

Low global crude oil prices, a positive base effect, and tight monetary policy kept consumer price inflation benign at an average of 4.8% in the first 4 months of FY2015 (Figure 3.4.3). Although food inflation ticked up slightly in June as the prices of vegetables and pulses rose, it quickly corrected in July on better supply. Food inflation has stayed well below rates observed in recent years as increases in procurement prices moderated for the third consecutive year, rural wage growth stabilized, and food supply management improved with checks on hoarding and encouragement for imports. Core inflation has trended downward and now hovers just above 4%.

With inflation slowing, the central bank in January started reducing its main policy rate, the repo rate, by a cumulative 75 basis points, with the last cut of 25 basis points taking place in June (Figure 3.4.4). It has since refrained from further rate cuts to balance inflation risk. A hardening of core inflation and the possibility of an agricultural shortfall from a weak monsoon are downside risks to the maintenance of price stability; mitigating factors include the continuation of low crude oil and other commodity prices. The authorities have been concerned that only a fraction of the policy rate reduction has been passed on to borrowers in the form of lower lending rates. To improve the transmission of monetary policy, the central bank has mooted a proposal requiring banks to calculate their base rate, which sets the structure of customer lending rates, according to their marginal cost of funds, which is sensitive to changes in policy rates.

The ratio of commercial banks' nonperforming assets to all assets rose further to 4.6% in March, while the ratio of restructured assets rose to 6.5%, pushing the ratio of all stressed assets to total assets up to 11.1% from 10.0% a year earlier (Figure 3.4.5). The stressed-asset ratio at private banks stands at 4.6%, while that of public sector banks, which account for about 70% of lending, reached 13.5%. Lending in five areas—mining, iron and steel, textiles, infrastructure, and aviation—account for more than half of stressed loans. To improve the performance of banks in the public sector, the government is appointing new bank management and has taken steps to strengthen lending standards and improve the credit culture. To resolve bad assets including willful defaults more quickly and effectively, the central bank has proposed a stringent scheme for strategic debt restructuring that would have banks take majority stakes in stressed companies, expedite the conversion of debt into equity, and bring in new management to run the enterprise.

Despite signs of economic recovery, credit growth has continued to ebb, dropping to less than 10% in 2015. Low inflation and substitution away from bank credit toward cheaper fund sources such as commercial paper and external borrowing appear to be factors sustaining the slow expansion in bank credit.

3.4.3 Inflation

- Core consumer price index
- Food consumer price index
- Consumer price index

% change, year on year

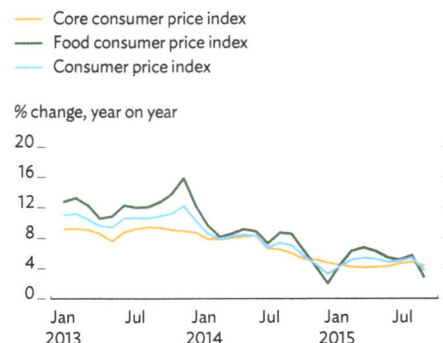

Sources: CEIC data company (accessed 25 August 2015); ADB estimates.

3.4.4 Policy interest rates

- Reverse repo rate
- Repo rate
- Marginal standing facility rate
- Interbank call money rate

%

Source: Bloomberg (accessed 24 August 2015).

3.4.5 Nonperforming and restructured loans

- Restructured loans
- Nonperforming loans

% share of loans and advances

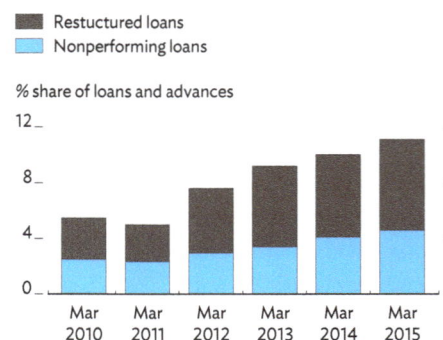

Source: Reserve Bank of India. http://www.rbi.org.in

The federal government deficit is expected to narrow to 3.9% of GDP in FY2015 from 4.1% in FY2014 (Figure 3.4.6). Data for the first 4 months of the fiscal year point to a deficit equal to nearly 70% of the targeted deficit, which is slightly higher than average in the 4 previous years. Tax revenue grew by a robust 17.9%, well above the target, on strong expansion in excise duty collection augmented by higher excise duties on petroleum products and the withdrawal of exemptions for various consumer durables. Custom duties and service tax collections remained strong, but slumping collections of income and corporate taxes point to continuing sluggishness in the corporate sector. Despite strong growth in overall tax revenue, revenue accruing to the central government grew by a tepid 4.8% with higher transfers to states mandated by the Finance Commission in January 2015. Nearly Rs126.3 billion (0.1% of GDP) was raised through divestment of public shares in the first half of FY2015, a record for the past 7 years.

Despite strong revenues, the fiscal deficit from April to July was higher than average because of significant growth in expenditure. Encouragingly for economic growth, capital expenditure grew by an impressive 39%, well above the 25% target, on higher outlays for electric power, roads, and shipping. Although low commodity prices reduced fuel subsidies, current expenditure grew by 16.5%, also significantly above the 2.5% target.

The current account deficit in the first quarter of FY2015 improved to 1.2% of GDP from 1.6% a year earlier, helped by moderate monthly trade deficits (Figure 3.4.7). The strong performance reflects a smaller trade deficit at $34.2 billion and lower net outflows from the primary income account. Trade deficit shrinkage from a year earlier occurred with a 12.1% fall in imports that reflected mainly the sharp fall in oil prices, which have accounted for about 35% of imports. Lower prices for other commodities were also a factor. Import volumes of goods other than oil and gold inched up on some strengthening of domestic demand. Food imports increased as the government worked to augment domestic supplies ahead of a doubtful monsoon. Exports, which are substantially smaller than imports, contracted by 16.7%. Exports of refined petroleum products dropped by 53.1%, primarily because of a large fall in crude oil prices but also in part due to reduced export volume. Other exports fell by 7.2% on lackluster demand in key markets. Readymade garments and pharmaceuticals were among the few categories that saw some growth.

Net foreign direct investment inflows reached $10.2 billion in the first quarter of FY2015, up by 29.1% from the quarter a year earlier, led by investments in computer software and hardware, automobiles, and telecommunications. Following a long period of large net portfolio capital inflows from foreign institutional investors, the first quarter of FY2015 saw the strong inflow in April erased by net outflows in May and June as investors everywhere grew averse to risk. Inflows picked up a bit in July before falling sharply again in August as investors sold $2.6 billion in stock (Figure 3.4.8). Equity markets worldwide were spooked by worries over the outlook for the global economy and a possible tightening of US monetary policy (Figure 3.4.9). A rise in real interest rates helped to boost deposits by nonresident Indians significantly to $5.8 billion in the first quarter of FY2015.

3.4.6 Federal budget indicators

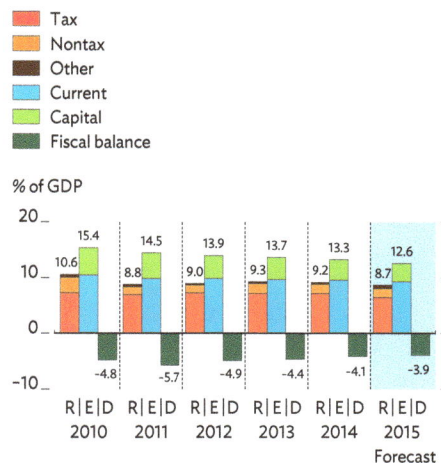

R = revenue, E = expenditure, D = deficit financing.
Note: Years are fiscal years ending on 31 March of the next year.
Source: Ministry of Finance Union Budget 2014–2015. http://www.indiabudget.nic.in

3.4.7 Trade indicators

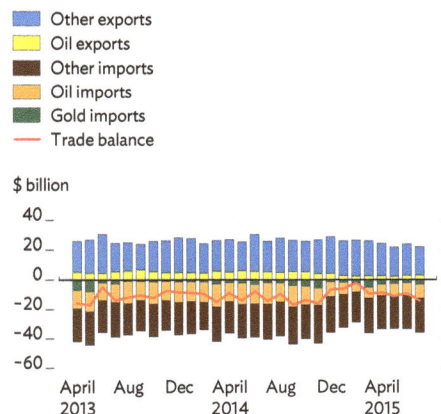

Source: CEIC Data Company (accessed 9 September 2015).

3.4.8 Portfolio flows

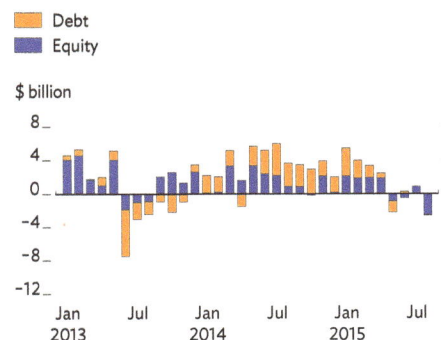

Source: Securities and Exchange Board of India.

To manage exchange rate volatility, the central bank has been intervening on the spot and forward markets. A healthy external position and low inflation allowed the Indian rupee to remain broadly stable in real effective terms in the first 5 months of FY2015 as it depreciated by about 6% against a strengthening US dollar (Figure 3.4.10). International reserves increased by $10 billion to $352 billion in the period (Figure 3.4.11).

Prospects

The forecasts in *ADO 2015* assumed improved growth in the advanced economies, a normal monsoon, monetary easing, the clearing of some structural bottlenecks, and robust growth in the government's capital expenditure. This *Update* takes into account decelerating growth in the major industrial economies and the People's Republic of China, the monsoon faltering a bit after a good start, and some forward movement on structural reform despite action on some key reforms being delayed.

A pickup in the pace of investment is vital for sustained economic recovery. While investment conditions have improved in recent quarters, significant challenges remain. Clearing the bottlenecks of stalled investment projects is likely to provide a fillip to investment. The Project Monitoring Group, set up in mid-2013 to resolve issues that were stalling large infrastructure projects, cleared projects worth an additional $45 billion in the first half of 2015 to bring the total of projects resolved to nearly $150 billion, equal to 7.0% of GDP. Data from the Centre for Monitoring Indian Economy shows that the value of stalled projects was reined in for the fourth consecutive quarter in April–June 2015, with much of the reduction from government projects. While there was an encouraging increase in the value of new projects announced in the second half of 2014, this figure fell in the first 2 quarters in 2015 (Figure 3.4.12). Moreover, important reforms that would further boost growth but remain pending under parliamentary deadlock include simplifying the domestic tax system by introducing a common goods and services tax, amending the law on land acquisition so that it balances social safeguards with the requirements of the industry, and labor reform to make manufacturing more competitive.

Manufacturing is improving, albeit slowly. While the Nikkei purchasing managers' index reached in July its highest in 6 months, the services purchasing managers' index has been mixed and more volatile, returning to growth in July after contracting for 2 months (Figure 3.4.13). Moreover, the Organisation for Economic Co-operation and Development composite leading index for India has been, after a multiyear decline, on an upswing from the fourth quarter of 2014. However, the central bank's industrial outlook survey shows business confidence weakening slightly as optimism ebbs regarding order books, imports, and capacity utilization (Figure 3.4.14). Slower growth than anticipated in the major industrial economies, including the US, and the currencies of some major trading partners weakening against Indian rupee are likely to tamp down exports of merchandise and tradable services in finance, telecommunications, and business.

3.4.9 Stock price indexes

- Sensex
- MSCI ACAP excluding Japan
- Emerging markets excluding Asia

Index, 1 Jan 2009 = 100

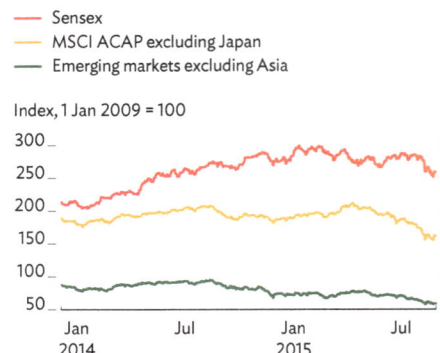

Source: Bloomberg (accessed 9 September 2015).

3.4.10 Exchange rates

Real effective   Nominal

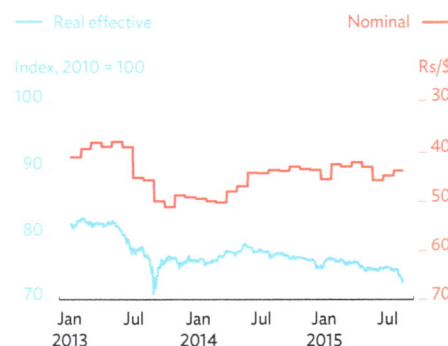

Source: Bloomberg (accessed 24 August 2015).

3.4.11 International reserves

- Gold and special drawing rights
- Foreign exchange reserves

$ billion

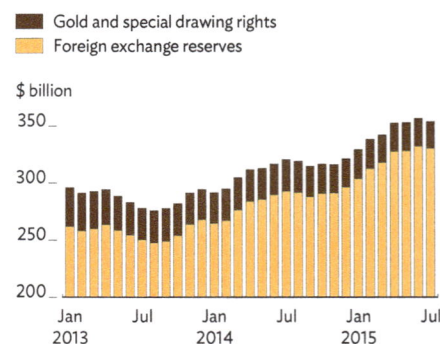

Source: CEIC Data Company (accessed 4 September 2015).

Some policy headroom exists for improving growth. The sharp drop in consumer price inflation in July and August left some scope for monetary easing in the second half of FY2015. Moreover, banks' fuller transmission of the policy rate cuts undertaken in the first half of 2015 would bolster growth prospects. However, for lower lending rates to substantially boost demand for credit, further progress is needed toward economic reform and strengthening business confidence (Figure 3.4.15). Although fiscal headroom is constrained by the objective of narrowing the budget deficit to 3.9% of GDP, improving the expenditure mix would boost economic growth.

Monsoon rainfall has been 12% below normal despite a strong opening in June. Summer crop planted area is only marginally larger than last year, when a monsoon constrained sowing. A weak monsoon through September would likely affect winter crops, further hampering weak rural demand as well as agricultural output.

The weak monsoon, flagging external demand, and stalled parliamentary action on structural reforms, including a revamped domestic tax system and eased restrictions in land acquisition and labor, are expected to slow the economy. With growth in the industrial economies strengthened by policy action but still falling short of earlier assumptions, growth is revised to 7.4% in FY2015 from the 7.8% projected in *ADO 2015*, and to 7.8% in FY2016, also lower than forecast. The revisions reflect the expectation that advancing reform and boosting investor confidence will likely take some months and that global markets pose a risk if they are roiled by exaggerated reactions to events such as the expected US move to increase policy interest rates. As the government's plans to roll out the uniform goods and services tax in April 2016 are apparently on hold, the substantial benefits promised by this major economic reform will be deferred.

Consumer inflation is likely to remain within the central bank and government target of 4% ±2 percentage points. Despite the deficient monsoon, food inflation is expected to remain benign because minimum support prices increased only modestly in 2015 and the government moved proactively to contain inflation volatility. Low global crude oil prices are expected to hold down fuel inflation—though rupee depreciation poses a downside risk. Core inflation hovered around 4.5% in the early months of FY2015 and is expected to remain subdued by tight monetary policy, constrained rural demand, and improved inflation expectations (though they rose marginally in the most recent quarter). Consumer inflation is expected to edge up during the second half of FY2015 as the favorable base effect wanes. Nevertheless, inflation is expected to average 5.0% in FY2015, in line with the forecast in *ADO 2015*. Improved growth and an uptick in prices for commodities, including crude oil, are expected to boost inflation to 5.5% in FY2016.

Nearly 70% of the budgeted fiscal deficit was spent in the first 4 months of FY2015, generating some fiscal pressure. However, it could subside in the coming months as revenue gets a boost from public enterprises' dividend payments and asset sales, which typically occur in the second half of the fiscal year. The government could resort to expenditure control in the final months of the year. The decline in subsidies to 1.6% of GDP appears realistic given low crude oil prices

3.4.1 Selected economic indicators (%)

	2015		2016	
	ADO 2015	Update 2015	ADO 2015	Update 2015
GDP growth	7.8	7.4	8.2	7.8
Inflation	5.0	5.0	5.5	5.5
Current acct. bal. (share of GDP)	-1.1	-1.1	-1.5	-1.5

Source: ADB estimates.

3.4.12 New investment projects announced

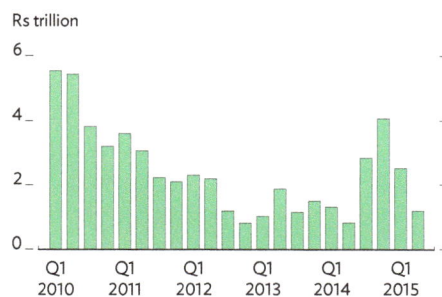

Q = quarter.
Note: Years are fiscal years; Q1 is April–June.
Source: Centre for Monitoring Indian Economy.

3.4.13 Purchasing managers' index

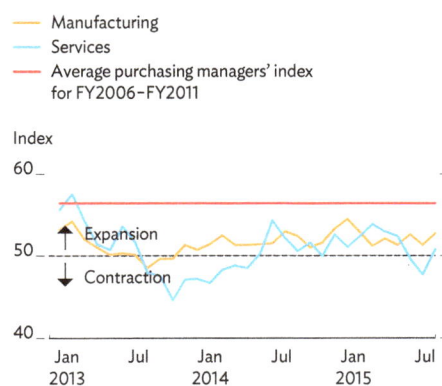

Note: Nikkei, Markit.
Source: Bloomberg (accessed 24 August 2015).

and steps taken to deregulate diesel prices, introduce cash transfer for the cooking gas subsidy, and cap some fuel subsidies. The reduced subsidy bill frees fiscal resources for infrastructure investment and a buffer in case receipts from divestment fall short of the ambitious target. Improved manufacturing performance bodes well for collections of excise and corporate taxes, though continued import contraction could squeeze custom duties.

The import bill is expected to shrink with the projected 37% decline in the average crude oil price in FY2015. The rise in real interest rates and the government's push to convert investment from physical gold to certificates backed by gold will contain gold imports. Imports other than gold and oil are likely to improve a bit during the rest of the year along with domestic demand, but not enough to offset the decline in value of petroleum imports. Overall imports are therefore expected to contract by about 10% in FY2015. The slump in exports over the past few months is likely to continue with listless global demand and a drop in exports of refined oil products. Growth in services exports is likely to be modest, affected by the slowdown in the industrial economies. Remittance inflows are expected to remain stable. On balance, the current account deficit is expected to be 1.1% of GDP, significantly narrower than in recent years.

Some recovery in oil prices and improved demand for industry and investment will likely push import growth to 8.0% in FY2016. Exports are also likely to recover, growing by 3.5% as higher petroleum prices boost the value of exports of refined petroleum products and as external demand improves. The current account deficit is expected to widen marginally to 1.5% of GDP.

Inflows of foreign direct investment are likely to remain strong. The government is striving to attract additional inflows by lifting limits on foreign direct investment and making business easier to conduct. However, portfolio flows are likely to moderate. With more than 85% of the cap utilized, scope for additional foreign investment in the bond market is limited. Equity flows are likely to remain volatile, with sentiment driven by economic developments in the industrial economies and the People's Republic of China, progress on structural reform, and India's own growth prospects.

3.4.14 Industry outlook survey

— Order books
— Capacity utilization
— Business situation
— Imports

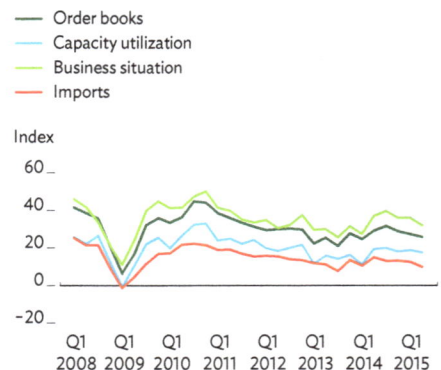

Q = quarter.
Note: Years are fiscal years; Q1 is April–June.
Source: Reserve Bank of India. http://www.rbi.org.in

3.4.15 Bank credit growth

— Nonfood credit
— Large industry

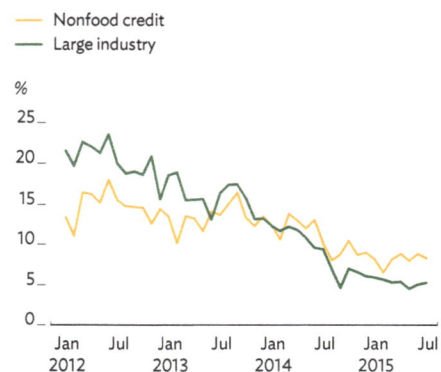

Source: Bloomberg (accessed 9 September 2015).

Indonesia

Stronger public investment in infrastructure is now seen to pull the economy out of a slowdown that persisted in the first half of 2015. Infrastructure upgrades, reform to attract private investment, and some recovery in exports next year should spur expansion in 2016. However, growth in both years will undershoot earlier projections. As inflation is subsiding more gradually than anticipated, forecasts for this year and next are raised. Turbulence in financial markets has rattled the rupiah despite an improved current account.

Updated assessment

GDP growth slowed to 4.7% year on year in the first half of 2015 as investment and household consumption both decelerated (Figure 3.5.1). Growth in fixed investment eased to 3.9% even as the government that took office in October 2014 introduced a number of reforms to revive investment (Figure 3.5.2). Although the government doubled the infrastructure budget for 2015, only 10% was disbursed in the first 6 months, mainly because of budget revisions undertaken early in the year and time taken to appoint senior ministry officials. Investment in buildings and infrastructure rose by 5.1%, but investment in machinery and equipment fell by 3.3%.

Household consumption remained relatively robust, moderating slightly from 2014 because of higher inflation and tighter consumer credit. Expanding by 5.0%, household consumption contributed more than half of GDP growth. Good harvests in the first half and government cash payments to compensate low-income earners for higher fuel prices helped to support incomes and consumption spending. Government consumption grew by 2.5%, recovering from a sharp slowdown in the first half of 2014. Net external demand made a solid contribution to GDP growth as imports of goods and services fell by 4.6% in real terms, a much steeper decline than the 0.5% fall in exports of goods and services.

By sector, services and manufacturing grew at a slower pace than a year earlier, but still generated most of the increase in GDP. Services expanded by 5.4% and contributed half of growth. Continued rapid expansion of communication was a major contributor to services growth. Manufacturing grew by a modest 4.2% as growth slowed in the food and beverages subsector, which accounts for one-quarter of manufacturing. Growth in construction eased to 5.7% in line with more subdued overall investment and delays on government-led projects.

3.5.1 Demand-side contributions to growth

- Household consumption
- Nonprofit institutions serving households
- Government consumption
- Gross fixed capital formation
- Stocks
- Net exports
- Statistical discrepancy
- Gross domestic product

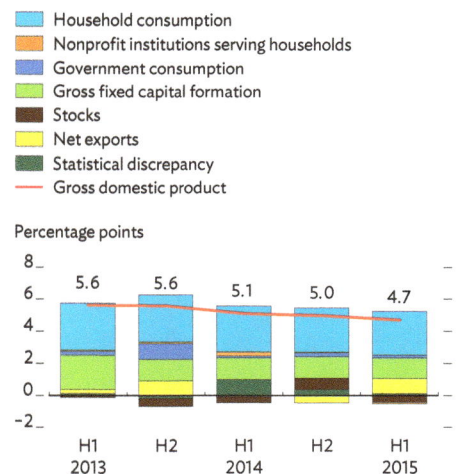

Percentage points

H = half.

Sources: CEIC Data Company; Haver Analytics (both accessed 4 September 2015).

3.5.2 Fixed investment

Share — Growth —

% of GDP — % change, year on year

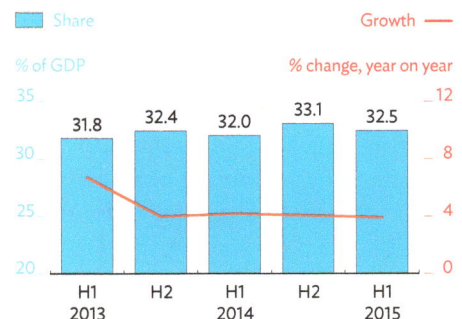

H = half.

Source: Haver Analytics (accessed 4 September 2015).

This chapter was written by Edimon Ginting and Priasto Aji of the Indonesia Resident Mission, ADB, Jakarta.

Agriculture performed well in the first half, expanding by 5.4% on higher rice production made possible in part by the increased planting of high-yielding varieties. Palm oil and natural rubber production fell, though, on weaker global demand and prices. By contrast, declining crude oil extraction and weak commodity prices cut mining output by 3.6%.

In the 12 months to February 2015, the economy generated 2.7 million new jobs, or fewer than the 3.0 million new entrants into the workforce in that period. Manufacturing, community services, and wholesale trading accounted for most of the new jobs. An increase in formal employment of 3.4 million jobs and a decline of 660,000 jobs in the informal sector indicated improved quality of employment. However, a lack of jobs may have contributed to a rise in poverty to 11.2% in March 2015 from 11.0% in September 2014.

Inflation abated only gradually from 8.4% at the end of last year to average 6.9% over the first 8 months of 2015 (Figure 3.5.3). The government raised prices of gasoline and diesel after slashing fuel subsidies in November 2014, and it increased prices for cooking gas and electricity for all but low-income groups as part of its effort to improve the targeting of subsidies. Import restrictions on some staples such as beef put upward pressure on food prices despite a good rice harvest. Core inflation, excluding fuel and fresh food, was about 5% in the first half.

Bank Indonesia, the central bank, reduced its policy interest rate by 25 basis points to 7.5% in February this year then kept the rate unchanged. Growth in credit slowed to 10.4% year on year in June 2015 from 17.2% in June 2014, reflecting soft demand for loans and higher bank interest rates.

The trade surplus rose sharply in January–June. Merchandise exports fell by 12.4% in US dollar terms on unexpectedly weak demand in major markets such as the People's Republic of China (PRC) and lower prices for export commodities. Merchandise imports fell in US dollar terms even more steeply than exports, by 17.7%, because of rupiah depreciation, decelerating investment, and a drop in oil imports stemming from both lower oil prices and lower consumption in the wake of the fuel subsidy cuts. Consequently, the trade surplus rose by 79% to $7.2 billion, which, coupled with lower deficits in services and primary income, narrowed the current account deficit to $8.6 billion, equal to 2.0% of GDP, from $13.0 billion in second half of 2014 (Figure 3.5.4).

After smaller surpluses in the capital and financial accounts, the balance of payments posted a $1.6 billion deficit. Foreign direct investment was fairly buoyant at $9.0 billion, compared with $10.2 billion in the first half of 2014. Net inflows of portfolio investment at $14.6 billion were down 13.1% from a year earlier. Gross international reserves fell by $6.6 billion to $105.3 billion in 2015 to August, largely reflecting repayment of private external debt and, to a smaller extent, the central bank's sales of foreign currency to support the rupiah (Figure 3.5.5). Reserves in August covered 6.9 months of imports and government debt repayments.

Indonesia's financial markets and the rupiah weakened sharply in August, the falls triggered by the stock market slide and renminbi devaluation in the PRC and by expectations of a rise in US interest rates.

3.5.3 Policy and inflation rates

Source: Haver Analytics (accessed 4 September 2015).

3.5.4 Current account components

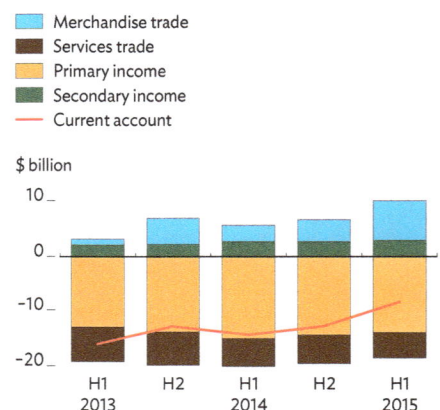

H = half.
Source: Haver Analytics (accessed 4 September 2015).

3.5.5 Gross international reserves and exchange rate

Sources: Haver Analytics; Bloomberg (both accessed 4 September 2015).

However, net sales of shares by foreign investors in August and the rise in yields on government bonds still were far below those at the height of the "taper tantrum" in June 2013. Foreign investors' holdings of rupiah-denominated government bonds rose by $4.6 billion in the first 8 months despite substantial net outflows in August. Standard & Poor's, citing improved fiscal policy credibility, revised up its credit rating outlook for Indonesia to positive from stable in May 2015, which helped to support financial markets. Nevertheless, the rupiah depreciated by 13.7% against the US dollar in 2015 to early September.

Prospects

The new government's economic policy priorities were to accelerate infrastructure development and implement bold reforms to spur investment. The administration doubled the budget for infrastructure in 2015 and implemented several reforms, but the impact on economic growth has been delayed largely by slow fund disbursement. Projections in this *Update* assume that the government will achieve stronger infrastructure investment from the second half of 2015 and will follow through on other investment reforms.

The role of public investment is increasingly important as recovery in private investment has been weaker than anticipated. By the end of August, the rate of capital budget disbursement had improved to about 30%. The government has taken steps to accelerate budget execution that, in tandem with an annual pattern of much higher outlays in the fourth quarter, aim to sharply raise the rate of capital budget disbursement to 80%–85% by the end of 2015.

Further, the government injected additional capital into state-owned enterprises involved in infrastructure and will allow some of them to borrow directly from international financial institutions with government guarantees to build infrastructure. Local administrations are encouraged to tap their accumulated surpluses for public investment and face penalties imposed by the central government if they underspend their budgets. Importantly, officials have advanced the bidding for most projects in the 2016 budget to the second half of 2015 to speed implementation. Progress has also been made in accelerating land acquisition for infrastructure.

As anticipated, government revenue will likely fall short of an ambitious tax revenue target set early in 2015 due to slowing economic activity and lower revenue from oil and international trade. Nevertheless, to accommodate funding for infrastructure, the government moved in August to widen its budget deficit to the equivalent of 2.2% of GDP from an original target of 1.9%. The actual deficit in 2014 also was 2.2% of GDP. This year's deficit could end up slightly wider to accommodate additional countercyclical spending to help lower-income groups announced in September. By late August, the government had raised 83% of its targeted budget financing from debt issuance. Additional funding is expected from bilateral and multilateral development partners.

The budget proposed for 2016 maintains an expansionary fiscal stance. It includes a more realistic revenue target and a fiscal deficit equal to 2.1% of GDP. Spending on health is to rise by 43%, and spending

3.5.1 Selected economic indicators (%)

	2015 ADO 2015	2015 Update	2016 ADO 2015	2016 Update
GDP growth	5.5	4.9	6.0	5.4
Inflation	5.5	6.7	4.0	5.1
Current acct. bal. (share of GDP)	-2.8	-2.5	-2.4	-2.1

Source: ADB estimates.

3.5.6 Consumer and business confidence indexes

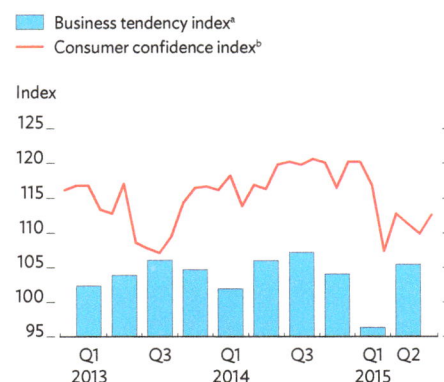

Q = quarter.
[a] From a quarterly Statistics Indonesia survey of business executives.
[b] From a monthly Bank Indonesia survey of households.
Note: A score above 100 means that respondents are optimistic and vice versa.
Source: Haver Analytics (accessed 4 September 2015).

on infrastructure by a further 8%. If approved, the budget will reduce electricity subsidies and improve the targeting of subsidies for fertilizer and housing for the poor.

Policy reforms are expected to stimulate private investment, though its recovery has been delayed by such factors as weak external demand. Reforms include a new one-stop service for investment licensing and the encouragement of private investment in selected infrastructure through public–private partnership. The impact of these reforms, announced earlier this year, was partly negated by moves to tighten some restrictions on business, such as more stringent requirements for employing foreign workers and higher import duties on a number of products. In September the government unveiled a package to revive investment that further simplifies or removes regulations that hinder business, expands tax incentives for priority industries, accelerates strategic projects, and allows foreign ownership of high-end properties.

Next year, a pipeline of public infrastructure projects will help to spur private investment, as will the projected improvement in demand from the major industrial economies and lower domestic inflation.

Household consumption is expected to remain fairly robust through the second half and, from late this year, should get support from decelerating inflation. Pay rises for the civil service and tax breaks for low-income earners, both effective from July this year, will further encourage consumer spending. Additional civil servant salary increases are proposed in the 2016 budget. Consumer confidence weakened earlier this year on concerns about the cut in fuel subsidies and rupiah depreciation, but it has since stabilized (Figure 3.5.6).

Bank Indonesia has loosened macroprudential policies to support lending for housing and car purchases. Credit growth is expected to pick up gradually from the subdued pace at midyear (Figure 3.5.7). In the near term, the central bank is expected to maintain a focus on stability issues, but anticipated lower inflation in 2016 should provide room for a gradual reduction in interest rates to stimulate the economy.

Exports will continue to struggle this year in the face of unexpectedly subdued growth in many of Indonesia's trading partners before improving in 2016 on better prospects for major industrial economies—this despite some continuing drag from the slowdown in the PRC. Imports will remain constrained by the rupiah's depreciation. Net exports are seen making a significant contribution to GDP growth in the second half of this year.

From the production side, the manufacturing purchasing managers' index in August showed signs of improvement, as softer declines in output, new orders, and employment suggest a possible rebound in the months ahead (Figure 3.5.8). Construction will benefit from stronger investment in infrastructure, and growth in services will likely gather momentum next year as business and consumer sentiment improves. A drought caused by El Niño could, however, disrupt agriculture.

On balance, GDP growth is projected to edge up to 5.1% in the second half of 2015, putting full-year growth at 4.9% (Figure 3.5.9). In 2016, growth is seen accelerating to 5.4% on stronger investment and external demand. Both projections are 0.6 percentage points below those in *ADO 2015*. Current account deficits will be narrower than

3.5.7 Credit growth

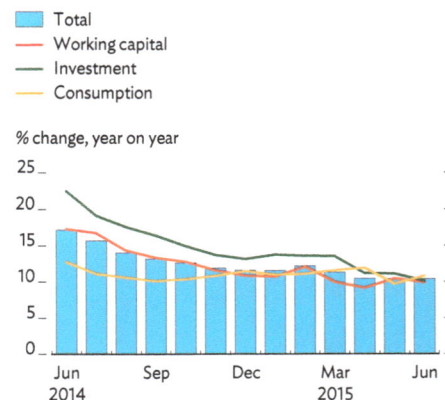

Note: Total, Working capital, Investment, Consumption

% change, year on year

Source: CEIC data company (accessed 4 September 2015).

3.5.8 Manufacturing purchasing managers' index

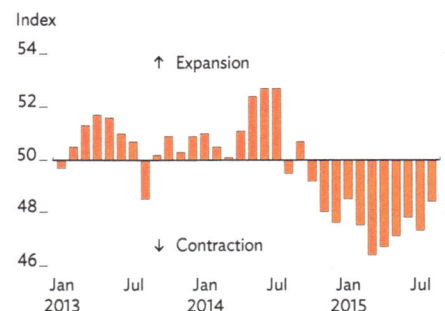

Index

↑ Expansion

↓ Contraction

Note: Nikkei, Markit.
Source: Bloomberg (accessed 4 September 2015).

3.5.9 GDP growth

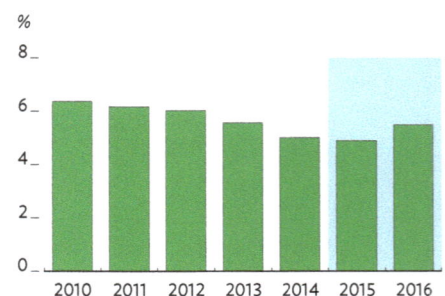

%

Source: Asian Development Outlook database.

previously anticipated, largely the result of the sharp fall in imports and much lower payments for imported oil. Merchandise imports continued to fall at a faster pace than exports in July, pushing up the trade surplus (Figure 3.5.10). Next year, improved demand from major industrial economies together with the impact on trade of rupiah depreciation should keep the current account deficit shrinking. The balance of payments is expected to show a deficit this year due to declining portfolio inflows and then return to surplus in 2016.

Inflation is projected to decelerate to 4%–5% in December after the anniversary of the November 2014 fuel price hike removes it from the base. However, the average rate for 2015 is now seen at 6.7% in light of unexpectedly high inflation in the first 8 months and the potential impact of El Niño on food production. Inflation next year is forecast to average 5.1% (Figure 3.5.11).

Domestic risks to the projections center on further delays in infrastructure investment, which would significantly damage growth, and slow progress on structural reform. If El Niño weather conditions are more severe than expected, rice production will fall sharply, pushing up inflation and eroding rural incomes. To mitigate risks from El Niño, the government has increased food stocks and eased import quotas for staples. It has also funded the digging of wells and reservoirs, and distributed 20,000 irrigation pumps to farmers.

Global financial market turbulence poses a risk given Indonesia's need to finance fiscal and external deficits. Still, the country's resilience under market volatility has improved, in part owing to a more flexible exchange rate and market-driven adjustments to bond yields. Current account deficits are narrowing, and the cut in fuel subsidies has strengthened the fiscal outlook. To manage risks, Bank Indonesia has curbed foreign exchange speculation by reducing the cap for approved US dollar purchases without an underlying transaction. Further, the central bank now requires that corporations hedge 20% of their external debt by December 2015 and 25% by 2016. The Financial Services Authority has allowed companies to buy back shares without requiring approval from a shareholders' meeting. The government has a bond stabilization framework under which it can buy back government bonds from the market. Indonesia maintains contingent funding facilities with development partners in case access to capital markets becomes too restrictive, and the central bank has established currency swap arrangements with the central banks of the PRC, the Republic of Korea, and Japan. Indonesian banks' nonperforming loans at midyear were 2.6% of total lending and their capital adequacy ratio was, at 20.1% well above the 8.0% regulatory minimum.

Reforms to spur larger inflows of foreign direct investment would further mitigate the country's external vulnerability by improving the mix in its current account financing and diversifying exports.

3.5.10 Trade indicators

Source: Haver Analytics (accessed 4 September 2015).

3.5.11 Inflation

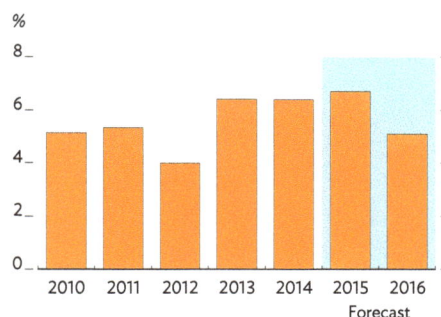

Source: Asian Development Outlook database.

Malaysia

Private consumption expanded in the first half of 2015 despite a new tax that dampened spending from April, but weak exports and slowing investment weighed on economic growth. For the year as a whole, GDP growth is seen decelerating as expected, before the pace picks up slightly in 2016. Inflation this year will undershoot the earlier projection. Forecasts are lowered for current account surpluses.

Updated assessment

Buffeted by headwinds that include a slump in commodity prices and soft demand for hydrocarbons and other exports, Malaysia's economy has slowed this year. GDP growth decelerated to 5.6% in the first quarter and 4.9% in the second, putting growth in the first half at 5.3% (Figure 3.6.1).

Private consumption generated most of the growth in GDP, accelerating to expand by 7.6% in the first half of 2015 from the first half of 2014. Consumer spending was underpinned by wage rises, modest growth in employment (up by 1.6% in the 12 months through June), and government cash transfers, including flood relief payments early in 2015. Growth in private consumption moderated after April, however, when the government implemented a long-planned 6.0% tax on a broad range of goods and services, aiming to diversify its sources of revenue away from the oil and gas industry. One reason for the moderation in spending was that consumers had brought forward some purchases to beat the new tax.

The government maintained growth in its consumption expenditure at 5.5% in the first 6 months, but government fixed investment fell by 3.7%, in part because some projects by state-owned enterprises reached completion. Private sector fixed investment continued to decelerate but still grew by 7.5% (Figure 3.6.2). Fixed investment overall increased by 4.0% in the first half, compared with 6.8% a year earlier.

Net external demand dragged down GDP growth, the result of weakness in export markets. Exports of goods and services fell by 2.2% in volume terms during January–June, outpacing a 0.9% decline in imports.

By sector, services grew by 5.7% and contributed most of GDP growth from the supply side. Growth in government services eased, and the goods and services tax dampened activity in wholesale and retail trade. Solid demand for data communication services maintained near double-digit expansion for information and communication technology.

Growth in manufacturing slowed to 4.9%. Electronics output, which had rebounded in the first half of 2014, fell in the 6 months to June

3.6.1 Demand-side contributions to growth

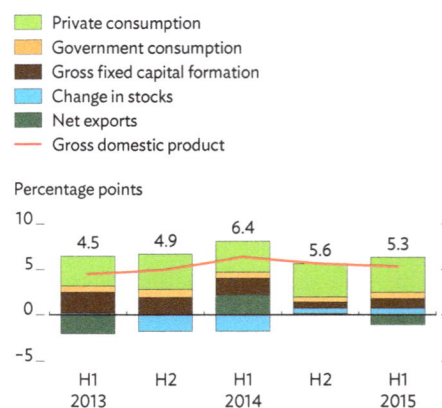

- Private consumption
- Government consumption
- Gross fixed capital formation
- Change in stocks
- Net exports
- Gross domestic product

Percentage points

H = half.
Source: Haver Analytics (accessed 2 September 2015).

3.6.2 Fixed investment growth

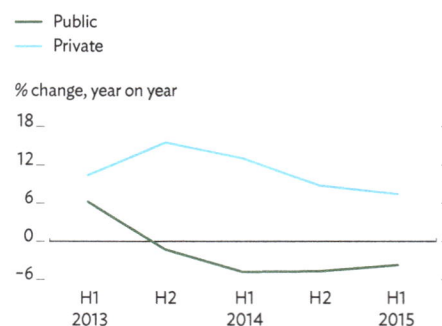

- Public
- Private

% change, year on year

H = half.
Source: Haver Analytics (accessed 2 September 2015).

This chapter was written by Gary Krishnan of the Southeast Asia Department, ADB, Manila.

this year. Construction also decelerated from a year earlier, though it still recorded robust expansion of 7.7%. Output from mining quickened to 7.8%, driven partly by a new oilfield offshore of Sabah state.

Agricultural production was flat in the first half of 2015. Small increases in the production of food and natural rubber were offset by lower production of palm oil caused by floods.

Inflation braked sharply early this year as fuel prices fell, then accelerated to 3.3% in July, largely reflecting the new goods and services tax and the impact on import prices of ringgit depreciation (Figure 3.6.3). Rising vegetable prices caused by bad weather contributed to higher inflation in July. Still, average inflation for the first 7 months was, at 1.7%, unexpectedly low and below that of a year earlier. The producer price index fell by 6.0% over the first half owing to lower global prices for oil and other commodities.

Bank Negara Malaysia, the central bank, kept its policy interest rate at 3.25% through the first 8 months, having raised the rate by 25 basis points in July 2014 to dampen inflationary expectations ahead of the goods and services tax. Growth in loans outstanding to households moderated to 8.7% year on year in June 2015, though loans to businesses picked up to increase by the same 8.7%. The rate of increase in broad money supply (M3) slowed to 3.9% in July.

Cuts in subsidies for fuel helped the federal government to narrow its fiscal deficit to 2.8% of GDP in January–June from 3.5% in the first half of 2014. Government operating expenditure barely increased, contrasting with a 7.9% rise in the first half of 2014. Development spending rose after shrinking a year earlier. Higher tax income, despite the slump in prices for oil and gas, increased total revenue by 4.9%. The federal government's debt rose to an estimated 53.8% of GDP by midyear from 51.4% in mid-2014.

Trade and current account surpluses narrowed in the first half. Merchandise exports fell by 13.7% to $89.7 billion owing to declines in exports of commodities and resource-based manufactured products such as refined petroleum (Figure 3.6.4). Demand in major markets was unexpectedly weak, and prices dropped for oil, liquefied natural gas, and some agricultural commodities. Exports of electronics and electrical products slowed. As for export destinations, the steepest falls were recorded in shipments to Japan, the Republic of Korea, and Taipei,China.

Merchandise imports fell by 12.0% to $75.7 billion. Imports of intermediate and capital goods declined, reflecting the disappointing export and investment results, but buoyant private consumption drove an increase in imports of consumer goods. The outcome was a 21.9% narrowing of the trade surplus to $14.0 billion. This and a much wider deficit in services, due in part to a decline in tourist arrivals, slashed the current account surplus by more than half to $4.8 billion, equal to 3.1% of GDP.

The financial account posted net outflows of $7.6 billion mainly on outward portfolio investment, leaving the balance of payments in deficit by $2.0 billion, equivalent to 1.3% of GDP (Figure 3.6.5). International reserves fell by 18.3% to $94.7 billion through August from the start of 2015, still enough to cover 7.4 months of imports and equal to short-term external debt. The fall in reserves reflected efforts by the central bank

3.6.3 Inflation and policy rate

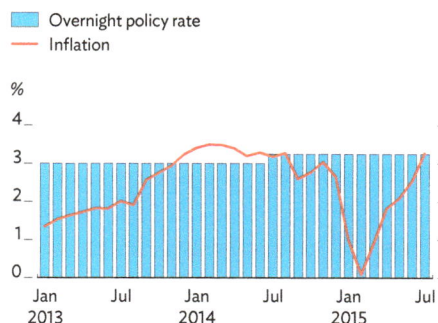

Sources: Haver Analytics; Bank Negara Malaysia. 2015. Monthly Statistical Bulletin. July. http://www.bnm.gov.my (accessed 2 September 2015).

3.6.4 Merchandise trade indicators

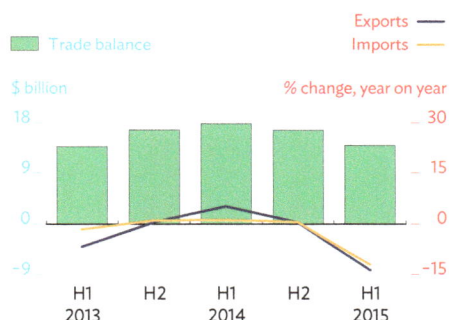

H = half.
Source: Haver Analytics (accessed 2 September 2015).

3.6.5 Balance of payments components

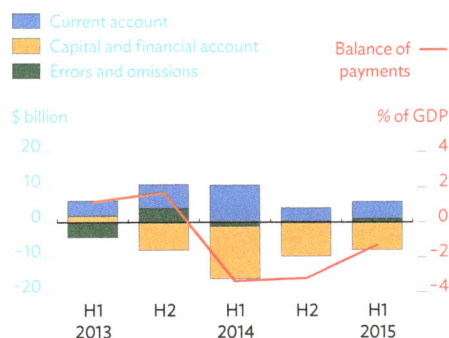

H = half.
Source: Haver Analytics (accessed 2 September 2015).

to support the ringgit as it came under downward pressure largely from the slide in exports and capital outflows. Investor concerns about the finances of the government-owned investment company 1Malaysia Development added to pressure on the ringgit in August. From the start of this year to early September, the ringgit depreciated by 16.5% against the US dollar.

Malaysia's external debt as a ratio to GDP rose to 68.1% in the 12 months to June 2015 from 66.0% a year earlier. More than half the external debt was medium to long term, and 60% was denominated in foreign currencies. The share of short-term external debt declined by nearly 5 percentage points to 42.9% over the 12 months to June this year.

Prospects

Economic growth is projected to moderate further through the second half of 2015, with GDP still seen expanding by 4.7% for the year, down from 6.0% in 2014, a 4-year high. In 2016, growth is expected to pick up gradually, assuming better global trade and economic performances and some recovery in prices for oil and other commodities (Figure 3.6.6).

Domestic demand will be constrained through the second half by lower earnings from oil and other commodities and by wavering consumer and business confidence (Figure 3.6.7). A number of factors point to more muted growth in private consumption: slowing growth in credit to households, high household debt equal to 87.9% of GDP, and signs of softening in the labor market. The number of unemployed rose by 16.6% in the 12 months to June 2015, nudging up the unemployment rate to a still-low 3.1%.

The goods and services tax will temper growth in private consumption, though concerns about its impact on prices have been alleviated somewhat by its exemptions for food staples, electricity for most households, and government and transportation services, as well as the removal of sales and services taxes that it replaces. Further, government measures compensate lower-income earners for higher prices, and income tax rates have been reduced for individuals and firms.

Business sentiment has been dented by the lackluster prospects for exports, the depreciation of the ringgit, a slide in domestic stock prices, and spare manufacturing capacity. Conditions in Malaysian manufacturing have deteriorated this year, according to the manufacturing purchasing managers' index (Figure 3.6.8). In August, new orders contracted at the fastest rate in almost 3 years, dragging down manufacturing production and purchasing. Manufacturers reported that they shed staff in August for a third consecutive month.

Construction moderated in the second quarter of this year, with slower growth across the residential, nonresidential, and civil engineering subsectors. Housing approvals fell by 14.8% in the first 5 months of 2015 from a year earlier.

Still, investment projects continue to roll out under the government's Economic Transformation Programme to upgrade industry and infrastructure. Next year, investment is expected to strengthen on prospects for improved economic growth in the major industrial economies and firmer prices for oil and other commodities.

3.6.6 GDP growth

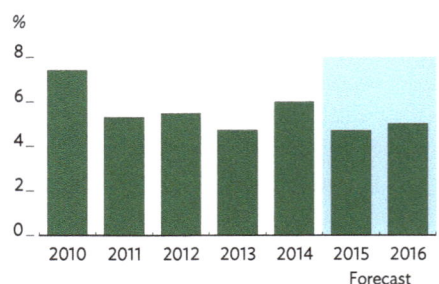

Source: Asian Development Outlook database.

3.6.1 Selected economic indicators (%)

	2015		2016	
	ADO 2015	Update	ADO 2015	Update
GDP growth	4.7	4.7	5.0	4.9
Inflation	3.2	2.4	2.9	2.9
Current acct. bal. (share of GDP)	3.3	2.7	4.5	3.2

Source: ADB estimates.

3.6.7 Business and consumer confidence

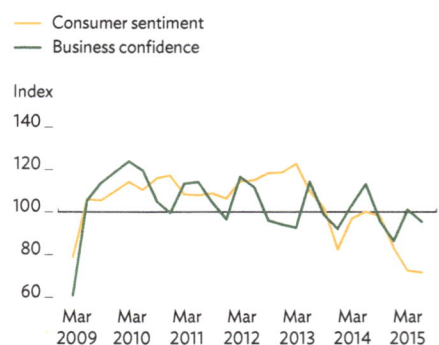

Note: Above 100 indicates improvement in business conditions and rising consumer confidence.
Source: CEIC Data Company (accessed 3 September 2015).

A decision by Fitch Ratings in June 2015 to maintain its long-term foreign currency credit rating for Malaysia at A–, while revising up its outlook for the rating to stable from negative, was good news for the investment climate. In revising up its outlook, Fitch cited the narrowing fiscal deficit and associated reforms to reduce subsidies and introduce the goods and services tax. However, it also noted that government debt and contingent liabilities continue to climb and that the current account surplus is narrowing.

Leading economic indicators compiled by the government in June showed the economy likely to expand at a slower rate in the months ahead. The Prime Minister established in August a special economic committee of public and private sector representatives to recommend policies to support growth. While the government is constrained from offering substantial new fiscal stimulus by its pledge to shrink the fiscal deficit, narrowing the gap to 3.2% of GDP in 2015, and to balance the budget and cut public debt by 2020, its budget this October is expected to provide some additional measures to support domestic demand in 2016.

Regarding monetary policy, the central bank said in August that its policy settings were appropriate to support economic growth. Concerns about high household debt and capital outflows could weigh against easing interest rates.

As inflationary pressures have been weaker than previously anticipated, the inflation forecast for this year is lowered to 2.4% (Figure 3.6.9). Firmer domestic demand, higher oil prices, and the ringgit's depreciation will put moderate upward pressure on the inflation rate in 2016, offset to some degree by the fading impact of the goods and services tax next year.

Export income has been considerably weaker than anticipated in *ADO 2015*, a result of disappointing economic growth in export markets and the steep slide in prices for oil and gas. Customs data showed some improvement during June and July for exports of electrical and electronic products, palm oil, and rubber, but export income for crude oil, refined petroleum products, and liquefied natural gas plunged in those months from the same period in 2014. Exports are seen picking up in 2016, though imports will also rise in line with a projected better performance in investment. This *Update* lowers forecasts for current account surpluses to 2.7% of GDP in 2015 and 3.2% in 2016 (Figure 3.6.10).

Looking to the medium term, the government unveiled in May its Eleventh Malaysia Plan, 2016–2020, which targets annual average GDP growth of 5.0%–6.0%. Average growth during the previous plan period, 2011–2015, is estimated at 5.3%. Inflation for the new 5-year plan period is targeted at below 3.0%. The goal of the plan is to raise gross national income per capita from $10,200 expected this year to $15,690 in 2020, lifting Malaysia into the category of high-income nations.

The plan's strategy emphasizes boosting productivity by, among other things, building rail and road infrastructure and broadband networks, investing in skills development, fostering small and medium-sized enterprises, and encouraging sustainable development. Private investment is targeted to rise by an average of 9.4% per year in real terms through 2020, and public investment by 2.7%.

3.6.8 Manufacturing purchasing managers' index

Note: Nikkei-Markit.
Source: Bloomberg (accessed 3 September 2015).

3.6.9 Inflation

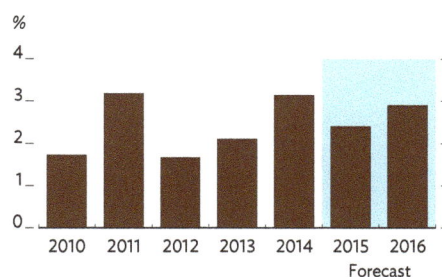

Source: Asian Development Outlook database.

3.6.10 Current account balance

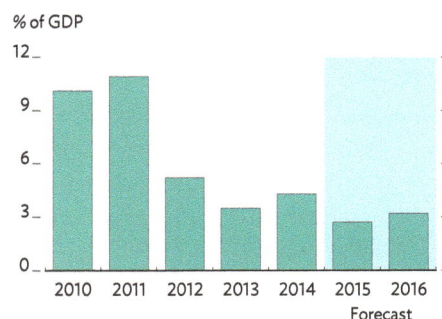

Source: Asian Development Outlook database.

Pakistan

Low oil prices, continued economic reform, and gradually improving domestic security strengthened the economy in FY2015. Inflation declined, the current account deficit narrowed, and foreign reserves increased. For FY2016, this *Update* maintains the *ADO 2015* forecast for growth but trims those for inflation and the current account deficit. More rapid and durable growth requires structural reform to improve tax revenues, energy supply, and the business climate.

Updated assessment

Provisional GDP growth of 4.2% in FY2015 (ended 30 June 2015) matched the *ADO 2015* forecast and was led by services as growth in manufacturing slowed (Figure 3.7.1). Buoyant 5.0% expansion in services reflected an upturn in finance and insurance and a rebound in general government services. Industrial growth was crimped by a slowdown in large-scale manufacturing to 3.3% owing to continued power shortages and weaker external demand. The resilience of small-scale manufacturing and construction sustained industrial growth at 3.6%, nearly a full percentage point lower than a year earlier. Agriculture growth remained modest at 2.9% as improvement in livestock compensated for weakness in the major crops.

Consumption, the largest component in GDP, expanded by 5.1% in FY2015, reflecting a 16.0% nominal increase in government consumption and a smaller rise in private consumption. Total investment improved marginally to equal 15.1% of GDP in FY2015 as the government continued spending on infrastructure. Private fixed investment slipped to equal 9.7% of GDP from 10.0% a year earlier, even with better credit conditions, because of energy constraints and the generally weak business environment that has depressed investment for several years.

Headline inflation sharply declined to average 4.5% in FY2015. Inflation for both food and other items dropped significantly, reflecting adequate food supplies and the transmission into domestic prices of lower global prices for oil and other commodities. By July 2015, year-on-year inflation had fallen by 6.0 percentage points to 1.8% (Figure 3.7.2). Exchange rate stability and a significant reduction in government borrowing from the State Bank of Pakistan, the central bank, helped contain inflation expectations.

With the sharp decline in inflation, the main policy interest rate was reduced by a cumulative 3 percentage points to 7% from November 2014 to May 2015 (Figure 3.7.3). To further strengthen monetary policy transmission and tame volatility in short-term interest rates,

3.7.1 Supply-side contributions to growth

- Agriculture
- Services
- Industry
- Gross domestic product

Percentage points

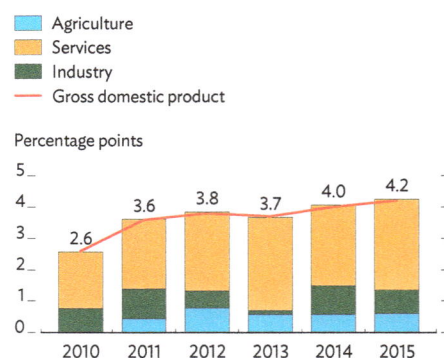

Note: Years are fiscal years ending on 30 June of that year.
Source: Ministry of Finance. Pakistan Economic Survey 2014–15. http://www.finance.gov.pk (accessed 4 September 2015).

3.7.2 Inflation

- Food
- Other
- Headline

%

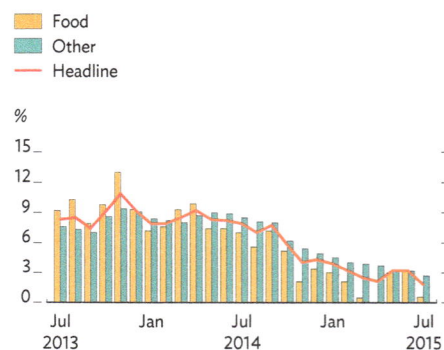

Source: State Bank of Pakistan. Economic Data. http://www.sbp.org.pk (accessed 12 August 2015).

This chapter was written by Farzana Noshab of the Pakistan Resident Mission, ADB, Islamabad.

the central bank introduced from 1 June 2015 a new policy target for the money market overnight rate, set between the repo rate floor and the reverse repo rate ceiling of an interest rate corridor now tightened from 250 basis points to 200. In line with monetary policy, market interest rates have fallen since January 2015. To enhance central bank independence as it designs and implements monetary policy, a revised State Bank of Pakistan Act has been submitted to Parliament.

Official data for the consolidated general government deficit (combining federal and provincial fiscal deficits and excluding grants) shows a decline to 5.3% of GDP in FY2015 from 5.5% a year earlier, reflecting higher tax revenues. Tax revenues including a natural gas levy increased by 17.7% during FY2015. The Federal Board of Revenue net tax revenue collection grew by 14.2% to PRs2.58 trillion but was marginally short of its revised target of PRs2.60 trillion. Nontax revenue fell by 15% despite higher central bank profits and larger inflows under the Coalition Support Fund (CSF).

Total expenditure in FY2015, at 19.7% of GDP, declined by 0.3 percentage points from FY2014, as a small increase in interest payments was offset by power subsidies falling to 0.9% of GDP and lower spending on general government services. Spending under the consolidated public sector development program increased marginally and, at 3.6% of GDP, was about the same as in the previous year. But total development expenditure for the year fell as other development expenditures and spending on net lending to public sector enterprises dropped by 0.9 percentage points.

A significant decline in government borrowing from the central bank left the burden of budget financing in FY2015 to be met largely by commercial banks. Borrowings from commercial banks increased to PRs1.4 trillion as net retirement of debt to the central bank reached PRs462 billion (Figure 3.7.4). Net credit to the private sector increased by PRs209 billion, down from PRs371 billion in the previous year. Loans for fixed investment increased significantly, mainly benefitting construction, real estate, and some manufacturing industries. Loans for working capital declined as prices for imported commodities fell.

The current account deficit narrowed to 0.8% of GDP in FY2015 from 1.3% in FY2014 (Figure 3.7.5). The reasons were lower prices of oil imports (which had been 35% of the total), larger inflows under the CSF, and robust workers' remittances. The 18% decline in expenditures on oil imports was offset to some extent by increased imports of machinery and metal products, as well as of food and transport equipment.

A 3.7% decline in exports outpaced a 1.3% decline in imports to marginally widen the trade deficit. Textile exports, comprising over half of exports, declined by 1.0% as much lower prices for cotton and yarn offset gains from sales of textiles with higher value added, including those shipped to the European Union under the Generalized System of Preferences Plus scheme. A lower services account deficit came about from inflows of $1.5 billion under the CSF. Growth in workers' remittances remained robust at 16.5%.

Foreign exchange reserves rose from $9.1 billion in June 2014 to $13.5 billion a year later, enough to cover over 3 months of imports of goods and services (Figure 3.7.6). External account vulnerabilities

3.7.3 Interest rates

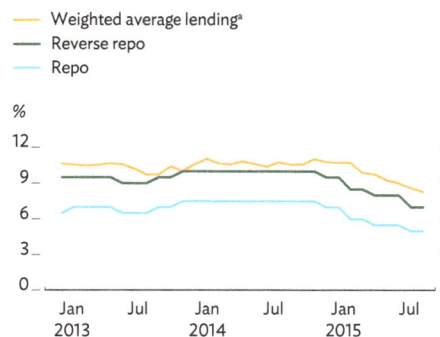

ᵃ On gross loan disbursements during the month, but also including loans repriced, renewed, or rolled over during the month.
Source: State Bank of Pakistan. Economic Data. http://www.sbp.org.pk (accessed 12 August 2015).

3.7.4 Budget borrowing from banks

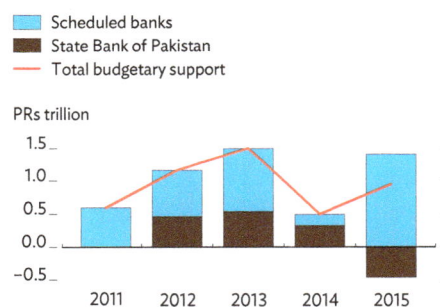

Note: Years are fiscal years ending on 30 June of that year.
Source: State Bank of Pakistan. Economic Data. http://www.sbp.org.pk (accessed 12 August 2015).

3.7.5 Current account components

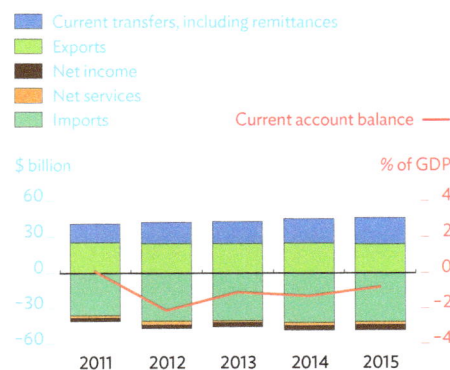

Note: Years are fiscal years ending on 30 June of that year.
Source: State Bank of Pakistan. Economic Data. http://www.sbp.org.pk (accessed 12 August 2015).

receded in the face of this substantial gain, which derived from the effect of lower prices for oil and other imports on the current account, the issuance of international sharia-compliant bonds, disbursements from bilateral and multilateral development partners, and spot market purchases by the central bank. The rupee remained stable, marginally appreciating to PRs101.3 per $1 during FY2015. However, in real effective exchange rate terms, it appreciated by 8.8% over the year, with likely adverse implications for export competitiveness (Figure 3.7.7).

Prospects

GDP growth is expected to edge up to 4.5% in FY2016, assuming continued low prices for oil and other commodities, the expected pickup in growth in the advanced economies, and some alleviation of power shortages, especially for manufacturing. Torrential rains and floods across the country in July 2015 are likely to adversely affect agricultural output and some farmers' incomes. Manufacturing, construction, and mining are expected to benefit from budgetary incentives and planned investments in infrastructure under the government's ongoing Economic Corridor program. Prospects for large-scale manufacturing remain subject to progress on power supply, which has constrained growth in recent years.

On the demand side, consumption is expected to remain the key growth driver, supported by higher salaries and robust remittances. Lower real interest rates should help private credit demand and investment. Ongoing military operations in various parts of the country are gradually repairing domestic security, reversing the deterioration that saw net foreign direct investment contract from over $5 billion in FY2008 to $600 million in FY2015 (Figure 3.7.8). Also expected to raise investors' confidence is ongoing reform to improve the business environment. Plans to build an economic corridor linking Kashgar in the People's Republic of China to the Pakistani port of Gwadar were announced in April, and this could significantly boost private investment and growth in the coming years.

The government is implementing structural reform to make energy provision financially sustainable by improving collections to stem the accumulation of payables to the industry, while reducing operating costs and losses in the next 3 years. Power tariffs are being adjusted upward toward cost-recovery levels. Other ongoing structural reforms aim to privatize public enterprises in energy, transport, finance, and manufacturing and to improve the business climate, trade regime, and tax administration. Progress has been slow, but the sale of government shares in public sector entities in FY2015 raised $1.7 billion, and measures are being implemented to automate tax payment and thereby facilitate and encourage tax return filing.

The federal budget for FY2016 (Figure 3.7.9) projects a further reduction in the consolidated general government deficit (excluding grants) to 4.3% of GDP, achieved through higher tax revenues, the continued rationalization of energy subsidies (Figure 3.7.10), and a sizeable provincial surplus. Total tax revenues are targeted at 12.1% of GDP, or 1.1 percentage points higher than in FY2015. Most of this

3.7.6 Foreign reserves and exchange rate

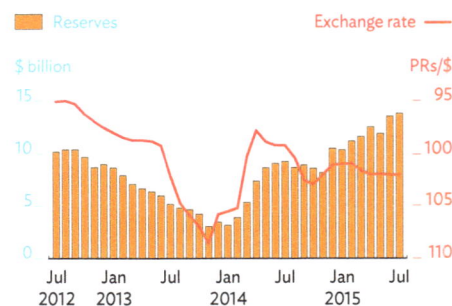

Source: State Bank of Pakistan. Economic Data. http://www.sbp.org.pk (accessed 12 August 2015).

3.7.7 Exchange rate indexes

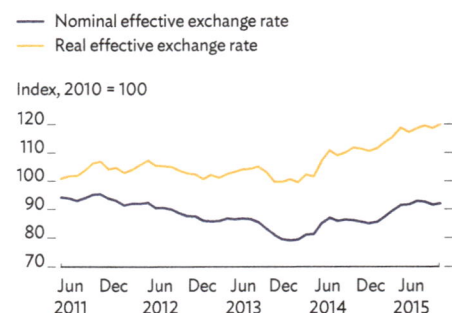

Source: CEIC Data Company (accessed 1 September 2015).

3.7.8 Foreign direct and portfolio investments and financial account

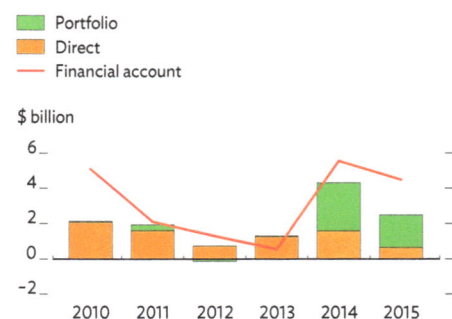

Source: State Bank of Pakistan. Economic Data. http://www.sbp.org.pk (accessed 12 August 2015).

3.7.1 Selected economic indicators (%)

	2015		2016	
	ADO 2015	Update	ADO 2015	Update
GDP growth	4.2	4.2	4.5	4.5
Inflation	5.8	4.5	5.8	5.1
Current acct. bal. (share of GDP)	-1.0	-0.8	-1.3	-1.0

Source: ADB estimates.

increase is expected to come from new measures to boost tax collection and further eliminate tax exemptions (Figure 3.7.11). Nontax revenues as a percentage of GDP are projected to be 0.3 percentage points down from FY2015, assuming lower central bank profits and smaller CSF inflows.

The consolidated public sector development program has been boosted for FY2016 to equal 4.9% of GDP, up by 1.3 percentage points over FY2015. Other development spending is budgeted to increase by 31% to equal 0.5% of GDP, including a rise in the allocation for cash transfers under the Benazir Income Support Program to about $1 billion. The 2016 federal budget allocates 11% of its consolidated public sector development program budget to begin work on the transport and energy infrastructure for the economic corridor linking Kashgar to Gwardar. The budget continues to rely on domestic sources for deficit financing, supplemented by external financing and higher privatization proceeds equal to 0.2% of GDP.

Notable risks to the budget estimates include failure to achieve a significantly higher provincial fiscal surplus and the Federal Board of Revenue collecting less tax than projected. So far, the provincial fiscal surplus has remained below budget estimates, contributing to higher deficits. Fiscal consolidation requires greater effort from provinces considering that their combined share of federal revenues transfers were set to 57.5% under the 2011 National Finance Commission award for the allocation of fiscal resources. Negotiations for the next award, expected in 2016, should provide a mechanism by which the provinces and the federal government can address this challenge under the Council of Common Interest.

Inflation is expected to average 5.1% in FY2016, slightly higher than in FY2015, as oil prices are expected to slowly recover. Inflationary pressures may come from higher food prices in response to possible supply shortages following floods in July 2015. Meanwhile, tariffs on natural gas were raised in August 2015. An increase in oil prices is a risk to the forecast, as it would push up transportation costs and increase monthly electricity bills through fuel price adjustments to tariffs. Monetary policy is expected to remain supportive, as the policy rate was cut by another 50 basis points in the September 2015 policy statement, and the objective continues to be to maximize growth while maintaining low inflation.

The current account deficit is expected to widen marginally to 1.0% of GDP in FY2016, assuming slightly higher oil prices. Exports are expected to increase only slightly after 2 years of stagnation, as manufacturing continues to suffer under energy shortages and low cotton prices may see only a modest increase. The increase in imports will be contained by the slight expansion in domestic growth and benign global prices. Robust growth in remittances should continue to cushion any deterioration in the current account.

3.7.9 General government budget

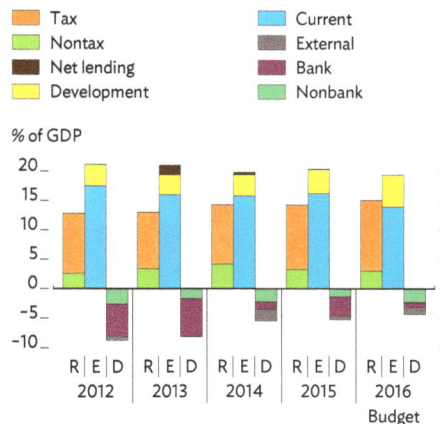

R = revenue, E = expenditure, D = deficit financing.
Note: Years are fiscal years ending on 30 June of that year. Data refer to consolidated federal and provincial governments. Net lending includes statistical discrepancy. Nonbank includes privatization proceeds.
Source: Ministry of Finance. Pakistan Economic Survey 2014–15. http://www.finance.gov.pk

3.7.10 Subsidies

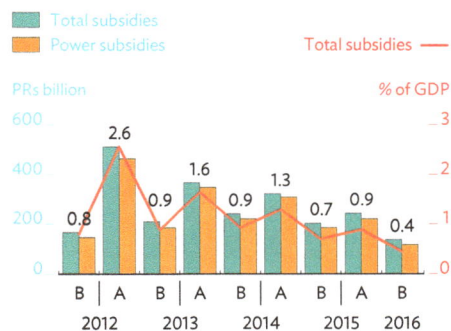

B = budget, A = actual.
Note: Years are fiscal years ending on 30 June of that year.
Source: State Bank of Pakistan. Economic Data. http://www.sbp.org.pk (accessed 4 September 2015).

3.7.11 Federal Board of Revenue tax collection

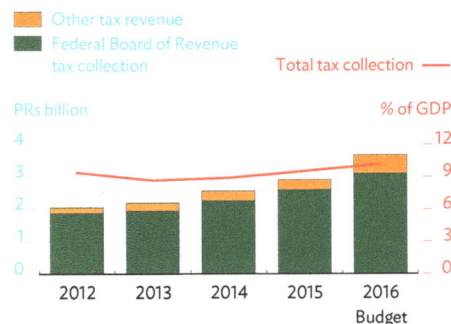

Note: Years are fiscal years ending on 30 June of that year.
Source: State Bank of Pakistan. Economic Data. http://www.sbp.org.pk (accessed 4 September 2015).

Philippines

Domestic demand held up in the first half of 2015, but net external demand dragged on GDP growth. A stronger outcome based on improved fiscal spending is expected in the second half. Growth for the year as a whole is now seen at 6.0%, revised down from March, and edging higher in 2016. Inflation projections are trimmed for both years. Further progress on reform will be vital to maintain the momentum of growth.

Updated assessment

Though a pickup in government spending in the second quarter lifted GDP growth to 5.6% from 5.0% in the first, expansion in January–June at 5.3% was the lowest since 2011. Domestic demand remained firm, with solid growth in private consumption and investment. However, net external demand weighed on GDP growth, the result of a sharp rise in imports in real terms and virtually flat real exports of goods, albeit partly offset by higher services exports (Figure 3.8.1).

Household consumption accelerated from 2014 to rise by 6.1% and remain the biggest contributor to GDP growth on the demand side. Stronger consumption spending, particularly on food, beverages, and transportation, was supported by higher employment, low inflation, and rising remittance inflows from overseas Filipinos. About 700,000 new jobs were generated in the 12 months to July 2015, mainly in services, and the unemployment rate fell to 6.5% from 6.7% in July 2014. Remittances rose by 5.3% to $13.4 billion in the first half, the rate of increase about the same in peso terms. Private investment recorded robust expansion, as illustrated by a 10.4% increase in purchases of machinery and equipment and a 12.6% rise in private construction.

Government expenditure rebounded in the second quarter from a sluggish performance early in 2015. Growth in government consumption quickened to 3.9% in the second quarter, and public construction jumped by 20.4% after a slump early in the year (Figure 3.8.2).

By sector, services and manufacturing were the main drivers of GDP growth (Figure 3.8.3). The expansion of services, which comprise over half of economic output and employment, decelerated to 5.8% in the first half but still generated nearly two-thirds of overall growth. Major contributors were retail trade, business process outsourcing, tourism, and real estate services.

Growth in manufacturing, which generated one-fourth of the increase in GDP, slowed to 5.3% on sagging demand for export products. The subsectors contributing the most to growth in manufacturing were food processing, chemicals, and communication equipment.

3.8.1 Demand-side contributions to growth

- Private consumption
- Government consumption
- Fixed investment
- Change in inventories
- Net exports
- Statistical discrepancy
- Gross domestic product

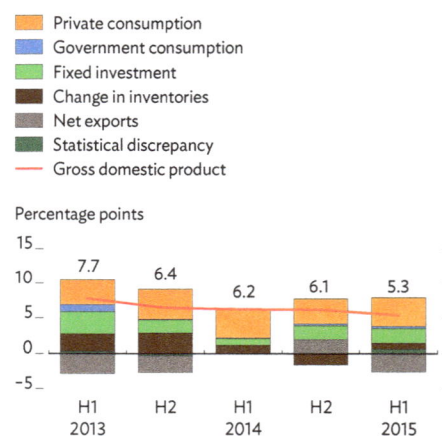

H = half.
Source: CEIC Data Company (accessed 4 September 2015).

3.8.2 Growth in real government spending

- Government consumption
- Public construction

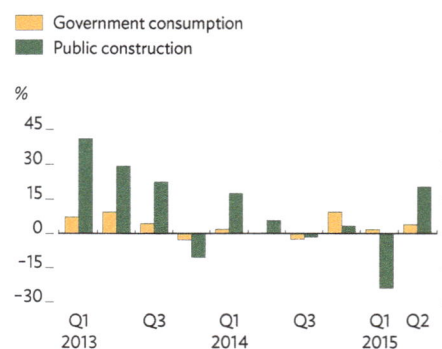

Q = quarter.
Source: CEIC Data Company (accessed 4 September 2015).

This chapter was written by Sona Shrestha and Teresa Mendoza of the Philippines Country Office, ADB, Manila.

However, agricultural output was flat in the first half compared with the same period in 2014 due to drought caused by El Niño. Rice and maize production fell in the second quarter after marginal increases in the first 3 months.

Inflation ebbed to 0.6% year on year in August 2015, and it averaged 1.7% in the first 8 months (Figure 3.8.4). Low rates of inflation this year stem from the slide in global oil prices and slower increases in food prices, with rice imports supplementing domestic supplies. The central bank maintained its policy interest rates at 4.0% for overnight borrowing and 6.0% for overnight lending, having raised them by 50 basis points between July and September 2014. Liquidity (M3) growth decelerated from the end of 2014 to 8.5% year on year in July.

Underspending by the government produced a fiscal surplus equivalent to 0.2% of GDP in the first half. Expenditure excluding interest fell below target even as it rose by 10.6% year on year. Higher tax receipts from tobacco and alcohol sales and more stringent tax enforcement helped to generate a 16.3% rise in government revenue. To accommodate increased spending, particularly for infrastructure and social services, the government set a budget deficit ceiling for 2015 at 2.0% of GDP, similar to that set in 2014 (the actual 2014 budget deficit was 0.6% because spending targets were missed).

In the external trade accounts, merchandise exports fell by 12.9% in US dollar terms in the first half, widening the trade deficit by 6.3% from a year earlier (Figure 3.8.5). Exports of mineral products, fruit, and vegetables fell, reflecting both weak external demand and low commodity prices. Exports of manufactured goods also fell on lower shipments of electronics, processed food, and beverages. Higher shipments of coconut products and some manufactured goods such as chemicals and machinery and transport equipment tempered the export decline.

Merchandise imports declined by 8.3% in US dollar terms, reflecting sharply lower prices for oil and a decline in imports of raw materials for the manufacture of electronic products. Buoyant imports of capital and consumer goods illustrated the strength of private consumption and investment. Growth in remittances and services receipts, mainly from business process outsourcing and tourism, increased the current account surplus to $4.7 billion in the first half, equal to 3.3% of GDP.

Gross international reserves rose by 1% to $80.3 billion in August from the end of 2014, covering 10.3 months of imports. By mid-September, the Philippine peso had fallen by 4.6% against the US dollar since the end of 2014 as funds flowed from developing economies, including the Philippines, into the strengthening US dollar.

Prospects

Economic activity is projected to accelerate in the second half, with full-year growth projected at 6.0% (Figure 3.8.6). The forecast is trimmed from *ADO 2015* largely as a result of slow public spending early in the year.

The rebound in government spending since the first quarter is expected to spur economic growth through the rest of this year and

3.8.3 Supply-side contributions to growth

- Agriculture
- Manufacturing
- Other industries
- Services
- Gross domestic product

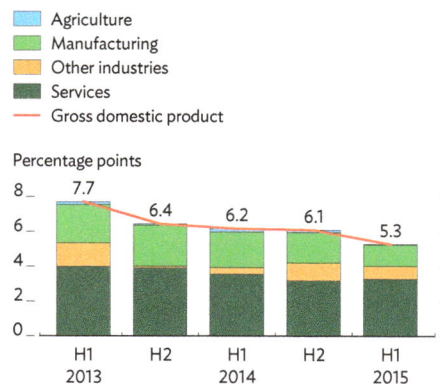

H = half.
Source: CEIC Data Company (accessed 4 September 2015).

3.8.4 Inflation and policy rates

- Overnight borrowing rate
- Inflation

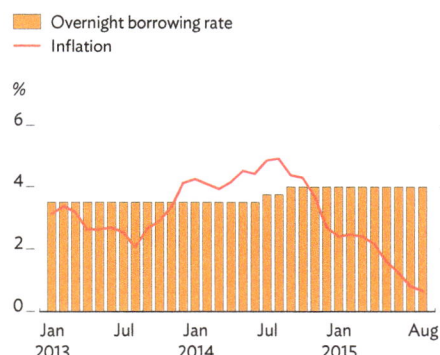

Source: CEIC Data Company (accessed 4 September 2015).

3.8.5 Merchandise trade indicators

- Trade balance
- Export growth
- Import growth

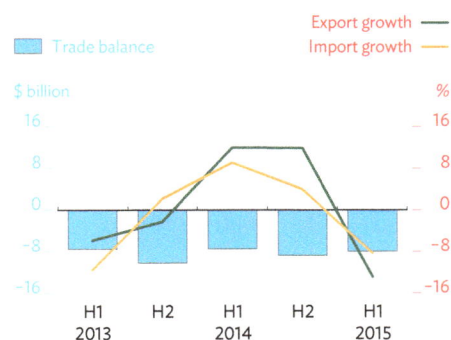

H = half.
Source: CEIC Data Company (accessed 18 September 2015).

into 2016. To speed up budget execution, the government has enhanced project preparation, procurement, and monitoring. Public expenditure excluding interest has accelerated since April, posting 31% growth year on year in July with a substantial increase in construction (Figure 3.8.7). A low base effect—the result of a Supreme Court ruling in July 2014 that slowed budget disbursements in the second half of last year—should help to keep growth in government spending elevated through the rest of this year.

Election-related spending will support domestic demand through May 2016, when elections are scheduled. GDP growth is forecast to rise to 6.3% in 2016 on stronger recovery in the major industrial economies that should benefit Philippine exports and investment inflows.

Private investment and household consumption are expected to maintain solid growth. Favorable indicators for investment include sustained growth in outlays for commercial vehicles and industrial machinery, rising imports of capital goods, and expanded credit. Lending to the private sector rose by 13.4% year on year in July. Foreign direct investment inflows amounted to $2.0 billion in the first half, though they fell short of those in the year-earlier period. Surveys by the central bank show that business and consumer sentiments are generally positive.

Lower global fuel prices are benefiting consumers and businesses alike because the Philippines imports more than 90% of its oil requirements. Private consumption is projected to remain robust in light of low inflation and growth in employment and remittances (Figure 3.8.8).

Net exports are seen as a drag on GDP growth through 2015 against a backdrop of soft external demand and buoyant import volumes. Next year, exports are projected to improve in line with better prospects for the industrial economies. As export growth is expected to outpace import growth, net external demand is seen contributing to GDP growth in 2016.

Fiscal policy is likely to support a quickening of economic growth in 2016. The government's proposed budget for next year targets a 15.2% rise in spending from the 2015 budget, with significant increases in social services and infrastructure investment, including programs for the continued rehabilitation of areas battered by Super Typhoon Haiyan late in 2013. The 2016 budget is equivalent to 19.5% of GDP as projected by the government.

By sector, services will continue to be the major driver of growth, with business process outsourcing, tourism, and retail trade expected to perform well. Revenue from business process outsourcing is estimated by the industry to climb to $21 billion in 2015 from $18 billion in 2014. Tourist arrivals rose by 8.7% year on year to 3.1 million in the first 7 months of this year. Tourism accounts for 12.5% of total employment. Buoyant private spending will underpin growth in retail trade.

Manufacturing has drawn support from domestic demand at a time when external demand is subdued. Factories that produce cement, glass, iron, and steel are benefitting from brisk construction. Manufacturers of processed food and other consumer goods are gaining from growth in household expenditure. Next year, export-oriented manufacturing is expected to trend up as some important export markets strengthen.

3.8.1 Selected economic indicators (%)

	2015		2016	
	ADO 2015	Update	ADO 2015	Update
GDP growth	6.4	6.0	6.3	6.3
Inflation	2.8	2.0	3.3	3.0
Current acct. bal. (share of GDP)	4.0	3.7	3.6	3.6

Source: ADB estimates.

3.8.6 GDP growth

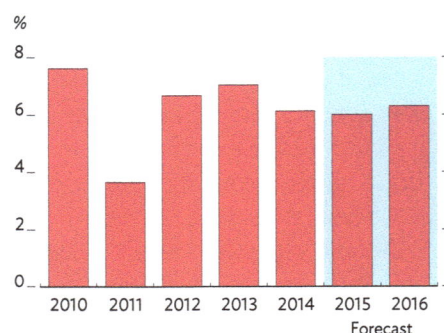

Source: Asian Development Outlook database.

3.8.7 Fiscal indicators

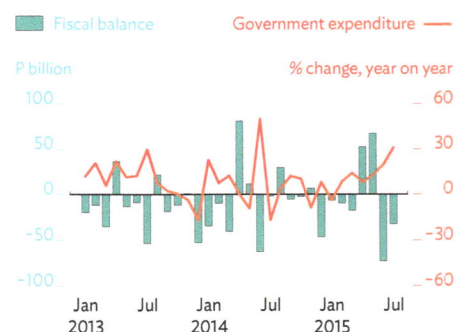

Note: Government expenditures exclude interest payments.
Source: CEIC Data Company (accessed 4 September 2015).

Construction expanded at a double-digit pace in the first half of 2015, and its prospects look bright because of high demand for housing and offices. Rebounding public investment and progress on the government's renewed public–private partnership program will fuel the construction pipeline. From the revival of the program in 2010 to August 2015, the government awarded 10 projects worth $4.2 billion.

Upward pressure on inflation could come from drought induced by El Niño, if it reduces harvests and hydropower output, and from peso depreciation this year. Still, inflation has been milder than expected, prompting downward revisions to forecasts. In 2016, inflation is seen accelerating to average 3.0% as global prices for oil and other commodities edge higher (Figure 3.8.9).

Provided year-average inflation stays within the central bank's 2%–4% target range, as expected, the monetary stance is likely to remain accommodative to economic growth.

Increases in remittances and services exports, together with lower costs of imported oil, will sustain current account surpluses. This *Update* trims the forecast for the current account surplus in 2015 to 3.7% of GDP owing to weak merchandise exports. The forecast for the current account surplus in 2016 is maintained at 3.6%.

Risks to the outlook include unexpectedly slow growth in the People's Republic of China and in the large industrial economies, which would weigh on exports and investment. The risks from volatile capital flows are mitigated by the country's solid macroeconomic fundamentals and robust banking system. Current account surpluses are underpinned by resilient remittances and services income. External debt as a share of GDP declined to 26.1% in March 2015. Banks' nonperforming loans are low at 2.3% of total lending, and their capital adequacy ratio at 17% is above regulatory requirements. El Nino would, if severe, have an impact on prices of food, water, and electricity and also hurt rural incomes.

The economic outlook for next year is subject to more uncertainty than usual as the outcome of elections will have an important bearing on policy. Raising public investment and continued efforts to strengthen budget execution will be needed to deliver social programs and address infrastructure shortcomings. Pressing ahead with public–private partnership reform, including through continued improvements to the legal and regulatory frameworks and project development and monitoring, will also be crucial. The Competition Act adopted in July 2015 aims to promote investment by creating a level playing field for business. Recent amendments to the Cabotage Law allow foreign-owned vessels into domestic routes to promote competition and reduce shipping costs. The effective implementation of these reforms and further progress in improving regulatory efficiency to reduce the cost of doing business will be key to raising private investment to drive stronger growth and generate more jobs.

3.8.8 Personal remittances

Q = quarter.
Source: CEIC Data Company (accessed 4 September 2015).

3.8.9 Inflation

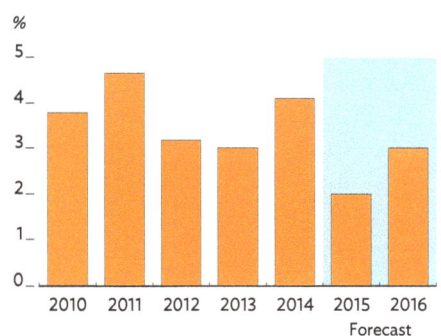

Source: Asian Development Outlook database.

Thailand

Tepid economic recovery in the first half of 2015 depended on government expenditure while private sector activity lagged. GDP growth this year will fall short of that projected in March, though a pickup is still seen for 2016. Consumer prices have declined in 2015 and will likely edge up gradually next year. Buoyant tourism receipts and a sharper fall for the value of imports than exports indicate that current account surpluses will be larger than previously anticipated.

Updated assessment

A recovery in government expenditure and slightly higher private consumption generated a modest 2.9% GDP growth in the first half of 2015, which improved on the first half of 2014, when political disruption and a military coup flattened economic growth (Figure 3.9.1).

Public fixed investment rebounded by 30.9% year on year, which, together with accelerated growth of government consumption spending to 4.0%, contributed most of the increase in GDP. To spur growth, the government launched a program of soft loans from state-owned financial institutions to small businesses and raised cost-of-living allowances for government employees. Its fixed investment focused on small and medium-sized infrastructure and water-management projects. Budget execution improved as the budget disbursement rate rose to 72.0% in the first 3 quarters of FY2015 (ending 30 September 2015), even as disbursement for capital works fell short of the target.

Lackluster private sector activity dampened the recovery. While private consumption increased, in contrast with a decline a year earlier during the political turmoil, the rise was a feeble 2.0%. Factors that hampered consumption spending included falls in farm incomes owing to drought and lower prices for agricultural commodities, slowing growth in wages, and high household debt. Toward cushioning the decline in rural incomes, the government is subsidizing production costs for rice and rubber farmers and offering funds for community investment projects in drought-affected districts.

Private fixed investment was flat in the face of subdued private consumption, weak exports, and low industrial capacity utilization. It was the recovery in public sector outlays that lifted total fixed investment by 6.4% in January–June, after contractions in the 2 previous full years (Figure 3.9.2).

Net external demand contributed slightly to GDP growth in January–June, mainly because of a 31% rebound in tourist arrivals, which had dived in early 2014 during street protests and the intervention by the military (Figure 3.9.3). Earnings from tourism

3.9.1 Half yearly GDP growth

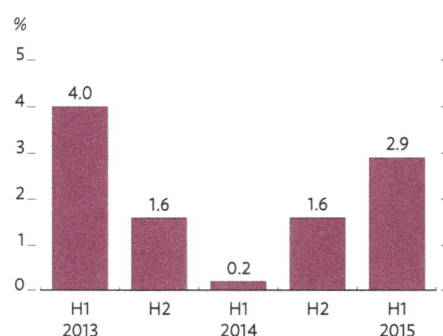

H = half.
Source: CEIC Database Company (accessed 4 September 2015).

3.9.2 Fixed investment growth

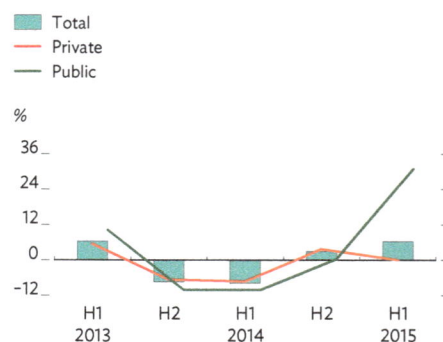

H = half.
Source: National Economic and Social Development Board. http://www.nesdb.go.th (accessed 4 September 2015).

This chapter was written by Luxmon Attapich of the Thailand Resident Mission, ADB, Bangkok.

pushed up services exports by 19.2% in real terms. Exports of goods fell by 3.2% in the same period. Imports of goods and services were little changed in real terms from the first half of 2014.

From the production side, the rise in tourist arrivals in the first half contributed to 5.4% growth in services. Higher inbound tourism boosted air transport and hotels and restaurants. Construction, too, rebounded in the first half, by 20.1%, as the government ramped up spending.

By contrast, manufacturing remained slack due to weak domestic and external demand. Output fell in computers and electronics, among other industries. Automobile production started to recover in the first 3 months but then fell again in April–June. Manufacturing overall grew by a slight 0.9% in the first half. Agriculture performed poorly, contracting by 5.3%. Drought and lower prices hurt the production of rice, natural rubber, and palm oil. Shrimp production turned up, though, after having fallen in the previous year.

Consumer prices have slipped, the result of a decline in prices for fresh food, lower global oil prices, and sluggish domestic demand (Figure 3.9.4). The consumer price index fell by 0.9% in the first 8 months of 2015 compared with the same period in 2014. Core inflation, excluding fuel and fresh food, remained positive at an average of 1.1% through August. By midyear, the impact of the drought was nudging up food prices.

In light of the unexpectedly weak economic recovery and easing consumer prices, the Bank of Thailand, the central bank, reduced its policy interest rate in March 2015 and again in April, to 1.50%. Commercial banks lowered lending rates, but growth in credit to the private sector was subdued in July at 5.3% year on year after having decelerated for some time.

Trade and current account surpluses rose in the first half. Merchandise exports fell by 4.9% in US dollar terms, hit by soft demand in many markets, the end of Generalized System of Preferences benefits for Thai products in the European Union from the start of 2015, and lower prices for rice, natural rubber, and sugar. Merchandise imports fell more sharply than exports, by 8.7% in US dollar terms, reflecting lower prices for imported oil, reduced demand for inputs for export-oriented industries, and weak private investment (Figure 3.9.5). This produced a higher merchandise trade surplus of $15.3 billion. After accounting for net earnings from services, the current account surplus more than doubled to $12.3 billion, equal to 6.0% of GDP. Capital and financial accounts recorded smaller net outflows of $914 million. The balance of payments, after errors and omissions, showed a large surplus of $7.3 billion. Gross international reserves were $156.9 billion in July 2015, or cover for 8.1 months of imports.

Outflows from capital markets and lower domestic interest rates contributed to a 4.3% depreciation of the Thai baht against the strengthening US dollar over the first 8 months. In trade-weighted nominal effective terms, the baht was unchanged between the end of 2014 and July 2015. The Bank of Thailand relaxed capital controls in April and August, following through on a capital account liberalization plan from 2012.

3.9.3 Tourism indicators

Source: Bank of Thailand. http://www.bot.or.th (accessed 4 September 2015).

3.9.4 Inflation and policy interest rate

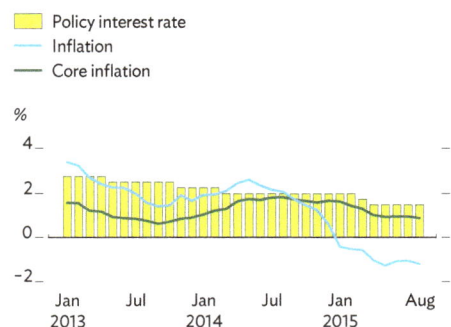

Sources: Bloomberg; CEIC Data Company (both accessed 11 September 2015).

3.9.5 Trade indicators

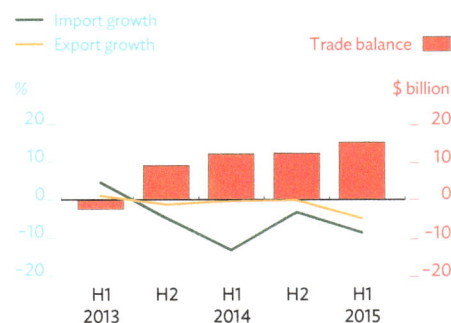

H = half.
Source: CEIC Data Company (accessed 4 September 2015).

Prospects

Economic growth in the second half of 2015 is expected to ease from the pace set in the first 6 months such that growth for the year falls short of the forecast in *ADO 2015* (Figure 3.9.6). Not only has recovery in domestic demand been unexpectedly weak, particularly for private consumption and investment, but forecasts for economic growth have been lowered for major export markets including the large industrial economies, the People's Republic of China, and much of the rest of Asia.

The Thai economy started the second half on a weak note with year-on-year declines in July for indexes tracking private consumption and manufacturing as well as falls in the value of merchandise exports and imports and low private investment (Figure 3.9.7). Government spending and tourism, by contrast, continued to grow.

Next year, GDP growth is seen accelerating by just over 1 percentage point to 3.8%, assuming the timely implementation of large infrastructure projects planned by the government.

The government is stepping up efforts to help rural areas, where drought and low prices for agricultural products have eroded incomes. In August the cabinet approved a plan to spend B6.5 billion on almost 5,000 small projects aimed at creating jobs for 2 million households, mainly in rural areas. The cabinet has also endorsed a program of interest-free 5-year loans to be provided through 59,000 village funds and a separate program to grant to 7,000 subdistricts B5 million each for construction and repairs.

These funds are likely to be disbursed quickly enough for private consumption to benefit later this year and in 2016. Gradual improvement in consumption spending next year should find support from better weather and some pickup in farm commodity prices. Nevertheless, high household debt will weigh on consumption. Rebased GDP data show household debt equal to almost 80% of GDP. The consumer confidence index continued on a downward trend to a 14-month low in July (Figure 3.9.8).

Private investment will likely be subdued at least through 2015 in view of slack consumer demand, lackluster prospects for exports, and low industrial production capacity (Figure 3.9.9). A stimulus package unveiled by the government in September for small- and medium-sized businesses is expected to provide a lift to investment mainly next year. The package includes B100 billion in soft loans, a B100 billion credit guarantee, a B6 billion venture-capital fund, tax breaks for existing businesses, and tax exemptions for start-ups.

To attract companies to establish their headquarters and trading centers in Thailand, the government is offering exemptions from import duties and tax on some categories of income. It will allow foreign companies to own land, bring in skilled staff, and own 100% of their Thailand-based operations. Foreign direct investment picked up to $9.4 billion in the first 6 months of 2015 in line with a rebound last year in the value of applications for investment privileges. Approvals for investment privileges had dried up during the earlier political disruptions.

Public investment is expected to remain robust, with a pipeline that includes road building and maintenance and water-management

3.9.1 Selected economic indicators (%)

	2015		2016	
	ADO 2015	Update	ADO 2015	Update
GDP growth	3.6	2.7	4.1	3.8
Inflation	0.2	-0.7	2.0	1.5
Current acct. bal. (share of GDP)	4.0	5.0	1.5	2.0

Source: ADB estimates.

3.9.6 GDP growth

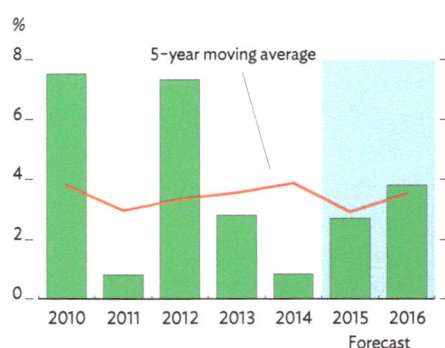

Source: Asian Development Outlook database.

3.9.7 Private consumption and investment

— Private consumption
— Private investment

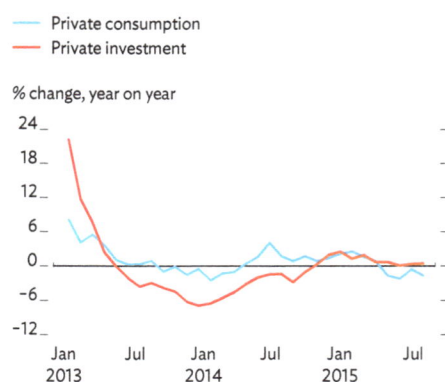

Note: Seasonally adjusted 3-month moving average.
Source: CEIC Data Company (accessed 11 September 2015).

projects. The cabinet has approved a plan to accelerate budget disbursement for small projects. Several large infrastructure projects—mass transit rail lines, highways, railways, and the expansion of Suvarnabhumi International Airport in Bangkok—are scheduled for bidding soon, with construction expected to start in 2016. Substantial government investment on large infrastructure projects would spur the private companies involved to expand capacity. The launch of major projects should provide a lift to business confidence in general.

Fiscal policy overall is set to stimulate growth. The government's budget for FY2016 calls for a 5.6% increase in expenditure and a wider fiscal deficit equal to 2.9% of GDP, though this reflects in part efforts to reduce off-budget spending by bringing more projects on to the budget.

The decline in consumer prices is projected to bottom out as base effects moderate the slide in fuel prices and the drought pushes up prices for some fresh food. Nevertheless, the consumer price index is now seen declining by 0.7% in 2015, reversing a small increase forecast in March, before it turns up again in 2016 as domestic demand improves and global oil prices edge up. Core inflation is likely to be close to 1.0% in 2015 and to trend up gradually next year. In this context, monetary policy is expected to remain accommodative to economic growth.

Weak exports and a sluggish domestic economy, together with the anticipated increase in US interest rates, augur some further depreciation of the baht against the US dollar. The benefit to Thailand's export competitiveness is likely to be modest, though, as the currencies of rival exporters are also depreciating against the US dollar. The value of merchandise exports is projected to fall in 2015, a third consecutive year of decline, before rising in 2016 when growth in major industrial economies improves. The upward momentum in tourist arrivals seen this year is expected to continue in 2016. Merchandise imports will remain weak through this year, rising in 2016 on expanded public infrastructure investment and in line with the pickup in exports. In light of unexpectedly low imports, forecasts of current account surpluses are revised up from March.

For the longer term, concerns are growing that efforts to expand exports on the basis of price competitiveness will become more difficult, and that Thailand needs to develop export products with higher value added. Labor-intensive industries such as textiles and clothing are relocating to neighboring countries with lower wages. Thailand lags in terms of research and development, ranked 31 overall out of 144 in *The Global Competitiveness Report 2014–2015* of the World Economic Forum but lower at 67 for innovation. Enhancing research and development will require, in turn, substantial improvements to the Thai education system.

3.9.8 Consumer confidence and business sentiment indexes

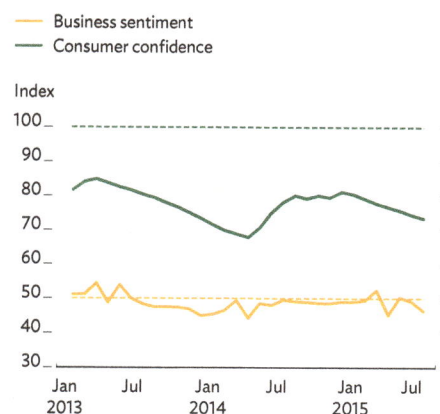

Note: A reading of less than 100 for consumer confidence and 50 for business sentiment denotes deterioration.
Source: Bank of Thailand. http://www.bot.or.th (accessed 10 September 2015).

3.9.9 Capacity utilization

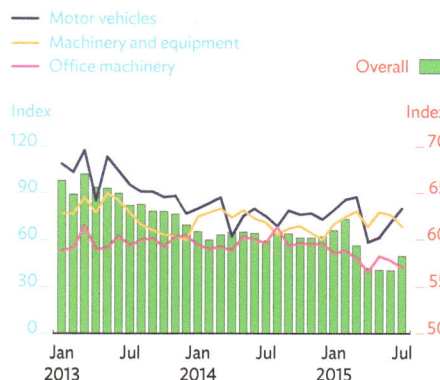

Source: CEIC Data Company (accessed 10 September 2015).

Viet Nam

Strong economic growth in the first half of 2015, driven by buoyant private consumption and foreign direct investment, prompts upward revisions to growth forecasts. Inflation in 2015 is lower than was anticipated in March and is seen rising moderately in 2016. Exports of manufactures continue to expand, but a surge in imports is eroding the current account surplus.

Updated assessment

GDP growth sped to 6.3% in January–June, the fastest first-half pace since 2010 (Figure 3.10.1). The acceleration was driven by industry, which expanded by 9.1% over the same period in 2014 and contributed nearly half of total growth. Manufacturing output was particularly strong, increasing by 9.9% as foreign-invested factories boosted the production of goods for export. New mineral investments helped the mining subsector to expand by 8.2%, recovering from contraction in the first half of 2014. Construction accelerated to grow by 6.6% owing to a modest recovery in the property market and to higher investment in infrastructure.

Growth in services was little changed at 5.9% in the first half. A pickup in wholesale and retail trade was offset by a drop in tourism that saw visitor arrivals fall by 11.3%. Agriculture, forestry, and fisheries recorded modest growth at 2.4%, half a percentage point down from a year earlier due to bad weather and weak commodity prices.

On the demand side, low inflation encouraged robust 8.9% growth in private consumption. Investment also improved as gross capital formation increased by 6.9%, lifted by faster credit growth and rising disbursement of foreign direct investment (FDI). However, net external demand weighed on GDP growth because a rapid increase in imports of goods and services, reflecting stronger investment and consumption, exceeded growth in exports.

Inflation subsided to 0.6% year on year in August 2015, a steep decline from a peak of 23.0% in August 2011. In the first 8 months of this year, inflation averaged just 0.8% (Figure 3.10.2). Lower global oil and commodity prices have held down transportation and food prices.

Moderating inflation allowed the State Bank of Viet Nam, the central bank, to maintain an accommodative monetary stance. Since early 2012, it has lowered policy interest rates by a cumulative 850 basis points, including a reduction of 50 basis points in March 2014. This year, the monetary authority has kept the refinancing rate at 6.5% and the discount rate at 4.5%. Average commercial bank lending rates have fallen from a high of 17.0% in 2012 to 9.5% in the first half of 2015.

3.10.1 Supply-side contributions to growth

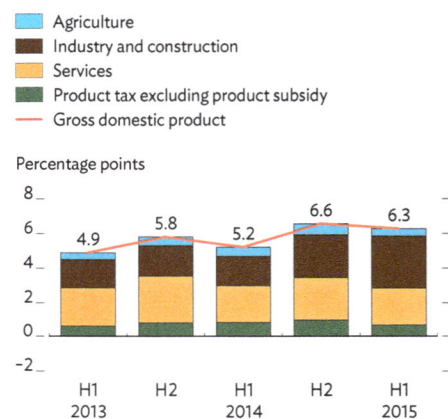

- Agriculture
- Industry and construction
- Services
- Product tax excluding product subsidy
- Gross domestic product

Percentage points

H = half.
Source: General Statistics Office of Viet Nam.

3.10.2 Inflation

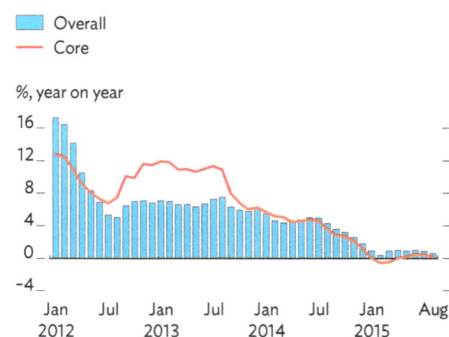

- Overall
- Core

%, year on year

Source: General Statistics Office of Viet Nam.

This chapter was written by Aaron Batten, Chu Hong Minh, and Nguyen Luu Thuc Phuong of the Viet Nam Resident Mission, ADB, Ha Noi.

Declining lending rates, together with a restoration of consumer and investor confidence, propelled credit growth to an estimated 17.1% year on year in mid-2015. Growth in M2 broad money supply increased to 15.6% year on year (Figure 3.10.3).

Fiscal policy remains expansionary. Budget expenditure increased by 10.5% in the first half, and the budget deficit widened to 3.7% of GDP from 3.0% a year earlier. Government revenue grew by 8.0%. Income from taxes on natural resources fell sharply, but this was more than offset by higher revenue from taxes on international trade, personal income, and retail sales. With global oil prices falling well below the budget forecast of $70 a barrel, the government has sought to compensate for lost revenue by increasing duties on petroleum products and strengthening its tax and duty collection efforts. Nevertheless, containing the budget deficit to the target of 5.0% of GDP for 2015 as a whole may be a challenge in light of the continued weakness in global oil prices.

After several years of substantial surpluses, the current account has come under pressure from the surge in imports. Merchandise imports climbed in the first half by an estimated 16.7%, measured on a balance-of-payments basis and in US dollars, against a 9.3% rise in merchandise exports. Strong import demand, the result of FDI-financed capital investment combined with rising domestic consumption, has overridden the impact on the trade balance of lower prices for imported commodities. Exports, still growing at a solid pace, were driven by an almost 25% jump in shipments of manufactured products, including electronics, garments, and footwear, according to customs data.

The trade surplus fell in the first half, slashing the current account surplus to the equivalent of an estimated 0.3% of GDP from 6.2% in the first half of 2014. Taking into account a substantial surplus in the capital account, bolstered by net FDI disbursements that rose by 15.6%, the balance of payments surplus equaled an estimated 3.9% of GDP (Figure 3.10.4).

The central bank, aiming to support the country's international competitiveness and responding to the depreciation of other Asian currencies, devalued the Viet Nam dong against the US dollar three times in the first 8 months of 2015, adjusting the reference rate by 1% each time. In August it also widened the currency's trading band from 1% to 3% on either side of the reference rate. Combined with the expectation of further currency depreciation in other Asian economies, this contributed to a 3.4% decline in the dong black market rate in August (Figure 3.10.5). Foreign exchange reserves increased to an estimated 2.8 months of import cover at the end of June 2015 from 2.7 months at the end of 2014.

Banks have seen their nonperforming loans (NPLs) decline this year, helped by stronger economic growth and a modest recovery in the property market. The ratio of NPLs to banks' total loans outstanding fell from 4.8% in December 2014 to 3.7% in June 2015. The full enforcement of enhanced asset classification and provisioning requirements in April 2015 has reduced the scope for discrepancy between reported NPLs and higher estimates based on international

3.10.3 Credit and money supply growth

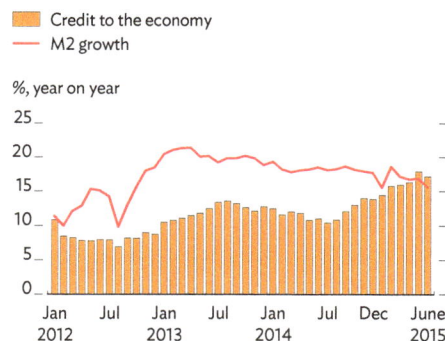

Sources: State Bank of Viet Nam; ADB estimates.

3.10.4 Balance of payments indicators

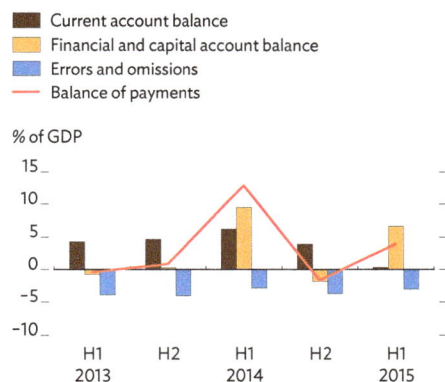

H = half.
Sources: State Bank of Viet Nam; International Monetary Fund; ADB estimates.

3.10.5 Exchange rate

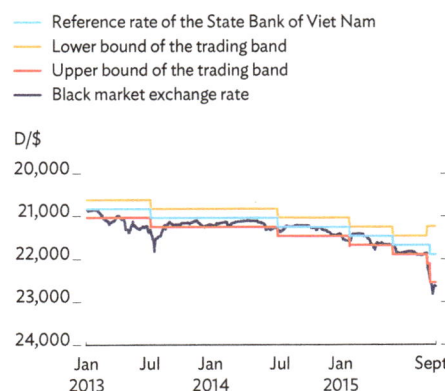

Sources: State Bank of Viet Nam; ADB observations.

standards. These new requirements have also strengthened prudential supervision of the financial sector.

The Viet Nam Asset Management Company, established by the government in 2013 to acquire, restructure, and sell NPLs, had purchased about $9 billion worth of bad debt by August 2015. Since March 2015, its efforts have been supported by regulations enabling the company to increase its capital base, expand purchases of NPLs, and resell acquired assets to nonresidents.

Prospects

Economic growth is expected to accelerate through the second half of 2015, underpinned by rising private consumption, export-oriented manufacturing, and foreign direct investment. This *Update* lifts the growth forecasts published in *ADO 2015* to 6.5% for 2015 and to 6.6% for 2016 (Figure 3.10.6).

Private consumption is benefitting from low inflation, improved consumer confidence, and growth in nonfarm wage employment. A 2014 labor market survey showed 800,000 people moving each year from agriculture and its low productivity and pay into better-paid enterprise and employment in other sectors.

Manufacturing continues to attract substantial FDI inflows. Of $84.8 billion in new FDI commitments from 2011 to August this year, 70% was to expand manufacturing, largely to produce exports. FDI disbursements rose to $8.5 billion in the first 8 months of this year (Figure 3.10.7). The average monthly value of exports from foreign-invested firms increased sharply from almost $3 billion in early 2010 to $10 billion in August 2015.

Foreign-owned firms now generate 70% of total exports, up from half 5 years ago. Domestic enterprises have been much less successful at integrating into global markets. Exports from domestically owned firms have languished at $2 billion–$4 billion per month since January 2010 (Figure 3.10.8).

Other signs pointing to further economic growth include the manufacturing purchasing managers' index, which signaled expansion in manufacturing for 24 consecutive months to August 2015, though a softening in export orders since June indicates that growth in manufacturing may moderate (Figure 3.10.9).

The outlook for trade and investment is bolstered by the relaxing of restrictions on foreign investment in the domestic share and property markets, and by the conclusion in August of a Viet Nam–European Union free trade agreement. Projected stronger economic growth in the major industrial economies in 2016 will support exports and capital inflows, offset in part by the impact from slowing growth in the People's Republic of China.

Fiscal policy will remain supportive of growth, though it could tighten in 2016. The government has increased spending and borrowing since 2011 to support economic recovery. Public debt, including loans guaranteed by the government, is expected to rise to about 62% of GDP by the end of 2015. Public external debt, which is mostly long-term concessional loans, has remained at around 28% of GDP over the past

3.10.1 Selected economic indicators (%)

	2015		2016	
	ADO 2015	Update	ADO 2015	Update
GDP growth	6.1	6.5	6.2	6.6
Inflation	2.5	0.9	4.0	4.0
Current acct. bal. (share of GDP)	3.1	0.5	1.5	1.0

Source: ADB estimates.

3.10.6 GDP growth

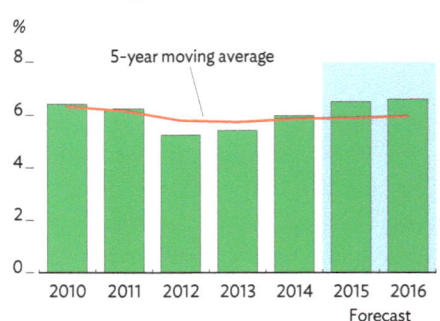

Source: Asian Development Outlook database.

3.10.7 Implemented foreign direct investment

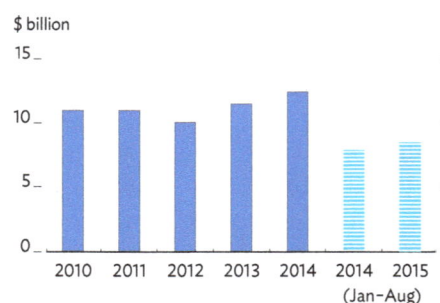

Source: General Statistics Office of Viet Nam.

3.10.8 Sources of exports

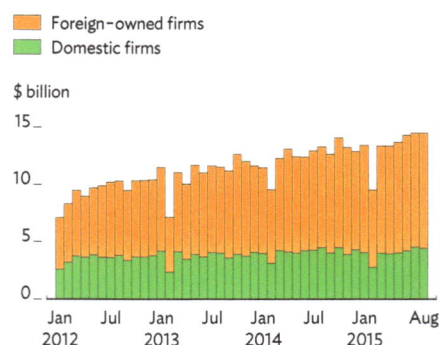

Source: General Statistics Office of Viet Nam.

3 years, limited by increasingly complex procedures to mobilize official development assistance. Higher-cost domestic debt is estimated to rise to 33% of GDP this year (Figure 3.10.10). Debt servicing is expected to absorb 15% of total government revenue in 2016.

Concerns about public debt and debt servicing are expected to prompt the government to rein in expenditure growth to narrow the budget deficit, starting in 2016. The challenge will be to manage this tightening in a gradual, predictable manner that avoids disrupting the economy's upward momentum.

Growth in credit this year looks likely to exceed the government's initial target of 13%–15% and is projected to quicken into 2016. Demand for credit is increasing, and the reported improvement in NPLs and bank balance sheets will facilitate the expansion of lending. Moreover, the central bank relaxed limits on banks using short-term funds for longer-term lending. A program to consolidate or close small, weak banks should further strengthen the financial system. The central bank is encouraging consolidation to reduce the number of banks by almost half by 2017.

Inflation is expected to edge up to 2.0% year on year by December 2015 owing to higher domestic demand, strong credit and money supply growth, increases in gasoline prices and electricity tariffs earlier this year, and the impact on import prices of the 3% devaluation of the dong. Nevertheless, inflationary pressures this year have been even tamer than anticipated in *ADO 2015*, so the year-average forecast is revised down to 0.9%. Inflation is still seen rising to 4.0% in 2016. Such modest inflation may pave the way for lower interest rates.

Current account surpluses will be lower than forecast in March on account of the surge in imports and more subdued growth in exports. Also, growth in remittance inflows slowed to 4.8% of GDP in the first half of 2015 from 5.6% in the first half of 2014. The forecasts for the current account surplus are lowered to 0.5% of GDP this year and less sharply to 1.0% in 2016. Over the medium term, surpluses are expected to grow as more foreign-invested factories come into production and lift exports.

Gradual progress is being achieved toward improving the performance of state-owned enterprises. The government partly privatized 61 state firms in the first half of 2015, following on from 143 in 2014. The official target for a further 228 to be thus equitized this year looks ambitious, and many of these exercises are expected to take place later, in 2016 and beyond. One obstacle is a lack of strategic investors willing to participate in initial public offerings of shares. The easing of foreign ownership restrictions on companies listed on the stock market aims to address this shortcoming, though foreign investors may still be discouraged by concerns over corporate governance and financial transparency.

El Niño weather patterns developing across the Pacific this year present a risk to the outlook. Extended dry weather could amplify existing drought conditions that have damaged coffee and rice production and, if prolonged, could further decelerate growth in agriculture while pushing up food prices into 2016.

3.10.9 Purchasing managers' index

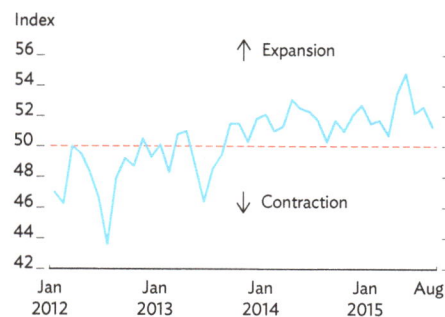

Note: Nikkei, Markit.
Source: Bloomberg (accessed 2 September 2015).

3.10.10 Public debt

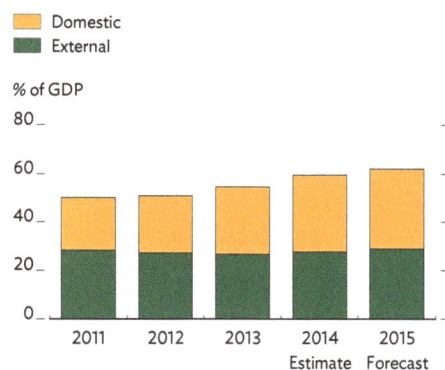

Sources: Government of Viet Nam; World Bank; International Monetary Fund; ADB estimates.

STATISTICAL
APPENDIX

Statistical notes and tables

The statistical appendix presents selected economic indicators for the 45 developing member economies of the Asian Development Bank (ADB) in three tables: gross domestic product (GDP) growth, inflation, and current account balance as a percentage of GDP. The economies are grouped into five subregions: Central Asia, East Asia, South Asia, Southeast Asia, and the Pacific. The tables contain historical data for 2012–2014 and forecasts for 2015 and 2016.

The data are standardized to the degree possible to allow comparability over time and across economies, but differences in statistical methodology, definitions, coverage, and practices make full comparability impossible. The national income accounts section is based on the United Nations System of National Accounts, while the data on balance of payments are based on International Monetary Fund accounting standards. Historical data are obtained from official sources, statistical publications, and databases, as well as from documents of ADB, the International Monetary Fund, and the World Bank. Projections for 2015 and 2016 are generally ADB estimates made on the bases of available quarterly or monthly data, though some projections are from governments.

Most countries report by calendar year. The following record their government finance data by fiscal year: Armenia; Azerbaijan; Brunei Darussalam; the Cook Islands; Hong Kong, China; Kazakhstan; the Kyrgyz Republic; the Lao People's Democratic Republic (Lao PDR); Samoa; Singapore; Taipei,China; Tajikistan; Thailand; and Uzbekistan. The Federated States of Micronesia, Nauru, the Republic of the Marshall Islands, and Palau report government finance and balance-of-payments data by fiscal year. South Asian countries (except for the Maldives and Sri Lanka), Myanmar, Samoa, and Tonga report all variables by fiscal year.

Regional and subregional averages are provided in the three tables. The averages are computed using weights derived from gross national income (GNI) in current US dollars following the World Bank Atlas method. The GNI data for 2009–2013 are obtained from the World Bank's World Development Indicators Online. Weights for 2013 are carried over through 2016. The GNI data for the Cook Islands are estimated using the Atlas conversion factor. Because Myanmar and Nauru have no GNI data, they are excluded from the computation of all subregional averages and totals.

The following paragraphs discuss the three tables in greater detail.

Table A1: Growth rate of GDP (% per year). The table shows annual growth rates of GDP valued at constant market price, factor cost, or basic price. GDP at market price is the aggregation of value added by all resident producers at producers' prices, including taxes less subsidies on imports plus all nondeductible value-added or similar taxes. Constant factor cost measures differ from market price measures in that they exclude taxes on production and include subsidies. Basic price valuation is the factor cost plus some taxes on production, such as those on property and payroll taxes, and less some subsidies, such as those on labor-related subsidies but not product-related subsidies. Most countries use constant market price valuation. Fiji, Pakistan, and Sri Lanka use constant factor cost, while the Maldives and Nepal use basic price. The series for Taipei,China is changed to accommodate its adoption of the chain-linking method. Because Sri Lanka rebased its national accounts from 2002 to 2010, *ADO 2015* GDP growth forecasts are not comparable with current estimates and have been omitted.

Table A2: Inflation (% per year). Data on inflation rates represents period averages. The inflation rates presented are based on consumer price indexes. The consumer price indexes of the following economies are for a given city or group of consumers only: Afghanistan for Kabul (until 2011), Cambodia for Phnom Penh, the Marshall Islands for Majuro, Solomon Islands for Honiara, and Nepal for urban consumers.

Table A3: Current account balance (% of GDP). The current account balance is the sum of the balance of trade in merchandise, net trade in services and factor income, and net transfers. The values reported are divided by GDP at current prices in US dollars. For Cambodia, the Lao PDR, and Viet Nam, official transfers are excluded from the current account balance. Because Sri Lanka rebased its national accounts from 2002 to 2010, the *ADO 2015* current account balances as a percentage of GDP are not comparable with current forecasts and are therefore omitted.

Table A1 Growth rate of GDP (% per year)

	2012	2013	2014	2015		2016	
				ADO 2015	Update	ADO 2015	Update
Central Asia	5.6	6.6	5.1	3.5	3.3	4.5	4.2
Armenia	7.2	3.3	3.5	1.6	1.2	2.3	2.0
Azerbaijan	2.2	5.8	2.8	3.0	3.0	2.8	2.8
Georgia	6.4	3.3	4.8	2.0	2.0	2.5	2.5
Kazakhstan	5.0	6.0	4.3	1.9	1.5	3.8	3.3
Kyrgyz Republic	−0.1	10.9	3.6	1.7	1.7	2.0	2.0
Tajikistan	7.5	7.4	6.7	4.0	3.5	4.8	4.2
Turkmenistan	11.1	10.2	10.3	9.7	9.5	9.2	9.2
Uzbekistan	8.2	8.0	8.1	7.0	7.0	7.2	7.2
East Asia	6.6	6.8	6.5	6.5	6.0	6.3	6.0
China, People's Rep. of	7.7	7.7	7.3	7.2	6.8	7.0	6.7
Hong Kong, China	1.7	3.1	2.5	2.8	2.4	2.9	2.7
Korea, Rep. of	2.3	2.9	3.3	3.5	2.7	3.7	3.4
Mongolia	12.3	11.6	7.8	3.0	2.3	5.0	3.0
Taipei,China	2.1	2.2	3.8	3.7	1.6	3.6	2.6
South Asia	5.2	6.4	6.7	7.2	6.9	7.6	7.3
Afghanistan	11.9	3.4	1.7	2.5	2.5	3.5	3.5
Bangladesh	6.5	6.0	6.1	6.1	6.5	6.4	6.7
Bhutan	6.4	3.5	4.0	6.8	6.7	7.0	7.0
India	5.1	6.9	7.3	7.8	7.4	8.2	7.8
Maldives	1.3	4.7	6.8	6.3	5.9	5.1	5.9
Nepal	4.6	3.8	5.1	4.6	3.0	5.1	4.8
Pakistan	3.8	3.7	4.1	4.2	4.2	4.5	4.5
Sri Lanka	9.9	3.8	4.2	–	6.3	–	7.0
Southeast Asia	5.8	5.1	4.4	4.9	4.4	5.3	4.9
Brunei Darussalam	0.9	−2.1	−2.3	−1.5	−1.5	0.8	0.8
Cambodia	7.3	7.4	7.1	7.3	7.0	7.5	7.2
Indonesia	6.0	5.6	5.0	5.5	4.9	6.0	5.4
Lao People's Dem. Rep.	7.9	7.9	7.4	7.0	6.7	7.2	7.0
Malaysia	5.5	4.7	6.0	4.7	4.7	5.0	4.9
Myanmar	7.1	8.3	7.7	8.3	8.3	8.2	8.2
Philippines	6.7	7.1	6.1	6.4	6.0	6.3	6.3
Singapore	3.4	4.4	2.9	3.0	2.1	3.4	2.5
Thailand	7.3	2.8	0.9	3.6	2.7	4.1	3.8
Viet Nam	5.2	5.4	6.0	6.1	6.5	6.2	6.6
The Pacific	5.7	3.8	6.7	9.9	6.7	4.8	3.9
Cook Islands	4.1	−1.7	−1.2	2.1	2.1	−0.3	−0.3
Fiji	1.4	4.7	5.3	4.0	4.0	4.0	4.5
Kiribati	3.4	2.4	3.8	1.5	3.0	1.5	2.0
Marshall Islands	4.7	3.0	0.5	3.5	3.5	1.5	1.5
Micronesia, Fed. States of	0.1	−4.0	−2.2	2.3	0.0	5.1	4.0
Nauru	4.9	4.5	10.0	8.0	6.8	5.0	5.4
Palau	4.0	0.1	8.0	8.0	10.0	6.0	9.0
Papua New Guinea	7.7	4.9	8.4	15.0	9.0	5.0	3.0
Samoa	0.4	−1.9	1.2	2.5	2.3	2.2	1.9
Solomon Islands	4.8	2.9	−0.2	3.0	3.0	3.5	3.5
Timor-Leste	6.4	2.8	7.1	6.2	6.2	6.6	6.6
Tonga	0.5	−2.7	2.1	2.4	2.4	2.6	2.6
Tuvalu	0.2	1.3	2.0	2.0	2.0	2.0	2.0
Vanuatu	1.8	2.0	3.6	−0.5	−1.0	4.0	4.5
Average	6.2	6.4	6.2	6.3	5.8	6.3	6.0

– = incomparable data.

Table A2 Inflation (% per year)

	2012	2013	2014	2015		2016	
				ADO 2015	*Update*	ADO 2015	*Update*
Central Asia	5.1	5.8	5.7	6.7	8.1	6.6	7.5
Armenia	2.6	5.8	3.0	4.6	4.6	4.1	4.1
Azerbaijan	1.1	2.4	1.4	6.0	6.0	5.5	5.5
Georgia	−0.9	−0.5	3.1	5.0	4.3	5.0	5.0
Kazakhstan	5.1	5.8	6.7	6.0	8.9	6.2	7.9
Kyrgyz Republic	2.8	6.6	7.5	10.5	11.0	10.0	11.5
Tajikistan	5.8	5.1	6.1	10.0	10.0	6.5	7.0
Turkmenistan	5.3	6.8	6.0	7.0	7.0	6.5	6.5
Uzbekistan	12.1	11.2	8.4	9.5	9.5	10.0	10.0
East Asia	2.6	2.4	1.9	1.7	1.4	2.2	2.1
China, People's Rep. of	2.6	2.6	2.0	1.8	1.5	2.3	2.2
Hong Kong, China	4.1	4.3	4.4	3.3	3.2	3.4	3.3
Korea, Rep. of	2.2	1.3	1.3	1.3	0.8	2.1	2.0
Mongolia	14.3	9.9	12.8	8.9	7.6	7.7	7.6
Taipei,China	1.9	0.8	1.2	0.5	−0.5	1.0	0.5
South Asia	10.1	9.0	6.2	5.1	5.0	5.6	5.5
Afghanistan	6.2	7.4	4.6	5.0	2.0	5.0	4.1
Bangladesh	8.7	6.8	7.4	6.5	6.4	6.2	6.2
Bhutan	10.2	8.8	9.6	7.0	6.6	6.8	5.9
India	10.2	9.5	5.9	5.0	5.0	5.5	5.5
Maldives	10.9	4.0	2.4	3.0	1.6	2.5	2.5
Nepal	8.3	9.8	9.1	7.7	7.2	7.3	9.0
Pakistan	11.0	7.4	8.6	5.8	4.5	5.8	5.1
Sri Lanka	7.5	6.9	3.2	2.0	2.0	5.0	5.0
Southeast Asia	3.8	4.2	4.1	3.1	3.0	3.1	3.3
Brunei Darussalam	0.2	0.3	−0.2	−0.2	−0.2	0.4	0.4
Cambodia	2.9	2.9	3.9	1.6	1.3	2.7	2.7
Indonesia	4.0	6.4	6.4	5.5	6.7	4.0	5.1
Lao People's Dem. Rep.	4.3	6.4	4.2	3.5	1.5	4.0	3.0
Malaysia	1.7	2.1	3.1	3.2	2.4	2.9	2.9
Myanmar	2.8	5.7	5.9	8.4	8.4	6.6	6.6
Philippines	3.2	3.0	4.1	2.8	2.0	3.3	3.0
Singapore	4.6	2.4	1.0	0.2	−0.2	1.5	1.0
Thailand	3.0	2.2	1.9	0.2	−0.7	2.0	1.5
Viet Nam	9.1	6.6	4.1	2.5	0.9	4.0	4.0
The Pacific	5.5	5.0	3.2	5.0	4.2	4.1	4.4
Cook Islands	2.8	2.6	1.6	1.3	2.4	1.4	1.4
Fiji	3.4	2.9	0.5	2.5	2.5	2.5	3.0
Kiribati	−3.0	−1.5	2.6	1.0	1.0	1.5	1.5
Marshall Islands	4.3	1.9	1.3	1.4	1.4	1.3	1.3
Micronesia, Fed. States of	6.3	2.1	0.7	2.4	1.0	2.6	1.0
Nauru	−0.5	1.4	5.0	8.0	11.4	3.0	10.0
Palau	5.4	2.8	4.0	3.4	3.0	3.4	3.0
Papua New Guinea	4.6	5.0	5.2	7.0	6.0	5.0	6.0
Samoa	6.2	−0.2	−1.2	2.5	1.9	2.0	2.0
Solomon Islands	5.9	5.4	5.2	5.0	2.0	5.5	2.8
Timor-Leste	10.9	9.5	0.7	2.8	1.8	4.0	3.0
Tonga	3.3	0.7	2.3	0.4	0.4	1.0	1.2
Tuvalu	1.4	2.0	3.3	1.0	2.0	1.0	2.0
Vanuatu	1.4	1.4	0.4	4.0	4.0	2.0	2.5
Average	4.1	3.8	3.0	2.6	2.3	3.0	3.0

Table A3 Current account balance (% of GDP)

	2012	2013	2014	2015		2016	
				ADO 2015	Update	ADO 2015	Update
Central Asia	3.2	1.9	2.4	−0.2	−3.2	0.2	−1.6
Armenia	−10.0	−7.6	−7.3	−9.2	−8.7	−8.3	−8.3
Azerbaijan	21.4	16.6	16.0	12.0	6.0	13.4	8.0
Georgia	−11.4	−5.7	−9.8	−12.0	−10.5	−10.5	−10.0
Kazakhstan	0.5	0.4	2.1	−1.0	−5.2	−1.3	−3.2
Kyrgyz Republic	−15.1	−14.1	−15.0	−16.0	−16.0	−15.0	−15.0
Tajikistan	−2.5	−2.9	−9.1	−5.9	−5.9	−4.8	−4.8
Turkmenistan	0.0	−7.3	−5.9	−8.4	−8.4	−6.2	−6.2
Uzbekistan	1.2	1.6	1.2	0.9	0.9	1.1	1.1
East Asia	3.1	2.5	3.1	3.3	3.3	3.0	3.1
China, People's Rep. of	2.5	1.6	2.1	2.3	2.3	2.0	2.2
Hong Kong, China	1.6	1.5	1.9	2.6	2.3	2.5	2.2
Korea, Rep. of	4.2	6.2	6.3	7.0	7.0	6.3	6.3
Mongolia	−27.4	−25.4	−12.5	−8.0	−5.0	−15.0	−7.0
Taipei,China	9.9	10.8	12.3	12.5	12.0	13.0	12.0
South Asia	−4.1	−1.4	−1.3	−1.0	−1.1	−1.3	−1.5
Afghanistan	3.9	3.7	3.9	1.4	1.4	−1.0	−1.0
Bangladesh	−0.3	1.6	0.8	−0.5	−0.8	0.5	−0.5
Bhutan	−21.7	−27.3	−25.8	−30.6	−25.6	−30.6	−24.6
India	−4.8	−1.7	−1.5	−1.1	−1.1	−1.5	−1.5
Maldives	−8.4	−5.2	−7.4	−6.3	−8.9	−6.1	−9.0
Nepal	5.0	3.4	4.6	2.7	5.1	3.5	−1.0
Pakistan	−2.1	−1.1	−1.3	−1.0	−0.8	−1.3	−1.0
Sri Lanka	−5.8	−3.4	−2.6	−	−2.9	−	−3.6
Southeast Asia	2.6	2.2	3.1	3.1	3.0	2.9	2.7
Brunei Darussalam	38.8	29.4	20.8	25.0	9.0	26.5	11.0
Cambodia	−9.6	−14.9	−11.7	−12.9	−12.3	−12.7	−12.2
Indonesia	−2.7	−3.2	−3.0	−2.8	−2.5	−2.4	−2.1
Lao People's Dem. Rep.	−28.5	−30.6	−25.0	−21.2	−20.3	−17.3	−17.0
Malaysia	5.2	3.5	4.3	3.3	2.7	4.5	3.2
Myanmar	−4.3	−5.1	−7.1	−6.8	−6.8	−5.0	−5.0
Philippines	2.8	4.2	3.8	4.0	3.7	3.6	3.6
Singapore	17.2	17.9	19.1	18.9	19.8	19.3	18.7
Thailand	−0.4	−0.7	3.3	4.0	5.0	1.5	2.0
Viet Nam	5.9	4.5	4.9	3.1	0.5	1.5	1.0
The Pacific	10.0	13.0	5.7	13.9	9.1	14.4	7.9
Cook Islands	...	...	...	...	...	...	...
Fiji	−2.1	−17.1	−9.9	−9.8	−9.8	−8.7	−8.7
Kiribati	−1.7	14.2	17.1	−53.0	−4.5	−48.4	−9.7
Marshall Islands	−7.8	−12.4	−9.4	−9.9	−9.9	−11.4	−11.4
Micronesia, Fed. States of	−12.6	−10.1	2.8	11.2	−1.3	6.4	−2.5
Nauru	...	...	...	...	...	...	...
Palau	−10.1	−8.8	−5.0	−6.4	−6.1	−8.1	−7.6
Papua New Guinea	−53.4	−31.0	−11.0	13.5	4.4	15.0	4.2
Samoa	−8.7	−2.6	−8.0	−10.9	−6.9	−9.4	−5.4
Solomon Islands	1.3	−4.1	−8.1	−15.5	−8.5	−15.0	−13.0
Timor-Leste	211.3	181.3	75.1	55.0	52.2	51.6	46.5
Tonga	−8.8	−1.9	−1.4	−4.5	−4.5	−6.0	−6.0
Tuvalu	25.5	26.2	27.3	−37.2	−37.2	−21.4	−21.4
Vanuatu	−6.5	−3.3	−5.7	−10.0	−15.0	−7.0	−13.0
Average	1.8	1.9	2.4	2.5	2.5	2.3	2.3

... = data not available, − = incomparable data.

www.ingramcontent.com/pod-product-compliance
Lightning Source LLC
Chambersburg PA
CBHW061220270326
41926CB00032B/4783